HATS IN THE RING

HATS IN THE RING

An Illustrated History of American Presidential Campaigns

TEXT BY

EVAN CORNOG

ILLUSTRATIONS SELECTED BY AND CAPTIONS BY

RICHARD WHELAN

RANDOM HOUSE　　NEW YORK

Design by **BTD**NYC

Library of Congress Cataloging-in-Publication Data

Cornog, Evan.
    Hats in the ring: an illustrated history of American presidential campaigns/Evan
Cornog and Richard Whelan.
       p. cm.
    Includes index.
    ISBN 0-679-45730-5 (acid-free paper)
    1. Presidents—United States—Election—History. 2. United States—Politics and
government. 3. Presidential candidates—United States—History. 4. Presidents—
United States—Election—History—Pictorial works. 5. United States—Politics and
government—Pictorial works. 6. Presidential candidates—United States—History—
Pictorial works. I. Whelan, Richard, 1946– II. Title.
E176.1.C793 2000
324.973—dc21
                                     00-027578

Acknowledgments

It is our pleasure to acknowledge the many debts we have incurred in the process of creating this book, especially to the following: Melanie Jackson, our agent; our editors at Random House, Ann Godoff, Kate Niedzwiecki, and Sean Abbott; the book's designer, Beth Tondreau; the copy editor, Lynn Anderson; the production editor, Sybil Pincus; the production director, Kathy Rosenbloom; and the fact-checker, Ariel Hart.

We wish to thanks the staffs of all the collections that provided us with visual material, as cited in the illustration captions. We also want to express our deep appreciation to Cornell Capa for his generosity in permitting us to reproduce so many of his great photographs from his twenty years of covering American politics. Our special debt to David J. and Janice L. Frent is acknowledged below.

The material in this text is drawn from a wide range of works in American history—biographies of political leaders, treatises on the American political party system, in-depth studies of particular historical periods or movements, published diaries and letters of political figures. Serious students of presidential elections owe particular thanks to Arthur M. Schlesinger, Jr., for his general editorship of the *History of American Presidential Elections*. This history, which now runs to ten volumes and four thousand pages, provides scholarly essays on each election as well as voluminous primary materials such as speeches and party platforms.

The author of the text of this book wishes to acknowledge two sections in particular from among the many works consulted. The description of the dinner honoring William Dean Howells at the start of the chapter on the 1912 race was inspired by—and drawn from—Henry R. May's splendid intellectual history of the era, *The End of American Innocence*. And the use of John Maynard Keynes's generous assessment of Herbert Hoover was a nod to Richard Hofstadter's essay on Hoover in *The American Political Tradition*, a book that more than fifty years after its publication still repays close attention.

The authors wish to express their warmest gratitude to David J. and Janice L. Frent, who over the past three decades have assembled the vast and definitive David J. and Janice L. Frent Political Americana Collection, which spans the entire history of American presidential campaigns, including a staggering array of memorabilia ranging from buttons to banners, from novelties to campaign biographies. The collection, which is by far the largest in private hands, also concentrates in depth on a broad spectrum of political, patriotic, and social causes, including woman suffrage, Prohibition, the civil rights movement, and Vietnam. Items from this unparalleled collection have illustrated many books, including the two-volume work *Running for President,* edited by Arthur M. Schlesinger, Jr., Fred L. Israel, and David J. Frent.

Contents

Introduction

The idea of doing this book arose quite simply from a single photograph in an auction catalog. The photograph, of a young man in the uniform of a "Wide Awake" supporter of Abraham Lincoln in the 1860 election (see p. 107), seemed to us to embody the remarkable amalgam of serious purpose and carnival spirits that has characterized the process of choosing a President. It seemed to us that a narrative history that tried to make sense of all American presidential elections, and of the images that attended and often helped determine them, would both entertain and instruct (much as election events are intended to do). One of our assumptions has been that the images and symbols of an election are as freighted with meaning, and as "valid" a political medium, as the more explicitly issue-oriented material inscribed in party platforms and spoken at debates.

Dealing with such a broad sweep of the nation's history in a single volume has required making many choices, and we have had to leave out images, and issues, that may be missed. But we felt it was important to cover all the presidential elections, and to do so in a way that would allow readers to appreciate how much has changed—and how much has stayed the same—in the way we choose our chief executive. Some readers may be surprised to learn how vitriolic and irresponsible were some of the campaigns involving the revered Founding Fathers of the nation. Others may find it surprising that an early start has been part of the wise candidate's approach for well over a century. Still others may find it charming to see how long the tradition of the reluctant candidate survived, adopted as a pose by men whose ambition could scarcely be contained, let alone concealed.

This book can be read straight through, as a single coherent narrative, but individual chapters can also be read in isolation. Various overarching themes of American political life—the rise and fall of political parties, the expansion of political participation, the growing importance of foreign policy in elections as the nation emerged as a world power, the changing role of the news media in the electoral process, the central role of slavery and the rights of African Americans in the political discourse of the United States—have been embedded in the narrative rather than treated separately. And while this book looks specifically at presidential elections, it includes enough material about contemporary nonelection issues and problems in the nation so that the electoral debates can be understood within the larger context of their times.

Political history can be very narrow, and certainly there are tremendous historical forces that, although they have transformed the nation, have seldom been explicitly discussed in election campaigns. But because a President must appeal to the entire nation to win election—and because voters choose a President on the basis of many things, not merely his stands on important issues—the choice the voters make and the way they make it reveal much about what America is, and what Americans would like it to be.

HATS IN THE RING

The Patriot King

WASHINGTON AND THE ELECTIONS OF 1789 AND 1792

The first two elections for President of the United States were utterly different in process, scope, and intention from any of the elections that followed, yet because of the titanic stature of George Washington, the elections of 1789 and 1792 have profoundly influenced the shape of presidential politics for two centuries. Washington established the ideal of what the presidency should be, and candidates from his time forward have sought to portray themselves as being, in some fashion, like the first President. They have appropriated his name and his symbols, but none has managed to embody the qualities that made Washington the model President.

George Washington was in fact what countless of his actual and would-be successors have wished to be taken for: a disinterested patriot who accepted the office of President of the United States out of duty and obligation, not to satisfy ego or ambition. Washington's eminence, universally accepted among that unusually eminent group of men called the Founding Fathers, meant that there would be no contest for the presidency as long as he wished to stand for the office. So Washington himself had very little to do with the practices that have come to govern campaigning and elections in the United States. Indeed, he would have found any effort to campaign for office offensive to his and his compatriots' notion of leadership, which was based on the idea of the "patriot king." This ideal of a sovereign had been defined for Washington's generation by the writings of Henry St. John, First Viscount Bolingbroke, an English Tory of the early eighteenth century. A patriot king, Bolingbroke wrote, was above faction and party and governed in the interest of the entire nation, rather than carrying out the desires of narrower interests. Such a king, Bolingbroke declared, "will put himself at the head of his people in order to govern, or more properly to subdue, all parties." Washington himself aspired to embody this model, and most of his contemporaries thought he succeeded.

George Washington's reputation so dwarfed that of other heroes of the Revolution that even when Thomas Jefferson and Alexander Hamilton had become bitter political opponents in the 1790s, they were united in their admiration for him.

1789: NEW YORK AS THE NATIONAL CAPITAL

NEW YORK SERVED as the national capital from 1785 to 1790. For most of this period, the government of the United States was conducted by Congress under the Articles of Confederation ratified in 1781. When the new government established by the Constitution convened in New York City in the spring of 1789, it met in City Hall, which had been lavishly remodeled to house the national government. Pierre Charles L'Enfant, who would later create the master plan for the city of Washington, D.C., was hired to spruce up the building, which had been constructed around the beginning of the eighteenth century. L'Enfant added a two-story Doric portico, marble floors were laid inside, the ceilings were painted, and crimson damask draperies provided an elegant touch. New Yorkers took pride in the renovations, grumbled about the expense ($65,000), and made it clear that they expected that this "Monument to the Munificence of the Citizens" (as the city's Common Council phrased it) would be suitably appreciated by the national government.

The most desired form of appreciation would, of course, be the selection of New York by the new government as the permanent national capital. The principal rival (in the minds of New Yorkers, at least) was Philadelphia, which at the time was the largest and most sophisticated American city. New York, by contrast, had suffered two major fires during the Revolutionary War and had been occupied by the British for almost the entire conflict. Despite its rough edges, New York still hoped to be chosen as the capital, and various plans were advanced to make the prospect seem attractive. One proposed to erect a modern Acropolis on the Heights of Brooklyn, across the East River from New York (the city still occupied only the southern tip of Manhattan Island). Lewis Morris, a New York signer of the Declaration of Independence, suggested that his Bronx estate, Morrisania, would serve the nation well as a capital.

In the end, neither the expensively spruced-up Federal Hall (on the terrace of which Washington took the oath of office as President on April 30, 1789) nor the then-sylvan charms of the Bronx or Brooklyn cast a sufficient spell to keep the federal government in New York. The selection of a national capital, unsurprisingly, became the subject of a political deal. In the summer of 1790, the new Congress was deadlocked over the financial proposals of Treasury Secretary Alexander Hamilton.

He had, after all, led the Continental Army to victory against the might of Great Britain, in spite of the fact that the government he was fighting to establish and preserve could not keep his men supplied with food, clothing, or weapons. He had managed to contain mutinies of the misused troops and to keep his equally disgruntled officers from threatening the civil government when their own grievances went unmet. And when these crises had passed and the war was over he had put aside power and returned, like the ancient Roman hero Cincinnatus, to his plow. After peace came, in 1783, Washington returned home to Mount Vernon, finished (he thought) with public office.

Many, including leading Virginia figures such as Thomas Jefferson and James Madison, opposed Hamilton's financial plan. Hamilton and Jefferson happened to run into each other on the steps of President Washington's residence, and eventually they reached agreement on a deal whereby they would allow Hamilton's proposals to pass in return for Hamilton's support of a bill to situate the capital on the banks of the Potomac, granting Philadelphia a ten-year stint as capital while the new Federal City was constructed.

Again, Washington's immense prestige played a role—it was thought considerate to place the capital closer to his home at Mount Vernon. The price the nation paid for placing its political leaders in a city that had no other reason to exist is hard to reckon, but comparing Washington with Paris or London may give some idea. Of course, there were many (Thomas Jefferson first among them) who viewed urban life as the ultimate corruption. But we may well ponder (as the historians Stanley Elkins and Eric McKitrick have done) how our history might have been different had the capital remained in New York or Philadelphia, surrounded by the bustle of commerce and the stimulation of intellectual and artistic activity.

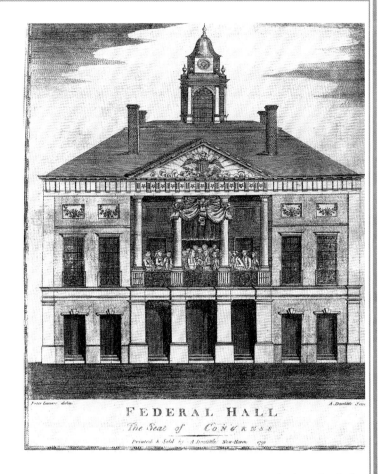

FEDERAL HALL
The Seat of Congress
Printed & Sold by A. Doolittle New-Haven 1790

Washington's inauguration at Federal Hall. Engraving by Amos Doolittle.
LIBRARY OF CONGRESS.

The United States was to be a republic, not a monarchy, and a government had to be created that somehow allowed for a patriot king without putting a new despot in place of George III. One vital difference was that the American leader would be elected to his office. The initial rules for presidential contests were devised by the delegates to the Federal Convention in Philadelphia in the summer of 1787. As those delegates drafted the nation's Constitution, they had to establish the powers of the nation's executive and determine how the executive was to be chosen. Both the political experience of the colonial period and the political rhetoric of the

Brass button commemorating Washington's first inauguration. Such buttons were to be sewn onto clothing.

THE DAVID J. AND JANICE L. FRENT POLITICAL AMERICANA COLLECTION.

American Revolution had taught Americans the danger of a strong executive. Many American propagandists had viewed the taxes and trade restrictions passed by the British Parliament in the decade before the Revolution as the outcome of excessive influence over that body by the king's ministers. This influence was referred to as "corruption"; the mere existence of such influence was thought to be corrosive of liberty. This bias against strong executive powers had been expressed in various ways in the constitutions adopted by the states during the Revolution—New York, for example, lodged the power of appointment in a Council of Appointment rather than vesting it in the governor.

The actual experience of fighting the Revolutionary War, however, and the problems of the national government under the Articles of Confederation (the nation's original charter, which had been passed by Congress in 1777 and ratified in 1781) had persuaded George Washington and others that a strong executive within a strong national government was essential to the nation's survival. The Constitution itself had come into being in part because Washington was eager to improve inland navigation but found that quarrels between states constantly retarded the carrying out of improvements. In 1785, his efforts had resulted in an agreement between Virginia and Maryland to improve navigation on the Potomac River. This agreement had led, the following year, to a larger meeting at Annapolis to discuss commercial issues between the states; the result of the Annapolis convention was a report, written by Alexander Hamilton, that urged a meeting of delegates from all the states in Philadelphia in 1787 to revise the Articles of Confederation.

The resulting Constitutional Convention went beyond the original mandate to revise the Articles and presented to the people of the United States an entirely new Constitution. That it succeeded in doing so is largely attributable to the presence of George Washington as president of the convention and as the presumed first President of the United States. If the convention had contemplated bestowing executive powers on Patrick Henry, John Adams, or George Clinton, earlier proposals for a plural executive, or for short and unrenewable terms for the President, might well have been adopted. But Washington's very presence calmed the fears of those who dreaded the consequences of an overly strong executive. As a result, the Constitution called for a strong presidency—an office worth campaigning for.

Washington himself was uneasy about accepting the presidency, in part because when he had retired from the army in 1783 he had made it clear that his retirement was to be permanent. When friends began to urge him to accept, he fretted that he might be thought guilty of "inconsistency and ambition" if he agreed to accept the office. His genuine reluctance to take the job was particularly troublesome to Alexander Hamilton, who saw that only Washington could provide the foundation of a strong federal government. In the summer and fall of 1788, he wrote a series of letters to Washington, urging him to accept the obvious will of the people. Hamilton, an acute judge of character, appealed to Washington's large concern for his own reputation when he suggested that it would be "inglorious in such a situation not to hazard the glory however great, which he might have previously acquired." The implication that Washington's reluctance to accept the presidency might be seen as self-regarding was exactly calculated to bring Washington forward, and so he came.

No one but Washington himself doubted his fitness for the job or the nation's desire to have him fill the office. James Madison, writing from New York to Jefferson in Paris in the fall of 1788, stated that the choice for President "unites the conjectures of the public." It was well that it should be so, because Congress had decreed a rather hasty process for the first election, and confusion was minimized by the obvious lack of dispute over who was to fill the office. Congress had provided that presidential electors were to be chosen the first week in January and to cast their votes a month later. In most states the choice of electors was left to the legislature, in some the people chose electors directly, and the remaining states concocted election methods that were a hybrid of popular and legislative choice.

Washington's election was a foregone conclusion, but the selection of a Vice President was a very different matter. Washington stated that any person of sound federal principles would be acceptable to him, and since the President and Vice President had to be from different states, a non-Virginian was required. One logical choice was John Adams, a revolutionary leader from the populous state of Massachusetts, a person of obvious gifts and strong character. But some felt that he came on a bit too strong. Madison, in the same letter to Jefferson in which he spoke of the public's united support for Washington, said (writing partly in the private cipher they used to keep the sensitive parts of their correspondence safe from prying eyes) that Adams had "made himself obnoxious to many, particularly in the Southern states" and worried that he might "even intrigue for premature advancement" to the presidency.

How, one might ask, could such an intrigue be carried out? The answer lay in the Constitution's provisions for electing the President and Vice President, which did not allow electors to specify which vote was for the top of the ticket and which was for the second spot. The problem had been quickly grasped by Alexander Hamilton, who wrote in January 1789, "Every body is aware of that defect in the

	Washington	Adams	Huntington	Jay	Hancock	R. H. Harrison	Clinton	Rutledge	Milton	Armstrong	Telfair	Lincoln
New Hampshire	5.	5.	—	—	—	—	—	—	—	—	—	—
Massachusetts	10.	10.	—	—	—	—	—	—	—	—	—	—
Connecticut	7.	5.	2.	—	—	—	—	—	—	—	—	—
New Jersey	6.	1.	—	5.	—	—	—	—	—	—	—	—
Pennsylvania	10.	8.	—	—	2.	—	—	—	—	—	—	—
Delaware	3.	—	—	3.	—	—	—	—	—	—	—	—
Maryland	6.	—	—	—	—	6.	—	—	—	—	—	—
Virginia	10.	5.	—	1.	1.	—	3.	—	—	—	—	—
South Carolina	7.	—	—	1.	—	6.	—	—	—	—	—	—
Georgia	5.	—	—	—	—	—	—	2.	1.	1.	1.	
	69.	34.	2.	9.	4.	6.	3.	6.	2.	1.	1.	1.

Whereby it appears that George Washington, Esq. Was unanimously elected President;—And John Adams Esq. Was duly elected Vice President, Of the United States of America.

Mr. Madison came from the House of Representatives with the following verbal message:—Mr. President, I am directed by the House of Representatives to inform the Senate, that the House have agreed, that the notifications of the election of the President and of the Vice President of the

United States Senate journal for April 6, 1789. Each of the sixty-nine electors had two votes. The first column of numbers shows that all cast one vote for George Washington, thereby unanimously electing him President. The remaining columns show that thirty-four of the electors cast their second votes for John Adams, making him Vice President, and the other thirty-five distributed their second votes among ten candidates.

1792: THE FIRST POLITICAL PARTIES

ALTHOUGH POLITICAL PARTIES EMERGED in the first decade of the republic's existence under the Constitution, the Founding Fathers considered the idea of parties repulsive, and they insisted both to others and to themselves that they were not creating a party system. The Founding Fathers were, after all, men of the Enlightenment, and in the Age of Reason it was supposed that matters of public policy could be decided by a careful examination of the facts of the case. When a conclusion was arrived at, those advancing the solution to the problem expected it to be accepted as the clear answer; when opposition surfaced, it was often seen as being motivated by some factional interest. It was hard for these new American leaders to accept the idea that individuals applying their reason could arrive at different conclusions, and as a result opposition was attacked as being self-interested and contrary to the public good. It was a shrill kind of politics, one that found it necessary, for example, to portray Washington and Adams as British toadies and "monarchists" and Jefferson and Madison as "anarchists" and servants of France.

The public interest, of course, appeared different to Boston merchants and backcountry farmers, to Carolina slaveholders and Philadelphia Quakers. At first glance it would seem difficult to understand why this first generation of American politicians had such a hard time grasping the idea of a legitimate opposition. After all, the formation of the national government under the Constitution had provoked a great debate across the country about the principles under which the nation should be governed: What powers should be granted to the federal government and which reserved to the states? How powerful should the executive branch be? How should individual liberties be preserved? But the Constitution had been ratified, and many took that fact to overshadow the debates that had preceded

constitution which renders it possible that the man intended for Vice President may in fact turn up President." (For more on this problem, see the election of 1800.) Hamilton—wanting to prevent a tie in electoral votes and eager to weaken the power of the Massachusetts statesman by reducing the number of votes for him— saw an opportunity in this constitutional flaw and urged various political allies to make sure that a few Adams votes were diverted to other candidates.

When the electors met and voted on February 4, 1789, Washington was elected unanimously (with 69 votes), but Adams won the second spot with a mere 34 votes, a humiliatingly low total (not even a majority). When he learned of Hamilton's scheme to deprive him of votes, the proud and prickly Adams became Hamilton's enemy, with serious consequences.

As the leader of the new republic progressed through Alexandria, Baltimore, and Wilmington on his way to New York, where he was to be inaugurated, he was feted with parades, grand dinners, and ceremonies. His route through New Jersey was at times strewn with flowers as young women sang odes or danced in his honor.

ratification. The great issues had been resolved, many voters decided, and so government could proceed without the debilitating influence of faction.

Faction, however, proved stronger. And as political differences deepened during the 1790s, political parties coalesced around the divisions in the national government. The accepted ideology of the time still held parties to be abhorrent, and in many places a respected individual could hold himself above party strife and still wield power, but parties were nevertheless coming to life.

The Federalist Party, which included George Washington, Alexander Hamilton, John Adams, and others, drew its greatest support from New England. The Federalists were fearful of granting too much power to the people, and the New England states were linked by commerce to Britain and the British colonies in the Caribbean and thus were interested in national policies favorable to trade and protective of maritime interests. The French Revolution, and the consequent execution of the French king and queen, was seen by many Federalists as a warning about the consequences of unleashing the mob. They were not, as Jefferson sometimes fulminated, monarchists. They did accept that the ultimate source of power was the people. They felt, however, that this raw power had to be harnessed by an elite in order for it to find prudent expression in governmental action.

The Republicans, as the group aligned with Jefferson and Madison came to be called, were more trusting of the people and less insistent upon the prerogatives of the elite (although the Republican leaders were hardly plebeian). The Republicans of the 1790s still found the word "democratic" to be pejorative, connoting excess, rabble, demagoguery. But within a generation the party moved to the left and by the time of Andrew Jackson had shifted so far as to adopt the name "Democratic" Party. The party's old name lay fallow for a generation, until a new organization arose in the 1850s and revived the name of the Republican Party.

Washington accepted these tributes with his customary formal dignity. An elegantly decorated barge ferried him from New Jersey to Manhattan, and on April 30, 1789, standing on a balcony overlooking Wall Street and dressed in a suit of brown homespun, chosen to symbolize his encouragement of American manufacturing, Washington took the oath of office as first President of the United States.

The united support for George Washington did not mean that the measures he advanced would be approved uncritically, however, and his first term was marked by the development of two camps of political leaders, one led by Hamilton, Washington's secretary of the Treasury, and the other by Secretary of State Jefferson and his Virginia ally James Madison. By the time the 1792 elections came around, disagreements over domestic and foreign policy had turned these loose alliances into embryonic political parties. Hamilton's economic policies had won the administration support in New England and among the merchants of the port cities, while many in the more agrarian, slaveholding South shared Jefferson's distaste for the course Hamilton was steering. Washington, disgusted with all the feuding, asked Madison

*George Washington arriving
at Manhattan's Battery for his
inauguration, 1789.*
COLLECTION OF THE NEW-YORK
HISTORICAL SOCIETY.

in May of that year to draft a farewell address for him. But in spite of, or, rather, owing to, their other differences, Hamilton, Jefferson, and Madison all agreed that Washington would have to accept a second term. Jefferson urged Washington to stay in office, saying that only he could keep North and South together, and Edmund Randolph, the attorney general, suggested that it would be easier for Washington to prevent civil war—by staying in office—than it would be to stop a war once it had begun.

The threat to the Union posed by the vicious partisan politics of the middle 1790s was not as grave as it seemed in the summer of 1792, but then again it may have been Washington's willingness to stay in office that kept matters from degenerating as Randolph and others feared they might. Washington's election was again unanimous, and John Adams was again elected Vice President, but unanimity was never to return to the Electoral College.

Washington devised no electoral strategies, made no campaign trips, did no fund-raising, delivered no stirring campaign speeches, attended no political conventions. Yet his willingness to serve two terms in office had lasting consequences for the nation.

If the Constitution had been written with Washington in mind as President, the considerable powers allotted the President were not the only consequence of that situation. We are accustomed to hearing the Founding Fathers praised in unstinting terms and the Constitution memorialized as a nearly flawless creation. But the provisions for choosing the President and Vice President were deeply flawed, perhaps because most of the Framers' assumptions about presidential contests were wrong. They assumed that political parties would not arise. They assumed that the voters would retain the deferential attitude toward their leaders that had defined the politics of eighteenth-century America. They assumed that men who showed themselves to be ambitious for power would be spurned by the electorate. They assumed that the President and the Vice President should be the two most prominent politicians in the nation, not troubling to think what might happen if those two persons were rivals.

While Washington was still in office, these errors mattered little. But when he finally retired to his beloved Mount Vernon (establishing the two-term precedent in the process), the flaws of this newborn political system quickly grew prominent.

United States Senate journal for February 13, 1793, documenting Washington's reelection.

NATIONAL ARCHIVES.

Divided Government

ADAMS v. JEFFERSON, 1796

Although the Founding Fathers' hopes for avoiding party strife had proved futile, and despite the fact that Washington himself had been attacked in print—"If ever a nation has been deceived by a man, the American Nation has been deceived by Washington," the Philadelphia *Aurora* proclaimed—the presidency was clearly his to keep for as long as he wished to remain in office. Until he stepped down, the defects in the electoral system were of little importance. As for the vice presidency, although it had already given rise to electoral scheming, the prize itself was hardly worth the effort. The first man to hold the office, John Adams, wrote to his wife, Abigail, "My country has in its wisdom contrived for me the most insignificant office that ever the invention of man contrived or his imagination conceived."

The vast gulf between the importance of the President and the insignificance of the Vice President was not, however, recognized in the electoral system, which still failed to allow electors to distinguish which vote each was casting for President and which for the second office. Once Washington disappeared from the scene, the possibilities for electoral intrigue would expand, and in 1796 and 1800 the flaws in the system became clear.

But first there was the matter of Washington's intentions. Although in 1792 he had asked Madison to draft a farewell address for him, he had yielded to the entreaties of his closest advisers to serve at least part of a second term. But the second term had proved to be rockier than the first, with partisan feeling deepening and parties beginning their slow transformation from loose associations of like-minded leaders to broad-based popular organizations. The party splits of Washington's second term were aggravated by events in Europe. The opposing Federalist and Republican causes linked themselves to the fate of the two great Atlantic powers, Britain and France, respectively, which were engaged in the early stages of their decades-long struggle following the French Revolution.

The initial reaction to that revolution had been very favorable—here was the flattering situation of the greatest nation of Europe following the lead of the United States. But America's economic ties to Britain, which had been central to

Alexander Hamilton's financial system, meant that even as enthusiastic patriots were celebrating the new status of America's old ally France, powerful forces in the United States had many reasons to prefer closer ties to Britain. Of course, emotions were a bit confused, since it was King Louis XVI's army and navy that had helped America win independence. The declaration of the French Republic in 1792 may have swelled Republican breasts in the United States, but the subsequent execution of the king and queen outraged Americans when the news arrived early in 1793.

While Washington's cabinet kept the United States out of the war between Britain and France, individual members of that body had their own particular sympathies. Secretary of State Thomas Jefferson was a champion of the French Revolution and was happy for his political followers to try to capitalize on American enthusiasm for it. Alexander Hamilton, the secretary of the Treasury, was eager to keep relations with Britain as warm as circumstances allowed, and his followers were revolted by the excesses of the regicidal rulers of France. John Adams, the Vice President, had, like Jefferson, served America in France as a diplomat and had come home disliking the French as much as Jefferson had come home admiring them. Although Jefferson sought ways to avoid disappointing his enthusiastic followers, America's only plausible course was neutrality, and soon after news of France's declaration of war on Britain and Holland reached America in the spring of 1793, Washington duly issued a proclamation of American neutrality.

Despite Washington's proclamation, the European conflict was playing havoc with American shipping, with both British and French ships seizing hundreds of American vessels. Chief Justice John Jay had been dispatched to London to seek Britain's commitment to respect America's neutrality, as well as to resolve various matters left over from the Revolutionary War, such as the failure of the British to evacuate various frontier forts under the terms of the 1783 peace treaty. (The British countered that the United States had failed to observe some of the treaty's terms as well.) America's military weakness left Jay with little beyond moral suasion to use in his negotiations, and as usual that had little effect. Britain's desire to keep the American republic from growing too close to its French cousin was Jay's most powerful ally, and he managed to conclude a treaty that secured the return of the forts, although it won little from the British in terms of maritime concessions.

The treaty was greeted with outrage in America, where the news arrived just after Jay was elected governor of New York—and for a time that victory seemed likely to be the last major Federalist triumph. The treaty was ratified only after a bitter Senate debate (and even then James Madison attempted to block

1796

PRESIDENTIAL CANDIDATE (STATE) VICE-PRESIDENTIAL CANDIDATE (STATE)	PARTY	ELECTORAL VOTES
John Adams (Mass.)	Federalist	71
Thomas Pinckney (S.C.)		59
Thomas Jefferson (Va.)	Democratic-Republican	68
Aaron Burr (N.Y.)		30

Nine other men—some of them declared candidates and some (including George Washington) not—received a total of 48 electoral votes.

"It is a delicate thing for me to speak of the late election. To myself, personally, 'my election' might be a matter of indifference or rather of aversion. Had Mr. Jay, or some others, been in question, it might have less mortified my vanity, and infinitely less alarmed my apprehensions for the public. But to see such a character as Jefferson, and much more such an unknown being as Pinckney, brought over my head, and trampling on the bellies of hundreds of other men infinitely his superior in talents, services, and reputation, filled me with apprehensions for the safety of us all. . . . That must be a sordid people indeed— a people destitute of sense of honor, equity, and character, that could submit to be governed, and see hundreds of its most meritorious public men governed, by a Pinckney, under an elective govern- ment."

JOHN ADAMS IN A LETTER TO
HENRY KNOX DATED
MARCH 30, 1797

it in the House of Representatives by trying to withhold the funding needed to carry it into effect). But the consequences of the treaty proved more concrete than had been expected, with not only British forces' departure from the frontier forts but also a move by Spain to improve relations with the United States by allowing Americans free navigation of the Mississippi River. These diplomatic moves helped promote a surge of migration westward.

But in spite of the successes of George Washington's diplomatic efforts, opposi- tion voices, particularly in the partisan press, were loud and persistent. The growth of political parties during Washington's first administration had been accelerated in the spring of 1792 by a war of words that Hamiltonians and Jeffersonians waged in their respective newspapers, the *Gazette of the United States* and the *National Gazette.*

Amid all this George Washington remained President, and in spite of the calumnies in the newspapers (he was accused of being a secret traitor during the Revolutionary War and called the "scourge and misfortune of our country") he was certain to be re-elected if he chose to stand. But the man who had made clear his desire to retire to Mount Vernon would not be prevailed upon to seek a third term. The press attacks clearly rankled: he complained that he had been savaged in terms that would not even be used against "a common pickpocket" and listed among his reasons for leaving office his "disinclination to be longer buffited [*sic*] in the public prints by a set of infamous scribblers." Though his friends knew he intended to re- tire and the public was eager to know his plans, Washington remained silent on the subject throughout the summer of 1796, until September 17, when he delivered his "Farewell Address," warning against the twin evils he saw roiling his country's do- mestic tranquillity: the "baneful effects of the spirit of party" and "passionate at- tachments" to any foreign country or cause.

Washington's announcement came only seven weeks before electors were due to be chosen, and although his plans were suspected much earlier, the effect of his delay was to greatly reduce the amount of time that could be devoted to the sorts of activities dictated by "the spirit of party." Nevertheless, the address was, as the Fed- eralist Fisher Ames said, "a signal, like dropping a hat, for the party racers to start."

Who would the racers be? It was hardly an enviable task to succeed the Father of the Country, and Jefferson, when sounded by Madison on the subject the previ- ous year, had replied, "The question is forever closed with me." However, by 1796 Jefferson was certainly eager for the office, although he presented the proper fa- cade of disinterestedness and lack of ambition. Despite an equal affectation of in- difference, Vice President Adams also desired the office, though he did so more from a sense of personal entitlement than out of strong party feeling.

But partisan emotion was rising, and for the first time there was to be an actual contest for the presidency. The historian Page Smith has written that it is not unrea- sonable to consider the election of 1796 "the most important in our history," both because it was the first contested election and because the divisions in the country, exemplified in the struggle over the Jay Treaty, represented a serious threat to the maintenance of the Union—perhaps the most serious threat before the 1850s. Of

John Adams, by John Trumbull, 1793.
NATIONAL PORTRAIT GALLERY,
SMITHSONIAN INSTITUTION.

course, the rules under which this first contest proceeded were very different from those we know today. There was no campaigning yet—the tradition of disinterested leadership was still too strong to permit even the slightest hint of candidacy. Madison was so afraid that Jefferson would decline to be a candidate if asked directly that he avoided him that fall, not wishing to give Jefferson the chance to express his reluctance to take office. Adams was selected by the Federalist members of Congress. To run with Adams, the Federalists selected Thomas Pinckney of South Carolina, who had recently negotiated the treaty with Spain that had opened the Mississippi to American commerce—so recently, in fact, that he was aboard a ship returning from Europe at the time of the election and learned of his candidacy only after the results were in. The Republicans paid little attention to the second spot on their ticket, although the young Aaron Burr of New York, then a U.S. senator, campaigned for the office and actively toured New England on his own behalf.

Sixteen states chose electors in 1796, ten of them through their state legislatures and six through popular elections. Although the presidential candidates did not campaign, their supporters made efforts to garner votes in states such as Massachusetts and Pennsylvania where the voters picked the electors. Accusations that Adams was a monarchist were part of the Republican approach, and his past attempts to endow the office of President with what he thought would be sufficient grandeur (he favored referring to the President as "His Highness the President of the United States and Protector of the Rights of the Same") provided some support for the absurd charge. (Another proposed form of address was "His Elective Highness.")

But the greatest threat to the election of Adams came neither from Jefferson nor from France but from the scheming of members of his own party, led by Hamilton. Hamilton wished to continue to exercise the influence that Washington had granted him but recognized that Adams was too stiff-necked and willful to allow Hamilton such power. Pinckney, though, promised to be more easily influenced (or so Hamilton thought—Pinckney, still literally at sea, can have had no part in Hamilton's plot), so Hamilton sought to have some electors from Pinckney's home state cast away electoral votes for Adams and thus allow his running mate, Pinckney, to win the presidency. But Hamilton's plan was thwarted when some electors in New England got wind of the plan and dropped Pinckney's name from their ballots. The result of Hamilton's gambit was hardly what he desired: Adams was elected President (with 71 electoral votes), but because votes for Pinckney had been thrown away in the North (and because South Carolina's electors cast eight votes each for favorite son Pinckney and Jefferson), it was Jefferson, Hamilton's nemesis, who came in second (with 68 votes) and became Vice President.

For all the bungling that attended the outcome, the election of 1796 was terribly important. For the first time, power was passed from one president to another. There was scheming but no violence. Washington's decision to step down after two terms confirmed his reputation for disinterested leadership and set a precedent that was followed for a century and a half, and is now embedded in the Constitution. But the election, resulting in a Vice President openly opposed to the President in fundamental matters of policy, indicated more clearly than ever the defects in the Constitution's provision for electing the nation's executive. Had Hamilton's scheme succeeded, the consequences could have been dire (although it is possible that Pinckney would have refused to accept an office obtained so dishonorably). And one consequence of the plot would prove disastrous four years later, for the squandering of electoral votes showed that strict discipline was needed to prevent a repeat of the 1796 result, with a President from one party and a Vice President from the other.

In 1800, strict discipline would be maintained, with nearly calamitous consequences for the nation.

The Revolution of 1800

JEFFERSON v. ADAMS

If John Adams was eager to be elected President, he had no illusions that holding the office would make him happy. The morning after his victory, thinking about George Washington, he wrote in his diary, "Methought I heard him say, 'Ay! I am fairly out and you fairly in! See which of us will be the happiest!' "

Adams was not a man cut out for happiness in any case. Jefferson assessed him acutely: "He is vain, irritable, and a bad calculator of the force and probable effect of the motives which govern men." The new President disdained the scrum of politics and tried to assume Washington's mantle as a disinterested leader, but he lacked his predecessor's unique fitness for the role of patriot king. Adams's failure to take into account "the motives which govern men" was exemplified by his decision to retain Washington's cabinet, even though several of its members—in particular his secretary of state, Timothy Pickering, and his secretary of war, James McHenry—were loyal to Adams's rival Hamilton.

Division within the Federalists was only making things easier for the Republicans, who were developing their skills as opposition partisans and building the foundations of a national party organization. That the leader of this opposition was Adams's own Vice President only compounded the President's problems. Jefferson and Adams respected each other personally, and pointedly made known their mutual admiration in the weeks before Adams's inauguration. The two men met in Philadelphia early in March 1797 and discussed the country's most pressing international concern, relations with France. Adams wished to send a mission to Paris with either Jefferson or Madison as part of it, with a view to resolving the many areas of contention between the two nations. Jefferson said that he, as Vice President, should probably remain in America, and he predicted that Madison would decline such an appointment. (Perhaps both Virginians were eager to avoid responsibility for any failure that might attend the mission.) Adams's disappointment grew into bewildered exasperation when he raised the idea with Oliver Wolcott, his Hamiltonian secretary of the Treasury, who said that if Madison was named to the Paris mission, the cabinet would resign. That conversation took place on March 5, the day after Adams took the oath of office as President. The next day Jefferson informed Adams that Madison would certainly decline such an appointment if it were offered. The hopes for a bipartisan foreign policy were thus extinguished before Adams had been President three days.

The Jeffersonians may have desired to avoid the issues between the United States and France, but the President, having no such luxury, dispatched a mission to Paris composed of John Marshall, Charles Cotesworth Pinckney, and Elbridge Gerry with instructions to seek ways to end French attacks on American shipping. The Americans were treated with barely concealed contempt in Paris as Talleyrand, the French foreign minister, sought to extract money from the American government, both for his nation and for himself, and repeatedly sent intermediaries (referred to in American dispatches as "X," "Y," and "Z") to try to get the Americans to pay the demanded bribe. Pinckney exploded at one of these emissaries—"No! No! Not a sixpence!"—and Marshall was similarly resolute, although Gerry was more sympathetic to the French position. Such bribes were common practice, and France's victories on the battlefield had strengthened Talleyrand's hand and stiffened his resolve to extort everything he could from the Americans. When the Americans managed to avoid Talleyrand's various snares, the French threatened to escalate the war at sea.

A year to the day after Adams's inauguration, the first of the dispatches from the Paris mission reached Philadelphia, and Adams soon gave Congress a general idea of what had happened. As the cabinet considered a declaration of war, Congress decided it needed the full dispatches to reach its own conclusions, and one Republican member from Virginia accused the President of "keeping back all information." On April 2, 1798, the House called for the release of the dispatches.

For the Republicans, this was a grave error. The clarity with which France's duplicity was exposed, and the stern refusal of the Americans to traffic with Talleyrand, buoyed up the administration's popularity and even made John Adams himself a popular leader for a time. Jefferson carped that the "X.Y.Z. dish" had been "cooked up by Marshall," a Virginia Federalist, but most read the dispatches with greater objectivity and perception. The reluctance of congressmen to appear pro-French now made it possible for the Federalists to control the passage of legislation, and not only were Adams's requests for more warships and a stronger defense granted, but overenthusiastic Federalists in Congress enacted measures Adams had not requested, the notorious Alien and Sedition Acts.

Of these, the most serious threat to the developing American political process was the Sedition Act, which among other measures

1800

PRESIDENTIAL CANDIDATE (STATE) VICE-PRESIDENTIAL CANDIDATE (STATE)	PARTY	ELECTORAL VOTES
Thomas Jefferson (Va.)	Democratic-Republican	73
Aaron Burr (N.Y.)		73
John Adams (Mass.)	Federalist	65
Charles C. Pinckney (S.C.)		64

John Jay (N.Y.; Federalist) received 1 electoral vote.

made it illegal to circulate "false, scandalous and malicious" statements about public officials. Such statements were common in the highly partisan newspapers of the 1790s, and Adams and Jefferson had both been subjected to vile abuse. But enforcement of the Sedition Act was selective. A number of prominent Republican editors were fined and jailed under the law, while Federalist editors who blasted Jefferson were not prosecuted.

There is no question that France and Britain were attempting to manipulate American politics and politicians for their own geopolitical ends, and the weak and newly minted United States clearly had to defend itself against such manipulations. Although the Alien and Sedition Acts were too clearly partisan in their design and execution to be defended successfully on the grounds of "national security," the principal challenges to the laws were as intemperate as the laws themselves and would have a much longer-reaching influence over American politics and government. The Republicans denounced the government's measures as violations of the Constitution and of the rights of the sovereign states. In two of those states resolutions were introduced in the legislatures—in Virginia the proposal was drafted by James Madison, while Jefferson himself wrote the measure considered in Kentucky (although both men kept their authorship secret). Jefferson's version declared that since the Constitution was a document agreed to by the states (not by the "people," as the document's preamble stated), each state could determine for itself what federal acts were lawful and which were not. The principles laid out in the resolutions were to be used for decades to fight federal power, particularly as the sectional issues surrounding slavery became ever more hotly debated. But in the short run the resolutions were less important as theoretical statements about the Constitution than as the first planks in the Republican platform for the election of 1800.

The Republicans' fortunes had reached a low point in the elections of 1798, when the Federalists' tough stand against France had led to a stronger majority in Congress. By January 1799, Thomas Jefferson, who was actively organizing the Republicans for the 1800 campaign, was laying out his ideas in a letter to Elbridge Gerry of Massachusetts in which he stressed that he was for "a government rigorously frugal and simple" that relied, for defense, on "our militia solely, till actual invasion." As in the Kentucky Resolutions, he emphasized the proper limits of the federal government, calling for a small navy (Adams had established the Navy Department as part of his military buildup) and freedom of the press (as opposed to the Sedition Act).

In the practical realm of political tactics, both parties tried to alter the states' methods of choosing electors to be favorable (as they thought) to their candidates. Jefferson's Virginia changed from its earlier system of choosing electors by district to a statewide winner-take-all ticket. Adams's Massachusetts stripped the choice from the voters and lodged it in the legislature, where the Federalists could deliver the entire state to the favorite son. (In 1800, only five of the sixteen states would allow voters to choose the electors.) And in New York, which would be the pivot upon which the election turned, Republicans attempted to take the choice away

"During these past months enough abuse and scandal has been unleashed to ruin and corrupt the minds and morals of the best people in the world."

ABIGAIL ADAMS IN A LETTER
DATED MAY 4, 1800

from the legislature and substitute popular choice of electors by district, but the Federalists defeated the proposal.

As election year approached, the efforts of the Adams administration to improve relations with France finally began to bear fruit. Talleyrand became less high-handed, and Adams sent a new mission to France, which by September 1800 had managed to negotiate a satisfactory agreement. But this diplomatic success contained the seeds of defeat. More militant Federalists felt that Adams had capitulated to France, while the lessening of tensions between the two nations made the Republicans' sympathies for France less of a liability. Moreover, when the threat of war receded, the justification for the Alien and Sedition Acts evaporated with it.

The election of 1800 was a party contest, displaying a level of partisan feeling that would not be reached again for a generation. Although nationally parties were still little more than informal networks of like-minded leaders, real party organizations were developing in hotly contested states, such as New York, and in states with statewide popular tickets, such as Virginia. Although candidates would be expected to feign reluctance to put themselves forward for public office for decades to come, the practical work of selecting candidates, organizing campaigns, coordinating electoral efforts, and getting a coherent message to the voters through the press had to be done—and effectively. In Virginia the challenge was mostly one of form, because Jefferson's stature in the state guaranteed that he would carry it. But New York was a true battleground, and there the Republicans had to accomplish the more difficult task of winning control of the legislature, which would then choose the state's electors.

Jefferson's effort in New York was directed by Aaron Burr, who had been active in the state's politics for a decade and had managed in that time not only to offend many leading Republicans but also to make a potent enemy of Alexander Hamilton. But Burr was able, energetic, and eager to please Jefferson. The goal of winning the state legislature was a daunting one, but it was clearly crucial to Jefferson's chances (as the candidate himself perceived), and this was an argument Burr used to persuade many of the state's leading men to allow themselves to be put forward as candidates for offices that were beneath their station. George Clinton, for example, had served as governor of the state from 1777 to 1795 yet was cajoled into running for state assembly. Horatio Gates, hero of the great Revolutionary War victory at Saratoga, was on the same ticket, as were other men of high reputation. The Federalist ticket was less distinguished and its campaign less well organized. The election was held over three days (April 29–May 1), and during that time party activists worked ceaselessly to persuade voters to back their tickets. Burr's strategy proved the better, and the Republicans won.

The New York win had immediate and far-reaching consequences. In Philadelphia, Adams finally moved to rid his cabinet of those whose loyalty was to Hamilton, not to himself. Within a week of receiving the news from New York, Adams fired Secretary of State Pickering and Secretary of War McHenry. Adams had been reluctant to create deeper divisions within the Federalist ranks, but when Hamilton proved unable to deliver his state to his party, Adams felt that he might as well move ahead. On May 3, the Federalists met in congressional caucus and chose the ticket of Adams and Charles Cotesworth Pinckney. For the Republicans, one result of the New York victory was to suggest that some politician from that state ought to be given the second spot on the ticket—and who better than Aaron Burr, architect of the victory? On May 11, the Republican members of Congress caucused and nominated Burr as Jefferson's running mate.

Whether a state chose electors by popular vote or in the legislature, efforts to influence opinion were crucial to a party's success, and the Republicans in particular worked hard to make sure that the message voters heard was consistent. One strain, ever popular with parties that have languished in opposition for some time, was expressed by a New Jersey flyer that demanded of voters, "Is it not high time for a CHANGE?" Republicans attacked Adams as a closet monarchist; Adams's voluminous writings warned of the dangers of unbridled popular government, and some of his quite sensible statements on the subject were easily adopted to portray him as an enemy of the people. One Republican pamphleteer trotted forth heretical statements made by Adams—that "THE BRITISH CONSTITUTION IS, IN THE STRICTEST SENSE, A REPUBLIC" and that "AN HEREDITARY PRESIDENT AND SENATE FOR LIFE CAN ALONE SECURE YOU HAPPINESS." Then he asked his readers, "*When* and *where* will you look for relief?" (To Jefferson, he suggested.) Every effort was made to deprive Adams of the protective mantle of Washington and to associate him with the Federalist hard-liners who were in fact Adams's foes. He was made into the proud father of the Alien and Sedition Acts, and appeals were aimed at immigrant groups, such as Germans in Pennsylvania, to vote Republican.

The Federalist message was quite simple: Jefferson was (as one Connecticut partisan put it) a "howling atheist," a fellow traveler of the French Revolution. His coming to power would tear the country apart, destroy religion, assault property. Jefferson's scientific writings were scoured for passages that questioned the accuracy of the Bible, and these were then cited as evidence that Jefferson was irreligious. The Vice President's supporters went through remarkable contortions to defend him from the charge. One rising Republican politician, DeWitt Clinton of New York, writing under the name "Grotius," labored to explain away Jefferson's doubts about the great flood of Noah, saying Jefferson agreed that there had been a flood and merely questioned whether it had been universal, and suggesting helpfully that when Moses said, "All the high hills that were under the whole heaven were covered" he might have been using "synecdoche, a figure in rhetoric, where the whole is put for a part, or a part for the whole." How effective this argument was we don't know, but it was at least instructive. The various attacks on Jefferson were refuted at length by John Beckley, the former clerk of the House of Representatives, in the first campaign biography.

Federalist writers were also publishing defenses of Adams, and the leading intellect of the party, Hamilton, contributed the most important tract, *The Public Conduct and Character of John Adams, Esq., President of the United States.* Unfortunately for

"I should be deficient in candor were I to conceal the conviction, that he [Adams] does not possess the talents adapted to the Administration of Government, and that there are great and intrinsic defects in his character which unfit him for the office of Chief Magistrate."

ALEXANDER HAMILTON'S REMARK ABOUT HIS FELLOW FEDERALIST JOHN ADAMS, IN A PRIVATE LETTER PUBLISHED BY AARON BURR, WITHOUT AUTHORIZATION, AS *The Public Conduct and Character of John Adams, Esq., President of the United States* (NEW YORK, OCTOBER 24, 1800)

Adams, this turned out to be a nasty assault, accusing him of weakness in his dealings with France and assailing the dismissals of Hamilton's chums from the cabinet. Hamilton had circulated the privately printed pamphlet among his friends, but Burr obtained a copy and in the weeks leading up to the November elections excerpts appeared in Republican papers around the nation. After the vote, Hamilton again attempted to pervert the electoral process by trying to persuade members of his party to cast away some Adams votes and thus give the election to Charles Cotesworth Pinckney. (He was assuming that the Federalists would receive more electoral votes than the Republicans.)

Hamilton was trying one last time to take advantage of the flaw in the Constitution that prevented electors from specifying which vote was for President and which for Vice President. The development of political parties, unanticipated by the members of the Constitutional Convention just a dozen years before, had made the original provisions for electing the executive obsolete, and the experience of having a Vice President who opposed the President's policies had demonstrated how deeply flawed the process was.

But it was to be the Republicans, not the Federalists, who gave the final proof of the need to amend the Constitution. The election results in November gave Jefferson a clear, if narrow, majority of the votes over Adams—but not over Burr. Jefferson and his running mate each received 73 electoral votes. The failure of the party to pay much attention to the second spot on the ticket four years earlier was understood as a mistake, and in 1800 the party took the vice presidency seriously. Furthermore, Burr, who had campaigned for the job four years earlier, was miffed that Virginia had given him only a single vote. In 1800, the Republicans, grateful for the victory in New York and eager to promote party unity, delivered the state's entire vote to him. But so successful was party discipline that a tie vote resulted, and the election was thrown into the House of Representatives, where the lame-duck Sixth Congress, due to leave office March 4, would decide the issue in February.

Article II of the Constitution provided that if two candidates had an equal number of votes the House would elect the President, with each state delegation having one vote. So with sixteen states in the Union in 1800, nine states would have to vote for a candidate for him to be elected. The Republicans could count on the votes of only eight delegations, and as soon as a tie vote was apparent certain Federalists began scheming to throw the election to Burr, who, though a Republican, was thought to be less dangerous than the "atheistic" Jefferson. But for once Hamilton steered clear of the plot. After the Republican victory in the New York legislative elections that spring, he had urged Governor John Jay to lead an effort to have the lame-duck New York legislature give the vote to the people (Jay rejected the move), but when the alternative to Jefferson was Aaron Burr, Hamilton was for letting the Virginian succeed. Many Federalists in Congress, however, hoped to cut a deal with Burr and make him President in return for favorable consideration of their views, and it is unclear how open to such proposals Burr was. He stated that he had no de-

"Look at your houses, your parents, your wives, and your children. Are you prepared to see your dwellings in flames, hoary hairs bathed in blood, female chastity violated, or children writhing on the pike and the halbert?... Look at every leading Jacobin as at a ravening wolf, preparing to enter your peaceful fold, and glut his deadly appetite on the vitals of your country.... GREAT GOD OF COMPASSION AND JUSTICE, SHIELD MY COUNTRY FROM DESTRUCTION."

Connecticut Courant
(HARTFORD),
SEPTEMBER 29, 1800

Thomas Jefferson, by Rembrandt Peale,
1805.
COLLECTION OF THE NEW-YORK
HISTORICAL SOCIETY.

sire to displace Jefferson, but he never said he would decline the presidency if elected. Through thirty-five ballots the House remained unable to elect a President, but on the thirty-sixth the Federalists finally relented and Jefferson was elected. James Bayard of Delaware was the crucial changed vote, and he later claimed to have changed it only after receiving assurances from Maryland's Samuel Smith that Jefferson would not destroy the public credit or disband the navy.

After all the intrigue, the nation faced a new party in power and a Congress firmly in the hands of the Republicans. It was this peaceful handing over of power, even more than the different policies the new administration would pursue, that fully justified Jefferson's characterization of the result as the "Revolution of 1800." A greater revolution, or even dissolution of the Union, might have come about if

Aaron Burr, by John Vanderlyn, 1802.
COLLECTION OF THE NEW-YORK
HISTORICAL SOCIETY.

the Federalists' plot to deprive Jefferson of his victory had succeeded (or had Hamilton's effort to place Pinckney in the President's chair worked). Before the House voted, there were rumors that the lame-duck Congress would try to choose a President by law, and Jefferson predicted in a letter to James Monroe that "the middle states would arm" to oppose such a move. When we celebrate this historic transfer of power, we should not forget that the first months of 1801 were a perilous time for the young republic.

Hamilton is "an intriguant, the greatest intriguant in the world—a man devoid of every moral principle—a bastard and as much a foreigner as Gallatin."

JOHN ADAMS, AS QUOTED BY HIS SECRETARY OF WAR JAMES MCHENRY, MAY 31, 1800. ALBERT GALLATIN, WHO WOULD SERVE AS JEFFERSON'S SECRETARY OF THE TREASURY, WAS BORN IN SWITZERLAND.

Jeffersonians Triumphant, Burr Deposed

JEFFERSON v. PINCKNEY, 1804

On March 4, 1801, Thomas Jefferson and Aaron Burr were sworn into office as President and Vice President of the United States by the new chief justice, John Marshall. The nation's capital had moved to the pestilential banks of the Potomac the previous fall, and this was the first inauguration held in the new town. Jefferson struck a conciliatory note in his address: "We have called by different names brethren of the same principle. We are all Republicans, we are all Federalists."

Jefferson was both right and wrong. It was true that the great majority of both parties supported a republican form of government (in spite of all Jefferson and his supporters had done to brand John Adams a "monocrat" or monarchist), and there was also widespread support for the union of the states in a federal government (in spite of Jefferson's and Madison's resolutions of 1798 that had raised state sovereignty to heights that would, if realized, have effectively dissolved that federal union). But Jefferson was wrong in his suggestion that political factions or parties would disappear, as he ardently hoped they would. Jefferson had proved an effective party leader in the years before his election as President, but he was uncomfortable with the idea of parties and held to a set of ideas, inculcated in him during his Virginia boyhood, that saw partisan strife as a serious defect in government. For a time Jefferson's goal of partyless politics seemed to have been achieved: his triumph in the 1800 election ushered in the "Virginia Dynasty," the domination of the presidency for a quarter century by Jefferson and his fellow Virginians James Madison and James Monroe. By the end of that period Jefferson could have said, "We are all Republicans, there are no Federalists." But the *idea* of parties would prove stronger than the Federalist Party.

The political worldview shared by Jefferson and most of his contemporaries has been called "classical republicanism," and it took many shapes. Jefferson and Hamilton were both "republicans" in their own ways, but those ways were very different. Republics, in the common view, were fragile entities, liable to degenerate into tyranny. Rome and Greece offered telling examples, and English and American propagandists adopted classical pseudonyms such as Cato or Publius (the by-line over which *The Federalist* articles appeared) to evoke a whole chain of associations freighted with meaning for their audiences. Each party perceived the other as a grave threat to republicanism. Jeffersonian Republicans looked at recent events and saw a Federalist administration that was building a standing army, suppressing freedom of the press, and linking itself to the interests of wealthy merchants through the Hamiltonian financial system. Federalists saw Jefferson's appeal to the common man as an unwelcome importation of the excesses of France, whose republic had already degenerated into a military dictatorship, and which before the end of Jefferson's first term would be ruled by a self-proclaimed emperor.

Even though political parties were taking distinct shape by 1800, it was a generation before parties were accepted as a good thing. The divisions that existed were thought to be temporary. And they were rendered more harmful to the nation because those divided were men of the Enlightenment. Enamored of science and eager to free mankind from the shackles of the past, Jefferson and many like him felt that once the old forms of government were cast aside society could be administered for the common good by men who would disinterestedly perceive the country's needs and take steps to meet them. The example of George Washington did much to raise these high expectations. Rational, disinterested leadership had been the ideal of those who wrote the Constitution, and for that reason they had fashioned the process of electing a President on the assumption that the best approach was to elect as President and Vice President the two most prominent men in the country. The flaws in that approach had been partially exposed in 1796 and made apparent to all in 1800. But the solution to the problem brought political parties to a new eminence.

In 1800, the Federalist electors had remained firmly in their party's camp, although one elector from Rhode Island had voted for John Jay rather than Pinckney to avoid a tie with Adams in the Electoral College. Had that vote, or any of the other 129 votes cast by Federalist electors that December, gone to Burr, he would have defeated Jefferson. The Twelfth Amendment to the Constitution (ratified in 1804) solved the problem by requiring electors to cast distinct ballots for President and Vice President. Yet even as Congress was embedding the idea of political parties in the very fabric of the Constitution—for that is what the amendment did—some members professed themselves shocked to hear parties spoken of so baldly. "We have, I believe, for the first time in this House heard the term federal and republican applied to members of this House," lamented a Federalist congressman from Massachusetts.

The Twelfth Amendment went into effect just in time for the 1804 election, but the conduct of that election, and its result, might well

1804

PRESIDENTIAL CANDIDATE (STATE) VICE-PRESIDENTIAL CANDIDATE (STATE)	PARTY	ELECTORAL VOTES
Thomas Jefferson (Va.) George Clinton (N.Y.)	Democratic-Republican	162
Charles C. Pinckney (S.C.) Rufus King (N.Y.)	Federalist	14

An anti-Jefferson broadside.
LIBRARY OF CONGRESS.

have caused observers to wonder what place parties would have in the nation's future. Jefferson's first term in office did much to reassure those who had feared that he would introduce some form of French tyranny, and it encouraged the more democratic elements of American society. Taxes were reduced, but Hamilton's financial system was left substantially in place. The nation's military establishment was greatly reduced, but the course of the struggle between Britain and France left America largely untroubled. And in a single diplomatic coup, the United States purchased the vast French territory of Louisiana, thereby gaining vital control of the Mississippi River.

Thus Jefferson made a formidable candidate for re-election. The nation was at peace, taxes had been lowered, the Alien and Sedition Acts had been allowed to expire, and vast new territory was available to the nation's farmers, allowing them the sort of financial independence that republican theory saw as essential to responsible voting. Jefferson had written the Declaration of Independence, served as secretary of state, Vice President, and President, and was the finest composer of political rhetoric of his age. Even a powerful opposition party would stand little hope against him. And the Federalists were now hardly a party at all.

The defeat of John Adams had been a stern blow; the Federalists' power was waning around the nation. Even in New England the realization that Jefferson did not behave like a French despot had calmed fears and undercut the Federalists'

ABOVE LEFT: *Charles C. Pinckney.*
Engraving, c. 1800–1810.
NATIONAL PORTRAIT GALLERY,
SMITHSONIAN INSTITUTION.

ABOVE RIGHT: *George Clinton.*
Pastel attributed to James Sharples
or Felix Sharples, c. 1806.
NATIONAL PORTRAIT GALLERY,
SMITHSONIAN INSTITUTION.

credibility. As the Republicans organized and refined their political tactics, the Federalists remained tied to an earlier conception of disinterested patrician leadership and disdained the idea of making attempts to reach out to voters. Alexander Hamilton urged the party to move with the times (but he would soon be killed by Aaron Burr).

The Federalists' support for Burr after the election was thrown into the hands of Congress in 1801, along with Burr's cloudy conduct during that period, had alienated Jefferson from his Vice President. Therefore the Federalists continued to see Burr as a possible ally. With their party dead in the South and West (in part as a result of their opposition to the Louisiana Purchase), some thought they would be better off if the northeast portion of the nation seceded from the rest. Senator Timothy Pickering of Massachusetts thought Burr might be the man to bring New York into such a confederation, and he urged New York Federalists to support Burr in the state's 1804 gubernatorial race. But Hamilton, who had opposed the plot to elect Burr over Jefferson in 1800 (since even Jefferson was preferable to the unprincipled Burr), urged his fellow New York Federalists not to support Burr. Hamilton was so strident in his urgings that Burr challenged him to a duel and killed him.

With the passing of Hamilton the Federalists lost their leading intellect and a shrewd politician. Moreover, with Adams retired and Washington dead, the party

Rufus King, by Gilbert Stuart, 1820.
NATIONAL PORTRAIT GALLERY,
SMITHSONIAN INSTITUTION.

was poorly supplied with leaders of national stature. John Marshall, the chief justice
and a former secretary of state, was perhaps the party's best hope (and the opponent most feared by Jefferson), but he remained on the bench, where for the next
three decades he would prove the ablest defender of the bedrock principles of federalism. The Federalists essentially offered electors without naming a candidate, although it was understood that the Federalist electors expected to support Charles
Cotesworth Pinckney for President and Rufus King for Vice President.

Pinckney, educated in England and France, had served in the Revolutionary
War and had achieved a certain renown for his rejection of Talleyrand's grasping
entreaties during the XYZ Affair. His candidacy for Vice President in 1800, like his
brother Thomas's in 1796, had been the vehicle for a Hamiltonian plot against

John Adams, but Pinckney had played no role in that and was well respected in the party. He may have been respected outside the party as well, but he had little support. His running mate, Rufus King, was a former senator from New York who had recently returned from serving as the American minister in London. Jefferson's running mate that year would also be a New Yorker: George Clinton, the retiring seven-term governor, replaced Burr on the Republican ticket.

Jefferson again had a well-organized electoral machine to work for him and had recruited an editor, Samuel Harrison Smith, to publish the party line in the Washington *National Intelligencer,* which was then parroted by Republican papers throughout the country. But the Federalists, without a real national ticket or a national party, ran a campaign that was fatally inept. Old charges against Jefferson (atheism, failure to pay his debts, cowardice in fleeing the British invasion of Virginia during the Revolution when he was governor) were unearthed, and efforts were made to alarm voters about the supposedly exorbitant cost of the Louisiana Purchase. Jefferson had little need to worry. Disdainful of popular campaigning and disgusted by the Federalists' appropriation of Washington's birthday as an occasion for political rallies, he refused to reveal the date of his birth in order to prevent Republicans from turning the day into a partisan jubilee.

The election was a landslide. Jefferson collected 162 electoral votes to 14 for the Federalists. Even the old Federalist bastion of Massachusetts went for him. Jefferson was understandably confident after this result and wrote to a French friend, "The two parties which prevailed with so much violence when you were here, are almost wholly melted into one." But Jefferson's policies would give federalism one last chance at power before its final extinction, and very soon the Republicans would learn that the absence of an external threat simply allowed divisions to appear within their own ranks.

The Virginia Dynasty and Its Discontents

MADISON v. PINCKNEY, 1808

In November 1807, Thomas Jefferson revealed that he did not plan to seek a third term as President, adopting George Washington's two-term limit and helping to turn that voluntary limit into a political tradition. The 1808 campaign would see the first battle for a party's nomination, and it would also show that the Federalists were not as moribund as Jefferson had hoped. It was the diplomacy of Jefferson and his secretary of state and chosen successor, James Madison, that revived federalism's fortunes and at the same time sowed dissension within the ranks of the Republicans. Madison would face three rivals in 1808, two within his own party, in addition to Charles Cotesworth Pinckney, whose defeat in 1804 had seemed a final blow to the Federalists' hopes for the presidency.

Jefferson's triumph in 1804 had owed much to the improved treatment of American ships following the Adams administration's resolution of problems with the French in 1800. Since that time Europe's greatest impact on the United States had come with Napoleon's decision to sell Louisiana to help finance his war against Britain and her allies. But in the fall of 1805, the European conflict was redefined: Nelson destroyed the French and Spanish fleets at Trafalgar in October, and Napoleon crushed the Austrian and Russian armies at Austerlitz in December. Britain now commanded the seas, but Napoleon was supreme on the Continent. Thus locked in desperate conflict, neither nation cared much for the sensitivities of impotent neutrals.

That the United States was impotent owed much to the naval policies pursued by Jefferson, whose belief in small government had led to the dismantling of the naval establishment built up during Adams's term in office. (The classical republican ideology taught that maintaining a standing army was often the quickest route a nation could take from liberty to tyranny.) Alexander Hamilton had certainly hoped to use the army to project and consolidate the power of the federal government, and the navy Adams had created was to the Virginians a sinkhole of federal influence. Jefferson's secretary of the Treasury, Albert Gallatin, who had opposed the creation of the navy while a congressman from Pennsylvania, had slashed naval spending by more than 70 percent. The navy that remained was even weaker than it might have been as a result of one of Jefferson's most admired character traits: his scientific mind. Jefferson had concluded that the best naval force would be one composed of heavy gunboats that would lie at the entrances to American harbors and protect them. Informing Congress that gunboats were "in use with every modern maritime nation for the purpose of defence," he neglected to mention that those nations devoted vastly more effort to furnishing their navies with powerful, maneuverable frigates and ships of the line. Jefferson admitted that gunboats "can have but little effect toward protecting our commerce," but he maintained that this purely defensive navy would, unlike the stronger navy favored by Federalists, not "become an excitement to engage in offensive maritime war."

Jefferson and James Madison, his secretary of state, believed not only that a new kind of nation could be created but that a new kind of foreign policy could be made to serve that nation. Nowhere was their sense of limitless possibility more expansive—or less successful—than in their attempt to use commercial warfare to protect America from the naval predations of the great powers of Europe. In the aftermath of Trafalgar and Austerlitz, a series of ever-stricter limits on neutral trade was proclaimed by Britain and France. America's protests to both powers were largely ignored, which is hardly surprising considering that the United States was without any significant force to add weight to its complaints. Madison had long harbored his own pet theories on the efficacy of commercial warfare, theories entirely consistent with Jefferson's frugal approach to government and his own pacific nature. Both men believed that Britain, in particular, needed American raw materials far more than the United States needed British goods. The United States sold the British wheat, cotton, timber, and other vital supplies but in return bought mere "fripperies": fancy fabrics, expensive furniture, fine china. Americans could easily forgo those luxuries, at least for the period required to bring Britain and France to their senses. The theory took form in the Embargo Act, passed in December 1807, which decreed that, with a few stated exceptions, American ships in port had to stay there and those at sea would be made to remain in port once they returned.

The Embargo was a policy rooted in the Virginian experience of its chief proponents. And in Virginia the act had little enough practical effect at first. But in the port cities of the eastern seaboard, such as Boston and New York, the act shattered the economy. A British visitor who had remarked on New York's bustling state when he passed through in November ("an exact epitome" of London, he thought) returned in April to find that the city now presented a "melancholy appearance" and that grass was growing on the for-

1808

PRESIDENTIAL CANDIDATE (STATE) VICE-PRESIDENTIAL CANDIDATE (STATE)	PARTY	ELECTORAL VOTES
James Madison (Va.) George Clinton (N.Y.)	Democratic-Republican	122
Charles C. Pinckney (S.C.) Rufus King (N.Y.)	Federalist	47

George Clinton received 6 of New York's 19 electoral votes for the presidency.

In this etching by William Charles, the casket containing Peace, Plenty, Liberty, and Independence is in danger of smashing to the ground as a pro-French Jeffersonian (appropriately on the left in the engraving), favoring war with Britain, attempts to remove the pillar of Federalism. A pro-British Federalist simultaneously tries to remove the pillar of Democracy. Note the early appearance of the slogan "United we stand, divided we fall."

merly busy wharves. One response to such conditions was to seek to evade the law, and merchants did everything from hurrying their ships to sea before the regulations went into effect to engaging in outright smuggling. Since the kind of strenuous measures that would be needed to enforce the Embargo were distasteful to the Virginians, they declined to enact them. But even had the administration cracked down hard, the Embargo would not have achieved its goal. The Spanish rebellion against Napoleon's rule had opened the ports of Spain's American colonies to British vessels, and from those ports Britain could obtain supplies. Ineffective as the Embargo was as a diplomatic tool, however, it proved quite potent as a spur to Federalists and other opponents of the status quo.

Jefferson and Madison had been working together now for a quarter of a century and had been virtual partners in creating the Republican Party in the 1790s, savoring the great triumph of 1800 and the electoral successes that followed. Although Jefferson had declared his neutrality in the matter of a successor, this was a pious sham. In fact, he had made it clear that Madison was to be his heir, and only a person blinded by ambition could fail to understand this. James Monroe was such a person.

Monroe, a Virginian who had left the College of William and Mary in 1776 to join the Continental Army, had gone on to serve as congressman, senator, and governor of Virginia. He had been minister to England in 1803–06 and during this period had tried to secure protection for American shipping from unsympathetic British negotiators. In this he had been at a great disadvantage. The instructions Monroe had received from Secretary of State Madison were simply not realistic—among other things, Madison demanded that Britain end impressment (taking sailors off American ships to serve aboard British vessels), which may have been an unjust practice but was seen by Britain as crucial to the maintenance of her naval might. The treaty that Monroe negotiated (with the aid of William Pinkney, whose presence Monroe correctly took as a vote of no confidence in his skills) won some minor concessions but did not even mention impressment, and when it arrived in Washington, Jefferson and Madison declined to send it to the Senate for ratification. Upon learning that Virginia senator John Randolph and his allies were hoping to nominate Monroe as the candidate of the rock-ribbed Old Republicans, Jefferson wrote Monroe, "I see with infinite grief a contest arising between yourself and another, who have been very dear to each other, and equally so to me." Although Monroe took such statements of equal affection as demonstrations of Jefferson's real neutrality, Irving Brant correctly observes that "Jefferson's neutrality cloaked the strongest kind of wish that Monroe would avert impending evils by withdrawing."

Plans for a smooth succession from Jefferson to Madison were also challenged by a Republican aspirant from outside the Old Dominion. Vice President George Clinton, who had been one of the national leaders of opposition to the Constitution in 1788, felt that his long service to the nation, as well as the still unbroken precedent of having the Vice President rise to the presidency, meant that he should be chosen. His candidacy received support from some who felt that Virginia, having held the presidency for sixteen of the nation's twenty years under the Constitution, should let another state have a chance at the office. Although Clinton was in poor health and found even the light duties of the vice presidency fatiguing, his candidacy had the energetic direction of his nephew DeWitt Clinton, mayor of New York City and a former U.S. senator.

The Clintons had a particularly difficult task to perform. When the Republican members of Congress caucused on January 23, 1808, George Clinton was again nominated for the office of Vice President, this time as James Madison's running mate. The caucus was a trifle short on legitimacy—sixty Republican members stayed away—but of the eighty-nine present, eighty-three supported Madison for President and seventy-nine backed Clinton as his running mate. The vice presidency may have been worth little, but it was worth something, and DeWitt Clinton edited a statement of his uncle's to communicate distaste for the procedures of the

OPPOSITE: *James Madison.*
Stipple engraving, 1810.
NATIONAL PORTRAIT GALLERY,
SMITHSONIAN INSTITUTION.

caucus without disowning its nomination of George Clinton for the vice presidency.

The disruption caused by the Embargo and the divisions in the Republican ranks ought to have been heartening for the Federalists, but they had difficulty capitalizing on the opportunity. There was some thought of throwing the party's support to George Clinton, but the Vice President's long record of antifederalism made him unpalatable to much of the leadership. The Federalist Party was divided, too: on the one hand, the younger activists wanted to adopt the Republicans' campaign methods and use them to achieve Federalist ends; the older leaders, however, seemed more comfortable lamenting the nation's decline into the swamp of democracy than campaigning to reverse it. In August a group of Federalist leaders, meeting in New York City, concluded that it was best to field a real Federalist, so once again Charles Cotesworth Pinckney and Rufus King were selected for the Federalist ticket.

The campaign, such as it was, was waged in the nation's highly partisan newspapers. That partisanship could be fluid, depending on which party or candidate was most generous in its contributions. In New York the Clintons could offer lucrative state printing contracts, but Madison's supporters could offer federal emoluments, forcing publishers to choose one revenue stream or to vacillate wildly between the two camps. Both approaches were tried.

JAMES MADISON,
President of the United States.

Monroe's treaty with England was examined, Madison's instructions to his ministers were pored over, and the result was that Monroe's candidacy dissolved under the scrutiny. Charges that Madison had been spineless in dealing with the British were refuted, and the exposure of the extent of Britain's arrogance in dealing with American representatives appears even to have bolstered popular support for the Embargo. Clinton's support was mostly limited to New York.

Madison's support was too strong for local candidacies like Clinton's to have much effect, and outside New England the Federalists had little support. Shortly before the election, Jefferson made public a new set of diplomatic correspondence that again showed Madison in a good light, although such a last-minute boost was hardly needed. Madison won with 122 electoral votes, while Pinckney received 47 and George Clinton a mere 6, all from New York, which cast its 13 other votes for Madison.

The election broke one precedent—the succession of the Vice President to the presidency—and saw the rudimentary beginnings of another. Because the meeting of Federalists in New York in August 1808 was the first, halting step on the way to what would eventually become the nominating convention.

CHAPTER

6

Sectionalism Surfaces

MADISON v. CLINTON, 1812

The presidential election of 1812 was the closest—indeed, the only close—race between 1800 and 1824. It was the first to be contested in the midst of war, and it divided the nation along a North-South fault line to an extent that would not be surpassed until the momentous election of 1860.

There are many places one could start in trying to understand the election, but perhaps the simplest is the census of 1810. Virginia, which had been the most populous state from the country's inception, had been surpassed in population by New York, which was now the nation's largest state and would cast 29 electoral votes in the 1812 election to Virginia's 25. (Pennsylvania, too, had pulled even with the Old Dominion, with 25 electoral votes.) For twelve years New York had contented itself with the vice presidency. Now, many New Yorkers thought, it was time for Virginia to hand over the reins of power.

But to which New Yorker? George Clinton was a revered elder statesman and a hero of the Revolution; his two terms as Vice President seemed a strong case for his elevation to the presidency—at least to those who had not witnessed the decline of his physical and mental powers. Long before he died, in April 1812, it had been clear to informed politicians that he could not be President. But there was another Clinton, George's nephew DeWitt, who had dominated state politics for a dozen years and whose ambition was not satisfied by his position as New York City's mayor. At age forty-three he had been active in state politics for twenty-five years, writing a well-received series of letters attacking the federal Constitution in 1787 and 1788, and going on to serve in various state offices as well as winning election to the U.S. Senate and appointment to the mayoralty. Writing under the pseudonym "Grotius," he had advanced Jefferson's cause in the 1800 election, and as the leader of the Republican Party in New York State he had helped to engineer Aaron Burr's defeat in the gubernatorial race of 1804. But he was too ambitious to remain satisfied with supporting roles and too aware of the potential of American commerce and the possible glories of America's cities to embrace the Jeffersonian strain of complacent agrarianism. Furthermore, the Virginians, eager to keep power within their grasp, were trying to divide power in New York. They began giving to Daniel D. Tompkins, whose election as governor in 1807 had been engineered by DeWitt Clinton, patronage favors that were denied his first patron. There had even been a rumor during the 1808 election that a move was afoot in Washington to split New York into two states, thus weakening its political influence.

That influence arose not only from New York's increasing size but also from its geopolitical location, on the fault line between the Northeast and the South and West, between the remaining bastions of federalism and the Republican heartland of the slave states. Calculating Federalists had considered alliances with New York Republicans for years. Some in the party had dallied with the notion of supporting Burr in 1804, and a Federalist meeting in New York in 1808 had considered supporting George Clinton before backing Charles Cotesworth Pinckney. Hamilton's opposition (and then his death) derailed any notion of supporting Burr, and the senior Clinton's age and longtime antifederalism had foreclosed his candidacy. But DeWitt Clinton was more supple than his uncle and less tainted than Burr. And DeWitt was wooing the Federalists.

Clinton was working the party's leaders in the state legislature to advance the cause of the proposed Erie Canal and had won some acclaim for the hard line he had taken against a riotous disturbance of the Columbia College commencement exercises in 1811, using his position as a city magistrate to deal harshly with the disrupters and denouncing the "outrageous" assault on the college, which was still a haven of federalism. But he had also been a busy partisan in the previous decade, denouncing New York Federalists in terms some found hard to forgive and impossible to forget. All that notwithstanding, if the Federalist Party wished to align itself with a New Yorker, Clinton was the best choice it had. And when the Republican caucus of the New York legislature nominated him for President at the end of May, he was effectively its only choice.

Clinton himself was faced with a tricky situation. He certainly had to have the Federalists' support—he could not defeat Madison in a three-way race. But he would have no hope of winning with *only* the Federalists' support. There were many Republicans who felt it was time for a non-Virginian to occupy the White House and many who felt that Madison's leadership had been seriously flawed. Madison's own postmaster general had privately urged New York Republicans to go for Clinton, confiding that many in Congress wished to have an alternative to Madison.

It may be that the quality most lacking in Madison as President, the one so many "great" presidents have possessed, was luck. He was unlucky to be the successor to Thomas Jefferson, revered as the great founding figure of

1812

PRESIDENTIAL CANDIDATE (STATE) VICE-PRESIDENTIAL CANDIDATE (STATE)	PARTY	ELECTORAL VOTES
James Madison (Va.) Elbridge Gerry (Mass.)	Democratic-Republican	128
DeWitt Clinton (N.Y.) Jared Ingersoll (Pa.)	Federalist	89

the Republican Party (even though Madison had played an equal role as architect of the party). And he was unlucky to come to the presidency at a time when so many of his most fondly held Republican principles—opposition to a military establishment, extreme frugality in government, the efficacy of commercial warfare—were destined to be harshly tested and found wanting.

The Embargo had succeeded only in beggaring the nation's port cities and turning merchants into smugglers. The government's failure to provide military force to back America's diplomatic demands had led Britain and France to react lightly and snidely to those demands. The Twelfth Congress, which had convened in November 1811, contained new and hot blood. Soon the "War Hawks," led by the freshman member from Kentucky, Henry Clay, who had been elected Speaker, were advocating war with Britain. Some sought local territorial gains—against Canada to the north, Spanish Florida to the south—while others were simply fed up with the continuing abuse of America's rights as a neutral power.

Choosing to interpret certain French diplomatic moves as signaling acquiescence to American demands, Madison proclaimed that the United States would exercise its economic power against Britain. The British responded to the American threats with threats of their own, and the two nations lurched toward war. Madison recommended an expansion of the navy in preparation for the expected conflict, but Republican frugality and western sentiment against naval expenditures crippled those plans and left the United States with a total naval force less than a sixth the size of Britain's usual contingent in North American waters. Evidence of Britain's attempts to sow disunion by fanning opposition to the Embargo in New England increased Madison's bellicosity and underlined the sectional rift his economic warfare policies had widened. On June 18, 1812, that neutrality ended with an American declaration of war on Great Britain.

Madison remained firmly in command of the southern and western Republicans, and he received the unanimous nomination of the congressional caucus

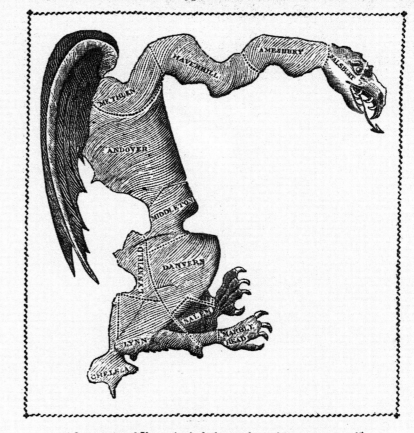

THE GERRY-MANDER.

A new species of *Monster*, which appeared in *Essex South District* in Jan. 1812.

" O generation of VIPERS *! who hath warned you of the wrath to come ?"*

In 1812 the Jeffersonian Republican governor of Massachusetts, Elbridge Gerry (who became Madison's running mate later that year), pushed through an electoral redistricting that ensured that the Republican majority in the township of Marblehead (one of the claws of the new monster, above) would outweigh the Federalist majority in eleven other townships. The artist Elkanah Tisdale embellished a map of the vaguely salamander–shaped district and coined a term that has remained in the political lexicon ever since.
LIBRARY OF CONGRESS.

DeWitt Clinton, by John Wesley Jarvis, c. 1816.

NATIONAL PORTRAIT GALLERY, SMITHSONIAN INSTITUTION.

(although a third of the Republican members were absent) shortly before the New York legislature nominated DeWitt Clinton. Madison had already received strong backing from his home state and from Pennsylvania, and if Clinton was to have any hope of unseating him he would need strong Federalist support. The Federalists were unsure what course to take. Some in New York, particularly Rufus King, were opposed to any alliance with Clinton; others saw him as the party's best chance. The most attractive alternative, Chief Justice John Marshall, was unfortunately from Virginia (thus depriving Madison's opposition of its anti–Virginia Dynasty ammunition) and too valuable on the court to risk in an election. Clinton met with leading New York Federalists in August, and in mid-September Federalist leaders from eleven states met secretly in New York City. They ultimately decided against an open endorsement of Clinton as being too divisive within the party and likely to hurt him outside it, and they merely urged voters to "support such candidates for P[resident]. & V.P. as would be likely to pursue a diff. Course" from the incumbent's. The logic was clear, but the rhetoric was cloudy.

This inconclusive result illustrates the central difficulty of Clinton's campaign. He needed to appeal both to Republicans who felt Madison was not the sort of dynamic leader the nation needed in wartime and to Federalists who wanted peace with England. A New York Committee of Correspondence had published a communication in August that was the closest thing there was to a Clinton platform, and it wafflingly stated that the candidate would display "vigor in war, and a determined character in the relations of peace." The document amplified some of the arguments that had been made in 1808 against the continuing control of the White House by Virginians and against congressional caucuses as the source of nominations and went on to suggest that Madison, although a distinguished patriot, had had his chance and should be replaced.

But Madison had no intention of being replaced, and he had solid backing among the Republican faithful. Local party organizations were strongest in the battleground states where neither party held a comfortable majority, particularly New York, Pennsylvania, and New Jersey. Although Clinton managed to win New York, both New Jersey and Pennsylvania supported Madison. The contest in New Jersey was closely fought, and to aid the President's chances Republicans there (and in South Carolina) sent Madison glowing public messages of praise, to which Madison replied with appropriate humility, asking voters to support the war effort. Madison's letter was then printed in Republican newspapers. The many shortcomings in the conduct of the war—notably General William Hull's humiliating surrender of Detroit to the British—managed to breathe hope but not life into Clinton's campaign. Pro-Clinton papers attacked Madison with vigor, but Madison's supporters delighted in pointing out the contradictions in the views of Clinton's backers in different parts of the country. New England (except Vermont), New York, and New Jersey went for Clinton, but his only other electoral votes came from Delaware and Maryland. Madison won by a margin of 128 to 89 in the Electoral College. Had Pennsylvania's 25 votes gone the other way, March 4, 1813, would have seen the inauguration of our first President Clinton. But Pennsylvania wasn't even close, and Clinton's defeat was the last, best chance the Federalists would have of winning national office.

The one significant Republican innovation during the campaign was Madison's public reply to his supporters in New Jersey and South Carolina. Although active campaigning was still taboo, this statement removed at least one layer of artifice. The September meeting of the Federalists has long been considered the first real political convention. But its shortcomings were emblematic of the Federalists' dilemma. The party had to win votes, yet its leaders were so contemptuous of the voters that their convention was held in secret. Clinton's attempt to be all things to all (anti-Madison) voters led Henry Adams to brand his candidacy "less creditable" than any other in American history. But Adams was writing a century ago, and Clinton's chameleon campaign would seem squeaky clean by modern standards. Perhaps his defeat illustrates the difficulty of pandering to the voters without the benefit of focus groups to tell the candidate exactly how to pander.

Good Feelings, or The Strange Death of the Federalist Party

THE REIGN OF JAMES MONROE, 1816, 1820

James Monroe had every reason to expect that he would follow James Madison as President in the 1816 election. He held the position of secretary of state, which had been the office of the President in waiting since 1801. He was a hero of the Revolution (the last to serve as President) and still wore the clothes of that era (powdered wig, tricorn hat, knee breeches) long after they had gone out of fashion. As he aged he had come to bear a striking resemblance to George Washington, and he had been a disciple of Thomas Jefferson for decades—he had even purchased an estate near Monticello. Thus carrying the imprimatur of both the Father of His Country and the Father of His Party, Monroe was the logical choice to succeed James Madison.

But the logic was not agreeable to all. After sixteen years of Virginia presidents, more states than just New York felt that their turn had come, or at least that a person from some state other than Virginia should occupy the office. Within the Republican Party there were several men with designs on the presidency. DeWitt Clinton had not given up hope, but his defeat four years earlier had derailed any chance at the prize in 1816. Henry Clay was already experienced in the ways of the capital city but was, at age thirty-nine, still a bit young. Daniel D. Tompkins, the governor of New York, was a favorite son of that populous power base. And there was William Crawford of Georgia, a former senator who had served as minister to France from 1813 to 1815 and had then been named secretary of war by Madison.

Crawford was only forty-four years old and was unwilling to challenge the man who so clearly was the favorite candidate of both Jefferson and Madison, both of whom remained publicly neutral. No doubt Crawford figured that he could afford to wait until Monroe had finished his service as President and then step into his shoes. He advised some of his supporters that he did not wish to challenge Monroe, but they were not to be quelled so easily. A notice appeared calling for a Republican caucus on March 12, 1816, and though there were insufficient members in attendance to place a candidate in nomination, those present called another meeting for the sixteenth. In spite of Crawford's wishes, his name was proposed, but Monroe won the nomination by a close vote of 65 to 54. This made Crawford particularly un-happy, since he had planned to issue a statement deferring to Monroe in order to secure the Virginian's backing in the future. Daniel D. Tompkins was given the second spot on the ticket, another recognition of New York's importance in the political calculus of the time. Monroe responded to his own nomination by stating, "I can only say that, should the suffrages of my fellow-citizens call me to that trust, I should feel a duty to enter on it." That was his only political statement of the campaign, and it was all he needed to say.

By now the Federalist Party was a walking corpse. What killed it was the very war that had for several years promised the party's revival and a renewed chance at national office. For a time, the War of 1812 seemed designed to prove the truth of nearly every substantive charge the Federalists had leveled against Jefferson and his followers. The army and navy, gutted by the Republicans' frugality, were filleted by the British, in spite of some impressive naval victories in single-ship contests. Madison's military appointees had blundered, and the Republicans' financial notions had left a federal government with insufficient credit to finance a real war. (One of the reasons Tompkins won the vice presidential nomination was that he had managed to put New York's credit at the service of the nation.) And of course the fact that there was a shooting war at all had demonstrated the inadequacy of the commercial warfare so proudly devised by Madison and Jefferson. The British sack of Washington, D.C., and the burning of the White House at the end of August 1814 was only the most lurid example of the Madison administration's incompetence in waging the war. The capital was so obviously poorly defended that, as rumors of a British attack grew in July, a mob demonstrated outside the White House and threatened to block the President and his family if they tried to flee.

During 1814, Federalist victories in state and local elections were on the rise, and, had the presidential election been held then, a Federalist candidate might well have had a chance. But by the spring of 1815, everything had changed—and in ways that finally laid the Federalist Party to rest. In the fall of 1814, representatives of five New England states had gathered in Connecticut for the Hartford convention and prepared a list of grievances and

1816

PRESIDENTIAL CANDIDATE (STATE) VICE-PRESIDENTIAL CANDIDATE (STATE)	PARTY	ELECTORAL VOTES
James Monroe (Va.) Daniel D. Tompkins (N.Y.)	Democratic-Republican	183
Rufus King (N.Y.) John E. Howard (Md.)	Federalist	34

1820

PRESIDENTIAL CANDIDATE (STATE) VICE-PRESIDENTIAL CANDIDATE (STATE)	PARTY	ELECTORAL VOTES
James Monroe (Va.) Daniel D. Tompkins (N.Y.)	Democratic-Republican	231

No one ran against Monroe in 1820. However, one member of the Electoral College (Governor William Plumer of New Hampshire) cast his vote for John Quincy Adams, and 3 other electoral votes were not cast at all.

James Monroe, by John Vanderlyn, 1816.
NATIONAL PORTRAIT GALLERY,
SMITHSONIAN INSTITUTION.

"So certain is the outcome
that no pains are taken to
excite the community on the
subject. It is quite worthy of
remark, that in no preceding
election has there been such a
calm respecting it."

RUFUS KING IN A LETTER
DATED NOVEMBER 5, 1816

demands to be presented to the government in Washington. Those demands had to do, first, with giving states more power to defend themselves (since the federal effort had proved so inept). Furthermore, the delegates proposed a series of constitutional amendments that would have deprived the South of the extra representation it had won in the "three-fifths" clause in the Constitution, which apportioned representation on a basis that counted each slave as three-fifths of a person (even though slaves, of course, could not vote). The Hartford convention also called for a ban on presidents serving a second term and on successive Presidents from the same state. Although some of the backers of the convention were thought to have favored secession, the actual demands passed were more modest. Yet modest as they were, by the time they might have been presented to Congress, the New Englanders had abandoned their protest.

The reason for that abandonment was a series of British retreats, both military and diplomatic. An American naval triumph on Lake Champlain was followed by the withdrawal of an invading British army back into Canada, crowned by Andrew Jackson's defeat of a seasoned British force at the Battle of New Orleans in January 1815. When news followed of the Treaty of Ghent, ending the war—the treaty had been completed before the Battle of New Orleans even took place—the entire disastrous war could be recast as a second American War of Independence. Britain's tolerant diplomacy had stopped short of insisting on a cession of American territory (which had been widely expected), and the treaty was hailed as a victory, the war remembered as a heroic triumph over adversity. In the light of such feelings, the Hartford convention was transformed from a reasonable protest into a treasonable assembly.

Although historians list Rufus King of New York as Monroe's Federalist opponent, one may search King's voluminous correspondence in vain for any mention of his candidacy. Electors from three states where the legislature still chose the electors—Massachusetts, Connecticut, and Delaware—cast a total of 34 votes for King, but Monroe's election was never in the slightest doubt once Crawford had decided to wait his turn.

In truth, the Federalists had little reason to oppose Monroe, since the Republicans had adopted so many of their opponents' leading arguments. In 1816, Congress chartered a new Bank of the United States, and Monroe had learned enough from his wartime experience in the cabinet to back the maintenance of a more professional army and navy. The Hartford convention, with its echoes of the Virginia and Kentucky Resolutions of 1798, only made clearer the fact that the Republicans had now become the party devoted to a strong union, while the remnants of federalism sought greater state autonomy. John Adams observed, "Our two great parties have crossed over the valley and taken possession of each other's mountain." Even internal improvements and a protective tariff were now acceptable to Republicans.

In the summer of 1817 the new President made a triumphal tour of northern states, and upon his arrival in Boston the local Federalist paper, the *Columbian Sentinel*, welcomed Monroe and proclaimed that he presided over a new time in the nation's history, an "Era of Good Feelings." Monroe himself had little love for partisan politics and accepted the situation as a happy realization of Jefferson's dream of a politics free of party passions. This had, after all, been the dream of the revolutionary generation—Monroe's generation—and he was glad to be the "instrument" by which the dream had been realized.

Yet the Era of Good Feelings was soon riven by major shocks: the financial panic of 1819, a serious economic decline, and then the controversy over the admission of Missouri into the Union, a controversy that erupted when northern congressmen tried to block the state from becoming a slave state and southern congressmen fought back with vigor. Off in Monticello, the struggle reached Jefferson's ears as a "fire bell in the night," sounding a warning of impending conflict over slavery. It would take forty years for the fire to break out, but the Missouri affair, resolved by the Missouri Compromise (which admitted Missouri as a slave state, balanced that with the admission of Maine as a free state, and barred slavery from the rest of the Louisiana Purchase north of latitude 36° 30′), placed the issue of slavery before the people with a new clarity.

Daniel D. Tompkins,
by John Wesley Jarvis, c. 1812.
COLLECTION OF THE NEW-YORK
HISTORICAL SOCIETY.

An economic recession and a struggle over slavery would seem to have been sufficient to have drawn forth a challenge to Monroe. After all, he was not a particularly revered figure. Those who knew him best had high words for his character—Jefferson said it was without a stain—but few spoke so highly of his intelligence or political shrewdness. Yet no opposition arose. His nomination was taken as a matter of course; the only attempt even to call a congressional caucus failed, apparently having been designed to replace Vice President Tompkins with Henry Clay. And the general election was more open than ever before to the will of the people, with 163 of the 235 electors being chosen directly by the voters. But the voters could hardly be bothered to vote. In

A campaign biography intended to increase the appeal of James Monroe to northern voters fed up with the Virginia Dynasty.
DAVID J. AND JANICE L. FRENT
POLITICAL AMERICANA COLLECTION.

"Surely our government may go on and prosper without the existence of parties. I have always considered their existence as the curse of the country. . . . The existence of parties is not necessary to free government."

JAMES MONROE

Virginia, which had a white population of around 600,000, only 4,321 voters showed up. According to Lynn W. Turner, "Probably less than 1 per cent of the male population went to the polls in 1820."

Monroe was satisfied. Nasty factionalism had been routed, and the republic could henceforth proceed under the rational and dispassionate guidance of the people's chosen leaders. But the members of Monroe's cabinet and ambitious politicians in many states were already eyeing the 1824 election. Monroe may have seen his elections as the beginning of a new era, but they actually marked the end of one. He was the last President to come from the revolutionary generation. He was the last of the Virginia Dynasty. And he was the last to believe that party could be extirpated from American political life. The Federalist Party had been vanquished and would trouble the Republicans no more. But the victory contained the seed of future discord, and the election of 1824 would allow that discord to grow. Out of the 1824 election would come a new era of politics, an era of party affiliations openly proclaimed. And in that new era political campaigns would become mighty contests of national parties, filled with images and oratory, parades and pomp.

CHAPTER

8

Free for All

ADAMS, JACKSON, CRAWFORD, CLAY, 1824

The election of 1824 signaled the end of several eras in the history both of the American presidency and of presidential elections. For the first time, the nation would elect a President who had not played a significant role in the American Revolution and the founding of the nation. For the first time since 1796, the nation would choose a chief executive who did not live in Virginia. For the first time since 1812, there would be a real contest for the presidency. And for the second and last time, the election would be decided by the House of Representatives, rather than by the Electoral College. It was a fitting conclusion to the ultimate Washington insiders' campaign.

Five men were considered to harbor serious and plausible designs on the White House. Three of these were members of President Monroe's cabinet: Secretary of State John Quincy Adams of Massachusetts; Secretary of the Treasury William H. Crawford of Georgia; and Secretary of War John C. Calhoun of South Carolina. The other leading contenders were Speaker of the House Henry Clay of Kentucky and Andrew Jackson, senator from Tennessee and a national hero since his victory over the British at the Battle of New Orleans on January 8, 1815. With the exception of Jackson, all the candidates were creatures of the capital.

The least well known of these men, Crawford, was in fact the front-runner in most people's minds for years before the election. As noted earlier, he could probably have had the presidency in the 1816 election but chose to defer to Monroe in the expectation that he could succeed the Virginian. As the 1824 election approached, he could count on the backing of many prominent Republicans and had the tacit support of James Madison as well as the active and invaluable assistance of Senator Martin Van Buren, who had developed his superb political skills in the bitter electoral contests of New York State. Of all the candidates, Crawford was the one most in tune with the states'-rights and small-government attitudes that Thomas Jefferson had tried to establish as the defining characteristics of the Republican Party.

Crawford's hopes rested on his popularity within the congressional caucus (which was now overwhelmingly Republican) and on support in the South and in

William H. Crawford. Engraving by
Asher B. Durand.
NATIONAL PORTRAIT GALLERY,
SMITHSONIAN INSTITUTION.

New York, where Van Buren hoped to use his influence to deliver the state's vote to the Georgian. Crawford's Treasury post enabled him to court supporters with patronage and other favors. But his bright hopes were nearly extinguished when, in the fall of 1823, he suffered a paralytic attack that left him bedridden and nearly blind, though his supporters attempted to minimize the seriousness of his condition and proceeded with their efforts to secure his nomination by the caucus. On Valentine's Day 1824, a poorly attended caucus that Van Buren had packed with Crawfordites gave the Georgian its tainted endorsement.

Crawford's illness had given encouragement to Henry Clay and his followers, who hoped that Clay would inherit the bulk of Crawford's support in the large states of Virginia and New York. Clay's talents were so manifest that on his first day as a member of the House of Representatives in 1811 he was chosen as Speaker, and he would remain prominent in national affairs until his death in 1852. Like Crawford, Clay was born in Virginia, and he had studied law with George Wythe, the legal mentor of Thomas Jefferson and Chief Justice John Marshall. But he had moved to Kentucky as a young man and styled himself a man of the West, a growing region where new states were eager to stake their claim to national prominence—and national office. He was a leading champion of an active government role in the economy, and his "American System" called for internal improvements and tariffs that would both help pay for the canals and roads the frontier states wanted and protect the rising manufacturing interests in the Northeast from European (chiefly British) competition. This program ought, in Clay's view, to win him support in both regions.

John C. Calhoun had been a champion of a strong national program when he first came to Congress (like Clay, he had been sworn in as a representative in 1811). He had distinguished himself in the House as an expert on military matters, and this had led to his appointment as James Monroe's secretary of war.

1824

PRESIDENTIAL CANDIDATE (STATE) VICE-PRESIDENTIAL CANDIDATE (STATE)	PARTY	ELECTORAL VOTES	APPROX. % OF POPULAR VOTE
John Quincy Adams (Mass.) John C. Calhoun (S.C.)	Democratic-Republican	84	32%
Andrew Jackson (Tenn.)	Democratic-Republican	99	42%
William H. Crawford (Ga.)	Democratic-Republican	41	13%
Henry Clay (Ky.)	Democratic-Republican	37	13%

The Twelfth Amendment to the Constitution stated that if no candidate received more than 50 percent of the electoral votes, the House of Representatives would choose the President from among the three candidates with the most electoral votes. Each of the 24 states then in the nation cast 1 vote, for the man favored by the majority of the state's congressmen. Adams received 13 votes: 7 from states he had carried in the popular election, 3 from Clay states, and 3 from states that Jackson had carried in the popular election. Jackson received 7 votes in the House, and Crawford received 4.

Calhoun looked for support in the South from those who found Crawford's states'-rights views unpalatable, and he hoped to win support in New York and particularly in Pennsylvania.

It was in Pennsylvania, however, that Calhoun's hopes were dashed and those of another candidate took off. Andrew Jackson was a popular hero because of his victory at New Orleans, but more sober minds in Washington worried about his willful nature and his tendency to exceed not only his orders but the bounds of civilized behavior. In Tennessee he was known as a man of fierce passions, a duelist whose harsh character could easily be read in his sharp features and stiff posture—the name "Old Hickory" had come to him from his troops in the War of 1812 in tribute to his toughness. Jackson's critics could (and did) rebuke him for his military adventures in Florida in 1817–18, in which he had turned a punitive expedition against the Seminole Indians into an imperial adventure that had aroused the justifiable anger of both Britain and Spain (among other actions, Jackson had hanged two British subjects with little cause after a hasty military court proceeding, then seized Pensacola, the capital of the Spanish province of West Florida). Most of Monroe's cabinet wished to disavow Jackson's outrages, but Secretary of State Adams appreciated the diplomatic possibilities of the general's forceful moves and eventually persuaded Monroe to support Jackson. Popular reaction was more positive, with Jackson again hailed as a military hero, and when Adams's diplomacy resulted in Spain's cession of Florida to the United States, Old Hickory's stock rose further. In 1822, the legislature in his home state of Tennessee recommended Jackson to the nation as the next President. Early in 1823, he indicated his willingness to run by issuing a suitably modest statement that while the presidency "should not be sought," at the same time "it cannot, with propriety, be declined." Skillfully playing the Washingtonian role of reluctant candidate (but without Washington's actual reluctance), Jackson gained popularity as 1823 advanced, and by early 1824 his standing in Pennsylvania was such that even Calhoun's strongest backers had to accept Jackson as the state's nominee for President, relegating Calhoun to their second spot. Calhoun then accepted the inevitable and limited his ambitions to the vice presidency.

While Jackson and Clay both represented the West and Crawford and Calhoun the South, the last candidate, John Quincy Adams, had the New England states all to himself. As the son of the second President, and as secretary of state, he was well known throughout the nation. But as the historian George Dangerfield observed, hardly any public servant had ever possessed "a finer mind or a more ungraceful personality." Prickly and self-willed, Adams was the antithesis of the glad-handing Henry Clay, and his squat, balding appearance carried none of the austere force that Andrew Jackson projected. Furthermore, Adams's independence of mind was reflected in his politics, as he remained unwilling to play the party political games that were the common practice of his opponents.

John C. Calhoun, attributed to Charles Bird King, c. 1818–1825.
NATIONAL PORTRAIT GALLERY, SMITHSONIAN INSTITUTION.

Henry Clay, by Charles Bird King, 1821.
IN THE COLLECTION OF THE
CORCORAN GALLERY OF ART,
WASHINGTON, D.C. MUSEUM
PURCHASE, GALLERY FUND, 81.9.

With four candidates, all nominally Republicans, the election became little more than a series of state contests, with each candidate trying to hold his geographical base and then pick up support in a few key states outside his region, the vote-rich states of New York, Pennsylvania, and Virginia being particularly sought after. Because there was a clear favorite in most states, the voter turnout was low, with only about a quarter of eligible voters making the trip to the polls.

Each candidate carried his home state but succeeded in varying degrees elsewhere. Crawford, though still seriously ill, carried Georgia as well as his native Virginia and picked up votes in three other states. Henry Clay took Kentucky, Ohio, and Missouri and won four of New York's 36 electoral votes. Adams won 26 of New York's votes, carried New England, and picked up a scattering of votes elsewhere. Jackson demonstrated his popularity in the West and also won Pennsylvania (with its 28 votes), along with the Carolinas. Jackson led with 99 electoral votes, Adams was second with 84, Crawford had 41, and Clay was last with 37. Calhoun was elected Vice President with 182 electoral votes. Under the terms of the Twelfth Amendment, only the top three presidential candidates could be considered in the House, so Clay's chances were finished.

Now, as the eliminated candidate and Speaker of the House, Clay was courted while the three remaining camps prepared for the February 9 vote that would decide who would be the next President. Under the rules laid down under the Constitution, each state had one vote; with twenty-four states then in the Union, thirteen votes were needed to elect. The members of the House had no obligation to vote as their states had voted (six of the twenty-four states still chose electors in the legislature, rather than by popular vote). Clay had to choose between Jackson and Adams, and Adams got his support. Like Clay, Jackson was from the West, and Clay's chances of succeeding a fellow westerner seemed slim. And although Clay disliked Adams (he felt that he himself, rather than Adams, should have been Monroe's choice for the State Department), Adams was, after all, a nationalist and a known quantity—unlike the unpredictable Jackson.

As Clay's intention of supporting Adams began to become clear in January, accusations of a quid pro quo surfaced in the press. Although this seriously misread Adams's character, it was believed by many, including Andrew Jackson. When the House convened on February 9, the election still hung in the balance. Twelve states were with Adams, seven were backing Jackson, and four were for Crawford. One state, New York, could either throw the election to Adams or leave the race tied with

John Quincy Adams. Engraving by Thomas Gimbrede, 1826.
NATIONAL PORTRAIT GALLERY, SMITHSONIAN INSTITUTION.

"If one took the calumnies of the most abandoned newspapers for the moral standard of this nation, it would be supposed that our Presidents, Secretaries, Senators, and Representatives are all traitors and pirates, and [that] the government of this people had been committed to the hands of public robbers."

Federal Gazette & Baltimore Daily Advertiser, JUNE 7, 1824

12 votes for Adams and 12 votes for his opponents. Exactly half of New York's congressmen had come out for Adams, but one more was needed to deliver the state (and the election) to him. The rest of the delegation was committed to other candidates, with the exception of Stephen Van Rensselaer, whose vast holdings along the Hudson made him the greatest individual landholder in New York. When Van Rensselaer, who was under pressure from New York's governor, DeWitt Clinton, to vote for Jackson, arrived at the Capitol the day of the vote, he was lobbied on Adams's behalf by Clay and Webster, and he took his seat still undecided. There (according to Martin Van Buren's account) he prayed for guidance. Looking down on the floor of the House chamber, he saw an Adams ballot, and, taking this as a sign

of God's will, he cast his vote for Adams. Alas, this was the only sign of divine favor to be visited upon the Adams presidency.

The night Adams learned of his election, he went to the White House, where he encountered Jackson, who was, Adams recorded in his diary, "altogether placid and courteous." But Jackson's demeanor, it turned out, concealed a hot anger and a desire for revenge that would be satisfied in the next election.

CHAPTER

9

A Grudge Match

JACKSON v. ADAMS, 1828

Few presidents have been as well prepared for the duties of office as the second Adams, and none has been less suited to the exigencies of politics. His entire term as President was little more than a prolonged wait for the taken-for-granted rematch between him and Jackson in the 1828 election. Adams, oblivious of the scandal that would almost inevitably follow from giving high office to the man whose change of heart had given him the presidency, named Henry Clay to his cabinet. Cries of "Bargain and corruption" greeted the news that Clay, whose support in the contested election of 1824 had secured the White House for Adams, would be the new secretary of state. And the cries did not fade. In 1826, Clay fought a duel with the eccentric Virginia senator John Randolph, who had likened Adams and Clay to Blifil and Black George, two unsavory characters from Fielding's *Tom Jones.*

In spite of such distractions, in December 1825 Adams presented an ambitious program to the nation in his first annual message to Congress. The national government would sponsor the construction of roads and canals (the Erie Canal, finished that year, had already proved a titanic success); a national university would cultivate the country's intellectual resources; a naval academy would refine the arts of war; an observatory (also built at government expense) would search the heavens and bring enlightenment to Earth. Tariffs would encourage domestic industries. Concluding his address and mindful of how completely his proposals went against the grain of Jeffersonian small-government notions, Adams urged the national government "not to be palsied by the will of our constituents."

But palsied the Congress was. Many members, indeed, were amazed at Adams's expansive notion of the federal government's domain. And Adams was the last person likely to win over a reluctant congressman. First of all, there was his manner, which Adams himself described as "cold" and "austere." This deficiency might have been overcome had Adams shown the slightest willingness to court support in the usual way: with political favors. But Adams refused to trade government patronage for votes. In fact, he even refused to remove those in his administration, including members of his cabinet, who were using their own patronage to establish political

Andrew Jackson's wife, Rachel Donelson Robards Jackson, by an unidentified artist. LIBRARY OF CONGRESS.

organizations opposed to him. Not only did Adams spout the antiparty rhetoric of the previous generation, he actually believed it. He was the last President to do so.

By 1828, presidential elections had become popular affairs, no longer under the sway of state legislatures. Only two of the twenty-four states voting that year (Delaware and South Carolina) still allowed the legislature to choose electors, so direct appeals to voters were more important than ever. By this time most states had arrived at something like white manhood suffrage, and the new voters were courted by the most sophisticated political organizations developed thus far. Running mates were selected with an eye to political advantage. Jackson, who had little Washington experience, ran with John C. Calhoun, who was Adams's Vice President; Adams was paired with Treasury Secretary Richard Rush of Pennsylvania, a swing state rich in electoral votes. Jackson's campaign apparatus was overseen by the New Yorker Martin Van Buren, the wiliest party tactician of the time, whose stature and abilities earned him the nickname "The Little Magician." Another able partisan, James Buchanan, directed Jackson's supporters in Pennsylvania. Their strategy was essentially sectional, writing off New England as irretrievably in the Adams camp and viewing the South as so unlikely to support the President as to need little attention from the Jackson forces. The West, where Clay fancied he was powerful, and the populous states of Pennsylvania and New York were the focus of the Jackson strategy. Jacksonians in Congress proposed tariff legislation designed to wound New England while granting a boon to the West and the middle states. The interests of the South, which as usual was opposed to tariffs, were largely ignored. The result, known as the Tariff of Abominations, made little economic sense but did pay political dividends.

But this perversion of trade policy was as close as the campaign would come to real issues. Personal recriminations and scurrilous accusations, served up by each side's well-financed partisan press, were the meat of the campaign. Jackson's side was led by Duff Green's *United States Telegraph*, the *Albany Argus*, and the *Richmond Enquirer*. Prominent Adams papers included the Washington *National Journal* and the *Massachusetts Journal*. Other newspapers loyal to one candidate or the other would reprint and sometimes amplify the charges made in these leading party organs.

The accusations against the President were varied, often laughable, and apparently effective. One line of argument tried to link the younger Adams to the hated Alien and Sedition Acts passed during his father's admin-

1828

PRESIDENTIAL CANDIDATE (STATE) VICE-PRESIDENTIAL CANDIDATE (STATE)	PARTY	ELECTORAL VOTES	APPROX. % OF POPULAR VOTE
Andrew Jackson (Tenn.) John C. Calhoun (S.C.)	Democratic	178	56%
John Quincy Adams (Mass.) Richard Rush (Pa.)	National Republican	83	44%

istration and to tie him to the perceived crimes of the defunct Federalist Party. Thus, one paper declared that Adams had the support of all the surviving delegates to the Hartford convention. The studious and frugal Adams, whose diary shows him writing sonnets and construing an oration of Cicero for his son Charles, was branded a slave to luxury, a pleasure-seeking King John II, who slaked his appetites at the public trough. Surely the most grotesque accusation against Adams was the charge that he had pimped for the czar while minister to Russia, procuring a beautiful American girl to satisfy the despot's desires. And through it all the ostinato bass line of "Bargain and corruption" sounded continually.

Jackson, too, was pilloried, with nearly as little regard for the truth. He was infuriated by the story circulated by his opponents that his mother was a prostitute and a mulatto. The most painful attack was the one directed against his marriage. His wife, Rachel, had formerly been married to one Lewis Robards, who had decided that the bachelor Jackson, then living in the same house as the Robardses, was having an affair with his wife. Whatever the truth of this accusation, Jackson and Rachel fled together to Natchez, Mississippi, and later married, apparently be-

"Ought a convicted adulteress and her paramour husband to be placed in the highest office of this free and Christian land?"

CHARLES HAMMOND,
View of General Jackson's Domestic Relations in Reference to His Fitness for the Presidency, 1828

Andrew Jackson, by James Barton Longacre. Sepia watercolor, 1828.
NATIONAL PORTRAIT GALLERY,
SMITHSONIAN INSTITUTION.

"You know that he [Jackson] is no jurist, no statesman, no politician; that he is destitute of historical, political, or statistical knowledge; that he is unacquainted with the orthography, concord, and government of his language; you know that he is a man of no labor, no patience, no investigation; in short that his whole recommendation is animal fierceness and organic energy. He is wholly unqualified by education, habit, and temper for the station of President."

PRO-ADAMS PAMPHLET, 1828

Medal distributed in support of Andrew Jackson's second bid for the presidency. Such medals were intended to be strung on ribbons for wearing.
DAVID J. AND JANICE L. FRENT POLITICAL AMERICANA COLLECTION.

OPPOSITE: *The 1828 "Coffin Handbill" accusing Andrew Jackson of having personally committed a murder and of being responsible for a number of murders and unjust executions, carried out either at his orders or by troops under his command.*
LIBRARY OF CONGRESS.

lieving that the divorce Robards was seeking on the grounds of adultery and abandonment had come through. It had not, and Rachel and Andrew married a second time in 1794 after the divorce became final. This innocent error was turned into a sex scandal, and Jackson never forgave Clay and Adams for not doing what they could to stop the accusations. His resentment became forged into cold steel when Rachel died of a heart attack soon after Jackson's election, her death hastened, he believed, by the slanders.

Another line of attack on Old Hickory grew out of his record during the War of 1812, the very foundation of his national popularity. In 1813, he had ordered six soldiers shot for mutiny, and a Philadelphia editor supporting Adams circulated an account of the incident that was highly unfavorable to General Jackson, the account printed as a broadside with six coffins representing the victims of Jackson's wrath. The "Coffin Handbill" also detailed other acts allegedly showing the general's cruel nature, including his participation in an Indian massacre during the War of 1812 and other atrocities committed during the Seminole War of 1818. Here the accusers were more on the mark, as the thousands of Choctaws, Chickasaws, Creeks, Seminoles, and Cherokees who died on what came to be called the Trail of Tears (which led west to Indian Territory, now Oklahoma) would discover.

However such accounts of genocide may move us today, they were probably not the most effective arguments in the United States of 1828, where Indians were considered "savages," and no impediment to American westward movement was respected except rivers, swamps, and mountain ranges. Jackson had something more important than rhetoric on his side; he had a political organization that understood the power of the enlarged electorate and worked hard to use that power to ensure victory. Rallies were arranged, barbecues were stocked with food and drink, and bands played to entertain Jackson supporters, who sported hickory leaves in their caps to demonstrate their allegiance. Although historians have rightly questioned the degree to which Jackson and his supporters were true champions of the common man, they certainly understood that the development of a broader electorate demanded that a candidate try to appeal to the ordinary citizen. Adams, on the other hand, had no interest in appealing to anyone, and his supporters were often

Some Account of some of the Bloody Deeds
OF
GENERAL JACKSON.

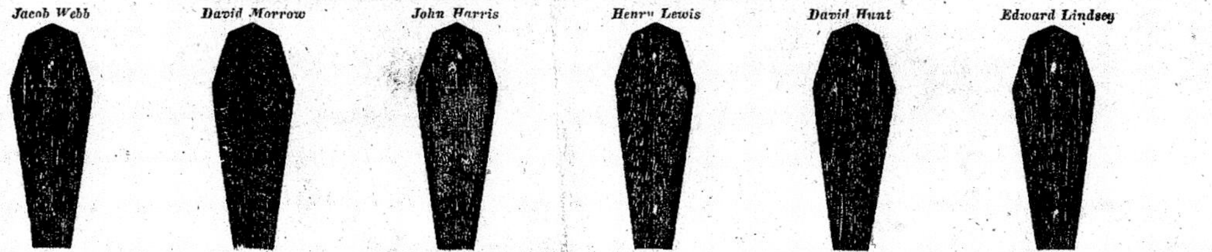

A brief account of the Execution of the Six Militia Men.

As we may soon expect to have the *official* documents in relation to the SIX MILITIA MEN, arrested, tried, and put to death, under the orders of General Andrew Jackson, this may not be an improper time to give to the public some of the particulars of their execution, as we have them from "AN EYE WITNESS;" who appeals to Col Russell, for the truth of every word he relates.

—

Harris was a Baptist preacher, with a large family. He had hired as a substitute for three months. This was the case with most of them. They were ignorant men, but obstinate in what they believed right, and what they had been told by their officers was right.—They were all sure they could not be kept beyond three months, and they gave up their musquets, and had provisions dealt out to them, from the public stores, before they left the camp.—This confirmed their convictions that they were right and doing what was lawful.

Col. Russel commanded at the execution. The Militia men were brought to the place in a large wagon. The military dispositions being made, Col. Russell rode up to the wagon and ordered the men so descend. Harris was the only one who betrayed feminine weakness. The awfulness of the occasion; his wife and nine children; the parting with his son; and the fear of a quickly approaching ignominious death! quite overcome him, and he sunk in unmanly grief. No feeling of military pride could brace him up.

Col. Russel, doubtless, felt as a man, but he felt also for the pride of the army, and desired to animate the men with fortitude. "You are about to die, "said he, by the sentence of a Court "Martial—die like men; *like soldiers.* "You have been brave in the field—"you have fought well—do no discredit to your country, or dishonour to the "army, or yourselves, by any unmanly "fears. Meet your fate with courage."

Harris attempted to make some apology for his conduct, but while he spoke, he wept bitterly. The fear of death, the idea that he should never again behold his wife and little ones, and his son weeping near him, had taken such entire possession of his mind that it was impossible he should rally.

Lewis, the gallant Lewis, said in a clear and manly tone, "Colonel, I have "served my country well. I love it "dearly, and would, if I could, serve "it longer and better. I have fought "bravely—*you know* I have, and HERE "I have a right to say so MYSELF. I "would not wish to die in this way"—here his voice faltered, and he passed the back of his right hand over his eyes—"I did not expect it: But, I am now "as firm as I have been in battle, and "you shall see that I will die as be- "comes a soldier, you know I am a "brave man." "Yes, Lewis, said the Colonel, you have always behaved like a brave man." Other sentences were uttered, other declarations were made, and words of comfort spoken, but they were lost on me: my attention, says an Eye Witness, being chiefly directed to Lewis.

Six coffins were ranged as directed, and on each of them knelt one of our condemned American Militia Men.—Such a sight was never seen before! I trust to God it never will be seen again! Six soldiers were detailed and drawn up to fire at each man. What an awful duty! Their white caps were drawn over the faces of the unhappy men.—Harris evidently trembled, and I could almost persuade myself that the heart of Lewis was enlarged, and that his bosom rose with manly courage to meet death. The fatal word was given and they all fell.

As we approached the scene of blood and carnage, Lewis gave signs of life; the rest were all dead—he crawled upon his coffin. After the lapse of a few minutes he said—I give his very words: "Colonel"—the Colonel was close to him—"Colonel, I am not killed, but I am sadly cut and mangled." His body was now examined and it was found that but four balls had wounded him. "Colonel," said he, "did I behave well." "Yes, Lewis"—said the Colonel in the kindest tone of voice—"like a man." "Well sir," said he, "have I not atoned for this offence? *Shall I not live?*" The Colonel was much agitated, and gave orders that the Surgeon should, if possible, preserve his life. They did all that skill and humanity could do—it was all of no avail. Poor Lewis expressed a great desire to live—"not," said he at one time, "that I fear death, "but I would repent me of some sins, "and I desire to live yet a little long- "er in the world." He suffered inconceivable agony, from his wounds, and died on the fourth day.

Many a soldier has wept over his grave. He was a brave man and much beloved. He suffered twenty deaths.—I have seen the big drops chase each other down his forehead with pain and anguish. There was much sensibility and sympathy throughout the camp.—I would not have, unjustly and unnecessarily, signed this death warrant for all the wealth of all the Indies. The soldier detailed to shoot Lewis had, from strong feelings of sympathy, or mistaken humanity failed to shoot him—but four balls had entered his body.

"An Eye Witness" appeals to Col. Russell, who he thinks now lives in Alabama, for the perfect truth of this sketch. He does not fear but the Colonel will keenly recollect and faithfully depict the horrors of the day on which six Americans were shot to death under his command—but not by his orders.

The order bears date the very day after *General Jackson* returned in triumph to New Orleans, and the day before he joyfully went, under triumphal arches, to the Temple of the living God; where, says the historian, "they *crowned* their adored General with laurels." The order for the execution of these six unhappy men bears date January 22, 1815. His crown of laurels had not yet withered, when blood, the life's blood of his countrymen, of his fellow soldiers, flowed plentifully by his order. May that order and its consequences, sink deep into the hearts of the American people and steel them against him who had no flesh in his obdurate heart; who did not feel for Man; in the midst of Joy and Revelry, almost in the more immediate presence of his Creator, who issued the fatal order to put his fellow creatures to death, and to make their wives & children, widows and orphans.

MOURNFUL TRAGEDY;

Or, the death of Jacob Webb, David Morrow, John Harris, Henry Lewis, David Hunt, & Edward Lindsey—six militia men, who were condemned to die, the sentence approved by Major General JACKSON, and by his order the whole six shot.

O! DID you hear that plaintive cry
Borne on the southern breeze?
Saw you JOHN HARRIS earnest pray
For mercy, on his knees?

Low to the earth he bent, and pray'd
For pardon from his chief;
But to his earnest prayer for life
JACKSON, alas! was deaf.

"Spare me"—he said—"I mean no wrong,
"My heart was always true:
"Frist for my county's cause it beat,
"And next, great Chief, for you.

"We thought our time of service out—
"Thought it our right to go:
"We meant to violate no law,
"Nor wish'd to shun the foe.

"Our officers declared that we
"Had but three months to stay;
"We served those three months faithfully,
"Up to the latest day."

"No one suspects intended wrong;
"The judgment only erred:
"In such a case, O noble Chief,
"Let mercy's voice be heard.

"At home an aged mother waits
"To clasp her only son;
"A wife, and little children—this arm
"Alone depend upon.

"Cut me not off from those dear ties;
"So soon from life's young bloom;
"O 'tis a dreadful thing to die,
"And moulder in the tomb!

"Sure mercy is a noble gem
"On every Chieftain's brow;
"More sparkling than a diadem—
"O exercise it now.—"

'Twas all in vain, John Harris' pary'r,
'Tis past the soul's belief!
Hard as the flint was Jackson's heart;
He would not grant relief.

He order'd Harris out to die,
And five poor fellows more!
Young, gallant men, in prime of life,
To welter in their gore!!

Methinks I hear the muffled drum,
And see the column move;
—Lo here they come—how sad their looks:
Farewell to life and love!

See six black coffins rang'd along—
Six graves before them made;
Webb, Lindsey, Harris, Lewis, Hunt,
And Morrow kneeled and prayed.

They kneel'd and pray'd, and tho't of HOME,
And all its dear delights.
The deadly tubes are levell'd now—
The scene my soul affrights!

Sure he will spare! Sure JACKSON yet
Will all reprive but one—
O hark! those shrieks! that cry of death!
The dreadful deed is done!

All six militia men were shot;
And O! it seems to me
A dreadful deed—a bloody act
Of needless cruelty.

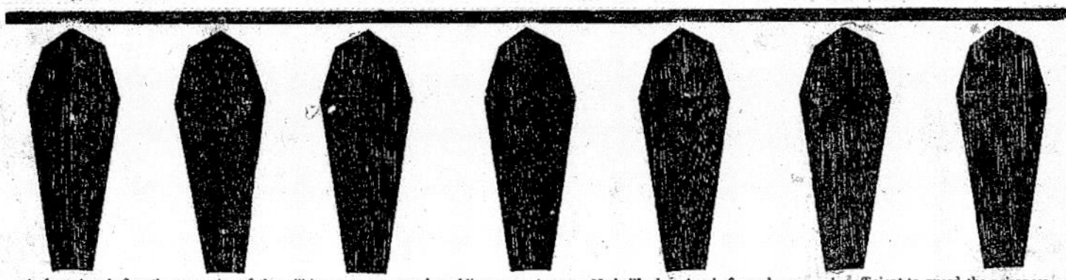

A short time before the execution of the militia-men, seven regular soldiers were shot near Nashville, by a band of regulars scarcely sufficient to guard the prisoners.—They were confined in a house, and taken out and executed one at a time, there being scarcely enough men for the purpose of executing and guarding at the same moment. An eighth soldier was to have been executed at the same time. He was a young man, who had deserted one month before his time had expired. General Jackson doomed him to die with the others. He was saved by a writ of habeas corpus from Judge M'Nairy, who fell under Jackson's displeasure for snatching this one victim from his blood-stained hands. If Jackson's army had been at hand, no doubt M'Nairy would have shared the fate of Judge Hall and Judge Fromentin. Capital punishments in an army, are designed for example as well as for penalty; but in this case it was a transaction of horror to peaceful citizens: no army was there to witness the bloody tragedy He has ever been a man of "blood and carnage."

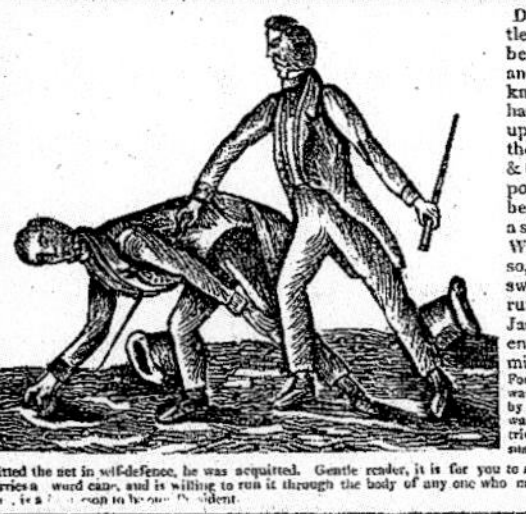

Do not be startled, gentle reader at the picture before you. It is all true and every body ought to know it. Gen. Jackson having made an assault upon Samuel Jackson, in the streets of Nashville, & the latter not being disposed to stand still and be beaten, stooped down for a stone to defend himself. While in the act of doing so, Gen. Jackson drew the sword from his cane and run it through Samuel Jackson's body, the sword entering his back and coming out of his breast.—For this offence an indictment was found against Gen. Jackson, by a grand Jury, upon which he was subsequently arraigned and tried. But finding means to persuade the petit jury that he committed the act in self-defence, he was acquitted. Gentle reader, it is for you to say, whether this man, who carries a sword cane, and is willing to run it through the body of any one who may presume to stand in his way, is a [illegible] person to be our President.

Poor JOHN WOODS; he was a generous hearted, noble fellow as ever lived, who had volunteered in the service of his country. He was on guard one day at Fort Strother—the officer of the guard had permitted him to go to his tent, and snatch a hasty breakfast; whilst disposing of his scanty meal, seated on the ground beside his skillet, an upstart little officer, who was not Woods' equal at home, ordered him to pick up and carry off some bones that lay scattered about the place—Woods refused, and the little officer attempted to compel him. At this instant, Gen. Jackson, having heard the dispute, came out of his tent, and without knowing any thing of the merits of the case, repeatedly vociferated—"*Shoot the damn'd rascal!—Shoot the damn'd rascal.*" For this offence, the unfortunate, the gallant Woods, was tried, condemned and shot. Before his trial, Gen. Jackson used this language to the court-martial. "*By the immortal God! if you find him guilty I will not pardon him!*" And he kept his promise; though he did offer a pardon provided he would enlist in the regular service—Thus perished as noble a fellow as ever lived, for as trifling an offence as ever took the life of man!!!

On the 27th day of March, 1814, General Jackson had found at an Indian village, at the bend of the Tallapousie, about 1000 Indians, with their *squaws* and *children*, "running about among their huts." The following is an account of the sanguinary massacre which took place;—it is Gen. Jackson's own, and therefore must be received as sufficient evidence against himself. He says:—"DETERMINING TO EXTERMINATE them, I detached Gen. Coffee with the mounted men, and nearly the whole of the Indian force, early on the morning of yesterday, to cross the river about two miles below the encampment, and to surround the bend in such a manner as that none of them should escape by attempting to cross the river." The result he then details:—"*Five hundred and fifty seven were left dead on the Peninsula, and a great number of them were killed by the horsemen in attempting to cross the river*; IT IS BELIEVED THAT NO MORE THAN TEN ESCAPED. WE CONTINUED to DESTROY *many of them who had concealed themselves under the banks of the river, until we were prevented by the night.* THIS MORNING WE KILLED 16 WHICH HAD BEEN CONCEALED."

We ask you to pause and reflect that the above tragic narration of cold-blooded and merciless cruelty, is taken from an official communication made by General Andrew Jackson.

The General, after sleeping (with what composure, we cannot say) thro' the night ensuing the tragedy we speak of, awoke in the morning surrounded by the corpses of "five hundred and seventy" fellow creatures, to cause, by way of worthy afterpiece, sixteen others to be dragged from their concealments, and put to death in cold blood. We cannot boast of more than common sensibility, but we must think that to witness such an act, would make ours a little cold also. What are the general's words?—these: "this morning we killed sixteen which had been concealed"—and the man who acts and speaks thus; who has half as much blood upon his conscience, as he has upon his hands,—he, forsooth, is to be called the peer and *like* of Washington, the happy warrior,—

————————"he
Whom every man at arms could wish to be!"

But it is time to have done with the unpleasant subject. We will observe in addition to the details already given, that the village was burnt, and several women and children killed. In conclusion, we ask our fellow citizens, whether Genl. Jackson, though he has contributed largely to the military reputation of our country, has not done enough to disqualify him, in the eyes of the people as virtuous as they are free, for the office he seeks at their hands.

Gen. Jackson, detailing his progress among the Indians, in the course of which, men, WOMEN and CHILDREN, were indiscriminately "exterminated," their towns burnt and their country laid waste, with the utmost complacency and *sang froid*, says, in his letter dated, "Camp before St. Marks, April 9, 1818"—"Capt. M'Ever having hoisted English colours on board of his boats, Francis *the Prophet*, Hocomochemutcho and *two others*, were *decoyed* on board. *These have been hung to-day!*" Reader, mark the perfect indifference with which Gen. Jackson shoots, hangs or stabs his fellow beings, with or without trial, and the more than callous, aye, even exulting composure, with which he details his horrid and bloody deeds! If the Indians, according to the customs of their nation, put to death a prisoner, all the feelings of our nature rise into indignation against them. With what feelings then should we contemplate the *decoying* and the cold-blooded murder of prisoners, by a civilized man, in the face of the laws and customs of his country!

"FRANKLIN, Tenn. September 10, 1818.

A difference which had been for some months brewing between Gen. Jackson and myself, produced on Saturday, the 4th inst. in the town of Nashville, the most outrageous affray ever witnessed in a civilized country. In communicating the affair to my friends and fellow-citizens, I limit myself to the statement of a few leading facts, the truth of which I am ready to establish by judicial proofs.

1. That myself and my brother, Jesse Benton, arriving in Nashville on the morning of the affray, and knowing of Gen. Jackson's threats, went and took lodgings in a different house from the one in which he staid, on purpose to avoid him.

2. That the General and some of his friends came the house where we had put up, and commenced the attack by levelling a pistol at me, when I had no weapon drawn, and advancing upon me at a quick pace, without giving me time to draw one.

3. That seeing this my brother fired upon General Jackson, when he had got within eight or ten feet of me.

4. That four other pistols were fired in quick succession; one by General Jackson at me; two by me at the General; and one by Col. Coffee at me. In the course of this firing, General Jackson was brought to the ground; but received no hurt.

5. That daggers were then drawn. Col. Coffee and Mr. Alexander Donaldson made at me, and gave me five slight wounds. Captain Hammond and Mr. Stokeley Hays engaged my brother, who being still weak from the effect of a severe wound he had lately received in a duel, was not able to resist two men. They got him down; and while Capt. Hammond beat him on the head to make him lie still, Mr. Hays attempted to stab him, and wounded him in both arms, as he lay on his back parrying the thrusts with his naked hands. From this situation a generous hearted citizen of Nashville, Mr. Summer, relieved him. Before he came to the ground, my brother clapped a pistol to the breast of Mr. Hays, to blow him through, but it missed fire.

6. My own and my brother's pistols carried two balls each; for it was our intention, if driven to arms, to have no child's play. The pistols fired at me were so near that the blaze of the muzzle of one of them burnt the sleeve of my coat, and the other aimed at my head at a little more than arms length from it.

7. Capt. Carroll was to have taken part in the affray, but was absent by the permission of General Jackson, as he has proved by the General's certificate, a certificate which reflects I know not whether less honor upon the General or upon the Captain.

8. That this attack was made upon me in the house where the Judge of the District, Mr. Searcy, had his lodgings! Nor has the civil authority yet taken cognizance of this horrible outrage.

These facts are sufficient to fix the public opinion. For my own part, I think it scandalous that such things should take place at any time; but particularly so at the present moment, when the public service requires the aid of all its citizens.—As for the name of *courage*, God forbid that I should ever attempt to gain it by becoming a bully.—Those who know me, know full well that I would give a thousand times more for the reputation of Croghan in defending his post, than I would for the reputation of all the duellists and gladiators that ever appeared upon the face of the earth.

THOMAS HART BENTON, *Lieut. Col. 39th Infantry.*

And now a member of the Senate of the United States.

"General Jackson's mother was a COMMON PROSTITUTE, brought to this country by the British Soldiers. She afterwards married a MULATTO MAN, with whom she had several children, of which number General JACKSON is one!!!"

Truth's Advocacy, CINCINNATI, OHIO, JANUARY 1828

elitists who expected a kind of deference from the common man that was no longer forthcoming.

The election proved a huge victory for Jackson. The common man came out to vote, and he voted for Old Hickory. Three times as many votes were cast in 1828 as in 1824, and the 56 percent of the vote that Jackson took was the largest majority achieved in the nineteenth century.

John Quincy Adams left Washington the night before the inauguration, piqued that Jackson had not paid the traditional courtesy call and unwilling to see his rival installed in office. The crowd of men and women of all classes who turned out for the inaugural festivities at the White House grew so rowdy that Jackson had to be extracted from the uproar by a group of friends, and damage to the White House was avoided only through the wise expedient of moving the bowls of punch onto the lawn to lure the carousers outdoors. Reflecting on 1828's squalid mud bath of an election campaign, the historian Edward Channing wrote, "On the whole, possibly it was more honorable to have been defeated in 1828 than to have been elected."

CHAPTER
10

Old Nick and Old Hickory

JACKSON v. CLAY (AND WIRT), 1832

The election of 1832 included both clearly drawn ideological differences between the two major candidates and copious bad blood between Andrew Jackson and members of his own party. It carried forward the development of American political institutions, making the nominating convention the new standard for selecting candidates. And, like the election four years before, it was a personal triumph for Andrew Jackson.

The most bitter of the animosities was between Jackson and his Vice President, John C. Calhoun, whose presidential ambitions had been stalled by Jackson's emergence in 1824 and by his victory in 1828. Given Jackson's age (he would be sixty-five by the time of the 1832 election), Calhoun was hoping that the way would be open for him that year to win the presidency at last. Jackson resented Calhoun's presumption and, early in 1829, found new reason to dislike his Vice President when Calhoun and his allies, together with their wives, attempted to banish from Washington society the new wife of Secretary of War John H. Eaton. Peggy Eaton was a tavern keeper's daughter, and her first husband had recently killed himself (some attributed the suicide to her relations with Eaton), opening the way for the Eatons' nuptials four months later. Secretary of State Martin Van Buren, a widower, extended every courtesy to Mrs. Eaton. President Jackson, to whom the entire affair was all too reminiscent of the smear campaign that had (in his view) driven his beloved wife, Rachel, to an early grave just weeks earlier, stood by Eaton and grew closer to Van Buren.

Soon the President had another reason to detest Calhoun. In 1830, it was revealed to Jackson that Calhoun, who had always pretended to Jackson that he had supported the general's actions in Florida in 1818, had actually denounced Jackson on the issue in meetings of Monroe's cabinet. Calhoun then attempted to defend himself in a long pamphlet, which only succeeded in making the matter public and caused Jackson to break with him definitively. Van Buren later engineered a cabinet reshuffle in which he left the State Department and accepted the post of minister to Great Britain. But while Van Buren was settling into his duties in London, Calhoun

The rejected Minister,
We never can make him President,
without first making him Vice-president.

In 1831 the Senate refused to approve Jackson's appointment of Secretary of State Martin Van Buren as ambassador to Britain. The infuriated Jackson vowed that he would make Van Buren Vice President first and then President.
LIBRARY OF CONGRESS.

arranged a tie vote in the Senate on Van Buren's appointment, allowing himself the pleasure, as Vice President, of casting the deciding vote against it. "It will kill him, sir, kill him dead!" the South Carolinian gloated to an ally. But this petty revenge backfired as severely as the Peggy Eaton affair had; Jackson decided that Van Buren would be his vice presidential nominee in 1832.

This was made official at the first national convention of what was coming to be called the Democratic Republican (soon to be simply the Democratic) Party. At the convention, held in Baltimore in May, no vote on a presidential nominee was undertaken as the meeting simply accepted the nominations of Jackson already made by the states. The issue was a vice presidential nominee; the hope was that by calling a national convention the Democrats would avoid a split in the party and thus guarantee victory in the general election. In pursuit of that goal, the rules of the convention stated that a nominee had to win the votes of two thirds of the delegates. Although there was considerable opposition to Van Buren from southerners sympathetic to Calhoun, there was no possibility that anyone other than Van Buren could meet the two-thirds requirement, and Van Buren was nominated on the first ballot.

If personal rivalries and vendettas were threatening to split the Democratic Republicans, their opponents were united behind the clear choice of the National Republicans, Henry Clay. This choice had been made at the National Republican convention, held in December 1831, also in Baltimore. Although deep hostility divided Clay from Jackson, there was also a clear ideological split between them. Clay championed a strong federal government that was actively involved in the nation's economic affairs, while Jackson was much more reluctant to expand federal responsibility for the economy. The issue that crystallized things in 1832 was the recharter of the Second Bank of the United States. The bank's charter in 1816 had been a major recognition by the party of Jefferson that

1832

PRESIDENTIAL CANDIDATE (STATE) VICE-PRESIDENTIAL CANDIDATE (STATE)	PARTY	ELECTORAL VOTES	APPROX. % OF POPULAR VOTE
Andrew Jackson (Tenn.) Martin Van Buren (N.Y.)	Democratic	219	55%
Henry Clay (Ky.) John Sergeant (Pa.)	National Republican	49	42%

South Carolina's 11 electoral votes went to John Floyd (Va.; Independent Democratic). Vermont's 7 electoral votes went to William Wirt (Md.; Anti-Masonic).

dency. A Whig editor in Philadelphia quickly recognized the blunder, and the Whig organization appropriated the cider jug and the log cabin as symbols of Harrison's (and thus the party's) identification with the common man, as opposed to the sneering elitism of the Democrats.

Harrison had in fact grown up in very comfortable circumstances in Virginia and lived in a large house in Ohio, but he was portrayed by his party as the salt of the earth, while President Van Buren, who had come from modest circumstances in New York (his father was a farmer and tavern keeper), was depicted as a profligate libertine. Van Buren was ensured renomination because of Andrew Jackson's unwavering support, but the Democratic hero's mantle could not protect Van Buren from the Whig vilification campaign. The President's table was set with gilded plates and golden spoons, falsely declared the Whigs, who even claimed that he had a golden coach. They accused him of being a dandy who kept the evidence of his gluttony contained within a whalebone corset. Whig versifiers compared the doughty Harrison to the ridiculous President:

Old Tip he wears a homespun suit,
He has no ruffled shirt-wirt-wirt;
But Mat he has the golden plate,
And he's a little squirt-wirt-wirt.

William Henry Harrison, by Albert Gallatin Hoit, 1840.
NATIONAL PORTRAIT GALLERY, SMITHSONIAN INSTITUTION.

Democrats responded by accusing Harrison of being illiterate and of having defaulted on his debts. And they belittled Harrison's military record—foolishly, in view of Van Buren's lack of military service.

"At thirty minutes past midnight, this morning of Palm Sunday, the 4th of April, 1841, died William Henry Harrison, precisely one calendar month President of the United States after his inauguration.

The influence of this event upon the condition and history of the country can scarcely be seen. It makes the Vice-President of the United States, John Tyler of Virginia, Acting President of the Union for four years less one month. Tyler is a political sectarian, of the slave-driving, Virginian, Jeffersonian school, principled against all improvement, with all the interests and passions and vices of slavery rooted in his moral and political constitution—with talents not above mediocrity, and a spirit incapable of expansion to the dimensions of the station upon which he has been cast by the hand of Providence."

JOHN QUINCY ADAMS IN HIS DIARY

A typical image of Harrison outside his purported log cabin. He was in fact born on the Virginia estate of his father, and when elected, was living in an elegant twenty-two-room manor house.

A mechanical "metamorphic" pull-card showing President Martin Van Buren first enjoying a "beautiful goblet of White-House champagne" and then grimacing when forced to drink "log-cabin hard cider" from an "ugly mug" labeled "WHH."

The emergence of Harrison marks an important advance in what was to become a theme of presidential contests from this time forward, the importance of military accomplishments as a measure of a possible president's worthiness. Most Presidents up to this time had come to office on the basis of other achievements. Washington, of course, had been a military hero, as had Jackson, and Monroe had served during the Revolution, but Jefferson, John Adams, Madison, John Quincy Adams, and Van Buren were all profoundly unmilitary, if not antimilitary, men. Of the four Whig presidential candidates between 1840 and 1852, three were generals, and after Abraham Lincoln all the Republican candidates for the balance of the century were Civil War veterans. Harrison, proclaimed the "Washington of the West," was a military man who, like Washington (and unlike Jackson), always showed a profound respect for civilian control of government.

The log-cabin-and-hard-cider campaign had a military tone with its frequent marches in support of Harrison. Whigs marched behind banners depicting Harrison's exploits, images of humble log cabins, and cider jugs (frequently dipping into their own jugs) and chanted, "Van, Van is a used-up man" and "To guide the ship, we'll try old Tip."

Images, not issues, were the centerpiece of the campaign. A Whig committee handled Harrison's correspondence to ensure that no unguarded opinion found its way into print. Both parties had reason to avoid a deep discussion of national affairs. Both drew support from across the nation, but the nation was divided into slaveholding states and free states, and the 1830s had seen a hardening of the lines. Fearing to alienate supporters on one side or the other, leaders of both parties kept mum on the matter, a course apparently approved by the voters, who turned out in record numbers (more than 80 percent of the eligible voters made it to the polls, compared with 58 percent four years earlier). Although the antislavery Liberty Party met in Albany, New York, in 1840 and nominated James G. Birney as its candidate, just 7,053 voters across the nation supported Birney. The country divided fairly evenly between the two major parties, with Harrison winning about 53 percent of the popular vote and Van Buren 47 percent. The electoral vote margin was far wider, 234 to 60, as Harrison carried nineteen of twenty-six states. The Whigs had won the battle of images.

PORTRAITS OF THE PRESIDENTS.

JOHN TYLER.

John Tyler, by Albert Newsam, 1846.
NATIONAL PORTRAIT GALLERY,
SMITHSONIAN INSTITUTION.

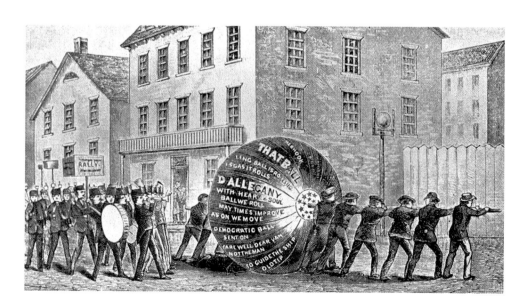

Harrison's campaign was the first in which large numbers of voters took to the streets. Rolling huge balls covered with pro-Harrison and anti-Van Buren slogans became a popular activity. On the ball shown here, the bottom four lines were the jingle

> *Farewell, dear Van.*
> *You're not the man*
> *To guide the ship.*
> *We'll try Old Tip.*

Old Tip was, of course, Old Tippecanoe: Harrison.
LIBRARY OF CONGRESS.

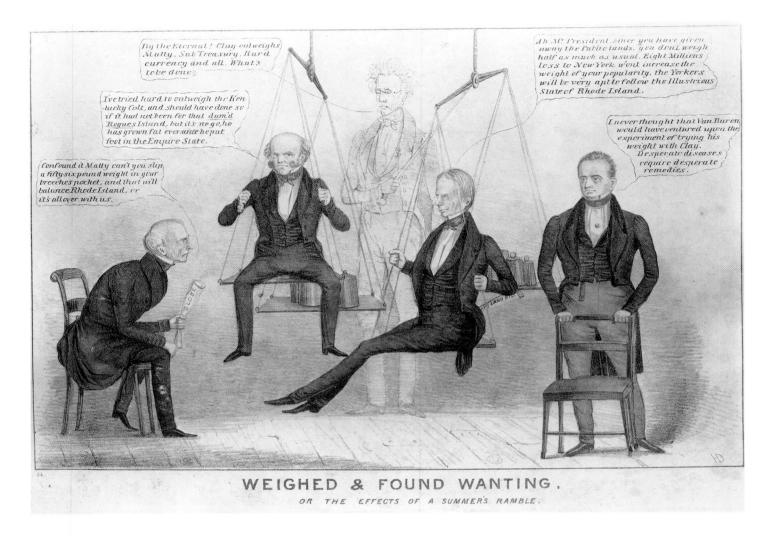

WEIGHED & FOUND WANTING.
OR THE EFFECTS OF A SUMMER'S RAMBLE.

Henry Clay outweighs Martin Van Buren as a suitable candidate for the presidency, while the distressed ghost of Jackson stands behind them, lamenting his protégé's inadequacy. Seated at left is Francis Blair, editor of the leading Democratic newspaper, The Globe; *at the right is Senator Thomas Hart Benton of Missouri, great-uncle of the artist of the same name.*
LIBRARY OF CONGRESS.

But images, of course, were not unrelated to issues. The depiction of Van Buren as a potentate living in gilded luxury must have had added power during a major recession, and the Whigs' expectation of victory was grounded in national discontent over the economy. Historians differ over whether the Whig triumph was founded on rational consideration of economic issues or irrational infatuation with campaign ballyhoo, but the lesson the politicians learned was clear: ballyhoo wins. For the balance of the century, parades and songs, slogans and picnics would remain a constant presence, whether candidates were avoiding the issues or confronting them head-on.

Sadly, the victor would have been better off taking the pension, the cider, and the cabin. Harrison, exposed to the elements during his inauguration, worn out by the duties of forming a government, and (incredibly) further taxed by doing the shopping for the White House, developed pneumonia and died just a month after taking office, leaving the nation in the hands of John Tyler, the first Vice President to be elevated to the presidency by death.

CHAPTER
13

Dark Horse and Darkening Skies

POLK v. CLAY, 1844

After Harrison died, some in Washington raised the question whether John Tyler would actually become President or would merely exercise the powers of the office while remaining Vice President. "His Accidency" decisively claimed both the title and the powers, however, and established a lasting precedent. Henry Clay, however, dominated the Whigs in Congress, and Tyler, who was resentful of his influence, began moving toward the Democrats, seeking to build a base of his own that would include the more liberal wing of the Whig Party and the more conservative elements of the Democratic Party. When Clay tried to push through a new national bank (after successfully repealing Van Buren's independent Treasury system), Tyler vetoed the measure. A second, milder measure was then passed, one that had originally had Tyler's support. But the President again vetoed the bill, whereupon the entire cabinet, with the exception of Secretary of State Daniel Webster, resigned. The glorious Whig victory of 1840 had been squandered.

The recession that had cost Van Buren a second term was finally abating as Tyler took office, and with economic improvement came a lessening of the divisions over economic policy that the Jacksonians had created and then exploited in their rise to power. But the economic chaos that erupted in 1837 undercut the more radical antibank sentiment, as did one more lasting fact: that the emerging entrepreneurial economy, whatever its inequalities, was proving remarkably successful at generating wealth. The egalitarian appeal of Van Buren's Democrats was diminished as Americans of both parties learned that there were many ways of getting rich, or at least rising. The Panic of 1837 had undercut the entire economy, but with the economy's revival in the 1840s came a concomitant revival of the most visible form of national growth in the nineteenth century: westward expansion. And the focus of expansionist aims, as the 1844 election approached, was Texas.

Anglo settlers had shown growing interest in Texas since the beginning of the century, and in 1821, as Mexico gained its independence from Spain, Stephen Austin was granted permission to establish the first Anglo-American settlement in Texas, along the Brazos River. By the middle 1830s, strains between the Anglos and

JAMES G. BIRNEY,
Eleventh President of the United States.

*An overly optimistic caption for
James G. Birney, the candidate
of the Liberty Party.*

DAVID J. AND JANICE L. FRENT
POLITICAL AMERICANA COLLECTION.

their Mexican rulers led to war, and after Sam Houston defeated Antonio López de Santa Anna at the Battle of San Jacinto in 1836, the independent Republic of Texas was formed. Like its sister republic to the east, Texas permitted slavery, and when Texas petitioned for annexation and admission to the Union as a state, the request sparked a controversy in Washington.

John Tyler, who saw this as an opportunity to further his aim of establishing a new political alignment, threw his support behind annexation. What looked like opportunity to Tyler looked like disaster to Clay and Van Buren, both of whom feared that annexation would harm the Union. Tyler, however, was President, and in 1843 he instructed his secretary of state, Abel Upshur (by this time Webster had resigned the post), to negotiate an agreement with the Republic of Texas. The plan had scant support in the North but was very popular in the South. Upshur had nearly completed the treaty when his duties took him aboard the warship *Princeton,* where he died when a cannon blew up near him. Tyler then appointed John C. Calhoun to succeed Upshur.

Calhoun, a brilliant political theorist, had his own presidential ambitions, which he had been pursuing, along different political tacks, for two decades. His championing of states' rights and slavery had narrowed his national appeal too much for him to win nomination for President, but in 1844 he played a crucial role in determining the outcome of the race. Calhoun completed Upshur's negotiations, and on April 22, 1844, the treaty was sent to the Senate. John Quincy Adams, still serving the nation as a congressman from Massachusetts, noted the fact in his diary, commenting that with the treaty "went the freedom of the human race."

Calhoun, of course, saw things differently, and one thing he saw was a great opportunity to damage his old rival Van Buren. Calhoun published an elaborate and heated argument linking the annexation of Texas with a defense of slavery. With antislavery sentiment growing in the North, Van Buren could not accept that link. Neither could Henry Clay. Five days after the treaty reached the Senate, both men published letters against annexation. The letters would keep both men from the presidency.

The 1844 Whig campaign had begun with the split with Tyler in 1841,

1844

PRESIDENTIAL CANDIDATE (STATE) VICE-PRESIDENTIAL CANDIDATE (STATE)	PARTY	ELECTORAL VOTES	APPROX. % OF POPULAR VOTE
James K. Polk (Tenn.) George M. Dallas (Pa.)	Democratic	170	50%
Henry Clay (Ky.) Theodore Frelinghuysen (N.J.)	Whig	105	48%
James G. Birney	Liberty	0	2%

and Clay, as the leader of the congressional Whigs, became the obvious choice to lead the party in 1844. He breezed to his party's nomination. Even Thurlow Weed, who had blocked Clay in 1840, came out for the Kentucky Hotspur early on. The Whig convention, held in Baltimore at the beginning of May 1844, was a coronation of Clay, with New Jersey's Theodore Frelinghuysen awarded the second spot on the ticket.

Van Buren had been expected to lead the Democrats, and, had the convention been held early (November 1843 was the preferred date of his backers), Old Kinderhook would have triumphed. But the Democrats did not meet until the end of May 1844, also in Baltimore. Van Buren's support among Democrats was a mile wide but an inch deep. In 1843, he had the backing of nearly all the party's major newspapers and leaders, but his popular support, perhaps undermined by the accusations made against him in 1840, was thin. The egalitarianism he championed was increasingly distasteful to the more prosperous members of the party, particularly in the South. A new center of gravity in the party was forming around the issues of expansionism and protection of southern interests (above all, preservation of the slave system). When Calhoun's "Texas bombshell" exploded and Van Buren came out against annexation, the ex-President's support began to evaporate.

James K. Polk, by Charles Fenderich, 1838.

NATIONAL PORTRAIT GALLERY, SMITHSONIAN INSTITUTION.

Both Van Buren and Clay had made it clear that their opposition to annexation arose from unwillingness to provoke a war with Mexico, and both, in spite of Calhoun's tactics, did everything possible to leave slavery out of the discussion. But many Democrats in the South and West were impatient. The problem was to find a candidate to take the nomination from Van Buren. Michigan's Lewis Cass had mounted a campaign and had some support, but he was such an unprincipled politician that few could accept him as the candidate, at least at the outset. Richard Johnson, the former Vice President, was still trying to parlay his supposed role as the slayer of Tecumseh into a leading part on the White House stage, but he was not a plausible nominee. Van Buren would have won on the first ballot but for the fact that the party retained the two-thirds rule it had first adopted in 1832. The simple majority he polled was not sufficient, and as the convention proceeded his strength began to fade. Support for Cass began to rise, and by the fifth ballot he had passed Old Kinderhook, although he was still far short of the two-thirds vote needed. While this was happening, the allies of James K. Polk of Tennessee were quietly pursuing the nomination for Vice President. Polk was a loyal Jacksonian, and as Speaker of the House had worked closely with President Van Buren during the 1830s. Polk had returned to Tennessee and been elected governor in 1839 but had then lost successive races to regain the office in 1841 and 1843. Andrew Jackson, whose support for Van Buren had lapsed over the Texas issue, suggested to Polk that the convention might deadlock and that Polk would be a fine compromise candidate. By the seventh ballot, with Van Buren's defeat apparent and Cass nearing success, others began to share Jackson's idea, and when a Massachusetts delegate, the historian George Bancroft, came to Polk's man Gideon Pillow to suggest it, Pillow was ready. Overnight, the two coordinated a lobbying campaign for Polk, and the next morning Polk emerged with strong support on the eighth ballot and swept to victory on the ninth. New York's Silas Wright was first selected as his running mate, but he declined and George Dallas of Pennsylvania was then named. News of the nomination was sent by Samuel F. B. Morse's new invention, the telegraph, directly to a telegraph office in the basement of the Capitol, where surprise greeted the nomination of Polk, the nation's first "dark horse" candidate.

The surprise of Polk's nomination provided ammunition for the Whig campaign, which asked, in newspapers and on banners, "Who is James K. Polk?" The obvious point was that Henry Clay was a person of national reputation, while Polk, if not exactly obscure, was not nearly as distinguished. It was a perfectly reasonable tactic, one that hearkened back to the idea of the Founding Fathers that the Presi-

Henry Clay defeats James Polk in this cartoon, as (from left to right) Daniel Webster, Theodore Frelinghuysen, Martin Van Buren, John C. Calhoun, Thomas Hart Benton, Andrew Jackson, and George Dallas look on.

LIBRARY OF CONGRESS.

POLITICAL COCK FIGHTERS.

THE PRESIDENTAL SWEEPSTAKES OF 1844.
Preparing to Start.

dent should be a person of national reputation. The Whigs also tried, in a rather ridiculous way, to make Clay seem worthy of respect as a military leader, even though he had not served in the armed forces. During the War of 1812, the Whigs said, he had been "as a general in chief over the intellectual power of the country" as a leader of the war hawks in Congress. And his parliamentary gifts had made him "the first Statesman of the Nation . . . whom posterity will place by the side of the father of his country."

The problem with these tactics was that the era of deference was over and the era of political parties had arrived. This was a time of strong party identification—in one county in Tennessee, the head of the Whig ticket had won by an identical margin in three consecutive annual elections. Clay also failed to recognize that hoopla, not reasoned argument, was the centerpiece of the campaign process. While Polk wisely spoke in generalities and dodged questions, Clay continued re-fining his position while attempting to show that he had been consistent all along. The shrewdest move of the campaign, even though it was an afterthought, was the

In spite of the continuing tradition of the ostensibly reluctant candidate, by 1844 the idea of presidential contests as sporting events was well established. The equestrian theme of the cartoon is appropriate, since James K. Polk, the eventual Democratic nominee and the winner of the election, was the first "dark horse" candidate.
LIBRARY OF CONGRESS.

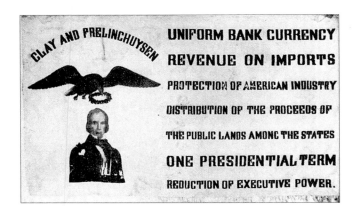

Campaign banner.

insertion of a plank into the Democratic platform that advanced America's claims to large portions of the Pacific Northwest, thus balancing geographically the party's enthusiasm for the annexation of Texas. The cry of "Fifty-four forty or fight," referring to the extreme northern limit of American claims against British Canada along the Pacific coast, became one of the hallmarks of the race.

The issue may also have blunted one of the charges made against Polk, that he was pro-British. This echo of earlier charges against Federalist candidates was supported by some Tory skeletons in the Polk family closet and by Polk's support for free trade (low or no tariffs), which the Whigs portrayed as subservience to the mighty British economy. Other old charges were trotted out against Henry Clay, including the supposed "corrupt bargain" with J. Q. Adams to conclude the 1824 election. Clay's personal life—he was a drinker, gambler, and womanizer, as well as a former duelist—was also used against him.

President Tyler tried to run on his own but dropped out when he discovered he was without support, and there was a fourth candidate, James G. Birney, again the nominee of the antislavery Liberty Party. With the issue of Texas focusing attention on slavery, Birney won 62,000 votes, nearly ten times as many as he had four years earlier, and probably cost Clay New York and the election.

The election proved very close, with fewer than 40,000 votes (out of more than 2.6 million cast) separating Polk from Clay. Expansionist sentiment, the antislavery vote in New York, and Clay's own natterings had helped Polk win. The day before he left office, John Tyler signed the bill inviting Texas to join the Union. Warned by the leading statesmen of both parties that annexation would lead to war with Mexico, the people voted for war. They soon got it.

The raccoon was the Whig Party's symbol, and the rooster (before the donkey came along) was the Democratic Party's. The rooster would continue to crop up on Democratic campaign items as late as 1948.

"Fictitious Partisanship"

TAYLOR, CASS, VAN BUREN, 1848

For a man who was mocked with banners that sneeringly asked, "Who is James K. Polk?" the dark horse candidate who became the eleventh President of the United States proved a remarkably competent chief executive. He worked tirelessly to master the demands of his office, and his extensive diary is filled with complaints about the unceasing stream of supplicants seeking government employment, contracts, handouts, and favors. During his 1844 campaign, Polk had promised that he would serve only one term, and so exhausted was he from that term that he died just three months after leaving office.

Polk had presided over the greatest expansion of American territory since Thomas Jefferson's Louisiana Purchase of 1803. The war with Mexico that Clay and Van Buren had prophesied in April 1844 had begun two years later, and a string of victories by American forces had led to a punitive peace for Mexico, which had ceded more than 500,000 square miles of territory to the United States, including the bulk of today's southwestern states and California. Using more peaceful means, Polk had also negotiated a settlement of American claims against British Canada in the Northwest, securing undisputed title to another 286,000 square miles of territory. Although some were disappointed that Polk had abandoned 54° 40′ without a fight, many voters were pleased with the swift fulfillment of what the magazine editor John L. O'Sullivan called in 1845 the nation's "Manifest Destiny" to expand across the continent.

The Mexican War had, naturally, provided a new roster of military heroes, and the martial tradition of the presidency was extended in the 1848 campaign. In fact, the successes of American generals in Mexico were evaluated with a view toward the 1848 race much the way early party caucus and straw poll results are sifted today. After winning a decisive victory at Buena Vista over Mexican forces commanded by the hated General Santa Anna, the butcher of the Alamo, Zachary Taylor was immediately anointed a front-runner for the presidency. His principal rival for military honors in Mexico was General Winfield Scott, a veteran (like Taylor) of the

Silk campaign ribbon.
LIBRARY OF CONGRESS.

War of 1812 and a far superior military leader. Scott had been backed for the Whig nomination for the presidency in 1840 by New York's Thurlow Weed.

It was irritating for Polk and the Democrats to have Whigs such as Scott and Taylor winning battles in Mexico. Scott had captured Mexico City in September 1847, but he had then quarreled with Polk over the peace talks and been relieved of his command. Scott, for his part, was irritated that his prospects for the Whig nomination were being compromised by Taylor, and he did his best to ensure that Taylor would have few chances for glory after Buena Vista. Scott was fat and vain, and he affected a formal, European style of military command that had earned him the nickname "Old Fuss and Feathers." The more rustic Taylor was dubbed "Old Rough and Ready."

The nicknames alone would seem to have predestined Taylor to win the Whig nomination; after all, the party's only presidential victory had come through embracing of the log cabin. But there were other contenders for the Whig throne, including Kentucky's Henry Clay, the quadrennial locust of Whig presidential campaigns. And Clay had proved himself prescient in asserting not only that the Texas issue would lead to war with Mexico but that the sectional divide in the nation would be deepened immeasurably.

Polk, of course, had brought the issue of Oregon and 54° 40′ into the 1844 race in order to finesse the matter, offering the possibility of new states to both North and South. But by this point the agitation against slavery in the North was not to be so easily quieted, and as the war with Mexico was getting under way David Wilmot, a Democratic representative from Pennsylvania, proposed an amendment to an appropriations bill stating that slavery should not be permitted in any territory obtained from Mexico as a result of the war. The measure, called the Wilmot Proviso, twice passed the House and twice died in the Senate. But it polarized opinion in both parties and widened the sectional fissures that Clay had made it his life's work to keep under control.

The stability of the two-party system during the previous decade had owed much to the determination of leaders on both sides to ignore the problems arising from slavery. Both parties drew strength from all sections of the nation, and neither wished to sacrifice its popularity in any region by taking too clear a stand. The new territories gained or secured under Polk made the issue impossible to avoid.

1848

PRESIDENTIAL CANDIDATE (STATE) VICE-PRESIDENTIAL CANDIDATE (STATE)	PARTY	ELECTORAL VOTES	APPROX. % OF POPULAR VOTE
Zachary Taylor (Ky.) Millard Fillmore (N.Y.)	Whig	163	47%
Lewis Cass (Mich.) William O. Butler (Ky.)	Democratic	127	43%
Martin Van Buren (N.Y.)	Free Soil	0	10%

The problem was severe in the Democratic Party, whose ranks included the loudest defenders of slavery as well as some of the most progressive politicians in the country, leftovers of the Locofoco days (see p. 86). New York's party split between the Barnburners, aligned with Martin Van Buren and his son, and the Hunkers, who were in sympathy with Polk and the party's southern wing. In 1848, the Democrats had three major contenders. The favorite was Lewis Cass, who had nearly won the nomination in 1844 before the Van Burenites had bolted to Polk. Silas Wright, the New York Barnburner who might have offered the most effective challenge to Cass, died in 1847, leaving the Democratic radicals without a serious candidate. The other major contenders for the nomination, James Buchanan of Pennsylvania and Levi Woodbury of New Hampshire, were, like Cass, opposed to the Wilmot Proviso.

The Democratic convention was held in Baltimore in May, and the New York Democrats sent two delegations, one of Barnburners, one of Hunkers. The party attempted to give each faction half the vote, but this didn't work, and New York was unrepresented at the gathering. Cass easily won the nomination, and William O. Butler of Kentucky was chosen as the vice presidential nominee. Butler had served with distinction in the War of 1812, fighting under Andrew Jackson, and had returned to the military in 1846 and fought in Mexico. It was Butler whom Polk had placed in command of American forces in Mexico when he stripped Scott of the

Hand-colored lithograph published by Nathaniel Currier, who in 1857 would form a partnership with James M. Ives.
NATIONAL PORTRAIT GALLERY,
SMITHSONIAN INSTITUTION.

1848: NEW YORK NOMENCLATURE

THERE IS A RICH LODE OF LANGUAGE that can be mined from the politics of just one state, New York, in the first half of the nineteenth century. New York's political life was of vital concern, in part because of its position as a capital of journalistic enterprise, in part because its 35 electoral votes (by 1852) were fully a fifth of the total needed to elect a President.

Some of New York's factions, such as the Burrites and the Clintonians, were named for their leaders. But many had more colorful names. One group opposed to the Clintonians was called the Quids (from the Latin *tertium quid,* a term used at the time to indicate political freelancers) and another the Coodies (after a character in a pamphlet that had attacked DeWitt Clinton following his loss to James Madison in the 1812 campaign). The adherents of New York City's Tammany Hall were for a while known as Martling Men (after a tavern in which they met) and later as Bucktails (after a party emblem worn on a hat). Martin Van Buren's supporters in the 1820s were called the Albany Regency (partly in reference to the prince regent in contemporary British politics, perhaps partly in recognition that those leading the party in Albany were simply acting on orders of their absent sovereign, Van Buren, who was in Washington serving as a U.S. senator).

In 1835, the Locofocos appeared on the scene. A Tammany Hall meeting was manipulated by party regulars so that their slate could be nominated before a group of more radical Democrats could object; the nominations made, the regulars extinguished the lights in the hall and fled. Prepared for this move, the radicals had brought candles and lit them with matches called "locofocos," which gave their name to the most radical, antibank Democrats.

post. Both Butler and Cass had risen to the rank of general in the army, so the Democratic ticket was well selected to counter a military man from the Whig side.

Taylor, though, had won his Buena Vista victory early, in 1847, so the Whig publicity machine had had time to build the image of him as "an American Cincinnatus"—yet another Whig incarnation of Washington. There was one serious complication: Taylor had no record of political affiliation. Not only had he never been active in the Whig Party (or, for that matter, as a Democrat) but he had never even voted. Taylor unveiled his political allegiance by saying that he was a Whig "but not an ultra Whig," which presumably excused his apathetic record. Taylor won nomination easily, and the Whigs selected Millard Fillmore of New York as his running mate. Fillmore provided both regional balance and a moderate antislavery past, which it was hoped would appeal to northern Whigs. Fillmore was the only person on either ticket who had not been a general.

Like the Democrats, the Whigs were divided over the issue of slavery. In Massachusetts, "Cotton" and "Conscience" Whigs split that state's Whig Party nearly as

Nativism gave us the Know-Nothings, and the Whigs of New York had their pro-Fillmore Silver Grays (from the flowing gray hair of one of their leaders, Francis Granger) and their anti-slavery Woolly Heads (a reference to the kind of hair slaves had). But it was the Democrats who brought party vocabulary in New York to its highest development: the antislavery Barnburners got their name from the story of the farmer who, discovering rats in his barn, burned down the barn to rid himself of the rats; in just that way, it was said, the Barnburners were willing to destroy the state's Democratic Party in order to rid it of proslavery elements. Their opponents in the party, the Hunkers, were so called because they were said to "hunker" (a blend of "hanker" and "hunger") after office; with the party in Washington increasingly dominated by southern Democrats, hope for federal patronage was brightest for those who were soft on slavery.

After the 1848 race, when so many Barnburners deserted the party to vote for Van Buren as the Free Soil candidate rather than for the "Doughface" Lewis Cass, a new division appeared among the Democrats, as the Hunkers divided between the Soft Shells, who were willing to let the Barnburners back into the party, and the Hard Shells, who were not.

It was, all told, a charming sort of name-calling.

Lewis Cass. Lithograph by Francis D'Avignon after a daguerreotype by Mathew Brady, 1850.
NATIONAL PORTRAIT GALLERY, SMITHSONIAN INSTITUTION.

badly as the Democratic Barnburners and Hunkers were split in New York, and the splits in each party were exploited by the other according to section. In the North, Democrats asked how Whigs "could stomach Taylor," a Louisiana slaveholder while Whigs branded Cass a "Doughface" (southern sympathizer). In the South, Whigs urged Democratic voters to embrace their fellow southerner Taylor, and Democrats responded by pointing to Fillmore's past antislavery sentiments.

Men in both parties who strongly opposed the extension of slavery (even in 1848, those actually favoring abolition were still perceived as being on the radical fringe) cast about for a new forum in which to express their views. Horace Greeley, who had done so much to help elect Harrison eight years earlier, pronounced the convention that had nominated Taylor a "slaughterhouse of Whig principles," and a number of leading Whigs broke with the party and called for an antislavery political convention to be held in Buffalo. Not long after that, the Barnburners in New York expressed their disapproval of Cass and nominated Martin Van Buren for President. Whigs and Democrats opposed to slavery met in Buffalo in August and nom-

"The country does not deserve a visitation of that pot-bellied, mutton-headed cucumber Cass."

HORACE GREELEY

inated Old Kinderhook as the Free Soil candidate. ("Free soil" meant land from which slavery was excluded; the party's slogan was "Free soil, free speech, free labor, and free men.")

Although the central issue of the time, slavery, was brought into the campaign in a major way for the first time with Van Buren's candidacy, much of the campaign was taken up by the usual exaggerated or simply false charges. Cass was branded a demagogue and a speculator; Taylor was dubbed a slave trader; and Van Buren was put down as a turncoat who had betrayed his old political friends to gain personal glory. Cass and Taylor, each trying to retain party strength in both the North and the South, said as little on the subject of slavery as possible. The London *Times* characterized the contest as one of "fictitious partisanship."

In 1848, there was one important procedural change: the election was held on the same day across the country. In the Log Cabin campaign of 1840, the voting had taken place between October 30 and November 10, depending on the state, and there had been many instances of voters crossing state lines to vote more than once. On November 7, 1848, nearly 3 million voters (all of them men, of course, and nearly all of them white) cast their votes. Perhaps the most telling result was that Van Buren's Free Soil candidacy drew 10 percent of the vote and held the balance of power in eleven states. Most important, Van Buren's popularity among New York's Barnburners diluted the Democratic vote (he polled more votes than Cass) and helped ensure that the state's 36 electoral votes went to Taylor. Taylor's final electoral vote margin was 163 votes to Cass's 127 (Van Buren did not carry any states); had New York voted for Cass, he would have won.

Henry Clay, reviewing the polls, judged that he would have won had he been the nominee. Nearing the end of his life, Clay would have one more great part to play on the national stage before his exit, one last effort to prevent the issue of slavery from dividing the Union. But his efforts would

General Zachary Taylor atop skulls of victims of the Mexican War. The Whigs deemed Taylor their candidate who was most "available," i.e., likely to win. Lithograph probably by Nathaniel Currier.

AN AVAILABLE CANDIDATE.
THE ONE QUALIFICATION FOR A WHIG PRESIDENT.

Manifest Destiny.

New Mexico,
California Chihuahua
Zacatecas. MEXICO, Peru,
Yucatan, Cuba.

A WAR PRESIDENT.

CASS

PROGRESSIVE DEMOCRACY.

Lewis Cass wielding the sword of "Manifest Destiny," a phrase coined in 1845 by John L. O'Sullivan, editor of the United States Magazine and Democratic Review. *Cass is here accused of wanting to extend American territory not only westward to the Pacific but also southward to annex Mexico and even Peru.*
LIBRARY OF CONGRESS.

succeed only in delaying the final crisis that had been building steadily since Thomas Jefferson had heard a "fire bell in the night" over the admission of Missouri to the Union nearly thirty years earlier. At that time, Clay had helped to negotiate the Missouri Compromise, and in 1850 the "Great Compromiser" would engineer one final, but futile, compromise.

The Democracy United

PIERCE v. SCOTT, 1852

On January 29, 1850, Senator Henry Clay of Kentucky, five times frustrated as a candidate for President, rose to offer the Senate of the United States a package of legislation that would, he promised, relieve the great sectional tensions that were threatening to tear the nation apart. "Taken together," he told his colleagues, "in combination, they propose an amicable arrangement of all questions in controversy between the free and slave states, growing out of the subject of slavery." For the North, Clay's proposals offered admission of California as a free state (which California had already determined to be) and prohibition of the slave trade in the District of Columbia (the sight of slave auctions in the nation's capital had become unacceptable to many northerners). For the South, there was a stronger fugitive slave law, a provision that slavery itself would continue in the capital, and a renunciation of congressional authority to interfere with the slave trade in or between the slave states themselves. Other parts of the plan dealt with the territorial claims of Texas and the organization of new territories in the Southwest. Clay's proposals were denounced by both abolitionists and die-hard supporters of the "peculiar institution" but found support among more moderate politicians. With his statement, Clay took the initiative on the central issue facing the Union away from President Taylor and set the terms for the presidential campaign of 1852, the last campaign for the Whig Party that he had helped found twenty years before.

The slavery controversy, fanned by the Mexican War and the Wilmot Proviso, had not diminished under Taylor's leadership. In October 1849, a Mississippi convention had called for a convention of proslavery delegates in Nashville the following June to examine the South's options, and Taylor had responded by stating that any attempt at disunion would be met by force. Clay, the conciliator, offered the nation an apparent way out of its troubles, although securing passage of what became known as the Compromise of 1850 proved beyond Clay's waning powers, and a new generation of leadership, embodied in the small but impressive form of Illinois's Stephen A. Douglas, the "Little Giant," would be needed to steer the compromise through Congress.

In early February, Clay spoke in Congress, combining a lucid defense of his compromise measures with a solemn warning to disunionists: "War and dissolution of the Union are identical and inevitable." A month later, Calhoun of South Carolina replied, although he was too ill to read his speech and had a copy of it read by a Virginia colleague. Unlike Clay, Calhoun had never been a great orator, but his power of thought was deeper. He was the great theorist of states' rights, an antifederalist until the end, whose brilliant formulation of a theoretical defense of the rights of the slaveholding states prompted the historian Richard Hofstadter to dub him "the Marx of the Master Class." He offered no optimism, simply excoriating the opponents of slavery and viewing the admission of California as a free state as the latest example of northern aggrandizement at the expense of the South. Three days later Daniel Webster rose to speak. Preparing to endorse the proposal, which would call much criticism down upon him back in Massachusetts, Webster opened by saying he was speaking not "as a Massachusetts man" or even as "a Northern man": "I speak today for the preservation of the Union. Hear me for my cause." His speech, conciliatory to the South, was hailed there as "Webster's apotheosis."

DAVID J. AND JANICE L. FRENT
POLITICAL AMERICANA COLLECTION.

The debate continued into the summer, when events took an unexpected turn. President Taylor had resented Clay's efforts to lead the nation and had even threatened military action against Texas, which was claiming part of the New Mexico territory. Then, while enjoying July 4 celebrations on a hot Washington day, Taylor refreshed himself with fruit and iced drinks. By that evening he was feeling quite ill, and five days later he was dead, the victim, perhaps, of typhoid fever. New York's Millard Fillmore, whom many in the South had feared because he had harbored some antislavery sentiments in the past, became the nation's thirteenth President. By the end of the month, Clay's bill had been defeated. But the new President was eager to make the compromise succeed, as were others who saw in Clay's proposals an opportunity for peace. It was Stephen A. Douglas who proposed that the various parts of the compromise be voted on individually by Congress. Presented as a package, the compromise could never succeed because too many of the items were unacceptable to some faction to build a majority. But each measure, on its own, might succeed, and so it transpired. Here, it was hoped by the leaders of both parties, the debate on slavery could end.

Another matter on which both parties agreed, especially as the nominating conventions approached, was that a military man was best suited for the presidency—that is, was most likely to win. With the loss

1852

PRESIDENTIAL CANDIDATE (STATE) VICE-PRESIDENTIAL CANDIDATE (STATE)	PARTY	ELECTORAL VOTES	APPROX. % OF POPULAR VOTE
Franklin Pierce (N.H.) William R. King (Ala.)	Democratic	254	51%
Winfield Scott (N.J.) William A. Graham (N.C.)	Whig	42	44%

O R N I T H O L O G Y .

Winfield Scott owed his depiction as a splendid turkey to his army nickname, "Old Fuss and Feathers." Scott, though personally opposed to slavery, was prepared to accept the status quo and hoped in this way to win votes in the South. Here he demands that Pierce, as the Democratic rooster, stop blocking his way across the Mason–Dixon Line.

of Taylor, the Whigs could still turn to the other great hero of the Mexican War, Winfield Scott. Scott was popular in the West, as the incumbent President, Fillmore, had become among southern Whigs, owing to his efforts to secure the compromise. New England still hoped that Webster could be the party's choice. The convention failed to make a choice until the fifty-third ballot, when Scott, "Old Fuss and Feathers," was selected.

The Democrats, too, had a deadlocked convention. Lewis Cass of Michigan was running again, hoping to avenge his loss to the Whigs four years before, but his support in the Midwest was undercut by Stephen A. Douglas, who at thirty-nine felt ready for his first run at the White House. From the East, Pennsylvania's James Buchanan had significant support, and William Marcy of New York also had a following, though smaller. The relative strength of the candidates, and the likelihood that none would have an easy time securing the two-thirds vote needed to take the Democratic nomination, had been apparent to some political operatives before the convention. Among these were the friends of Franklin Pierce of New Hampshire, whose principal qualifications were that he was an affable, good-looking man with few enemies, practically no political record (in spite of having served in both the House and the Senate), and an average career as a brigadier under Scott in Mexico. When the deadlock seemed unbreakable, his name was put forward and he won on the forty-ninth ballot. Pledged by the Democratic platform to support the compromise, Pierce managed for the moment to heal the rift in the Democratic Party, winning endorsement from Martin Van Buren as well as support in the South.

Scott, too, had accepted the compromise, and with both parties eager to avoid exacerbating the sectional tensions, the campaign itself degenerated into the usual round of parades and wild accusations. Democrats formed Granite Clubs and erected "Hickory Poles to the honor of Young Hickory of the Granite Hills" (a rather dubious effort to link Pierce to Andrew Jackson). Whigs paraded in praise of the man who had captured Mexico City and, borrowing from their unsuccessful tactics in 1844, asked, "Who is Franklin Pierce?" In an attempt to answer that question, Pierce got his old Bowdoin classmate Nathaniel Hawthorne to write his campaign

Major General Winfield Scott pulls the "presidential chair" out from under Franklin Pierce, who had been a mere brigadier general during the Mexican War.
LIBRARY OF CONGRESS.

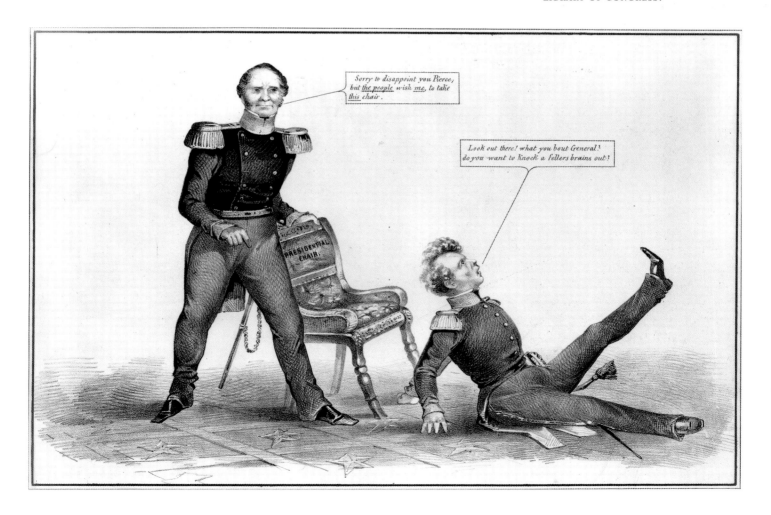

biography (Hawthorne's reward was appointment to the lucrative post of American consul in Liverpool).

Each party accused the other's candidate of unfairness to immigrants (the immigrant vote was growing rapidly). Scott's managers even planted Irish shills in the audience, and when they asked Scott a question he would warmly greet the lovely sound of "that rich Irish brogue." Pierce was accused of habitual drunkenness and of cowardice under fire in Mexico, while Scott was portrayed as a buffoon, a quarrelsome commander, a has-been. Pierce avoided most opportunities to appear in public, but Scott, trailing, went on an arranged tour of proposed sites for new military hospitals, where he found opportunities to address voters but often hurt his own cause with his poor oratory.

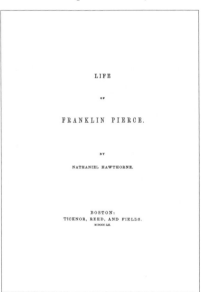

LIFE

OF

FRANKLIN PIERCE.

BY

NATHANIEL HAWTHORNE.

BOSTON:
TICKNOR, REED, AND FIELDS.
M DCCC LII.

Against a united Democratic Party, Scott had little chance, and his defeat was nearly total: he carried only four of thirty-one states. In New York on November 3, the day after the polling, the Whig diarist George Templeton Strong wrote of the defeat, "Till the day when Babylon the Great shall be cast down into the sea as a millstone, there will not be another such smash and collapse and catastrophe." Three days later, Strong was noting that the consensus was that "the Whig party is dead and will soon be decomposed into its original elements." The question now was: What would replace it?

LEFT: *Franklin Pierce. Daguerreotype by Mathew Brady.*
LIBRARY OF CONGRESS.

RIGHT: *In 1852 Franklin Pierce commissioned Nathaniel Hawthorne, his former classmate at Bowdoin College, to write a campaign biography. When Horace Mann heard about the project, he quipped that if Hawthorne succeeded in writing an inspiring biography of the undistinguished Pierce, it would be "the greatest work of fiction he ever wrote." In gratitude for a service well performed, the victorious Pierce rewarded Hawthorne with the lucrative post of American consul in Liverpool.*

In the biography Hawthorne states, "The two great parties of the nation appear—at least to an observer somewhat removed from both—to have nearly merged into one another; for they preserve the attitude of political antagonism rather through the effect of their old organizations, than because any great and radical principles are at present in dispute between them."

The contest was, then, more a matter of personalities than of parties. "It remains for the citizens of this great country to decide, within the next few weeks," wrote Hawthorne, "whether they will retard the steps of human progress by placing at its head an illustrious soldier [i.e., Scott], indeed, a patriot, and one indelibly stamped into the history of the past, but who has already done his work, and has not in him in the spirit of the present or of the coming time,—or whether they will put their trust in a new man [i.e., Pierce], whom a life of energy and various activity has tested, but not worn out, and advance with him into the auspicious epoch upon which we are about to enter."
LIBRARY OF CONGRESS.

CHAPTER

16

A House Dividing

BUCHANAN, FRÉMONT, FILLMORE, 1856

Franklin Pierce's victory in 1852 had been part of an overall Democratic triumph that had left the party with a two-thirds majority in the House of Representatives and a 37–25 majority in the Senate as the Thirty-third Congress convened. Pierce's own electoral victory and the strength of his party in Washington presented an opportunity for the Democrats to lead the nation in a time of trial, but that opportunity was dreadfully botched.

For Franklin Pierce, the time between election and inauguration was one of personal tragedy. He and his wife saw their only child, a boy of eleven, killed before their eyes in a train accident. Pierce arrived at the White House in a state of mourning, and his wife, who loathed the social obligations of political life, took to her bed. Even in the best of times, Pierce would have made an unlikely leader, but these were the worst of times, and Pierce offered little to the nation in the way of programs either foreign or domestic.

More sagacious political minds recognized in the huge Democratic triumph real problems as well as an opportunity. The last time a party had emerged from a presidential election so dominant was during James Monroe's Era of Good Feelings. That had ended with the schism of the old Jeffersonian Republican Party into the Adams and Jackson wings that had eventually become the Whig and Democratic Parties. Stephen A. Douglas of Illinois was aware of this precedent, troubled by Pierce's lassitude, and impatient to advance his own career, so he devised a strategy: eager to encourage construction of a railroad to the Pacific that would run west from Chicago in his own state of Illinois, the Little Giant proposed that the government encourage such a project, which would require organizing some western territories into new states. To foster migration westward, he also asked for a homestead bill to grant lands to settlers. As a sweetener to the South, which had its own hopes for a southern railroad to the Pacific, he suggested that the issue of slavery in the new states of Kansas and Nebraska be decided by the vote of the residents of those territories, following the principle of "popular sovereignty" that had been embraced in the Compromise of 1850. A neat package, it ignored the important fact

95

Metal pinback with a rebus of Buchanan's name: Buck + Cannon.

DAVID J. AND JANICE L. FRENT
POLITICAL AMERICANA COLLECTION.

that the earlier Missouri Compromise had "forever prohibited" slavery from the lands in the Louisiana Purchase north of 36° 30′ north latitude.

Douglas expected this set of measures to infuriate the Whigs and thus to unite Democrats against a common enemy. In January 1854, he persuaded Pierce to back the plan. But the atmosphere was too volatile, and many in the North saw the proposal as the clearest evidence yet that there was a great conspiracy afoot, a plot by the "Slave Power" to win control of the federal government and turn the lands to the west into degenerate bastions of slavery.

Although abolitionism was still a fringe position in much of the North, awareness of the plight of African-American slaves had been rising there for a quarter century. William Lloyd Garrison's *Liberator* had begun publication in 1831 (the year of Nat Turner's rebellion), and in 1838 a slave named Frederick Douglass fled slavery in Maryland and settled in Massachusetts, subsequently publishing his *Narrative of the Life of Frederick Douglass,* which revealed the inner workings of slavery from a slave's perspective. Then, in 1852, Harriet Beecher Stowe, who was not an abolitionist but who was outraged by the Fugitive Slave Act contained in the Compromise of 1850, published *Uncle Tom's Cabin,* which sold more than a million copies within a year and was pirated for stage performances across the North.

At the same time, another political movement was rising, one that also saw a malevolent conspiracy under way in the land and that portrayed the enemy in vivid and sentimental terms like those used by Stowe. This was nativism. In place of virtuous slave women menaced by lecherous overseers, the nativists frightened their audiences with images of chaste Protestant girls exposed to the supposedly libertine ways of the convent. Of course, the sort of depravity depicted by Stowe actually existed, while the Rabelaisian world of lascivious priests and nuns was a prurient fantasy. But the nativist fantasies arose from, even if they did not depict, social facts. Between 1845 and 1854, America had experienced a rush of immigration that was greater, in percentage terms, than during any other time in its history. Three million people had arrived in the United States in that period, a number equal to 14.5 percent of the nation's population in 1845. The potato famine in Ireland was driving hundreds of thousands of destitute Irish women and men to America each year. They were Catholics, and English-speaking Protestants had a long tradition of anti-Catholicism. Unable to get work except for

1856

PRESIDENTIAL CANDIDATE (STATE) VICE-PRESIDENTIAL CANDIDATE (STATE)	PARTY	ELECTORAL VOTES	APPROX. % OF POPULAR VOTE
James Buchanan (Pa.) John C. Breckinridge (Ky.)	Democratic	174	45%
John C. Frémont (Calif.) William L. Dayton (N.J.)	Republican	114	33%
Millard Fillmore (N.Y.) Andrew Jackson Donelson (Tenn.)	American (Know-Nothing)/Whig	8	22%

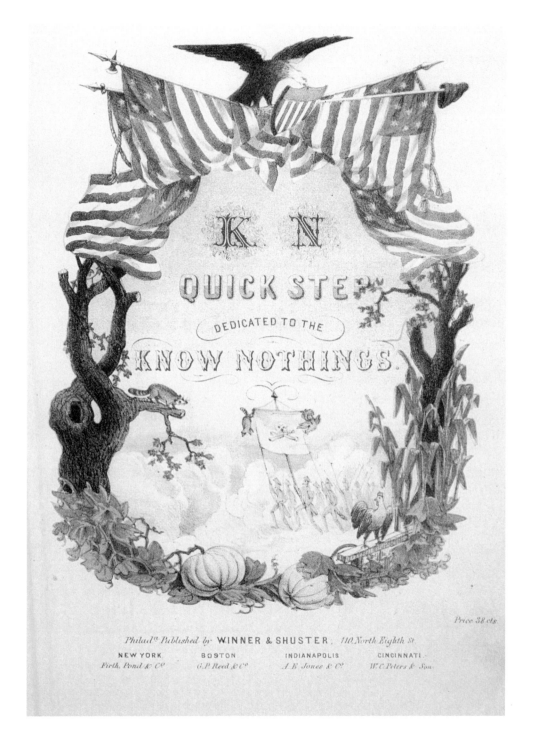

Cover of sheet music for a campaign song. Note the Whig raccoon and the Democratic rooster—both of them live in the foreground and both hanging dead from the marchers' skull-and-crossbones banner.
DAVID J. AND JANICE L. FRENT
POLITICAL AMERICANA COLLECTION.

Silk campaign ribbon.
DAVID J. AND JANICE L. FRENT
POLITICAL AMERICANA COLLECTION.

pitifully low wages, often fond of drink, and concentrated in cities, the Irish made for perfect villains—a threat to the wages of American-born workers, offensive to the rising temperance sentiment, and supposedly owing first loyalty to the pope in Rome.

1856: FOUR DAYS IN MAY

THE TURMOIL UNLEASHED BY THE KANSAS-NEBRASKA ACT and its provision to allow the citizens of both territories to decide whether slavery would be permitted once they achieved statehood was generally referred to as Bloody Kansas. Pro- and antislavery forces conducted campaigns of intimidation, and matters came to a head in the third week of May 1856, when three separate incidents escalated into bloody battles—in one instance, on the floor of the U.S. Senate chamber.

On May 21, a band of proslavery "border ruffians" attacked the "Free Soil" town of Lawrence, Kansas, burning the hotel and tearing apart the offices of the town's two newspapers. One person died in the violence. News of what sensationalist editors called the Sack of Lawrence appeared in the Washington newspapers on May 24, followed by later reports that described the town as being reduced to "a few bare and tottering chimneys."

The tone of the coverage of the attack on Lawrence was probably rendered more extreme by an event in Washington that had dominated the papers on May 23. The day before, Senator Charles Sumner of Massachusetts, a firebrand abolitionist, had been caned senseless by Congressman Preston Brooks of South Carolina. Sumner had offended Brooks with a blistering attack on slavery that included the suggestion that South Carolina senator Andrew P. Butler (Brooks's uncle) had taken a mistress. "I mean that harlot, Slavery," said Sumner.

The most bloody and brutal incident occurred in Kansas on the night of May 24–25. There a fanatical opponent of slavery named John Brown was heading toward Lawrence with other antislavery militiamen when he heard that the town had been destroyed. With biblical wrath he led a campaign of reprisal. Brown and his men butchered five proslavery men in the Pottawatomie Massacre.

It was against this bloody backdrop that the presidential campaign of 1856 unfolded.

FORCING SLAVERY DOWN THE THROAT OF A FREESOILER

Democrats (from left to right) Stephen A. Douglas, Franklin Pierce, James Buchanan, and Lewis Cass attempt to force slavery down the throat of a Freesoiler.
LIBRARY OF CONGRESS.

THE RIGHT MAN FOR THE RIGHT PLACE.

For Sale at N.º 2 Spruce S.t N.Y.

Millard Fillmore, "the right man for the right place," separating bearded John C. Frémont and James Buchanan.
LIBRARY OF CONGRESS.

    In the presidential election of 1856, nativism and sectionalism defined the campaign. The fruits of Stephen A. Douglas's Kansas-Nebraska Act had been the disaster of "Bloody Kansas," where pro- and antislavery forces had battled for control. Pierce and Douglas were both too closely associated with the problems in Kansas to win nomination from a Democratic Party that still hoped to appeal in all sections of the nation, so the party turned to James Buchanan, a Pennsylvanian sympathetic to the South who had had the good fortune to be out of the country on a diplomatic assignment and had thus avoided the Kansas-Nebraska taint.

    The Whig Party was fading fast, and the nativists hoped to replace it, thinking that nativism would have national appeal and provide a springboard to national power. But nativism proved less powerful than sectionalism, and the nativists split.

Silk badge.

The southern wing of the American Party (as it called itself, although its members were generally known as the Know-Nothings [see p. 86]) went for Millard Fillmore, the former President, who later received the endorsement of the pathetic remnants of the Whig Party. The North Americans (as that section's wing of the Know-Nothings was named) endorsed one Nathaniel Banks, a stalking horse who would later withdraw in favor of the nominee of another new party, which in 1854 had taken the name "Republican."

The Republican Party emerged as a strictly sectional party made up of northern Whigs and antislavery Democrats. They chose as their nominee John C. Frémont, an explorer and outdoorsman who had played a role in securing California for the United States in the Mexican War and whose political thinking was handled by others, including his wife, Jessie, the daughter of Missouri senator Thomas Hart Benton. A more logical choice would have been New York's William H. Seward, but Thurlow Weed, the wily master of the political back room, felt that the Republicans would inevitably lose in 1856 and wanted to save Seward for a better chance in 1860.

Frémont had served as a senator from the new state of California, and his career as explorer, combined with the romantic story of his courtship of Jessie Benton, made him good copy for Republican publicists.

Buchanan, as the Democratic nominee and in effect the only national candidate, was faced with the difficult task of avoiding taking any stands that could alienate either section. But the tradition of passive candidates and rhetorical pablum helped him. In the North, Frémont dwelt on the horrors of the Kansas situation and the audacity of the Slave Power, while in the South, Fillmore stressed the danger of papist influence and called for tougher restrictions on naturalization. Buchanan's followers painted him as a steadfast, cautious politician, which, for the most part, he was. He carried every slave state except Maryland (which went for Fillmore) and he did well enough in the North (carrying his populous home state of Pennsylvania, as well as four other northern states) to win the election. Buchanan had 174 electoral votes to 114 for Frémont and 8 for Fillmore.

With this election, the Democrats had become a southern party and would remain so for three quarters of a century.

A House Divided

LINCOLN, DOUGLAS, BRECKINRIDGE, BELL, 1860

In his inaugural address on March 4, 1857, James Buchanan predicted that the issue of slavery would be "speedily and finally settled" by the Supreme Court. Buchanan was terribly wrong, but he was basing his prediction on solid information. Two justices, Robert C. Grier and John Catron, had improperly informed the President-elect of the Court's impending decision in the Dred Scott case, which was announced a couple of days after the inauguration. Dred Scott, a slave, belonged to a doctor in Missouri but had spent years in the free state of Illinois and the Wisconsin Territory. He returned to Missouri and then sued for his freedom, arguing that his residence on free soil had made him free. The Court found against Scott, and vehemently so. The decision held first that Scott was not a citizen and thus had no right to sue in the federal courts; that in any case he was, at the time he brought the suit, back in Missouri, where slavery was permitted; and that the Missouri Compromise (which had barred slavery from the Wisconsin Territory) was unconstitutional because it violated the Fifth Amendment's prohibition against depriving a person of property "without due process of law." It was the first time the Court had found a law passed by Congress unconstitutional since the landmark case of *Marbury v. Madison* of 1803, which had established the concept of judicial review.

Like the Kansas-Nebraska Act of 1854, the Dred Scott decision lessened the hope that compromises of the sort engineered in the past by Henry Clay and others could succeed. The case made southern firebrands more aggressive and helped to persuade moderate northerners that there really was a Slave Power conspiracy aimed at extending slavery to the territories. Southerners had moved from an earlier defense of slavery as a "necessary evil" (due to the supposed inferior abilities of blacks, who, they said, would never succeed without the benevolent paternalism of the slave system) to strident claims that slavery was a positive good (and certainly a more humane labor system than the "wage slavery" faced by northern industrial workers).

As the year 1857 advanced, partisan warfare continued in Kansas, and eventually two competing elections were held to choose a constitution for the admission of

Kansas to the Union. The first election, on the proslavery "Lecompton Constitution" (named for the town where it had been drawn up), was boycotted by antislavery forces; the second, held early in 1858, was on a competing document that opposed slavery, and that referendum was boycotted by slavery's advocates. So each constitution won a vast majority in its separate election, leaving President Buchanan and Congress with a difficult choice. Buchanan supported the Lecompton version, Illinois senator Stephen A. Douglas opposed it, and the Democratic Party split along the fault line. The Democrats had won in 1856 in part because they had been the only remaining party of national scope, but now they, too, were split into two sectional factions.

The Democrats' internal problems were compounded by a rising challenge from the new Republican Party. The collapse of the Whig Party and the inability of nativism to supersede the sectional conflict had left the Republicans as the leading voice of opposition to Buchanan, the Democrats, and slavery. Strong in the old Northwest (Ohio, Indiana, Illinois, and so on) and gaining power in the Northeast, the party had important leadership in New York, where the master political operative Thurlow Weed had engineered the rise of William Henry Seward first to the governorship of New York and then to the U.S. Senate. Weed had held Seward back in favor of Frémont at the Republican convention in 1856, but 1860 was supposed to be Seward's year. He had opposed nativism in New York and had emerged as a vigorous Senate opponent of the Kansas-Nebraska Act and the Dred Scott decision. In October 1858, he told an audience in Rochester, New York, that the debate over slavery foretold an "irrepressible conflict" between the sections.

It was a theme that had been developed, in equally memorable but more eloquent terms, by an Illinois lawyer who, as a Whig, had served a single term in the House of Representatives in the late 1840s. Abraham Lincoln had returned to the practice of law after his brief stint in Washington, but the Kansas controversy and the Dred Scott decision had propelled him back into the public sphere, speaking out on slavery and the Union. The force of his logic, the elegance of his language, and the moderation of his position brought him many adherents, and in June 1858 he was nominated as

1860

PRESIDENTIAL CANDIDATE (STATE) VICE-PRESIDENTIAL CANDIDATE (STATE)	PARTY	ELECTORAL VOTES	APPROX. % OF POPULAR VOTE
Abraham Lincoln (Ill.) Hannibal Hamlin (Maine)	Republican	180	40%
Stephen A. Douglas (Ill.) Herschel V. Johnson (Ga.)	Democratic	12	29%
John C. Breckinridge (Ky.) Joseph Lane (Oreg.)	National Democratic	72	18%
John Bell (Tenn.) Edward Everett (Mass.)	Constitutional Union	39	13%

NATIONAL REPUBLICAN CHART

PRESIDENTIAL CAMPAIGN, 1860

Stephen A. Douglas.

the Republican candidate for the U.S. Senate seat held by Stephen A. Douglas. Speaking to the convention that had nominated him, Lincoln told the delegates:

"A house divided against itself cannot stand."
I believe this government cannot endure, permanently half *slave* and half *free*.
I do not expect the Union to be *dissolved*—I do not expect the house to *fall*—but I *do* expect it will cease to be divided.
It will become *all* one thing, or *all* the other.
Either the *opponents* of slavery, will arrest the further spread of it, and place it where the public mind shall rest in the belief that it is in course of ultimate extinction; or its *advocates* will push it forward, till it shall become alike lawful in *all* the States, *old* as well as *new*—*North* as well as *South*.

The balance of the election campaign revolved around the seven Lincoln-Douglas debates, where the issues of the day were explored in detail before rapt Illinois audiences. Douglas won that campaign, but there was a rematch looming, for Lincoln's performance in the debates had made him a national figure.

In one of the debates, in Freeport, Illinois, Douglas tried to reconcile his own doctrine of "popular sovereignty" (that each state should decide for itself whether to permit slavery) with the Dred Scott decision. The resulting "Freeport Doctrine," which suggested that territories could still bar slavery by the use of their police powers, offended southern Democrats but carried little weight with northerners. And when the Democratic convention came to order in April 1860, it was indeed a house divided.

The location could hardly have been less propitious for holding the party together. The Democrats met in Charleston, South Carolina, the epicenter of proslavery rhetoric and the place where, a year later, the first shots of the Civil War would rain down on Fort Sumter. Douglas had a slim majority of the delegates, but not nearly enough to win nomination under the two-thirds rule. The South had a working majority on the platform committee, where slots were allotted equally among the states, rather than being proportional to congressional representation, as was the case for the delegates. The committee divided on the platform's position on slavery, and the pro-Douglas majority of delegates voted down the platform majority's proslavery report in favor of a milder minority report, at which point the delegates from eight slave states walked out. The convention chairman subsequently ruled that to win nomination Douglas still needed to carry two thirds of the original number of delegates, and the convention soon adjourned, setting a June date to reassemble, this time in Baltimore, to select a candidate.

In May the focus switched to the Republicans, and again the choice of city was crucial. The Republicans met in Chicago, and Lincoln's advantages as a favorite son were skillfully capitalized on by Judge David Davis, who managed Lincoln's forces there. The candidate sent Davis a telegram reading, "I authorize no bargains and will be bound by none," but Davis, observing that "Lincoln ain't here," proceeded

to do what he had to do to win. The galleries were packed with pro-Lincoln demonstrators, and Seward and Weed were left to the side, with Lincoln winning on the third ballot. Hannibal Hamlin of Maine was chosen as his running mate.

When the Democrats reconvened in Baltimore the following month, a new issue emerged as the forces of Douglas and his opponents fought over the accreditation of delegates. When the Douglas forces prevailed, the South again walked out. On June 23, Douglas was nominated by the remaining Democrats as the leader of the northern wing of the party. The southern dissidents met at another hall in Baltimore and nominated John C. Breckinridge of Kentucky, Buchanan's Vice President, as the candidate of the southern wing. A fourth candidate, John Bell of Tennessee, sought to bridge the gap between North and South as the candidate of the new Constitutional Union Party.

The campaign itself was rather lackluster, in spite of (or perhaps because of) the magnitude of the question being decided. Few doubted that Lincoln's election would lead to war. The most colorful forces in the campaign field were Lincoln supporters called Wide Awakes. Ever vigilant to the threat of the Slave Power, the Wide Awakes marched in carefully choreographed parades, wearing glazed capes and

Abraham Lincoln, John Bell, and John C. Breckinridge.
NATIONAL MUSEUM OF
AMERICAN HISTORY,
SMITHSONIAN INSTITUTION.

The Republican Party convention
in Chicago.
LIBRARY OF CONGRESS.

Wide Awake march in New York City,
October 3, 1860. Wood engraving from
Harper's Weekly.
LIBRARY OF CONGRESS.

caps and carrying torches and colored transparencies emblazoned with campaign images and slogans. The Wide Awakes marched in a zigzag pattern that mimicked the usual course of a split-rail fence (in honor of Honest Abe, the rail-splitter). In New York City, ninety thousand Wide Awakes paraded along Broadway, singing rousing choruses of "Ain't You Glad You Joined the Republicans?"

Lincoln, of course, did not have to worry about how to tailor his appeal to reach both northern and southern voters, so he could concentrate on winning votes in the northern states. Douglas and Bell, the futile champions of compromise, together polled nearly 100,000 more popular votes than Lincoln, but even had their votes been united behind a single candidate, Lincoln's strength in the North would have carried him to electoral victory. In October, Douglas, foreseeing that Lincoln would win, took his campaign into the deep South, hoping to persuade those who heard him that the Union was the paramount consideration.

Douglas failed, and the cadenced march of uniformed, singing Wide Awakes along Broadway would soon be replaced by the steps of young men in other uniforms heading south to fight the Civil War.

Ambrotype of a Wide Awake, 1860.
COURTESY OF SWANN GALLERIES, NEW YORK.

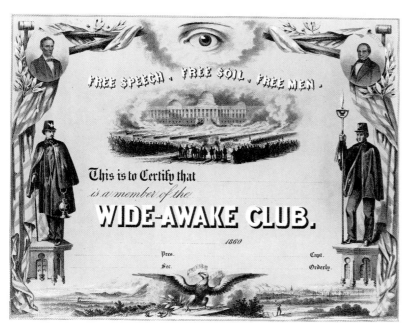

LIBRARY OF CONGRESS.

The Ordeal of Lincoln

LINCOLN v. McCLELLAN, 1864

The election of 1860 was the most fateful in the nation's history. That of 1864 was perhaps the most perilous.

Abraham Lincoln's victory in 1860 was the last straw for the South, and secession soon divided the Union. South Carolina led the defections on December 20, 1860. By February 1, 1861, Mississippi, Florida, Alabama, Georgia, Louisiana, and Texas had voted to secede. And it was again South Carolina that took the next, irrevocable step on the road to war, shelling the Union troops holding Fort Sumter in Charleston harbor on April 12, 1861. Lincoln responded with a call for volunteers, and four more states of the upper South—Arkansas, Tennessee, North Carolina, and Virginia—joined the Confederate nation. The bloodiest war in American history was under way.

Our knowledge that the Union won the war sometimes blinds us to the difficulty of the task Lincoln faced. The superiority of the Union in population (the North had more than twice as many inhabitants as the South, and black slaves made up almost half the South's population), together with its near monopoly of the nation's industrial capacity, makes the North's victory seem inevitable. But more important in determining the war's outcome was the opponents' will to fight. If the North had grown tired of war, the South might have obtained through negotiation the victory it could never win militarily. At the start of the war, a British correspondent pointed out that the area under Southern control was as large as European Russia (a comparison that brought to mind Napoleon's doomed Russian invasion of 1812) and predicted that the Union would have to come to terms, just as the British had been forced to do in the Revolutionary War.

Superior Southern generalship—and luck—helped the South win major victories early on, notably at the two battles of Bull Run in Virginia. Lincoln, desperate to find a good general, turned to George B. McClellan, who was appointed to the number two post in the army while just thirty-four years old. McClellan, called the "Young Napoleon" by the Northern press, was an able organizer. He managed to convert the raw recruits swelling the numbers of the Army of the Potomac into a well-drilled, confident fighting force. He excelled at inspiring troops on the parade ground, and his accomplishments received lavish praise. He took to posing with his hand tucked into his coat, à la Bonaparte, and recorded that he had heard suggestions that he accept "the Presidency, Dictatorship, etc."

Had McClellan proved as able on the battlefield as he was on the parade ground, he might well have been chosen President (if not dictator), but his organizational gifts were wedded to an unflappably timorous character. Through 1862, demands from Lincoln that he lead his army against the Confederate forces were met by McClellan with demands for more time, more men, and more supplies, while he denounced Lincoln and his cabinet as blunderers. (He called Lincoln a baboon.) McClellan was always convinced that his army was outnumbered three to one, though in fact the opposite was usually true. McClellan's caution became laughable when a Confederate withdrawal from a position on a hill a few miles from Washington, D.C., revealed that what the terrified capital and the Union commander had assumed to be a fearsome cannon positioned on the hill was merely a log painted to look like a cannon. The so-called Quaker gun made McClellan a laughingstock, and Lincoln continued his search for a fighting general.

The Quaker gun incident occurred shortly before the midterm elections of 1862 and probably added to the Democratic victories that November. Other factors that helped the opposition included a run of Union defeats and the tricky question of the aims of the war. Lincoln had won election in 1860 as a champion of the Union, not as an abolitionist. But war had a radicalizing effect on many in the North, while the defeats of the Northern armies made more attractive any step that might bring slaves into arms on the Union side. Commanders in the field issued orders emancipating slaves, and the slaves' labor in aid of the Union forces proved valuable. Ulysses S. Grant saw that accepting escaped slaves into Union lines "weakens the enemy," although McClellan felt that any radical step with respect to the slaves would "disintegrate" the army. Nevertheless, Lincoln decided on a radical step and on July 22, 1862, told his cabinet that he planned to issue an emancipation proclamation. Lincoln's supporters feared that it would harm the party in the election that fall, but

1864

PRESIDENTIAL CANDIDATE (STATE) VICE-PRESIDENTIAL CANDIDATE (STATE)	PARTY	ELECTORAL VOTES	APPROX. % OF POPULAR VOTE
Abraham Lincoln (Ill.; Republican) Andrew Johnson (Tenn.; Democratic)	Union	212	55%
George B. McClellan (N.J.) George H. Pendelton (Ohio)	Democratic	21	45%

In 1864 the Republican Party temporarily changed its name to the Union Party, both because it was dedicated to the reunification of the North with an emancipated South and because its ticket united the leading Republican with a Southern Democrat who had remained loyal to the Union. The party was variously known as the National Union or Union Republican Party.

Early in 1864 Uncle Sam reviews the lineup of possible candidates: (from left to right) Andrew Johnson, George McClellan (with drum), John C. Frémont, Lincoln, Secretary of the Treasury Salmon P. Chase, General Benjamin F. Butler, General Nathaniel P. Banks, General Franz Sigel, and Secretary of State William H. Seward.

Lincoln persevered, following Secretary of State Seward's advice to wait for a Northern victory before announcing such a step. After the bloody Battle of Antietam (where despite McClellan's ineptness the North turned back Robert E. Lee's army), the chance arrived, and with Lee's retreat the Emancipation Proclamation was announced, to go into effect on January 1, 1863. (Lincoln had stripped McClellan of command early in November 1862.)

The midterm elections were a triumph for the Democrats, who won in New York, Pennsylvania, Ohio, Indiana, and Illinois and overall took a majority of the votes in the free states. The progress of the war during 1863 raised Union hopes, particularly following the spectacular twin victories at Gettysburg and Vicksburg early that July. But later in the month draft riots roiled New York City and left more than a hundred people dead. The riots served as a reminder that support for the war—and for emancipation—was far from universal in the North. By early 1864, Lincoln faced a threat from within his own party, whose radicals felt he was too slow to advance their program. Two prominent Republicans, Salmon P. Chase, the secretary of the Treasury, and John C. Frémont, the Republican nominee in 1856, considered running against Lincoln. But they found that, however unpopular Lincoln might be among their friends in Congress and among various Republican elites, in the North he was the personification of the struggle to many, the "Father Abraham" who alone could see the nation through the ordeal. Lincoln accepted his party's nomination and, seeking to make the party's wartime name, the Union Party, more than a hollow slogan, jettisoned his first-term Vice President, Hannibal Hamlin, in favor of the pro-Union Tennessee Democrat Andrew Johnson.

At the end of August, the Democrats met in Chicago and chose George B. McClellan as their candidate. McClellan had to appeal both to prowar Democrats,

GRAND BANNER OF THE RADICAL DEMOCRACY,
FOR 1864.

The Radical Republicans, who confusingly called themselves the Party of the Radical Democracy, held a convention in Cleveland in May 1864 and nominated John C. Frémont, the unsuccessful Republican candidate of 1856. During the summer, much of the Republican leadership and press called for the withdrawal of both Lincoln and Frémont in favor of some candidate who could inspire enthusiasm and who would be certain of defeating McClellan.

The news of Admiral Farragut's victory in Mobile Bay (August 5) and of General Sherman's capture of Atlanta (September 2) greatly strengthened Lincoln's position. Finally, on September 22, Frémont agreed to withdraw from the race, transferring the Radical Republicans' support to Lincoln on the condition that the President force his moderate Republican postmaster general, Montgomery Blair, to resign. Lincoln accepted Blair's resignation the next day, and the Republicans became once again consolidated. Lithograph by Currier & Ives, 1864.

NATIONAL PORTRAIT GALLERY,
SMITHSONIAN INSTITUTION.

who sought a more martial commander in chief, and to antiwar, even Copperhead (Southern sympathizer) Democrats, who wanted an armistice that would end the war on very lenient terms. Although McClellan eventually decided he would have to insist that the war could end only with the restoration of the Union, the Democratic platform was filled with more defeatist sentiments and referred to "four years of failure" in the war under President Lincoln.

As August drew to an end, the Democrats were optimistic, and Lincoln was correspondingly depressed. In the White House on August 23, he wrote a memo assessing his chances:

> This morning, as for some days past, it seems exceedingly probable that this Administration will not be re-elected. Then it will be my duty to so co-operate with the President elect, as to save the Union between the election and the inauguration; as he will have secured his election on such ground that he can not possibly save it afterwards.

The next day, Lincoln wrote to one of his closest political allies, Henry J. Raymond, the editor of *The New York Times*, asking him to seek a peace conference with Jefferson Davis. Raymond was to seek Davis's agreement to a deal that involved the restoration of the Union, with all other matters to be decided later; failing that, he was to learn what terms Davis would accept and report the result to Washington.

In a war with many low points, this was one of the very lowest for Lincoln. But a new month brought new hope and a sea change in Lincoln's prospects. On September 1, General William Tecumseh Sherman took the city of Atlanta, and church bells rang throughout the North to celebrate the victory. (At the beginning of August, Union admiral David Farragut had won control of the port of Mobile, Alabama, sailing into Mobile Bay and then, after one of his fleet hit a mine—called a "torpedo" at the time—yelling to his helmsman, "Damn the torpedoes!" and signaling full steam ahead.) Although the main force of the Army of the Potomac was fighting a slow war of attrition in the Petersburg campaign, a force under Philip Sheridan won battles in the Shenandoah Valley later in September, and the Democratic platform's reference to the "failure" of Northern arms was becoming implausible. Nor was the opposition party helped by unsuccessful Confederate conspiracies to carry out sabotage campaigns in the North.

As the election approached, Lincoln found the Republican Party uniting behind him. Following the practice of the times, those holding office in the federal government were assessed campaign contributions to finance the incumbent's electioneering efforts. Republican papers attacked Democrats as "Copperheads," and the leading literary figures of the nation—Henry Wadsworth Longfellow, Ralph Waldo Emerson, Harriet Beecher Stowe, and others—wrote in support of Lincoln and the Union cause. The rash of Northern victories undercut McClellan's most promising theme, and the Confederate sabotage plots made it harder for Democrats to score political points off Lincoln's curtailment of civil liberties during the war.

Photograph of General George B. McClellan by the Mathew Brady Studio, 1863.
NATIONAL PORTRAIT GALLERY, SMITHSONIAN INSTITUTION.

The Union troops were vital not only for the victories they won that fall but also for the votes they cast. Eleven of the twenty-five Union states allowed soldiers to vote, and Lincoln did his best to make sure that their votes were counted. (He even asked Sherman to send soldiers from Indiana home to vote in the state elections there in October.) In some of those states soldiers voted for Lincoln by a margin of ten to one. Noncombatants also voted to retain Father Abraham, and Lincoln, who had so despaired for the Union in late August, was allowed to continue in office, having garnered 212 electoral votes to a mere 21 for McClellan.

A few days after the election, the President told a group that had come to serenade him in the White House that the election "has demonstrated that a people's government can sustain a national election, in the midst of a great civil war. Until now it has not been known to the world that this was a possibility."

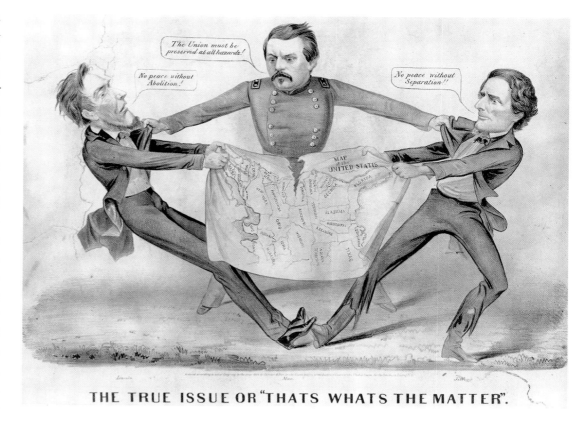

THE TRUE ISSUE OR "THATS WHATS THE MATTER".

McClellan trying to prevent Lincoln and Jefferson Davis from making the division between North and South irreparable. Lithograph by Currier & Ives.
LIBRARY OF CONGRESS.

CHAPTER
19

"Let Us Have Peace"

GRANT v. SEYMOUR, 1868

In April 1861, Wilmer McLean's house near Manassas Junction, Virginia, served as Confederate headquarters in the first major engagement of the Civil War, the Battle of Bull Run. Although the battle was a great victory for the South, McLean's house was severely damaged, and he moved to a more remote area near Appomattox Courthouse. There, four years later, war found McLean again, and it was in his home that Robert E. Lee surrendered his army to Ulysses S. Grant, the commander of the Union forces. The most devastating war in American history was over.

The transformations wrought by the Civil War were sufficiently grave that the historian Charles A. Beard concluded that it deserved to be considered a "Second American Revolution." Its importance was easy to comprehend for Americans in both North and South. Few Americans, whether in Pennsylvania or Virginia, Illinois or Texas, had not lost a near relation or a friend to the slaughter. The 600,000 Americans who died in the war amount to half the war dead in all American wars.

All those individualized losses were crystallized and embodied in a final loss, the assassination of Abraham Lincoln on April 15, 1865, just six days after Lee's surrender. The great issue of the war, the status of slavery, had been decided, and the "peculiar institution" was now defunct. But vital issues remained. What was to be the status of the freed slaves? How would the southern economy, which had depended on slave labor, recover? How would the rebels be punished? These issues, which would dominate the nation's Reconstruction period, would have been formidable in any case, but with Lincoln's death the difficulties increased enormously. Radical Republicans (a term applied at the time to those who favored equal political and economic rights for blacks) became even more dedicated to punishing the South and protecting the freed slaves. They came up against a strong opponent in President Andrew Johnson, a Tennessee Democrat picked as Lincoln's running mate in 1864 to show that the Union cause was bipartisan in the North. Johnson's highly conciliatory policies toward the South embittered the Radicals, who eventually led the effort in the House of Representatives that resulted in Johnson's impeachment and trial in the Senate in the spring of 1868.

Eighteen sixty-eight was an election year, of course, and the trial of Johnson had various effects on the race. One was to elevate the status of Chief Justice Salmon P. Chase, who presided over the Senate trial with an air of impartiality that impressed the Democrats (Chase had been Lincoln's secretary of the Treasury until he was appointed to the Supreme Court). Another was to make it clear that Johnson would not win the nomination of either party that year. So both parties would be selecting a new standard-bearer for the presidential race.

For a nation that had elected war heroes such as Washington and Jackson—and even William Henry Harrison—to the presidency, the logical place to look was among the heroes of the Union cause. Ulysses S. Grant was first among these, but General William Tecumseh Sherman and Admiral David Farragut also had their adherents. Grant had been a Democrat before the war, but his sensitivity to Lincoln's political needs and his responsiveness to Congress's requests had made him a favorite among the Republicans. Grant's innate conservatism had led him to work closely with Johnson until his own presidential possibilities were made clear to him. He had even accompanied Johnson on the latter's speech-making 1866 "swing around the circle" that had taken the President out to Chicago and back to the capital on a speaking tour in which Johnson had tried to justify his Reconstruction policies to the crowds. (Johnson's trip, timed to influence the 1866 congressional elections, was the first to use a campaign train for a whistle-stop tour, which was to become a staple of later contests.) Faced with hecklers at many stops, Johnson responded intemperately and further undermined his standing with the public. When Johnson moved to dismiss Secretary of War Edwin M. Stanton, an alleged violation of the Tenure of Office Act, the House voted for Johnson's impeachment. And Grant, who had served as interim secretary of war while Stanton was "suspended" from his duties by Johnson, moved into open opposition to the President.

Grant's career before the Civil War was hardly one to inspire visions of the presidency. While Lincoln was seeking the office in the 1860 election, Grant had been clerking in a leather store run by two of his brothers in Galena, Illinois. Grant had attended West Point, where he excelled in horsemanship but in no other pursuit, and he had followed a military career until a dreary posting and money worries had made him resign his commission in 1854. For the next seven years he had tried assorted vocations with scant success until war came and he joined the Union army as a colonel.

1868

PRESIDENTIAL CANDIDATE (STATE) VICE-PRESIDENTIAL CANDIDATE (STATE)	PARTY	ELECTORAL VOTES	APPROX. % OF POPULAR VOTE
Ulysses S. Grant (Ill.) Schuyler Colfax (Ind.)	Republican	214	53%
Horatio Seymour (N.Y.) Francis P. Blair (Mo.)	Democratic	80	47%

Grant's reputation rose as he won decisive victories in the western theater of war, culminating in the capture of Vicksburg on July 4, 1863, which opened the entire Mississippi to the Union and neatly complemented the simultaneous defeat of Lee's forces at Gettysburg. In March 1864, Lincoln put Grant in charge of all Union forces, and in just over a year Grant was accepting Robert E. Lee's surrender at Appomattox. Lee was certainly the more brilliant tactician, but Grant—understanding the central fact that he had far more men and supplies than Lee could ever command—had relentlessly pressed his advantage to victory.

When the National Union Republican Party (as Lincoln's party was now known) met in convention in May 1868, Grant was nominated on the first ballot, while Schuyler Colfax of Indiana, the House Speaker, was chosen as his running mate. Grant's letter accepting the nomination concluded with the simple plea "Let us have peace."

For the Democrats, the choice was not nearly so easy. Their convention, held at New York's Tammany Hall, brought together August Belmont, the wealthy banker of the party; William Tweed, the city's notorious Democratic boss; and a number of ex-Confederates, including Nathan Bedford Forrest, a former slave trader who had helped found the Ku Klux Klan to spread terror among freed slaves. But the Democrats knew that they could not overturn the result of the war at the polls, and the platform recognized that fact while trying to influence matters as much as possible in favor of southern whites. For example, it called for leaving any decision on the franchise to the individual states, whereas Congress had ordered black manhood suffrage throughout the South. (In this election, blacks could vote in only seven northern states, five of them in New England.) The Democrats also included a "soft-money" plank in the platform: the wartime inflation driven by the printing of "greenbacks" to finance the northern war effort had pleased borrowers (who could pay back their loans in depreciated currency) but angered creditors. The eastern capitalists who stood to lose by a soft-money policy gravitated toward the Republicans, while western farmers and merchants supported the Democrats. It was a dispute that would continue for the balance of the century, reaching its climax in William Jennings Bryan's "Cross of Gold" speech at the Democratic convention in 1896.

The Democratic champion of greenbacks was George Pendleton of Ohio, who had been George McClellan's running mate four years earlier. He led at the convention for the first fifteen ballots but then faded, and no other candidate seemed likely to prevail. New York's governor, Horatio Seymour, was a favorite of many but had repeatedly declined to run. But on the twenty-second ballot, as many (including Seymour) were planning a shift toward Chief Justice Chase (who had courted the Democrats all that year), Ohio put Seymour's name into nomination. Seymour tried to nominate Chase but was carried off bodily by his supporters and anointed by the convention. Francis P. Blair, a pro-Union politician from Missouri who opposed the Radical Republican program, was nominated for Vice President. Blair was an outspoken racist, expressing fears that intermarriage between whites and blacks would overturn the "accumulated improvement of the centuries" and proclaiming that only whites were capable of self-government.

The central issue of the campaign was Reconstruction, but personalities received their due attention. Grant's job in his brothers' leather shop provided a popular image of the general as a humble tanner called to the service of his nation, and "tanner" clubs sprouted up around the North to celebrate his rise. Grant refused to give campaign speeches but did tour western states with his fellow Union generals Sherman and Sheridan. While Frederick Douglass urged freed slaves to vote Republican, Democrats attacked Grant as a butcher and, with much of Reconstruction being carried forward under the eyes of federal troops, tried to fan fears that the general's election might result in a military dictatorship.

Seymour, in turn, was widely depicted in the Republican press as a Copperhead whose sympathy for the Southern cause had motivated his veto of a bill passed by New York's legislature to allow troops to vote in the 1864 presidential contest. Blair hardly needed detractors, as he made so many inflammatory statements that by the fall of the year Democrats were eager to remove both him and Seymour from the ticket and put Chase into Seymour's place.

While mudslinging in campaigns was old hat, there was a new and far darker element in the 1868 race, the terror campaign conducted against freedmen and other southern Republicans by the Ku Klux Klan and similar groups. In one incident in Louisiana an estimated two hundred blacks were killed by a white mob, and large- and small-scale incidents of terror took place across the South. In Louisiana and Georgia the terror campaign was so effective that the Republicans stopped trying to win those states for Grant; they were the only states of the defunct Confederacy to vote for Seymour. The terror campaign of 1868 set a precedent for southern opposition to Reconstruction over the next decade, and organized, often violent southern resistance to black voting rights would remain in place for a century.

But blacks did vote, risking their livelihoods, if not their lives, in the process. Democrats in the South evicted black Republicans from their lands, refused to grant credit, and took other measures to block black voters—but still blacks voted. About 500,000 blacks went to the polls, and Grant defeated Seymour by a 300,000-

1868: BLACK SUFFRAGE, WOMAN SUFFRAGE

THE ABOLITIONIST MOVEMENT was but one of the reform movements that grew to prominence in the decades before the Civil War. Rights for women, too, became a matter of public debate in those years, and supporters of both causes found homes in the Republican Party. When the war ended and the enfranchisement of African Americans offered the best hope to the Republicans of winning a significant political foothold in the South, the competing claims of black suffrage and woman suffrage split reformers.

At first it had seemed as though supporters of the two causes might work together: in 1866, the American Equal Rights Association was founded and included both the abolitionist Wendell Phillips and Elizabeth Cady Stanton, the women's rights advocate. But when another founder of the group, Theodore Tilton, declared that now was "the Negro's hour," Stanton replied that she "would sooner cut off my right hand than ask the ballot for the black man and not for woman." Facing a similar argument from Frederick Douglass, Stanton wondered if her opponents believed "the African race is composed entirely of males?"

The matter came to a head with the passage and adoption of the Fifteenth Amendment. Some champions of woman suffrage backed the amendment, even though it granted the vote only to black men; others, including Stanton and Susan B. Anthony, refused to support legislation that did not include votes for women. In 1869, two women's suffrage groups formed, the National Woman Suffrage Association (NWSA), with Stanton and Anthony, and the American Woman Suffrage Association (AWSA), led by Lucy Stone and Henry Blackwell. The AWSA felt certain that once black suffrage was secured, the Republicans would turn to voting rights for women. The party did put a brief mention of the subject into its 1872 platform (it was a "splinter," not a plank), but the matter was not mentioned again in the party's platform until 1916.

The NWSA took a harder line, and for the following generation the split in the women's movement hampered efforts to gain the franchise and to achieve other goals dear to advocates of women's rights.

Nast here attacks as militantly racist three groups that supported the Democrats: (from left to right) Irish Catholics, Confederate Army veterans, and New York millionaires. Published in Harper's Weekly, *September 5, 1868.*

LIBRARY OF CONGRESS.

vote margin in the popular vote (although the way the votes were distributed among the states meant that the black vote was not a crucial part of Grant's Electoral College margin of 214 to 80). With Grant's victory, Reconstruction was protected, and the development of a new Republican Party founded on "sound money" and fiscal conservatism was under way. Black votes, which had helped carry Grant to victory in the election just as black soldiers had helped carry him to victory in the war, would be given a greater chance to influence future elections. As a coda to the election, the lame-duck Congress passed the Fifteenth Amendment, guaranteeing to all Americans (male Americans, that is) the right to vote regardless of "race, color, or previous condition of servitude." Circumventing that amendment would prove vital to the maintenance of a Democratic lock on the South from the end of Reconstruction in 1877 to the Voting Rights Act of 1965.

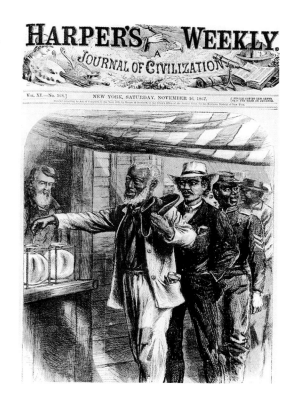

On the cover of Harper's Weekly, *Nast depicted African Americans of four different socioeconomic groups voting for the first time. They are (from left to right) a poor Southern farmer who was formerly a slave, a prosperous businessman or professional, a Union Army veteran, and a laborer. Published November 16, 1867.*

LIBRARY OF CONGRESS.

Until the 1930s leading contenders for the presidential nomination almost never attended their party's convention. Generally a small delegation was sent to the chosen candidate's home to notify him officially of his nomination (of which he would have been informed earlier by telegraph). His formal reply would be in the form of a letter for publication.

Grant ended his letter of acceptance with the phrase "Let Us Have Peace," which became the motto of his campaign.

DAVID J. AND JANICE L. FRENT POLITICAL AMERICANA COLLECTION.

20

Republican Fissures and Follies

GRANT v. GREELEY, 1872

No one familiar with Ulysses S. Grant's career before the Civil War would have predicted his great success as a general; one might, however, have forecast his disappointing performance as President. But however passive he was as chief executive, however prey to flattery and addicted to cronyism, those qualities never overshadowed his achievement as the military hero of the Civil War, especially in the eyes of veterans, freedmen, and others whose very identities had been forged in the conflict.

But there were those who saw a new world opening in America, a world that required different policies, more efficient and smaller government, and an end to sectional division. One of these men was Carl Schurz, a German-born Missouri senator who championed civil service reform, merit appointments to government offices, lower taxes, and freer trade (lower tariffs). From its inception, the Republican Party had included a significant faction whose greatest concern was advancing northern business interests, and with the great issue that had brought the party into existence, slavery, now resolved, those business interests became more clamorous and the remaining issues of the sectional conflict came to seem needlessly divisive.

Needless, that is, if one had no great concern for the status of blacks in America. The agenda of those who would form the short-lived Liberal Republican Party—Schurz among them—was to grant a general amnesty to ex-Confederates and to reduce federal interference in the former Confederate states (partly in the name of smaller government). Yet federal interference was crucial if black voters were to be allowed to exercise the franchise granted to them by the Fifteenth Amendment. The violence visited upon black Republicans in the 1868 presidential race continued in subsequent state elections. Defiance of the law became so general in some states that Congress passed a series of laws designed to guarantee enforcement of blacks' rights. Federal troops or U.S. marshals were employed to crack down on the Klan, with fair success. But such actions, crucial to the achievement of true "reconstruction" of the southern political system, were highly unpopular among white southerners, and the Liberal Republicans were willing to curtail them in the name of small government.

In a speech in Nashville in 1871, Schurz proclaimed the need for a new party to represent these views, and in May 1872 adherents of the new cause convened in Cincinnati to write a platform and select a candidate. Schurz had one in mind: Charles Francis Adams, son of President John Quincy Adams and minister to Great Britain during the Civil War. Adams was a skillful diplomatist, an able attorney, a serious historian, and a terrible politician. He was described by one contemporary as "the greatest iceberg in the northern hemisphere," and his chilly personal style was wedded to equally unseasonable political opinions. He complained that "the elite has little influence upon the political circles," apparently unaware that his father's defeat by Andrew Jackson in 1828 had spelled the end of public acceptance of such patrician sentiments.

Yet Adams was not alone in bemoaning the declining influence of the traditional elites. The Civil War had enriched many, and some of these newly wealthy men were using their money to buy influence in statehouses and in Washington. The danger to good government was real, as was the danger to the power and influence of those Adams included in "the elite." Many of those threatened supported the Liberal Republicans, and journals such as Edwin Godkin's *The Nation* and George William Curtis's *Harper's Weekly* called for reform and an end to the corruption and misgovernment of the Grant regime.

Adams would have been the candidate of most of these leaders of elite opinion, but he set forth such a conceited set of terms for accepting the nomination that he doomed his own chances. He wrote that his nomination would have to be "an unequivocal one," not to be "negotiated for," and that if he were to be chosen at Cincinnati, the delegates must express their support "in a manner to convince me" of their unconditional backing. The sentiment is pure Adams, but it is also representative of a flaw that pervaded the Liberal Republican movement. Eager to reform American political life, its members disdained to soil their hands by touching

1872

PRESIDENTIAL CANDIDATE (STATE) VICE-PRESIDENTIAL CANDIDATE (STATE)	PARTY	ELECTORAL VOTES	APPROX. % OF POPULAR VOTE
Ulysses S. Grant (Ill.) Henry Wilson (Mass.)	Republican	286	56%
Horace Greeley (N.Y.) B. Gratz Brown (Mo.)	Democratic/Liberal Republican	*	44%

Among the minor-party candidates were James Black (National Prohibition), Victoria C. Woodhull (People's Equal Rights), and William S. Groesbeck (Independent Liberal Republican).

*Because Greeley died before the Electoral College convened, 63 of his 66 electoral votes were distributed among Thomas A. Hendricks (Independent Democratic; 42 of the votes), B. Gratz Brown (Democratic; 18), Charles J. Jenkins (Democratic; 2), and David Davis (Democratic; 1).

the levers that moved the political mechanism. This flaw emerged clearly at their convention, and it doomed not only the nominee but the Liberal Republican movement as a whole. Adams led on the first ballot but did not achieve a majority, let alone the acclamation he had demanded. In second place was Horace Greeley, the eccentric editor of the *New York Tribune*. Schurz, serving as chairman of the convention, did nothing to block a sudden move to Greeley, and the editor was chosen, with Governor B. Gratz Brown of Missouri as his running mate.

Considering that the Liberal Republicans were depending on Democratic support in the general election, the choice of Greeley was incomprehensible. A founder of the Republican Party, Greeley had denounced the Democratic Party in the pages of the *Tribune* in a thousand colorful ways, all of which could be used against him. In fact, Greeley's genius as an editor had come in part from his great curiosity and limitless, if undisciplined, enthusiasm. Consistency was not a trait he valued highly. He had championed black rights but had also backed peaceful secession during the crisis following Lincoln's election. "Let the erring sisters go in peace," he had counseled. He beat the drum for abolitionism, vegetarianism, and spiritualism. One of his few consistent positions had been his support for a high protective tariff, a view that was opposite to that of most Democrats and Liberal Republicans. Even Greeley's former patron, the veteran New York politician Thurlow Weed, was amazed that any large group of men "outside of a Lunatic Asylum, would nominate Greeley for President." Weed's amazement was certainly shared by the Democrats, whose sole hope in the election was to link themselves

Thomas Nast here portrays Horace Greeley wearing his trademark white hat and holding a copy of the New York Tribune, *of which he had been editor until he resigned to become a candidate. Greeley proclaimed that the* Tribune *would not be a "party organ" during the campaign.*

Albert B. Paine, author of the classic 1904 biography of Nast, called the 1872 presidential contest "The Campaign of Caricature"—"the first great battle of pictures ever known in America." It was a vicious war of vituperation in which the two opposing generals were Nast, whose work appeared in Harper's Weekly, *and Matthew Somerville Morgan of* Frank Leslie's Illustrated Newspaper. *Morgan despised Grant as much as Nast hated Greeley, and the two cartoonists had a running battle in which each sought to outdo his competitor's effort of the previous week. The clear victor was Nast, whose sheer brilliance, and the uninhibited malice of his mind and his drawing pen, contributed not only to Greeley's electoral defeat but perhaps even to the candidate's death shortly after Election Day. Watercolor by Thomas Nast, 1872.*

NATIONAL PORTRAIT GALLERY, SMITHSONIAN INSTITUTION.

with the Liberals. Greeley's efforts to win the release of Jefferson Davis from prison won him some support in the South, but his long career as a Republican propagandist was an embarrassment there. And, in the biggest "negative research" effort in American politics up to that time, the Republican National Committee hired three hundred investigators to comb through back issues of the *Tribune* looking for past stands by Greeley that could be (and were) now used against him. The Democrats backed Greeley, although they refused to combine their organization with that of the Liberals.

For the regular Republicans, the matter was fairly simple: renominate Grant, "wave the bloody shirt" to remind everyone of the sacrifices of the Civil War era and recall Grant's heroic stature, and wait for victory. The convention did remove Colfax as the vice presidential candidate and replaced him with Senator Henry Wilson of Massachusetts.

In his cartoon "Diogenes Has Found an Honest Man," Nast depicts Greeley shaking hands with the notorious Boss Tweed, in whose downfall the previous year Nast's cartoons had played a decisive part.

LIBRARY OF CONGRESS.

THE WORKING-MAN'S BANNER.

FOR PRESIDENT.   FOR VICE-PRESIDENT.

TANNERY

ULYSSES S. GRANT   HENRY WILSON

"The Galena Tanner"   "The Natick Shoemaker"

PUBLISHED BY CURRIER & IVES   ENTERED ACCORDING ACT OF CONGRESS IN THE YEAR 1872 BY CURRIER & IVES IN THE OFFICE OF THE LIBRARIAN OF CONGRESS AT WASHINGTON   125 NASSAU ST. NEW YORK

LIBRARY OF CONGRESS.

Again the central issue of the campaign was Reconstruction. Support for black rights was surprisingly strong among northern Republicans, and the federal prosecution of the Klan had helped to create a much safer environment for southern Republicans than had existed in 1868. Grant wisely kept quiet during the campaign, allowing the Republican press to do the hard work for him. Notable for his exertions was the great cartoonist Thomas Nast, tormentor of New York City's Democratic boss, William Tweed. Nast now turned his pen upon the unfortunate Greeley. In 1868, Grant had said, "Let us have peace" and had been praised for his conciliatory tone. But when, four years later, Greeley had called on North and South to "clasp hands across the bloody chasm," Nast had drawn the editor shaking hands with John Wilkes Booth across Lincoln's grave. When state elections in August and September indicated a coming Republican success, Greeley embarked on a frenetic speaking tour, but he just made matters worse by saying, for example, that his earlier opposition to slavery might have been a mistake. Greeley's ineptness on the stump was exceeded only by his running mate's: Governor Brown had an unfortunate habit of speaking in public while conspicuously drunk.

The Liberals and their Democratic allies hoped to win by attacking the Grant administration. Grant's military background, combined with the steps the army was

LIBERTY. EQUALITY AND FRATERNITY.
UNIVERSAL AMNESTY.   IMPARTIAL SUFFRAGE.

FOR PRESIDENT.   FOR VICE-PRESIDENT.

HORACE GREELEY AND BENJ.N CRATZ BROWN
OF NEW YORK   OF MISSOURI

GRAND NATIONAL
LIBERAL REPUBLICAN BANNER FOR 1872.

taking to enforce federal law in the South, left him open to charges that he was seeking to set himself up as a military dictator. And Greeley's partisans attacked the poor quality of Grant's appointments; but, upsetting as those appointments were to members of the intelligentsia and to old-line leaders of the party, this proved not to be a potent election issue.

In Nast's cruelest depiction of Greeley, "The Next in Order . . . ," Greeley is reaching over Lincoln's grave to shake hands with the ghost of John Wilkes Booth.
LIBRARY OF CONGRESS.

In the end, the bloody shirt and Greeley's bumbling proved to be more than enough to carry the day for the Republicans. Grant won 55.6 percent of the popular vote, the highest percentage in any election between 1828 and 1904. Greeley, devastated first by the death of his wife just days before the election and then by the magnitude of his defeat, died before the month of November was over. As Grant began his second term as President in 1873, the nation plunged into the most devastating depression of the nineteenth century, an economic catastrophe that would help end the Reconstruction era and redefine American politics for the balance of the century.

The Nation Turns a Crooked Corner

HAYES v. TILDEN, 1876

The year 1876 marked the centenary of American independence, and the celebration of that event provided an opportunity to highlight the common traditions of North and South and to reflect on the achievements the nation had recorded in its first hundred years. A world's fair in Philadelphia provided the United States with a chance to display its manufacturing prowess, and, as it happened, 1876 was the year that American exports exceeded imports for the first time. At the Philadelphia Exposition, new inventions such as the telephone, the typewriter, and electric light proclaimed the promise of the new industrial age.

In literature, the publication of Mark Twain's *The Adventures of Tom Sawyer* showed the possibilities of distinctly American themes and uniquely American language and humor. At the same time, an increasing—and increasingly sophisticated—engagement with Europe was revealed in another of the year's books, *Roderick Hudson,* the first significant work by Henry James. Increasing sophistication in the country's scientific life was apparent, too: Johns Hopkins was founded, on the model of the finest German universities, and the American Chemical Society was established to advance American science. Greater organization was becoming apparent in leisure activities as well: baseball led the way with the founding of the National League that year. There were political foreshadowings as well, with the first attempt in Congress to amend the Constitution to prohibit the sale of alcoholic beverages. In the West, Sioux and Cheyenne warriors wiped out an army force under George Armstrong Custer at the Battle of Little Big Horn.

That year, the nation was still suffering through the severe depression that had begun with the Panic of 1873, and there were discordant assessments of how the country ought to manage its economy, particularly its monetary policy. Workers, too, were growing increasingly unhappy with their lot in the new economic order, and the excesses of the Gilded Age drew the nation's attention to the growing gap between the rich and the poor. People and parties differed, however, on the causes of these ills, and on the solutions to them. Many Democrats, particularly in the West, felt that inflationary monetary policies—the continued use of "greenbacks" as legal tender, rather than a deflationary return to a strict gold standard—were the key to a more just economy. Republicans and conservative Democrats viewed them as a recipe for catastrophe. In political life, the scandals of the Grant administration—his private secretary was found to be part of a tax fraud conspiracy called the "Whiskey Ring" and his secretary of war had to resign after being caught accepting a bribe—appalled Democrats and Liberal Republicans (many of whom had now joined the Democrats). To conservative Republicans, the highly organized corruption of Democratic Party machines in the big cities represented the danger of untrammeled democracy. The danger was even greater, in the minds of many, now that immigrants were arriving on American shores from China and from southern and eastern Europe—unfamiliar, even un-Christian, peoples.

In the face of all these concerns, the status of African Americans had fallen from the top of the Republican agenda, and the Grant administration had nearly abandoned its efforts to support black Republicans in the South. For three decades, the problem of slavery, the war, and then the consequences of emancipation had dominated the nation's political life. But ceaseless and ever-cannier resistance by southern whites, combined with ambivalence (at best) toward blacks even among white Republicans in the North, finally wore down the effort to guarantee that blacks would actually enjoy the rights promised in the laws passed under Reconstruction. Grant himself said in private that the Fifteenth Amendment (granting blacks the vote) might have been an error.

The election of 1876 provided a ratification of these new attitudes and brought an end to the era of Reconstruction. Blacks' voting rights in the South would be tenuous for another ninety years, giving the Democratic Party a reliable bloc of votes in presidential campaigns. And so powerful were the issues and feelings involved that when northern Democrats, in the 1960s, finally moved to redeem the promises of the Fifteenth Amendment and other Reconstruction-era changes, that move would cost the party the solid South it had relied on for so long.

Choosing a candidate for the Republicans was complicated. Grant had thoughts of trying for a third term, but the scandals involving some of his closest friends had exhausted his party's—and the public's—patience with him. James G. Blaine, a leading light of the party's reform wing, remained a favorite, despite his involvement in a couple of suspicious deals with

1876

PRESIDENTIAL CANDIDATE (STATE) VICE-PRESIDENTIAL CANDIDATE (STATE)	PARTY	ELECTORAL VOTES	APPROX. % OF POPULAR VOTE
Rutherford B. Hayes (Ohio) William A. Wheeler (N.Y.)	Republican	185	48%
Samuel J. Tilden (N.Y.) Thomas A. Hendricks (Ind.)	Democratic	18	51%

Among the minor-party candidates were Peter Cooper (National Independent), Samuel F. Cary (Greenback), and Green C. Smith (Prohibition).

The Democrats made much of "Honest Sam" Tilden's role in toppling Boss Tweed and boasted of the lack of corruption in his administration as governor of New York. Cover of sheet music.

railroad companies. When the Republican convention met in Cincinnati in June, an eloquent speech nominating him (and dubbing him the "Plumed Knight," a nickname that stuck) might have started a stampede for him, had not the convention hall's lighting system suddenly failed—perhaps, as his supporters suspected, thanks to an opponent's mischief. The meeting was adjourned to the following day, and the momentum for Blaine was lost.

The next day Blaine led on the first ballot and held steady until the sixth ballot, when his total rose and there was again a possibility of his securing the nomination. But several of the party's leaders, including New York's Roscoe Conkling and Indiana's Oliver Morton, opposed the too-reform-minded Blaine and moved instead to back Ohio's Rutherford B. Hayes, whose campaign had been engineered for just such

Two years before the election of 1876 it seemed quite possible that President Grant might decide to run for a third term, despite the charges of "Caesarism" being raised by that prospect. In 1874, while loyally defending Grant, Nast drew a cartoon in which he depicted the massive Republican vote as an elephant, an image so effective that the elephant was soon adopted as the official symbol of the Republican Party.

Here the elephant is about to fall into a trap as it and the other animals (including the New York Tribune as a giraffe and The New York Times as a unicorn) flee in panic from the braying of an ass (the New York Herald) wearing a lion's skin labeled "Caesarism."

Grant made it clear that he would not seek a third term, but he felt that if he were offered a third nomination, he would have "an imperative duty" to accept it. Such thoughts were, however, put to an end in December 1875, when the House of Representatives voted 233 to 18 to denounce a third term as "unwise, unpatriotic, and fraught with peril to our free institutions."

Nast's cartoon was published in Harper's Weekly, November 7, 1874.

a moment. Hayes and his handlers had assiduously avoided giving offense, and his record as a Union general (he had fought under Sheridan in the Shenandoah campaign late in the war), combined with the convention's being held in his home state, made him an easy compromise choice for the delegates. New York's William Wheeler, a shy and undistinguished congressman, was nominated as his running mate.

The Democrats met in St. Louis, the first time a major-party convention was held west of the Mississippi. The Democratic governor of New York, Samuel J. Tilden, was the overwhelming favorite for the nomination. A lawyer who had made a fortune in railroads and real estate, Tilden had been elected to New York's governorship in the 1874 election. He won the party's presidential nomination on the second ballot, and the runner-up, Governor Thomas A. Hendricks of Indiana, was given the second slot on the ticket, Hendricks's greenback sympathies balancing Tilden's fiscal conservatism.

Tilden's campaign suffered from that fiscal conservatism, as he refused to spend funds that might have helped him build larger majorities in some crucial states. The Republicans, too, ran a frugal campaign, devoting much of the treasure they raised from eastern capitalists and federal workers to the campaigns in Indiana and New York and essentially abandoning the Republicans of the South. Tilden and

These ballots from Massachusetts were typical of those used throughout the nation. Outside every polling place each party had a booth or table at which one picked up a ballot to be deposited into the ballot box. One voted not for individuals but for a party's entire slate.

DAVID J. AND JANICE L. FRENT
POLITICAL AMERICANA COLLECTION.

the Democrats promised southerners a return to "home rule," by which they meant white rule. In the North, the Republicans once again waved the bloody shirt and warned that electing a Democratic President would undermine the victory won at such great cost in the war.

The real bloody shirts that year belonged to black Republicans in the South, who were again the victims of terror and intimidation. Louisiana and South Carolina saw tremendous violence, with unnumbered beatings and murders in Louisiana and six blacks killed at the Hamburg Massacre in South Carolina that July. With Grant indifferent to the outcome of the election and unwilling to exercise federal powers to protect blacks any longer, white terror could prevail over black voters across the South.

The election was held on November 7, and by the following morning it seemed clear that Tilden had won. His popular-vote margin was a quarter of a million votes, and he seemed to have carried the entire South. The Republican leaders in New York checked with the offices of the strongly pro-Hayes *New York Times* to see how bad things were, and it dawned on them that if Hayes could secure the disputed electoral votes of Florida, South Carolina, and Louisiana (as well as one disputed vote in Oregon), the Republicans could eke out a 185–184 win in the Electoral College. So the party mobilized to achieve that. Money was dispatched south to aid the cause, and promises of patronage were tendered. Republican election boards certified Hayes's victories, and the results were forwarded to Congress.

The national mood was ominous, as once again sectional issues seemed likely to erupt into violence. "Tilden or War" proclaimed one Democratic newspaper, although Tilden himself seems to have been resigned to defeat as soon as the dispute began. To defuse the situation and resolve it, a bipartisan Electoral Commission was established with five members each from the Senate, House, and Supreme Court. With the Republicans in control of the Senate and the Democrats of the House, the deciding vote would come from the Supreme Court. The decisive vote there lay in the hands of Justice Joseph P. Bradley, a Republican with a reputation as a moderate. The commission awarded all the disputed electoral votes to Hayes, each time by a straight party-line vote of 8 to 7.

Yet the Democrats could still hope to influence things through their control of the House, and they threatened to filibuster the matter past the March 4 date for inauguration, which would have provoked an unprecedented constitutional crisis. There was plenty of room for negotiation, and talks between various Democratic forces and the Republicans had proceeded throughout the winter. The exact agreements reached are vague, but the essential conditions were that "home rule" would return to the South and a certain amount of federal money would be devoted to southern projects; in return, the southern whites would allow Hayes to become President and agree to honor the political rights of blacks under the post–Civil War legislation. An understanding was arrived at, and on March 2, 1877, in one of the low moments in American presidential elections, Hayes was certified as the winner by a one-vote Electoral College margin.

22

Politics Without Purpose

GARFIELD v. HANCOCK (AND WEAVER), 1880

Compared to the crucial election of 1876, which marked the end of the Civil War era, the election of 1880 was almost perfunctory. It could have served as a stage for the triumphal vindication of Samuel J. Tilden, the victim of party-line votes in the Electoral Commission four years earlier. But Tilden's health was poor, and he lacked supporters in his home state of New York. It could have provided the first three-term president, with Ulysses S. Grant again taking the highest office in the land. But that plot failed at the Republican convention. It could have brought forward the "Plumed Knight," James G. Blaine, but again there were too many Republicans who could not stomach the man or his (mild) reform policies. Few politicians, looking ahead from, say, two years earlier, would have predicted a contest between the Republican James Garfield and the Democrat Winfield Scott Hancock, but so it proved. And few, even at the time, could have named an issue in the campaign.

Patronage, local party squabbles, a colossal forgery, and cynical pandering to voters shaped the outcome of this squalid race. It was, in Mark Twain's term, the Gilded Age, not a golden age. In politics that gilt was the thinnest possible coating of glitter over base metal.

Rutherford B. Hayes was hardly a crusader, but even the mild reforms in appointments he undertook offended the conservative Republican "Stalwarts" led by New York's Senator Roscoe Conkling. Hayes said he wanted to be a one-term President, and few in his party lamented the news. Outside the party, his victory was so tainted by the "Fraud of 1877" that he would have been unlikely to succeed in any case. The Stalwarts needed a candidate for 1880, and the most attractive prospect was Ulysses S. Grant. He had been touring the world in the late 1870s, and the warm receptions he received abroad had elevated his status at home. Stalwarts urged Grant to continue his tour until the spring of 1880, when his return home could spark a move for his nomination. But Grant was weary of traveling and arrived back in the United States in the fall of 1879. The enthusiastic welcome he received came too early to build significant momentum toward the presidency, and the 1880 nomination started shaping up as a fight.

The leading opponent of the Stalwarts was James G. Blaine of Maine, who supported mild reforms in civil service. Blaine's backers were called "Half-Breeds," and those who avoided alignment with either group carried the label "Jellyfish." Personal ambitions, not political principles, separated the Stalwarts and Half-Breeds, and each side was fierce in its dedication to its own advancement. But the Plumed Knight's chances were not helped by the nominating speech he received from a Michigan millionaire named James Joy, who concluded his pathetic oration by calling for the assembly to nominate "James S. Blaine," provoking cries of "G., you fool, G.!" from the crowd.

For thirty-three ballots Grant and Blaine vied, Grant polling around 300 delegates, Blaine a score or so fewer, both far from the 379 needed. Meanwhile, the new senator-elect from Ohio, James A. Garfield, was supposedly managing the campaign of his fellow Buckeye, Treasury Secretary John Sherman. As chairman of the convention's rules committee, Garfield had played a prominent role in aiding the Blaine forces, but he had a gift for doing this without offending the Stalwarts. Handsome, with a decent record as a Civil War general, and hated by nobody, Garfield was emerging as everyone's second choice. He was, however, the first choice of Wharton Barker, a Philadelphia banker who was waiting his chance to secure the nomination for Garfield. Barker arranged for a few delegates to start casting votes for Garfield early in the process to keep his name in play. He managed to get a seat for himself on the platform from which speeches were given, and from there he signaled to hired agents situated around the hall, who, on his signal, would applaud when Garfield entered the hall or made a motion. Barker's plot was to wait out the deadlock he anticipated, then have Wisconsin switch to Garfield. Then, on the next ballot, Indiana, a key state, would follow suit. And that is just what happened on the thirty-fourth and thirty-fifth ballots. On the thirty-sixth Garfield was nominated. President Hayes judged that the nominee was not a "moral force"; Conkling, in plainer terms, said that Garfield had "no sand."

Sand or not, Garfield knew that to win in November a Republican nominee would have to take New York, and he was eager to patch things up with Conkling, New York's Republican boss.

1880

PRESIDENTIAL CANDIDATE (STATE) VICE-PRESIDENTIAL CANDIDATE (STATE)	PARTY	ELECTORAL VOTES	APPROX. % OF POPULAR VOTE
James Garfield (Ohio) Chester A. Arthur (N.Y.)	Republican	214	48.3%
Winfield S. Hancock (Pa.) William H. English (Ind.)	Democratic	155	48.2%

Among the minor-party candidates were James B. Weaver (Greenback-Labor) and Neal Dow (Prohibition).

In the front row of ballerinas appear
(from left to right) James Garfield,
Chester A. Arthur, Roscoe Conkling,
Winfield S. Hancock, James G. Blaine,
and Samuel J. Tilden. Cartoon by
Charles Kendrick, published in the New
York magazine Chic, September 1880.
NATIONAL PORTRAIT GALLERY,
SMITHSONIAN INSTITUTION.

First he offered the vice presidency to Conkling's lieutenant, Levi Morton, but was turned down. He next approached another Stalwart, Chester A. Arthur (like Garfield, an ex–Union general). Arthur went to consult with Conkling, who told him to drop the offer "as you would a red hot [horse]shoe from the forge." But Arthur was flattered by the offer. He told his chief, "The office of the vice-presidency is a greater honor than I ever dreamed of attaining," and announced that he intended to accept it.

The Democrats, meeting in Cincinnati, had one natural choice, the bilked nominee of four years earlier, Tilden. But the ailing Tilden refused to make clear his own wishes, flirting with the nomination but unwilling to pursue it directly. Pennsylvania's Samuel J. Randall, the Speaker of the House, had presidential hopes, as did Stephen Field, a Supreme Court justice from California. But the convention soon chose General Winfield Scott Hancock, with William English, a banker from Indiana, the vice presidential nominee. Hancock was a Union general who had won southern support with his mild military administration of Louisiana and Texas during Reconstruction. Finding a Union general who was liked in the South must have seemed like a gift to the Democrats, and one Hancock partisan promised, "Nominate Hancock, and the bloody shirt will be folded away."

Hancock was widely criticized for his political inexperience and for his southern sympathies. A widely publicized gaffe regarding the tariff issue (he called it a "local question") made him an easy target for ridicule. One Republican campaign pamphlet, entitled "A Record of the Statesmanship and Political Achievements of General Winfield Scott Hancock . . . compiled from the Records," consisted of seven totally blank pages and an eighth blank except for the word "FINIS" printed at its bottom. Cartoon by Thomas Nast, published in Harper's Weekly, *November 13, 1880.*

"A LOCAL QUESTION."
"WHO IS *TARIFF*, AND WHY IS *HE* FOR REVENUE *ONLY?*"

The platforms of both parties were long on rhetoric and short on tough positions, and one of the few places they differed was the tariff: the Democrats favored a tariff only to the extent needed for revenue, while the Republicans wanted a higher tariff to protect American industry. Returning prosperity had dampened enthusiasm for greenbackism a bit, and the champions of inflationary policies were forced to nominate their own candidate, Iowa's James B. Weaver. Weaver's chances were slight, because he backed such radical notions as woman suffrage, the eight-hour day, and federal efforts to protect the voting rights of blacks.

PUCK.

HE CARRIES THE PARTY.

THE PARTY CARRIES HIM.

JUST THE DIFFERENCE.

Austrian-born Joseph Keppler ranks second only to Thomas Nast as the greatest American political cartoonist of the nineteenth century. Most of his work appeared in the magazine Puck, *of which he was the founder and editor. Keppler—not Nast, who is usually given credit—was here the first to depict the Democratic Party as a donkey. He shows honest Hancock carrying a donkey branded with the letters "DP" for Democratic Party, blindered with "stupidity," and saddled with "pro-slavery Copperheadism," while Boss Thomas Kelly of Tammany Hall holds its tail. Contrarily, Garfield carries the personal shame of the Crédit Mobilier and De Golyer Contract scandals as he rides the white horse of the Republican Party.*
Lithograph from Puck, *July 28, 1880.*

The tariff proved a great issue for Garfield, largely because Winfield Scott Hancock had so little understanding of it and displayed that dim understanding to a reporter from a New Jersey newspaper early in October. He denied being for free trade, said he saw no harm in a little protection, and then offered the view that, ultimately, "The tariff question is a local question." Since the power to impose import duties is reserved to the federal government in the Constitution, this remark provoked mocking comment. It was a classic gaffe, and the Republicans used it to portray Hancock as laughably inadequate to the demands of the job. Some of the

By moving a lever on these campaign toys
(a devil's pointed tail in the case of
Hancock, on the right) one brought the
candidate's hidden arm into the position of
thumbing his nose at his opponent.
DAVID J. AND JANICE L. FRENT
POLITICAL AMERICANA COLLECTION.

The mount for a ferrotype. Hancock is a
rebus of the candidate's name: hand +
cock. Conveniently for this Democrat, the
rooster was still the most frequently used
symbol for the Democratic Party.
DAVID J. AND JANICE L. FRENT
POLITICAL AMERICANA COLLECTION.

Republican war chest that fall was spent on publishing "A Record of the Statesman-ship and Political Achievements of General Winfield Scott Hancock"—a set of blank pages.

For a time it appeared that Garfield had bumbled as well. A letter found on the desk of the editor of a Tammany newspaper in New York City, apparently in Garfield's own hand, discussed immigration and the labor market in politically dangerous ways. The letter, supposedly addressed to one H. L. Morey, said that employers should have the right to hire labor wherever they could get it most cheaply and that Chinese immigrants should continue coming until "our great manufacturing and corporate interests" were happy with the supply of surplus labor. After a cursory check of the handwriting, the letter was published on October 28. Garfield at first refused to comment (in part because he wanted to make sure that nobody in his office had sent such a letter in his name) but then denounced it as a fake. H. L. Morey turned out not to exist, and the letter was eventually proved to be a forgery. But it probably cost Garfield the states of California and Nevada, where Chinese immigration, and therefore anti-Chinese feeling, was highest.

The election was close: Garfield's plurality was fewer than 10,000 votes. In the Electoral College, however, he won by a margin of 214 to 155. Hancock carried the South but failed to break through in New York, which provided the margin of victory. The Greenback candidate, James B. Weaver, polled more than 300,000 votes.

The tawdryness of the election and the struggle for the spoils of victory had a final, tragic side. In July 1881, Garfield was shot in the back by Charles J. Guiteau, who (according to witnesses) cried out, "I am a Stalwart, and now Arthur is President." Garfield lingered some weeks before dying in September. His murder helped build support for what became the Pendleton Civil Service Reform Act, a first step toward limiting the excesses of the spoils system in the federal government.

CHAPTER

23

Political Poetry

CLEVELAND v. BLAINE, 1884

Some presidential campaigns leave legacies in the precedents they set: Jefferson's victory in 1800, for example, established the peaceful transfer of power to an opposition party. Some leave legacies in their consequences: Lincoln's victory in 1860 unleashed the Civil War. The campaign of 1884 supplied its own legacies: two passable couplets and a memorable alliterative phrase. Such was the politics of the 1880s.

The country was hardly short of burning issues. The status of African Americans in the wake of the Civil War was no less challenging to the nation than it had been a decade earlier, but the issue had been banished from national politics. Blacks were being denied the vote with increasing regularity, and as a result whites in the South had more voting power than their northern counterparts: blacks were counted in the apportionment of House seats, but since they were barred from voting, southern whites exercised disproportionate influence. Comparing five states each from North and South, each group of five having a total of 48 electoral votes, the historian John A. Garraty noted that in the five northern states 1,349,000 votes were cast while in their southern counterparts only 795,000 persons determined the allocation of those 48 votes.

Other Americans were left out, too, either politically or economically. Women, of course, could not yet vote, except in Wyoming and Utah. And the rapid transformation of America from an agricultural to an industrial nation was shattering old forms of labor relations and altering the look of the nation's cities. Waves of immigrants arriving from Europe were setting off new religious controversies, and anti-Chinese feeling in the West had resulted, in 1882, in the Chinese Exclusion Act, the beginning of a wave of immigration restrictions that would conclude with the draconian immigration law of 1924. Western farmers were feeling pressed by the increasing power of the railroads, which had become indispensable to their well-being but exacted a high price. Corruption in government, whether in Republican guise, as under President Grant, or in Democratic cities dominated by the

"Above all,

tell the truth."

GROVER CLEVELAND, 1884,
REPLYING TO HIS CAMPAIGN
MANAGERS WHEN THEY ASKED
HIM HOW TO RESPOND TO THE
REVELATION THAT THE NEVER-
MARRIED CANDIDATE DID
INDEED HAVE A SON. CLEVE-
LAND HAD LONG PROVIDED
FINANCIAL SUPPORT FOR THE
BOY AND HIS MOTHER.

likes of the Tweed Ring, had disconnected people from government and encouraged opposition to the status quo.

The most influential champions of reform were the "Mugwumps," Republicans opposed to the politics of patronage and cronyism (and to James G. Blaine). Leading editors, university presidents, and other members of the educated elite were drawn to the Mugwump cause (the derisive name, taken from an Algonquin word for "big chief," had been popularized by the New York *Sun*). Many of those who had backed the Liberal Republican campaign of Horace Greeley in 1872 now supported similar ideals under a more awkward label. The reformers had been dealt a sad blow with the murder of President Garfield, whose Stalwart replacement, Chester A. Arthur, espoused moderate reform but practiced spoilsmanship as usual. Anger over the lack of reform had helped Democrats pick up sixty-two House seats in the 1882 elections, and the passage of the Pendleton Act in 1883 had advanced the reform agenda. But Arthur was no friend of change. Nor, for that matter, was Blaine, although he was less hidebound in his dedication to political patronage than the Stalwarts. The contest for the Republican nomination would pit Blaine against Arthur.

For the Democrats, the early months of 1884 were largely a waiting game, with the party leaders marking time while Samuel J. Tilden mulled over his options. In the view of many, Tilden had a moral right to the nomination, owing to the way he had lost the 1876 race, and Tilden, in spite of his poor health, was not sure what to do. Not until June 10 did he withdraw his name from consideration, although the letter in which he did so left the door open should his party come to him and beg him to run, as he no doubt hoped it would do.

Tilden had a great appeal for the Democrats because he was from New York, a state they had to win if they were to defeat any Republican nominee. But there was another New Yorker, the new governor, Grover Cleveland, who had his own hopes for higher office. Cleveland had served as sheriff and then mayor in Buffalo and had won the governorship in 1882 largely on his reputation as a champion of clean government. As such, he had won the animosity of John Kelly, the Tammany boss, but such an enemy was very useful to a New York politician hoping to appeal to Democrats elsewhere in the country. Having Kelly as an enemy also endeared him to the Mugwumps. Cleveland's political man-

1884

PRESIDENTIAL CANDIDATE (STATE) VICE-PRESIDENTIAL CANDIDATE (STATE)	PARTY	ELECTORAL VOTES	APPROX. % OF POPULAR VOTE
Grover Cleveland (N.Y.) Thomas A. Hendricks (Ind.)	Democratic	219	49%
James G. Blaine (Maine) John A. Logan (Ill.)	Republican	182	48%

Among the minor-party candidates were Benjamin F. Butler (Greenback-Labor), John P. St. John (Prohibition), and Belva Ann Lockwood (Equal Rights).

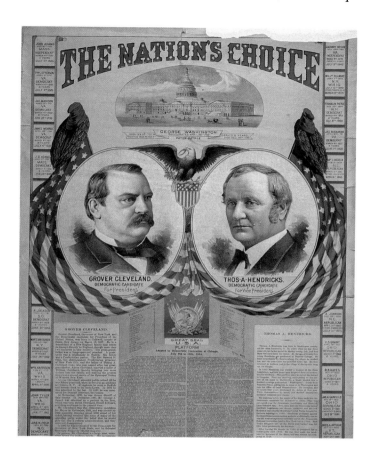

DAVID J. AND JANICE L. FRENT
POLITICAL AMERICANA COLLECTION.

agers pursued a stealth strategy, keeping Cleveland out of the papers but building relations with Democrats in the Midwest and elsewhere. Cleveland had no hope if Tilden put himself forward but might succeed if he could be everyone's second choice (the same strategy Garfield had employed in 1880).

The Republicans met first, in Chicago in June, and Blaine moved to victory on the fourth ballot. Senator John A. Logan of Illinois was chosen for Vice President. Early in July, the Democrats convened and, deprived of Tilden, nominated Cleveland on the second ballot. Thomas A. Hendricks of Indiana, Tilden's running mate in 1876, was again nominated to the second slot on the Democratic ticket.

The tone of the campaign was set for good on July 21, when the Buffalo *Telegraph* published a story that Cleveland had had an illegitimate child by a woman named Maria Halpin. Soon Blaine's supporters were chanting "Ma, Ma, where's my Pa?" "Going to the White House, Ha! Ha! Ha!" Cleveland admitted his involvement with Halpin and made no excuses. The issue continued to provoke comment throughout the campaign, but Cleveland's forthright response helped defuse the matter.

Forthright was not the term best applied to Blaine's handling of the "Mulligan Letters," incriminating documents that had already harmed him once, during his try for the Republican nomination in 1876. Blaine had been accused of some shady

*Grover Cleveland campaigning in the
then still independent city of Brooklyn,
New York. Wood engraving from
Harper's Weekly.*

dealings with railroad bonds carried out through the agency of a Boston broker. Letters from the broker's bookkeeper, James Mulligan, had been given to a House committee in 1876, but Blaine had managed to take control of them and had used them selectively to defend himself. Eventually the issue had died down, although it had hurt his presidential chances that year. In 1884, new letters emerged, including one designed to exonerate himself that Blaine had drafted and then sent to Mulligan with instructions to copy it in his own hand and mail the copy to the candidate. Along with those instructions was a final request: "Burn this letter." Blaine's tortured attempts to escape the consequences of this discovery stood in sharp contrast to Cleveland's forthright admission, and Democrats were soon rhyming on the streets, "Blaine, Blaine, James G. Blaine, the continental liar from the state of Maine," sometimes adding, as a coda, "Burn this letter, burn this letter, burn this letter."

New York was again the main prize in the campaign, the decisive state. Republicans were divided into several factions: those for Blaine, Stalwarts of the Arthur/Conkling stripe (lukewarm at best about the party's candidate), and the Mugwumps, who were attracted to Cleveland because of his reputation as a reformer. Another problem for the Republicans was that the Prohibitionists were offering a stronger candidate than usual, John P. St. John, the former governor of Kansas.

Democrats in New York were split as well, with Cleveland strongly supported by the "county democracy"—party leaders outside New York City—while Tammany Hall had no desire to see Cleveland elected. Blaine, too, had cultivated Irish support, and the Irish were powerful in Tammany. Also in the race was the former Union general Benjamin Butler, on the Antimonopoly-Greenback ticket. Butler could hope for little support in the South, since, as military commander in Louisiana, he had decreed that New Orleans women who refused to greet Union officers with courtesy would be treated as prostitutes. Butler was not a factor nationally, but the Republicans hoped he might siphon off votes from Cleveland in New York—hoped seriously enough to pay Butler $5,000 a week to carry on his race.

For a time Blaine made an effort to stress the tariff as an issue in the race, contending that without a protective tariff workers would lose their jobs. This protectionist stand helped with the Irish voters, who were for a tariff largely because the British were the global champions of free trade. But as the fall progressed and portents of a Democratic victory emerged, Blaine returned to the bloody shirt. Had Blaine been a Union general, this might have proved fruitful, since Cleveland had hired a substitute to replace him in the army (he had stayed home to support his

Cartoon by Bernhard Gillam, published in Puck, June 4, 1884, showing James Blaine as tattooed with all his crimes and misdemeanors. For months on end Puck attacked Blaine with as much graphic cruelty as that with which Nast had savaged Greeley in 1872. This cartoon of Blaine as the "Tattooed Man" was the most influential image of the 1884 campaign. Among the seated judges may be recognized the young Theodore Roosevelt (fourth from right), a New York State assemblyman who was a delegate to the 1884 Republican Party convention.
LIBRARY OF CONGRESS.

Cleveland, "Grover the Good," encounters Maria Halprin and their son outside the White House. In 1884 Cleveland's illegitimate son was ten years old. Cartoon by Frank Beard, published in September 1884.

widowed mother while his brothers went to war). But Blaine had not served, either. So he just waved the shirt and argued that allowing the Democrats back into the White House would be "as if the dead Stuarts were recalled to the throne of England, as if the Bourbons should be invited to administer the government of the French Republic."

At the end of the campaign, New York hung in the balance, and Blaine went to New York City to appeal to the state's voters. One of his stops was a meeting of ministers on October 29, a seemingly safe stop and one hardly likely to generate news. But as Blaine listened, the Reverend Samuel D. Burchard of the Murray Hill Presbyterian Church pledged that he and others like him "don't propose to . . . identify ourselves with the party whose antecedents have been rum, Romanism and rebellion." The attack on Roman Catholicism was dynamite, but Blaine either missed it or hoped that by failing to take note of it he might ensure that the remark would be ignored. When his turn came to speak, he uttered the usual platitudes and did not take Burchard to task for his prejudices. But a reporter from the Associated Press wire service, Frank Mack, had been there and seen that there was a big story, and soon it was on the wire nationally. For the remaining days of the campaign the Democrats attacked Blaine on the subject, and Blaine tried gamely to recover.

The race was one of the closest ever. Fewer than 30,000 votes (out of about 10 million) separated the candidates nationally, and in New York Cleveland's margin was fewer than 1,200 votes. Had Blaine responded adroitly to Burchard's remark, he might have carried the state. In fact, had the weather in Republican sections of upstate New York not been miserable on election day, he might still have won. But the Republicans faced more serious problems, and if there had not been Mugwump discontent the Republican nominee might well have won an easy victory. But Blaine didn't rise to the occasion, rain fell upstate, and the Mugwumps went for Cleveland.

In a poetic summation of a prosaic race, Democrats now called out:

Hurrah for Maria! Hurrah for the kid!
I voted for Cleveland,
And damned glad I did.

The Business of Campaigns

HARRISON v. CLEVELAND, 1888

If the campaign of 1884 provoked flights of doggerel, that of 1888 was all business. The central issue of the campaign, the tariff, engaged the passions of the nation's business leaders, and the Republican Party brought new professionalism to campaign management and, in particular, to fund-raising. The victory of the Republican nominee, Benjamin Harrison, in November was more than anything a tribute to a superior campaign organization.

President Grover Cleveland had won election in 1884 in part because of his reputation as a reformer. "Reform" carries connotations of innovation, of new approaches to old problems, but in Cleveland's case these connotations were incorrect. Cleveland's conception of reform, and of the executive office itself, was a throwback to an earlier era, not a harbinger of a new one. In civil service reform, the forward-looking Mugwumps wanted competitive exams and properly qualified appointees to bring modern efficiency to government organization. Cleveland's idea of reform was more in tune with Andrew Jackson's notions of rotation in office, and he liked to believe that any solid American citizen (which in his conception would have included no blacks or women) could fill just about any position of government. His efforts to reform the federal government were therefore a disappointment to many of his supporters. Old-line Democrats, expecting that with victory the traditional spoils of office would be divvied up among the faithful, were confronted by a more moralistic attitude; true reformers, hoping that Cleveland would remake the entire process of appointing civil servants, despaired over the slow pace and modest reach of Cleveland's reforms.

Cleveland may have been unimaginative, but he did not lack character, as he had demonstrated with his forthright response to the revelations about his romantic involvement with Maria Halpin. As his administration went forward, he eventually decided to face the most important economic issue, the protective tariff, and the huge surplus that had resulted from it, which was contributing to the deflationary path of the economy, meaning that debtors were being forced to pay back loans with money that was worth more, not less, than what they had borrowed. When he

Novelty scale with ceramic figures of Cleveland (left) and Harrison, who was to be the last full-bearded President. The figure of Harrison can be moved so that either candidate can outweigh the other.
DAVID J. AND JANICE L. FRENT POLITICAL AMERICANA COLLECTION.

was warned that opening this issue could cause him huge political problems, Cleveland responded, "What is the use of being elected or re-elected, unless you stand for something?"

He devoted his entire annual message in December 1887 to the issue. He pointed to the danger of the large surplus to the economy, tried to allay fears about jobs by showing that only about 15 percent of American workers were employed in industries protected by tariff rates, and went on to say that in any case the benefit to all from lower prices would outweigh any ill effects. But then Cleveland's notion of limited executive authority kicked in. Having laid out his plans in thoughtful detail, he deferred to the powers of Congress to legislate in such matters. The result was a bill that simply revised the tariff to be more favorable to the South.

On the Republican side, the great statesman remained James G. Blaine. But Blaine, weary of campaigns and unwilling to endure the kind of abuse that had been heaped upon him and his family in 1884, declined to run. He went on a grand tour of Europe for most of 1887 and 1888 and, when he was reached in Paris to comment on Cleveland's tariff proposals, dashed off a quick defense of the protective tariff that immediately defined the Republican strategy and so forcefully demonstrated his stature in the party that he had to issue another statement reiterating his disinclination to run for President. Second to Blaine in national reputation and Capitol Hill stature was Senator John Sherman of Ohio, the Treasury secretary under President Hayes and a champion of hard money and high tariffs. As a campaigner he lacked much—he was called "the Ohio icicle"—but in 1888 many Republicans felt that with Blaine refusing to run it was Sherman's turn. Other contenders on the Republican side included Michigan's governor, Russell Alger; Chauncey M. Depew of New York, attorney for the New York Central railroad; and Indiana's Benjamin Harrison.

Harrison had several significant advantages over his competitors. He had a famous name, being a grandson of President William Henry Harrison. He had served in the Union army in the Civil War, rising to brigadier general by the conflict's end. And he was from Indiana, one of the crucial swing states of the era. He was smart, worked hard, had not been involved in scandal, and had a reputation as a sensible compromiser. All of these qualities made him an appealing choice for the state party barons who controlled things. And

1888

PRESIDENTIAL CANDIDATE (STATE) VICE-PRESIDENTIAL CANDIDATE (STATE)	PARTY	ELECTORAL VOTES	APPROX. % OF POPULAR VOTE
Benjamin Harrison (Ind.) Levi P. Morton (N.Y.)	Republican	233	48%
Grover Cleveland (N.Y.) Allen G. Thurman (Ohio)	Democratic	168	49%

Among the minor-party candidates were Clinton B. Fisk (Prohibition) and Belva Ann Lockwood (Equal Rights).

Harrison found himself courted by some of the most important leaders. Blaine's man Stephen B. Elkins worked for him, as did Wharton Barker, who had choreographed the emergence of James A. Garfield at the Republican convention in 1880.

The Republicans met in Chicago in the middle of June. All the contenders fretted that the slightest incident could fan enthusiasm for the reluctant Blaine and that a true draft of the Man from Maine might persuade him to accept the nomination. A lengthy stalemate, then, was anathema to all the contenders. Sherman came into the hall with about half the votes needed for the nomination, taking 229 votes on the first ballot (the support of 416 delegates was needed to nominate), with Harrison a distant fourth. Candidates courted the party bosses, and the bosses sought the best deals they could make for themselves and their states, always predicated on finding a candidate who could beat Cleveland. Tough party bosses such as Nelson Aldrich of Rhode Island and Matthew Quay of Pennsylvania exacted quids for their quos, re-

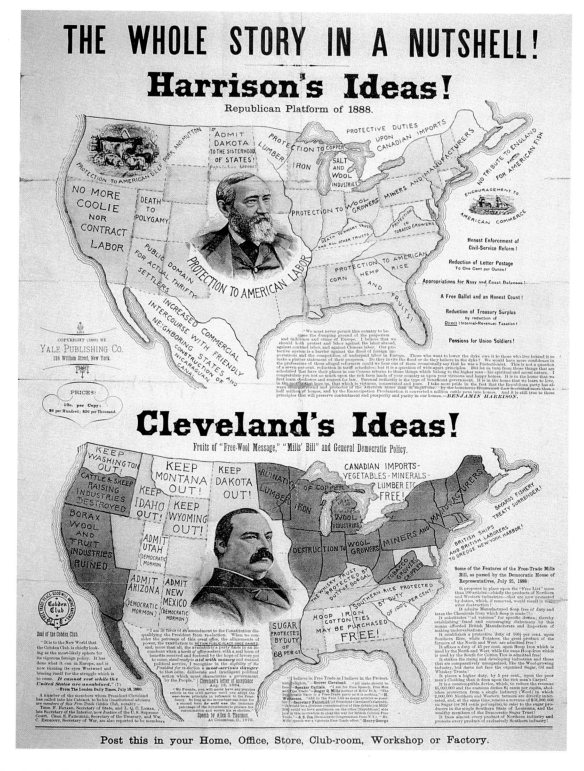

fusing to commit themselves until the spirit of the convention expressed itself. A few dozen delegates from the South were understood to be hawking their votes at $200 apiece. Blaine, still unwilling to run, reiterated his position by wire from Andrew Carnegie's castle in Scotland and in a prearranged code indicated that he favored Harrison. On the eighth ballot, Harrison was nominated, and he turned to the largest of the swing states, New York, for his running mate, Levi P. Morton, the loyal party man and able fund-raiser.

An even more able fund-raiser, Philadelphia's John Wanamaker, took charge of the party's money machine that fall, and it generated a quantity of campaign contributions that dwarfed anything yet seen. Wanamaker, who had made his fortune in the dry goods trade (he was a pioneer of the "money-back guarantee"), shook down Republican businessmen for $10,000 apiece, giving a sort of certificate in return for the contribution. In this way and others, Wanamaker probably produced more than $3 million for the race.

The Democrats, in contrast, were disorganized and poorly funded. Cleveland had been the presumptive nominee, but his idea of running a campaign was as outmoded as his notion of executive authority. With Washingtonian dignity he refused to stump for himself and even limited his written statements to the absolute minimum. The party had chosen as his running mate Allen Thurman, who at the age of seventy-four was unable to campaign with the vigor needed. The vice presidential nominee was supposed to do the actual speechmaking and touring, and with Cleveland holding himself unusually aloof it was even more important that the number two be a vibrant public person. Thurman's nickname, "The Old Roman," perhaps indicates how little suited he was to the role. Thurman was able to deliver a cogent attack on Republican tariff policies, but he would also treat his auditors to accounts of his illnesses, and on occasion he collapsed at the lectern, hardly presenting a dynamic image to a skeptical electorate. (The fact that Cleveland's first-term Vice President, Thomas Hendricks, had died suddenly after less than a year in office may have made the matter more sensitive.)

The money raised for the Republican campaign financed countless pamphlets in favor of protective tariffs that outlined the horrible unemployment and sorrow that would follow any embrace of the free-trade policies espoused by Britain. One California Republican even managed to drag the British into the campaign directly. George Osgoodby wrote to Lord Sackville-West, the British minister to the United States, posing as a former British subject named Charles Murchison. Which candidate, he asked the minister, should receive the support of a loyal friend of Britain? Sackville-West, clearly not a leading light of his nation or his family, expressed a preference for Cleveland, a colossal diplomatic and political gaffe. Osgoodby showed the reply to some friends, one of whom passed along a copy to Harrison Gray Otis, the editor of the *Los Angeles Times,* who held on to it until shortly before the election, when it could do the most harm. It ran on October 24, but Cleveland was so quick to demand the recall of the blundering diplomat that he somewhat defused the issue.

"America suffers from a sort of intermittent fever—what one may call a quintan ague. Every fourth year there come terrible shakings, passing into the hot fit of the presidential election; then follows what physicians call 'the interval;' then the fit again."

JAMES BRYCE,
The American Commonwealth,
1888

ELECTORAL COLLEGE

ALTHOUGH IT IS ALMOST A REQUIREMENT OF U.S. CITIZENSHIP to treat the Constitution as an inspired and nearly flawless document, the Founding Fathers did a remarkably bad job of arranging for the election of presidents. The flaw in the original method of casting electoral votes for President and Vice President (it did not allow electors to indicate which candidate was favored for the first office) was dramatically revealed in the election of 1800 and was soon fixed by the Twelfth Amendment. But the odd institution known as the Electoral College remains in place. It is the electoral equivalent of the human appendix—it serves no known purpose and is of interest only when something goes wrong.

In the Constitution, as amended, each state is assigned a number of electors equal to its number of senators and representatives in Washington. This perpetuates the bias in favor of less populous states that was adopted by the "Great Compromise" of 1787, when it was agreed that each state would have two senators, while its membership in the House of Representatives would be proportional to population. But the winner-take-all rule governing electoral votes returns the advantage to the large states, because bloc voting makes them the vital battlegrounds. (In each state, the winner, no matter how small the popular-vote margin, collects all the electoral votes.)

When there are viable third-party candidacies, concerns about the Electoral College rise, because if no candidate receives a majority of the votes in the Electoral College, the election is thrown into the House of Representatives, where each state has a single vote. The eight largest states have roughly half the nation's population but in such a case would cast only 16 percent of the vote. Although no election has gone to the House since 1824, the possibility remains, and the legitimacy of such an election could conceivably be highly dubious.

An even more dramatic possibility is also inherent in the system. Today, electors are not bound to vote as the states they represent voted (although they almost always do so). It is therefore possible that a group of rogue electors could conspire to thwart the expressed will of the voters.

Ultimately, though, that danger seems remote. American democracy rests upon the consent of the governed, and any blatantly illegitimate result would doubtless provoke such an outcry that it would be very difficult to uphold. But the possibility reminds us that the Founders, however inspired they were in the construction of a government, were not perfect.

Harrison's campaign was conducted very effectively. Discovering that their candidate could actually deliver a good speech but not wishing to risk a campaign swing of the sort that had hurt Blaine, Harrison's managers arranged for a string of visitors to come see him in Indiana, where the candidate would deliver carefully vetted greetings that would carry the right campaign message. This so-called front-porch campaign would become a standard over the next decade. For more active forays, Republican luminaries were sent around the country to stump for Harrison, with even James G. Blaine lending his considerable oratorical talents to the cause.

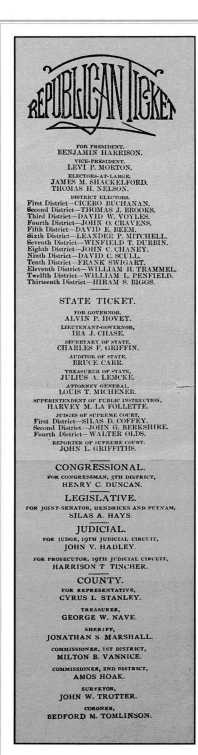

Republican ballot.

In Indiana—where there was no voter registration—thousands of Republican ballots, like this one from Hendricks County, were cast illegally in 1888, many by hired "repeaters," who returned over and over again to the polls, using a succession of names and disguises. Glass-sided ballot boxes and distinctively colored ballots for each party enabled the hovering party thugs to make sure that "bought" voters "stayed bought."

After his victory, the pious Benjamin Harrison solemnly remarked to Senator Matthew Stanley Quay (better known as Boss Matt Quay), chairman of the Republican National Committee, "Providence has given us the victory." Telling the story afterward, Quay exclaimed, "Think of the man! He ought to know that Providence hadn't a damn thing to do with it." He mused that Harrison would never know "how close a number of men were compelled to approach the gates of the penitentiary to make him President."

Corruption had always been a part of American elections, but its unprecedented extent and brazenness in 1888 triggered a reaction. Before the 1892 election, thirty-eight states would adopt the secret ballot to curb abuses. And in that election the citizens of Lockport, New York, became the first to try out the newly invented voting machines.

BOTH: NATIONAL MUSEUM OF AMERICAN HISTORY, SMITHSONIAN INSTITUTION.

The final days of the campaign saw both parties pouring dollars and speakers into the swing states. In Indiana, Harrison's home, money was freely spent to secure the votes of the estimated 20,000 Hoosiers whose votes were for sale.

Harrison's victory came because he carried both those crucial states, and he won in the Electoral College in spite of losing the popular vote nationwide by more than 90,000 votes. Cleveland rolled up unproductive margins in the South while narrowly losing states whose electoral votes could have saved him. Considering how completely outspent and outorganized the Democrats had been and how little Cleveland and how poorly Thurman had campaigned, the race was surprisingly close.

John Wanamaker had a final gift for those Republican contributors who had received certificates for their contributions. So awash in cash had the party been that it had not spent a significant portion of the funds received, so Wanamaker bet the remainder on the outcome of the race. Winning his bets, he was able to reimburse Harrison's backers generously.

CHAPTER
25

Two Honest Presidents Debating the Tariff and Evidence of Agrarian Unrest

CLEVELAND, HARRISON, WEAVER, 1892

In the election of 1892, President Benjamin Harrison faced ex-President Grover Cleveland in a contest dominated by earnest but vague debate over tariff policy. A Populist Party challenge mounted by General James B. Weaver garnered 8.5 percent of the popular vote and 22 electoral votes, but the principal contest was between Cleveland and Harrison, whose political views had much more in common than either party liked—or liked to admit.

Such a contest might be taken as a sign of a tranquil time in a nation's life, and looking at this and the previous three presidential elections, one might reach just such a conclusion. Once the aftermath of the Civil War was resolved by the election of 1876, the Compromise of 1877, and the abandonment of Reconstruction (and the rights of southern blacks), presidential elections had fallen into a somewhat tedious pattern of close contests between bland candidates decided in a few pivotal states. But the series of lackluster elections misrepresents life in the United States, which was undergoing profound changes in this period. The political system insisted on ignoring or containing these changes, but changes were taking place, and (as Weaver's candidacy portended) they would soon transform the political world.

Since 1877, workers, confronted with the vast economic power of huge new corporations (and the political power those corporations could purchase from either major party), had been forming large organizations of their own to confront the power of capital. The Knights of Labor grew rapidly in the 1870s, and in 1886 the American Federation of Labor was founded under the leadership of Samuel Gompers. As the election year of 1892 progressed, a 20 percent wage cut at Andrew Carnegie's Homestead, Pennsylvania, works spawned a great steel strike, and when Carnegie's man Henry Clay Frick sent in Pinkerton operatives to break the strike, there ensued a pitched gun battle in which three Pinkertons and ten strikers died. The Pennsylvania militia was then called in. Soon afterward, an anarchist tried to assassinate Frick, turning public sympathy away from the strikers (who had nothing to do with the anarchist) and leading to a complete defeat for the strikers and their union.

Pocket game.

Less dramatic events were transforming the country even more profoundly. At the end of the Civil War, there were 35,000 miles of railroad track in the country; by 1890, the figure was 166,000. Friendly legislators in Washington and state capitals poured vast public subsidies into the railroads, from which vast private profits were reaped. Farmers found they could now take their surpluses to distant markets, but only on terms dictated by the railroads. The railroads opened the West not only to farming but to urban development and provided an easy way for mining bosses and other employers to attract workers. In the West, many of those workers were Chinese, but animosity to cheap laborers by workingmen and racist attitudes led, by 1882, to the Chinese Exclusion Act, which barred nearly all further immigration of Chinese to the United States. (This explicitly racist policy remained in effect until 1943.)

Other waves of immigrants—Italian Catholics, Russian Jews, German socialists—were provoking new varieties of nativism, and "respectable" Bostonians and New Yorkers fretted over the "mongrelization of the races" and worried that democracy was in danger. Some looked into the matter historically and—although their education had celebrated the ancient republics of Greece and Rome—concluded that only Teutonic and Anglo-Saxon peoples had the requisite character to practice self-government.

Mechanization and more scientific farming methods (encouraged by the land-grant colleges that railroad expansion helped finance) allowed farmers to produce bumper crops, but oversupply then drove down prices, and railroads and banks could often exploit farmers to great profit. For many western farmers and ranchers, the world of the 1880s was filled with rapacious eastern capitalists, Republicans whose tariff policies made manufactured goods more expensive, and a Democratic Party beholden to the big-city political machines and their hordes of non-Protestant immigrant voters.

Various reform currents were percolating: woman suffrage, prohibitionism, civil service reform, and greater government control of railroads, among others. Radical notions of socialist or Communist hue also found adherents. Some of these reforms took root— by the 1892 election, for example, thirty-three of forty-four states had the secret ballot, and women

1892

PRESIDENTIAL CANDIDATE (STATE) VICE-PRESIDENTIAL CANDIDATE (STATE)	PARTY	ELECTORAL VOTES	APPROX. % OF POPULAR VOTE
Grover Cleveland (N.Y.) Adlai E. Stevenson (Ill.)	Democratic	277	46%
Benjamin Harrison (Ind.) Whitelaw Reid (N.Y.)	Republican	145	43%
James B. Weaver (Iowa) James G. Field (Va.)	People's (or Populist)	22	9%

were beginning to advance toward the vote. (By century's end, four states had enacted woman suffrage.) But reform was low on the agendas of the two major parties.

The Republicans had taken advantage of having control of the White House again to pass a very restrictive tariff named for William McKinley, the Ohio congressman who drafted the bill. When some prices quickly rose in response, voters took action, and the Democrats emerged from the 1890 midterm elections with 231 seats in the House of Representatives to 88 for the Republicans. The GOP was also hurt by the fact that the Fifty-first Congress had spent so lavishly on veterans' pensions and pet public works projects that it had been branded the "Billion-Dollar Congress."

Selection of the presidential nominees proceeded predictably. Harrison was the incumbent and as such had sufficient patronage power to ensure his renomination—unless, that is, James G. Blaine, his secretary of state, indicated he wanted the top job.

Cartoon from Frank Leslie's Illustrated Newspaper, *August 1892.*
LIBRARY OF CONGRESS.

Blaine was so respected (and Harrison so coldly regarded) that he could probably have had the job. But he was ill, depressed by the recent deaths of two of his children, and unwilling to put himself forward. Harrison won nomination easily and replaced the incumbent Vice President, Levi P. Morton, on his ticket with Whitelaw Reid, the owner of the *New York Tribune*.

Cleveland, too, had an easy time in spite of the efforts of his old New York enemies in Tammany Hall to find another candidate. Illinois's Adlai Stevenson (grandfather of the Democrat who lost twice to Dwight D. Eisenhower in the 1950s), a prosilver Democrat, was chosen as his running mate.

The biggest fireworks at any convention probably came with Ignatius Donnelly's opening remarks to the People's Party convention in Omaha in July. Eager

A campaign ribbon alluding to Harrison's illustrious grandfather, the hero of Tippecanoe.

to point out the division in society that the Democrats and Republicans were papering over, Donnelly, a former congressman who had written books on the lost continent of Atlantis and in support of Francis Bacon as the author of Shakespeare's plays, told the delegates, "The fruits of the toil of millions are boldly stolen to build up colossal fortunes for the few. . . . From the same prolific womb of governmental injustice we breed the two great classes—tramps and millionaires." The Populists asked for government ownership of railroads, telephones, and telegraphs, a graduated income tax, the secret ballot, and something called a "subtreasury plan," which involved federally funded and administered warehouses for agricultural products that would free farmers from economic tyranny.

The actual campaign was tame, at least for the two major-party nominees. The fact that each was a President cut down a bit on the name-calling, and neither nominee ran an active campaign (Cleveland out of personal preference, Harrison because his wife was dying). For a change the Democrats were better organized, and William C. Whitney, Cleveland's navy secretary, raised more than $2.3 million (about a tenth of that his own money). The uses of money were a bit different than in 1888. The secret ballot undercut the practice of purchasing votes; it made it hard to know if one had got one's money's worth. Whitney spent heavily on advertising and campaign publications and copied the Republicans' network of political clubs. He also arranged a truce between Cleveland and Tammany Hall, ensuring that Democrats in New York would get the state behind the nominee.

In fact, Cleveland won handily. He outpolled Harrison by about 400,000 votes and secured 277 electoral votes to Harrison's 145. Weaver polled just over a million votes and won 22 electors. Harrison, in mourning for his wife, who had died in the last week of October, felt more relief than disappointment on hearing the news of his defeat. Grover Cleveland entered the White House for a second time, the only person to serve two nonconsecutive terms as President. And, like Martin Van Buren in 1837, Cleveland found himself in office at the beginning of a great recession, which would expose the fault lines the parties had striven to hide for the past generation.

"*The Logic of the Situation*"

McKINLEY v. BRYAN, 1896

The Panic of 1893 got under way even before Grover Cleveland was inaugurated for his second term. Nervousness hit the New York stock market in February, and soon the jitters turned into real fear. Investors wanted to buy gold as a safe haven, and the federal government's reserves of the precious metal began to shrink as federal notes were redeemed for bullion. By early May, the government's gold reserves had fallen below $100 million and the stock market collapsed. "Industrial Black Friday," May 5, 1893, was the worst day in the market's history up to that point. Across the country, businesses that had overexpanded during the boom of the 1880s failed, including huge enterprises like the Union Pacific and Santa Fe railroads.

One victim of the panic was the governor of Ohio, William McKinley. He had cosigned some loans for a friend, and when the panic hit neither man could meet the obligation. McKinley's brilliant political manager, Marcus Alonzo ("Mark") Hanna, arranged for $100,000 to be raised to clear McKinley's debts. Others had less luck in escaping the consequences of the ensuing depression. A drought in the summer of 1894 hurt farmers, and for a time 20 percent of the workforce was unemployed. In 1894, Jacob S. Coxey, a wealthy Ohio businessman, started a march on Washington, leading a few hundred followers to petition for a federal jobs program that would employ the jobless to build roads. "Coxey's Army" became big news, and more than forty reporters followed Coxey's progress. Arriving at last on the steps of the Capitol, Coxey was beaten by police and then arrested for trespassing.

Industrial unrest took a more serious turn later that spring with a strike against the Pullman Palace Car Company, makers of the sleeping cars that dominated the American railroad market. Sparked by a company wage cut, the Pullman strike crippled rail traffic throughout the United States, beginning in late June, when the American Railway Union, led by Eugene V. Debs, refused to work on trains that carried Pullman cars. Early in July, President Cleveland decided to break the strike and obtained an injunction against Debs's union. He then sent federal troops against

A brass stickpin using McKinley's highly effective campaign promise of a "Full Dinner Pail" (forerunner of the lunch box) for American workers as a result of his protective tariff policy.

DAVID J. AND JANICE L. FRENT
POLITICAL AMERICANA COLLECTION.

the strikers, setting off riots across the country as strikers and troops battled. Riots also accompanied labor disputes in midwestern coal fields that year.

Amid all this turmoil the President remained persuaded that the cause of all these problems was the Sherman Silver Purchase Act of 1890, which had haltingly moved the country toward bimetalism. A devout believer in the gold standard, Cleveland had fought hard for repeal of the act, and once he had achieved it he expected the economy to improve. It did not. Presiding over a nation seemingly on the verge of class war, its economy in shambles, Cleveland was reviled within his party and throughout the country.

All this was good news for the Republicans, who scored huge gains in the 1894 midterm elections, picking up 117 seats in the House. As 1896 neared, they were confident they could win the White House. With Mark Hanna at its helm, McKinley's campaign moved quickly to advance his candidacy. Hanna took a house in Georgia in 1895, and when McKinley visited him the two men received southern Republican Party leaders. Although the South was unlikely to vote Republican (particularly since McKinley was a Union veteran), the states did send delegates to the Republican convention, and Hanna made sure McKinley had a head start on wooing them.

Other Republicans, too, recognized the opportunity that Cleveland's disgrace offered. House Speaker Thomas B. Reed was McKinley's most formidable foe, but his sharp tongue had alienated too many in the party for him to be nominated. By contrast, McKinley was a perfect candidate: a Civil War veteran with significant congressional experience, from a populous state, and with real skills as a speaker and a politician. Because his district was not a particularly safe one, McKinley had had to learn the politics of the broad center, and he was, according to the usually tart Henry Adams, a "marvellous manager of men." Furthermore, although he depended on Hanna for organization, McKinley was not the political puppet his opponents portrayed him to be. When the great Republican bosses sought to cut patronage deals in return for their support, McKinley and Hanna could hold them at arm's length, confident that the nomination was theirs.

McKinley's innovative campaign looked over the heads of the bosses and took the candidate's message directly to the people. McKinley easily won nomination at the Republican convention in St. Louis (as was still the

1896

PRESIDENTIAL CANDIDATE (STATE) VICE-PRESIDENTIAL CANDIDATE (STATE)	PARTY	ELECTORAL VOTES	APPROX. % OF POPULAR VOTE
William McKinley (Ohio) Garret A. Hobart (N.J.)	Republican	271	51%
William Jennings Bryan (Nebr.) Arthur Sewall (Maine)	Democratic/Populist	176	47%

Among the minor-party candidates were John Palmer (National Democratic), Joshua Levering (Prohibition), and Charles H. Matchett (Socialist-Labor).

tradition, he stayed home in Ohio, though he chatted with delegates on the telephone). He selected Garret A. Hobart, a Republican leader in New Jersey, as his running mate. The platform was foursquare behind the gold standard, and a small commotion occurred when a couple of dozen Republican silverites walked out. Watching the exodus was the former congressman William Jennings Bryan, now editor of the prosilver *Omaha World-Herald.*

The choice of the Republican nominee had been a foregone conclusion for months before the convention, but the choice of a Democrat was unpredictable. The party was badly split between silverites and more conservative eastern Democrats who favored the gold standard. The Populist revolt that had resulted in a third-party campaign that had secured more than a million votes in 1892 was still burning in the plains states and in the West, and also in parts of the South, where farmers looked on eastern bankers and industrialists (as well as immigrant workers) as hostile forces challenging their very existence. The Democrats had few promi-

A Bryan–Sewall bandanna. After 1896, bandannas, which had been the most popular category of campaign souvenirs since 1876, gave way almost entirely to graphic celluloid pinback buttons, the process for making which was patented shortly before the beginning of the 1896 campaign.

DAVID J. AND JANICE L. FRENT POLITICAL AMERICANA COLLECTION.

nent leaders other than the discredited Cleveland, and the likely nominee in the view of most professionals was former representative Richard P. Bland of Missouri, a prosilver leader.

Before choosing a nominee the convention had first to ratify a platform, and the great debate was to be over silver. Thirty-six-year-old William Jennings Bryan arranged to give the final speech in favor of a prosilver plank. Bryan was of limited experience and reputation, but he was a great speaker who blended rhetorical sophistication, a splendid voice, and a flair for drama. His speech began by trying to include his midwestern constituents under the heading "businessmen," since conservative Democrats were stressing that the party should do nothing to scare businessmen. "The mer-

*Campaign buttons and pins, 1896.
Because the silver-versus-gold issue was
central in that year's election, many items
played in one way or another on the
sixteen-to-one ratio of the values of the
two metals. A popular visual pun was a
clock face with the hands pointing to sixteen
minutes before one o'clock. Also popular
were gold bugs, derived from Edgar Allan
Poe's famous story; soon they were, naturally enough, countered by silver bugs.*
NATIONAL MUSEUM OF
AMERICAN HISTORY,
SMITHSONIAN INSTITUTION.

chant at the cross-roads store is as much a business man as the merchant of New York," he proclaimed. He then stated an agrarian bias that was almost Jeffersonian in its prejudice: "Burn down your cities and leave our farms, and your cities will spring up again as if by magic; but destroy our farms and the grass will grow in the streets of every city in the country." Then, in the famous conclusion of the speech, Bryan reached his peak: "You shall not press down upon the brow of labor this crown of thorns, you shall not crucify mankind upon a cross of gold." As he spoke the last clause, he held his arms out from his sides as if on a cross, then let them sink slowly to his sides again. The convention hall erupted. On the fifth ballot, Bryan was nominated the Democratic candidate for President, and soon another silverite, Arthur Sewall of Maine, was chosen as his running mate. If most were shocked by the outcome, Bryan was not. The day before the speech he told a friend, "I am the only man who can be nominated. I am what they call 'the logic of the situation.'"

Bryan's nomination upset the logic of the Populists, who had expected to have the prosilver turf to themselves. It seemed futile to run a Populist candidate against Bryan, although many despaired that union with the Democrats meant an end to populism. The party selected the southern Populist Tom Watson for Vice President to proclaim its independence but felt compelled to back Bryan.

The race itself was dramatic and innovative. Bryan, with little money—about $650,000, much of it from western silver-mine owners—and with his reputation resting on his gifts as an orator, decided to break with tradition and conduct a vigorous campaign of his own. His campaign took him, according to his own reckoning, more than 18,000 miles, and he gave more than six hundred speeches. As many as 5 million people may have seen the "Boy Orator of the Platte" speak that summer and fall.

*McKinley, on the front porch of his home,
in Canton, Ohio, welcoming the delegation officially notifying him that he had
received the Republican nomination.*
LIBRARY OF CONGRESS.

A slight turn of the circular overlay on this cardboard gimmick contrasts the prosperity that McKinley's election will guarantee with the ruin that Bryan's would cause.
DAVID J. AND JANICE L. FRENT
POLITICAL AMERICANA COLLECTION.

William McKinley ran a far wiser race and had the advantage of a much larger war chest. Hanna and his associates raised millions—how many is unclear, but $3.5 million is the most conservative estimate, and some think it might have been closer to $10 million. In any case, it dwarfed the amount the Democrats could raise, and the money was well spent. Voters were given 120 million pieces of pro-McKinley propaganda. His campaign buttons became ubiquitous. Travelers on rural roads passed posters of McKinley that bore the legend "The Advance Agent of Prosperity." Rather than touring the country, the Republican nominee let the country come to him, greeting visitors on his front porch in Canton, Ohio, listening politely to their remarks to him, then replying with some well-chosen words of his own. McKinley's campaign team carefully reviewed not only the candidate's remarks but those of his visitors (which had to be submitted in advance).

In the end, Bryan was soundly defeated. McKinley won with 51.1 percent of the popular vote to Bryan's 47.7 percent, and had a nearly 100-vote margin in the Electoral College. Bryan's agrarian appeal was great, but America was ceasing to be a nation of farmers. The workers of the cities seemed more persuaded by McKinley's promises that high tariffs and sound money would make their lives better than they were by Bryan's plans. The Democratic move to silver, coupled with Bryan's demonization of cities and industrialism, helped complete a shift in party balance that had begun in earnest with the 1894 races. The Democrats were making themselves into a sectional party, and by doing so they ceded dominance of political life to the Republicans for the next generation. Bryan had crucified his party upon a cross of silver.

"Bryan is begging for the presidency as a tramp might beg for a pie."

JOHN HAY, 1896.
(HAY WOULD BECOME
MCKINLEY'S SECRETARY
OF STATE IN 1898.)

Election on a World Stage

McKINLEY v. BRYAN, 1900

Seldom, in all the elections of the nineteenth century, does one hear a word about foreign policy. In the early days of the country, when independence was still an issue, Federalists and Jeffersonian Republicans debated matters of international moment, and the campaign of 1812 involved some discussion of the merits of the war that had begun that year, but foreign preoccupations were the exception, not the rule. The war with Mexico in 1846 brought a brief return of attention to international relations, but then indifference descended again. Not that other nations were left entirely out of the discussion. Candidates wishing to win the Irish vote found easy applause in attacking Great Britain—"twisting the lion's tail." Politicians wanting to appeal to nativist voters could denounce the "backwardness" of Roman Catholic lands or dwell on the "pagan barbarity" of China, but such tropes had little to do with reality, either foreign or domestic.

But between the first and second campaigns matching William McKinley against William Jennings Bryan, all of that changed. The United States emerged as a global power—or rather finally faced up to the fact that it had become a global power economically and decided to play the part politically and militarily as well. In short, America embraced imperialism.

Imperial ambitions had been present all along, of course. The first settlements in what is now the United States, Canada, and Mexico were part of the imperial designs of great European powers such as Britain, France, and Spain. The early history of the American colonies saw countless involvements in imperial wars in the Americas as men from Massachusetts and Virginia found themselves advancing the British cause against the French in Quebec or the Spanish in Cartagena. But the American Revolution bequeathed a powerful tradition of anti-imperial rhetoric to the new nation. After all, a country founded on the right of self-determination could hardly stay true to itself if it sought to deprive others of that right.

But the powers of rationalization are strong when principle is at odds with self-interest, and the leaders of the new nation soon found ways of justifying their conquest of lands occupied by Native Americans or settled by Spanish colonists. Racism played a role, and any outrage committed by an opponent—an Indian massacre of white settlers, the slaughter of the defenders of the Alamo—could be used to deprive that opponent of the degree of humanity that merited self-determination.

The United States was hardly alone in this. Dehumanization of one's enemies is a commonplace of warfare. In the late nineteenth century, European nations were engaged in a final orgy of colonial acquisition. Parvenu nations such as the recently unified Germany and Italy were trying to catch up with the seasoned imperial powers such as Britain, France, Spain, and the Netherlands. Sandy tracts of Africa, tiny atolls in the Pacific, any plot of land not already claimed by a world power was coveted.

Gold was one of the keys to, and one of the great changes in, the politics of the United States after 1896. South African mines were bringing more gold onto the world market, allowing the amount of money in circulation to expand (which was, after all, the principal goal of the silverites). And new gold discoveries in Alaska, as well as more efficient methods of extracting gold from ore, were raising America's indigenous gold supplies. The first shipment of Klondike gold arrived in San Francisco on July 14, 1897, and the balance of McKinley's term saw increasing prosperity.

The Spanish-American War was the turning point in America's progress from hemispheric power to global superpower, but the antecedents were many. There was James K. Polk's Manifest Destiny to expand to the Pacific and the desire of southern slaveholders to transplant American slavery to Cuba or Mexico in their efforts to expand the Cotton Kingdom. America's determination to govern events in the Western Hemisphere had been made explicit in the Monroe Doctrine of 1823, and American interventionism had made small steps under President Grant and, notably, under Secretary of State James G. Blaine, who presided over the first inter-American conference in Washington, D.C., in 1889. As the century neared its end,

Congress was financing expansion of the navy, influenced by the theories of Admiral Alfred Thayer Mahan, whose book *The Influence of Sea Power upon History, 1660–1783* (1890) stressed that for a nation to be great it had to have a great navy.

One of Mahan's most enthusiastic disciples was Theodore Roosevelt, who had served as a commissioner of police in New York City and had written a naval history of the War of 1812. Roosevelt was as-

1900

PRESIDENTIAL CANDIDATE (STATE) VICE-PRESIDENTIAL CANDIDATE (STATE)	PARTY	ELECTORAL VOTES	APPROX. % OF POPULAR VOTE
William McKinley (Ohio) Theodore Roosevelt (N.Y.)	Republican	292	52%
William Jennings Bryan (Nebr.) Adlai E. Stevenson (Ill.)	Democratic	155	46%

Among the minor-party candidates were Eugene V. Debs (Social Democratic), John G. Woolley (Prohibition), Wharton Barker (People's, or Populist), and Joseph Maloney (Socialist-Labor).

73.2 percent of the total electorate went to the polls on Election Day 1900. Since then, voter turnout has never hit 70 percent, and the percentage of eligible voters who actually bother to vote has declined steadily, with only small upward blips occasionally punctuating the downward sloping line on the graph.

McKinley's campaign manager, Cleveland millionaire Mark Hanna, is shown on the left in this cartoon by George Luks, who would go on to become one of the leading artists in the so-called Ashcan School of urban realist painting. Hanna had actually been quoted in the press as telling his top-hatted candidate, "It's better to be President than to be right," and dismissing Henry Clay (whose portrait hangs in the background) as an "ass" for having made his famous statement, in an 1850 speech, "I would rather be right than be President." Color lithograph from the Democratic magazine The Verdict, *March 13, 1899.*

sistant secretary of the navy as war with Spain approached, and he did everything he could to bring the war closer. Others were calling stridently for war, including the leading yellow journalists William Randolph Hearst and Joseph Pulitzer. Spain was fighting a brutal war of containment against an indigenous Cuban independence movement. The atrocities committed by the Spanish side became headlines in Hearst's *New York Journal* and Pulitzer's New York *World,* and their stories were repeated across the nation.

William McKinley was not eager to intervene in Cuba, and many in America opposed the imperial ambitions being fanned in the New York papers and elsewhere. Carl Schurz, Andrew Carnegie, the labor leader Samuel Gompers, and William Jennings Bryan all opposed intervention. But the explosion of the American battleship *Maine* in Havana harbor in February 1898 started public opinion rolling toward war. Although there was little reason to believe that the blast had been caused by sabotage (and an American naval inquiry in the 1970s concluded that an internal mishap had caused the disaster), outrage over the deaths of 260 sailors outweighed sober assessment of the situation. By the end of April, the United States was at war with Spain and soon triumphed. Theodore Roosevelt resigned his naval post and raised a volunteer regiment called the Rough Riders that rode to glory at the Battle of San Juan Hill in July. By November he had been elected governor of New York.

As the election of 1900 approached, it was clear that once again McKinley would face Bryan. Although Bryan had been defeated in the 1896 race, he had won many admirers—even the crusty Massachusetts senator Henry Cabot Lodge had admired Bryan's courage and determination in that race. Like Roosevelt, Bryan had volunteered for service in the war, although he had not had the opportunity to distinguish himself in action. But Bryan opposed the move of the victorious Americans to retain control of the conquered Spanish colonies. During the war, independence, the classic goal of colonial subjects, had been the goal for more idealistic Americans, but now the United States was moving to replace Spain as the colonial ruler of Cuba, the Philippines, and Puerto Rico.

Here, Bryan thought, was a winning issue. The Republicans were abandoning a central tenet of American political life, and by casting McKinley as King George III he hoped to awaken American anti-imperialism and win the election. With Adlai E. Stevenson of Illinois, the former Vice President, as his running mate, Bryan prepared to put up a good fight.

The Republicans were not unduly worried. McKinley had made good on his promise four years earlier to be the "Advance Agent of Prosperity," and with Bryan and the Democrats still embracing the now-lost cause of free silver, they anticipated little trouble. The only major decision facing the GOP at the convention was the choice of a running mate, Vice President Garret Hobart having died the year before. Teddy Roosevelt was a popular choice among the delegates, and although Mark Hanna opposed him, McKinley wanted to leave the choice of a running mate to the convention. Thomas Platt, the Republican boss of New York, liked the idea of ridding his state of Governor Roosevelt, who had shown himself to be a bit too independent in matters of patronage for Platt's liking. The delegates had their way, and with McKinley preserving a dignified distance from the campaign, vice presidential candidate Roosevelt toured the country in the Republican cause.

"Why Hanna Does Not Want Teddy Riding Behind McKinley." Cartoon by Horace Taylor, January 1900.

Bryan, with support from what remained of the Populist movement and the few Republican silverites, again barnstormed the land, making speeches that sought to ignite outrage over America's imperial break with its past. But voters showed little concern with the rights of dark-skinned peoples on distant islands, and Bryan's campaign foundered. Toward the end, he raised the matter of economic concentration, inequality, and the power of the trusts, but amid the country's general prosperity the message was not heeded. By embracing silver again, the Democrats had driven a significant portion of the party's eastern supporters into the Republican camp, and there many of them stayed.

Again Hanna's machine raised millions for McKinley, and now it could do so from a position of such strength that when one group of Wall Street contributors offered $10,000 with a few conditions attached, Hanna could calmly reject both the conditions and the money. With the charismatic Roosevelt out on the hustings and

William Jennings Bryan as the proponent of "free silver" and as the adversary of the industrial trusts and of American imperialism in Cuba and the Philippines.
DAVID J. AND JANICE L. FRENT
POLITICAL AMERICANA COLLECTION.

"Don't any of you realize that there's only one life between this madman and the Presidency?"

QUESTION SCREAMED AT THE 1900 REPUBLICAN CONVENTION BY MARK HANNA, MCKINLEY'S CAMPAIGN MANAGER, REFERRING TO VICE-PRESIDENTIAL NOMINEE—AND "MADMAN"— THEODORE ROOSEVELT

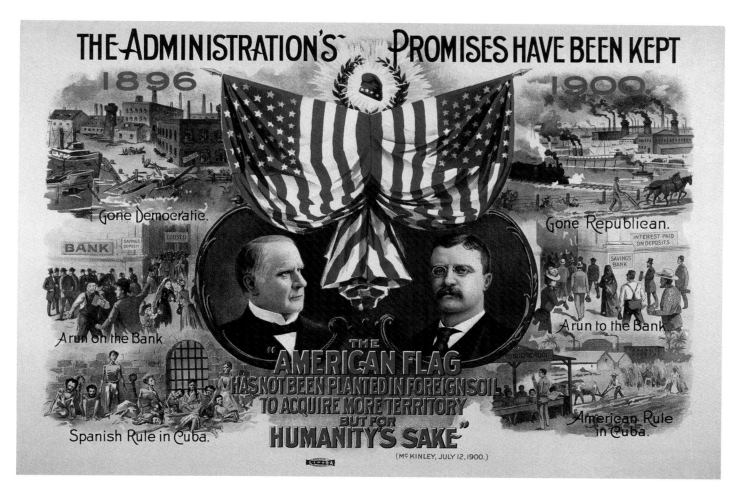

THE ADMINISTRATION'S PROMISES HAVE BEEN KEPT

1896

1900

Gone Democratic.

BANK

A run on the Bank

Gone Republican.

A run to the Bank

Spanish Rule in Cuba.

American Rule in Cuba.

THE AMERICAN FLAG HAS NOT BEEN PLANTED IN FOREIGN SOIL TO ACQUIRE MORE TERRITORY BUT FOR HUMANITY'S SAKE

(McKINLEY, JULY 12, 1900.)

the regal McKinley presiding over prosperity and an easy military victory, the Republicans coasted in November. The President took 292 electoral votes to Bryan's 155. McKinley won even Nebraska, Bryan's home state.

Six months into his second term, McKinley was shot by a deranged anarchist at a reception in Buffalo. He died on September 14, and Theodore Roosevelt was sworn in as President. Mark Hanna, now a U.S. senator, grieved for his slain friend and fumed over the result of his death: "Now look, that damned cowboy is President of the United States."

Teddy and the Bosses

ROOSEVELT v. PARKER, 1904

The assassination of McKinley in 1901 left many Americans grieving, not least the Republican bosses, who lamented that Teddy Roosevelt had become President. He had received the vice presidential nomination in part because the leadership felt he would do less harm as Vice President than as governor of New York. Now he was in a position to do plenty of harm, and that (thought the Republican leaders and their Wall Street allies) was what he proceeded to do.

Beginning in 1902, for example, Roosevelt used the Sherman Anti-Trust Act as the basis of a legal attack against the Northern Securities Company, a giant railroad concern that was backed by such important capitalists as J. P. Morgan and E. H. Harriman. Morgan went to the White House to work things out with Roosevelt: "If we have done anything wrong, send your man to my man and they can fix it up." But Roosevelt did not waver, and in 1904 the Supreme Court ordered Northern Securities to be dissolved. Other policies he championed, such as conservation and lower tariffs, also offended traditional business supporters of the Republican Party.

Another White House visitor created further political problems for the President. Only a month after he took office, Teddy Roosevelt invited Booker T. Washington to dinner at the Executive Mansion. Washington was the head of a black school in Tuskegee, Alabama, and the most prominent black citizen of the United States. In 1895, he had enunciated his accommodationist views of race relations—essentially, that blacks should stop fighting segregation and Jim Crow directly and work instead for their own advancement, arguing that once economic parity with whites was achieved other obstacles would disappear. This so-called Atlanta Compromise went well with the Supreme Court victory won by segregation in the case of *Plessy v. Ferguson* in 1896, which ruled that blacks could be served by "separate but equal" public facilities. Washington's cautious position was soon attacked by more militant black leaders, notably W.E.B. DuBois. But for many whites it was simply unacceptable that the President should share his dinner table with a black man. "No Southern woman with proper self-respect," wrote a Memphis editorialist, "would now accept an invitation to the White House."

It may seem surprising that Theodore Roosevelt, who in his foreign policy showed little sensitivity to the desires of nonwhite peoples, would risk his political standing at home to advance black rights. But it should be noted that one of the subjects of the dinner conversation was political patronage in the South. Roosevelt saw courting black voters as a way of building the Republicans' power base in the region and saw his influential guest as a good person with whom to pursue this goal. By the time Roosevelt had consolidated his control of the party, he had replaced about two thirds of the federal appointees in the South with his own men. A few of them were black, but when he chose a black man to fill a customs job in Charleston, S.C., the home of Fort Sumter, the Senate refused to approve the nomination. Roosevelt kept his man in the post by a series of interim appointments not subject to the advice and consent of the Senate.

Roosevelt's activist style was a radical departure from the sort of presidential leadership Americans had known for a generation. As the youngest President in American history—he became President at the age of forty-two—and with his colorful past as a writer and Rough Rider, Roosevelt was a much more engaging figure than the cautious McKinley had been. In contrast to his predecessors, Roosevelt had an expansive view of executive powers, founded in part on his imperialist foreign policy. He supported American suppression of the pro-independence movement in the Philippines led by Emilio Aguinaldo, in spite of the well-documented atrocities committed by American troops against the Filipinos. When Colombia refused to agree to his terms for land for an American Panama Canal project, Roosevelt backed a revolution that resulted in the creation of the independent nation of Panama, which promptly gave the United States the terms it wanted.

The President's dynamism often made his policies appear more radical than they in fact were, and he was an astute politician who understood that his popularity, although real, would fade if he moved too far in front of public opinion or too far away from the other leaders of the Republican Party. His trust-busting, for example, was directed against only the most outrageous examples of concentrated economic power, and his aim was to regulate the trusts, not destroy them. Once he was President, his imperial tendencies were tempered by his realization of the limits of American strength and the need of the country to fit into a global balance of power. In politics, too, he reached understandings

1904

PRESIDENTIAL CANDIDATE (STATE) VICE-PRESIDENTIAL CANDIDATE (STATE)	PARTY	ELECTORAL VOTES	APPROX. % OF POPULAR VOTE
Theodore Roosevelt (N.Y.) Charles W. Fairbanks (Ind.)	Republican	336	56%
Alton B. Parker (N.Y.) Henry G. Davis (W.Va.)	Democratic	140	38%

Among the minor-party candidates was Eugene V. Debs (Socialist), who received approximately 3 percent of the popular vote.

with his rivals and recognized that the judicious sharing of patronage was a wiser course than the unilateral exercise of appointive authority.

There were some Republicans who could not bear Roosevelt, and they looked to Ohio's Senator Mark Hanna as their best hope to challenge the President in 1904. Hanna's close relationship to the slain McKinley and his equally close ties to Wall Street promised emotional and economic support for Hanna's challenge. But in February 1904, Hanna died of typhoid fever, and at the Republican National Convention, held in Chicago, Roosevelt was unanimously nominated on the first ballot. But Republican leaders hostile to Teddy managed the nomination of the conservative Charles W. Fairbanks of Indiana as his running mate.

For Democrats, the rallying cry for the year was "Anyone but Bryan." The Boy Orator of the Platte, no longer a boy, had led the party to defeat in two consecutive elections, and its conservative wing had had enough of western populism and prosilver policies. Democrats looked again at Grover Cleveland, who was not interested in another race, and at Arthur Pue Gorman, a Republican senator from Maryland who was fiscally conservative but whose anti-imperialist attack on the popular Panama Canal treaty ruled out his candidacy. That left the party with the uninspiring choice of Alton B. Parker, a New Yorker who served as chief judge of the state's highest court. His personal reputation was clean; he favored states' rights and opposed black rights, which made him an acceptable choice in the South; and he had handed down some decisions mildly favorable to labor, thus offering an attraction to that part of the Democratic Party. But he was dull—terribly dull.

His leading Democratic opponent was far from dull. William Randolph Hearst had used his family's silver fortune to begin building one of the great newspaper empires in America. Hearst had supported Bryan in the past,

An appropriately pugilistic image of the candidates facing off, for Roosevelt was an enthusiastic amateur boxer. Cartoon by J. H. Pughe, published in Puck, *July 20, 1904.*

COURTESY OF THE THEODORE ROOSEVELT INAUGURAL SITE FOUNDATION AND THE BUFFALO & ERIE COUNTY LIBRARY.

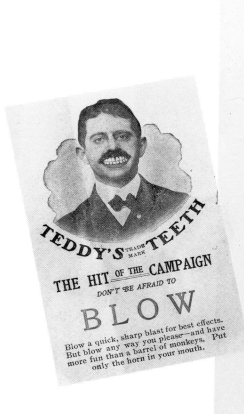

and it was now to Hearst that the Bryan forces turned at the convention, which met in St. Louis in the heat of July. But Bryan's allies were no match for the eastern conservatives who were determined to retake the party, and their man Parker easily won nomination. His running mate was Henry Gassaway Davis of West Virginia, who, at eighty, was the oldest person ever nominated to a major-party ticket. Davis owed his selection in part to his wealth and the expectation that he would contribute some of it to the campaign.

But money or no, the Democrats' campaign was practically nonexistent. Roosevelt, confident of victory, had no reason to leave the White House in search of votes. Parker was unwilling to abandon the traditional role of reluctant candidate, and only at the very end of the race did he campaign personally.

With Parker inactive, Democratic surrogates stumped for the ticket. In the last weeks before the election Bryan himself agreed to campaign for Parker, reasoning that a certain amount of party regularity might help encourage conservative Demo-

One of the most popular gimmicks of the 1904 campaign.
NATIONAL MUSEUM OF AMERICAN HISTORY, SMITHSONIAN INSTITUTION.

We favor a return to JEFFERSONIAN PRINCIPLES.

EXTRACTS from the DEMOCRATIC PLATFORM:

FOR PRESIDENT: ALTON B. PARKER.

FOR VICE PRESIDENT: HENRY G. DAVIS.

DEMOCRATIC

CANDIDATES.

Capital & Labor ought not to be enemies. The rights of Labor are certainly no less "vested," no less "sacred" & no less "inalienable" than the rights of capital.—We favor liberal appropriations for the care & improvement of the water ways of the country.— Open Door, but No Colonial Exploitation.— Ultimate Freedom for the Filipinos.—We denounce protection as a robbery of the many to enrich the few.— Gigantic Trusts a Menace to Nation.—Protection for All American Citizens abroad.— Investigation of corrupt Government departments.

COPYRIGHTED 1904 BY KURZ & ALLISON-CHICAGO.

crats to work for him if he should ever win the nomination again. It was not Bryan's finest hour—he made a point of attacking Roosevelt for his dinner with Booker T. Washington—and he probably did little to help Parker's chances. Democrats who could not follow Bryan in supporting Parker looked to minor-party candidates, such as the Socialist Eugene V. Debs, who won 400,000 votes that year.

All in all, it was an odd campaign. The Republicans were led by a progressive politician who did his best to improve his ties to the most conservative elements of his party—and secured large contributions from men such as E. H. Harriman and Henry Clay Frick. The Democratic candidate was a true conservative. The result was that in the midst of the so-called Progressive Era neither party was willing to present a platform of change. Differences over imperialist policies and practices were aired,

but voters were not deeply stirred about conditions in the Philippines or the proper status of Cuba. Prosperity, pride in America's new place in the world, and the charisma of Teddy Roosevelt proved such an overwhelming combination that the Democrats fell victim to the most decisive presidential mandate since Andrew Jackson's victory in 1832. Roosevelt won more than 57.9 percent of the popular vote, and, with Debs and other candidates drawing from the Democrats, Parker won less than 38 percent. Roosevelt, with 7.6 million votes, outpolled his Democratic rival by more than 2.5 million votes.

In his election-night enthusiasm at being elected to a term on his own, Roosevelt proclaimed that, although this was his first term in his own right, the fact that he had served the bulk of McKinley's term meant that he would not seek another term. He then proceeded to support progressive measures, prompting Henry Clay Frick to complain later, "We bought the son of a bitch and then he did not stay bought."

CHAPTER

29

The Commoner's Last Stand

TAFT v. BRYAN, 1908

During the 1904 campaign, Theodore Roosevelt had presented himself as a safe ally of the great business interests, but in his message to Congress in 1905, he offered proposals for greatly expanding the government's power to regulate business: to set railroad shipping rates, to audit corporations' internal books, and to intervene in labor disputes to protect the interests of the public. The following year, Upton Sinclair's novel *The Jungle* was published, and its grim scenes of brutal and unsanitary conditions in the Chicago stockyards prompted Roosevelt to back the Pure Food and Drug Act and the Meat Inspection Act, both of which increased government authority at the expense of private business. Roosevelt's actions were part of a widespread enthusiasm for new ideas of how government should work; the Progressive Era was in full swing. The progressives put much energy into reforming the political process, and in 1907 a bill was enacted that banned corporations from contributing to political campaigns.

Progressivism was anathema to those who, like Henry Clay Frick, felt that power was most safely lodged in the hands of men of property like himself, and many of the nation's wealthiest men were eager to see the last of Teddy Roosevelt. Fortunately for these men, Roosevelt was unwilling to renege on his commitment not to run in 1908. But in order to ensure that his reforms would not be eviscerated by his successor, T.R. did all he could to make certain that the nomination would go to his loyal lieutenant, William Howard Taft.

Taft and Roosevelt had the sort of partnership that often develops between men of widely different gifts and attributes. Roosevelt was energetic and impulsive, in love with command, and more eager to take actions than to weigh their consequences. Taft was by nature and training a judge, careful to consider all sides of a question and sensitive to the results of his decisions. Physically, too, the ponderous Taft contrasted sharply with the bantam Roosevelt. A man of Taft's temperament and integrity might easily have filled an important role in another era, but his deliberate style was painfully out of touch with the accelerating technological changes and the bubbling reformist spirit of the Progressive Era. Yet however slow Taft was at coming to decisions himself, he was an effective implementer of Roosevelt's policies, both as governor of the Philippines and, later, as secretary of war.

Given the divisions within the Republican Party, Taft seemed an effective choice. As Teddy's chosen heir, he could depend on the President's supporters, while his more cautious approach to the problems of the age made him more acceptable to the conservative, business-oriented sector of the party. Taft ran a shrewd campaign for the nomination, locking up the votes of southern Republicans and arriving at the convention in Chicago in June 1908 with all the votes he needed. But Taft's nomination did not mean that Roosevelt's partisans were firmly in charge. In fact, almost every other aspect of the meeting was controlled by the party's conservative elements, as demonstrated by the nomination of the "standpatter," or anti-progressive, James S. Sherman of New York for the vice presidency.

The Democratic nomination of Alton Parker in 1904 acknowledged that in spite of William Jennings Bryan's gifts as a public speaker and his diligence as a candidate, his two major issues—prosilver themes in 1896 and anti-imperialism in 1900—had been insufficiently popular among the voters. And although the nomination had managed to place the Democratic Party to the right of the Republicans, it had failed to draw much appreciation from the Wall Street interests the choice of Parker was intended to mollify.

Among the Democrats, leaders of real stature were so few that the best the party could do in 1908, against Taft and a divided Republican Party, was to throw Bryan into the fray one last time. Never a reluctant candidate, the man now called the "Great Commoner"—he had founded the weekly newspaper *The Commoner* in 1901 to keep his views before the public—was eager to run again. Following a world tour in 1906, he had arrived at an inflated estimate of the size and depth of his support. He had been hailed abroad as a symbol of American democracy and during his travels had learned that state conventions were putting his name forward for the nomination two years in advance of the election. Returning to the United States, Bryan was welcomed by large crowds in New York and gave a speech at Madison Square Garden on August 30, 1906, setting forth his platform for 1908. He backed popular election of U.S. senators (who were still chosen by vote of state legislatures) and informed his listeners that the income tax, "which some in our country have denounced as a socialistic attack upon

The object of this game was to get both balls at once into the circles at the center of Bryan's eyes.

NATIONAL MUSEUM OF AMERICAN HISTORY, SMITHSONIAN INSTITUTION.

1908

PRESIDENTIAL CANDIDATE (STATE) VICE-PRESIDENTIAL CANDIDATE (STATE)	PARTY	ELECTORAL VOTES	APPROX. % OF POPULAR VOTE
William Howard Taft (Ohio) James S. Sherman (N.Y.)	Republican	321	52%
William Jennings Bryan (Nebr.) John W. Kern (Ind.)	Democratic	162	43%

Again among the minor-party candidates was Eugene V. Debs (Socialist), who again received approximately 3 percent of the popular vote.

DAYTON
OHIO
FATT
MEN'S
TAFT
CLUB

"FATT" is a most appropriate anagram of "TAFT."
NATIONAL MUSEUM OF
AMERICAN HISTORY,
SMITHSONIAN INSTITUTION.

The letters B.S.A.C. on Roosevelt's shirt presumably stand for "Big Stick Athletic Club." Cartoon by Frank A. Nankivell, published in Puck, *March 4, 1908.*
COURTESY OF THE THEODORE
ROOSEVELT INAUGURAL SITE
FOUNDATION AND THE BUFFALO
& ERIE COUNTY LIBRARY.

wealth, has . . . the indorsement of the most conservative countries in the old world" and ought to be adopted in the United States. He went on to endorse government ownership of railroads, a proposal that was quickly denounced in papers and magazines as too radical for America.

But the lack of any serious challenger within the Democratic Party and the humiliating defeat of the conservative Democratic nominee in 1904 meant that such stumbles could not stop Bryan. And when the party met in Denver in July 1908, he was nominated on the first ballot. John Kern, from the perennial swing state of Indiana, was chosen to be his running mate.

Familiar faces had advanced easily to the presidential nominations of the two major parties, but the political world of 1908 was electric with new movements and ideas, as well as old ideas nearing realization. The battle for votes for women was accelerating, as was the struggle to pass legislation banning the sale of alcoholic beverages (seven states had adopted Prohibition by 1908). The two major parties faced challenges not only from prohibitionists but also from William Randolph Hearst's Independence Party and from the Socialists, led again by Eugene V. Debs. The vast concentration of wealth in the hands of the richest Americans, exemplified by titans such as J. P. Morgan and John D. Rockefeller, was a political issue employed by everyone from Debs to Roosevelt, who in 1908 spoke contemptuously of those who "regarded power as expressed only in its basest and most brutal form, that of mere money."

But progressive ideas were not the only ones around. The waves of immigration from southern and eastern Europe were increasing nativist sentiment within both major parties. Some of the opposition was cultural (they don't speak our language), some religious (they don't worship our God), and some political (they don't share our American beliefs). Nor were such feelings confined to the ignorant or the politically reactionary; some of the leading progressives shared them and worried whether immigrants from cultures where democracy was an alien concept could be assimilated into the American political tradition. In the South, lynchings were common enough to be of limited news value, and the subjugation of African Americans there and elsewhere was accepted unthinkingly by most white Americans.

William Jennings Bryan had the nomination, but he did not have much of a chance. Of the issues that had animated his earlier campaigns, silver was dead and anti-imperialism was a remote concern. Taft's ample figure filled the political center. Bryan advocated an income tax, and so did Taft. Bryan wanted direct election of senators, and Taft said this was not a partisan matter. Even traditionally Democratic papers such as *The Baltimore Sun* went for the Republican nominee.

With the center occupied, Bryan made a run to the left. He courted labor support and attacked Taft's judicial record, which was strongly probusiness. Speaking in Colorado near the end of September, he attacked the Republican Party as the "aristocratic party," and said that Roosevelt's "attempt to pick out his successor is a dangerous precedent." That it was a precedent a century old did not concern the Great Commoner.

This highly effective poster melds the facial features of Taft and Roosevelt, though the corpulent neck and body are clearly Taft's. DAVID J. AND JANICE L. FRENT POLITICAL AMERICANA COLLECTION.

William Jennings Bryan was a flamboyant and impassioned orator.

However tired Bryan's ideas were, and however unlikely he was to win, he pursued his goal with his customary assiduity, making as many as thirty speeches a day as the campaign wound to a close. Trains took him across the nation to deliver his message to crowds that were large but whose numbers included the curious as well as the committed. And although Bryan's oratory could always ignite fervor, that fervor did not necessarily last until election day.

Taft held to the dying tradition of the noncandidate running for office, making a few public statements but refusing to campaign in the vigorous fashion of Bryan. Roosevelt's efforts to aid Taft generally resulted in far more newspaper coverage than anything Taft himself did, although at one point T.R. felt compelled to advise his protégé to quit

Eugene Debs's "Red Special" train and band. Debs is standing directly under the "R" in PRESIDENTIAL, holding a child.

> "Men of ordinary physique and discretion cannot be Presidents and live, if the strain cannot be somehow relieved. We shall be obliged to always be picking our chief magistrates from among wise and prudent athletes, a small class."
>
> WOODROW WILSON, 1908, COMMENTING ON THAT YEAR'S CAMPAIGN, THE FIRST IN WHICH BOTH MAJOR CANDIDATES ACTIVELY STUMPED

playing golf during the campaign, as the rich man's sport set the wrong tone. Taft's religion was an issue for some: he was a Unitarian, a denomination seen by fundamentalist Christians as tantamount to agnosticism. Still, whatever difficulties Taft faced in the campaign were overcome by a strong revival of the economy in the fall of 1908, and Roosevelt's chosen successor won election with 321 electoral votes to Bryan's 162. Roosevelt then slipped off into an uncomfortable and brief retirement.

"The Bottom is Out of the Full Dinner Pail." A play on the McKinley slogan of 1896.
COURTESY SOTHEBY'S.

The High Tide of Progressivism

WILSON, ROOSEVELT, TAFT, DEBS, 1912

On March 3, 1912, many of the nation's leading writers met in New York City to celebrate the seventy-fifth birthday of the novelist William Dean Howells. Among those present were the historian Charles Francis Adams, the muckraker Ida M. Tarbell, and Alfred Thayer Mahan, whose works on the importance of a strong navy had profoundly influenced American foreign policy. Among those unable to attend (although they had sent letters of congratulation) were Henry James and Thomas Hardy. And lending the weight of his office and his presence to the evening was President William Howard Taft.

As was to be expected at a seventy-fifth-birthday celebration, the mood was one of culmination. This was appropriate both for Howells and for the American nation, which at this moment stood at the high tide of progressivism, with the most divisive class issues of the nineteenth century seemingly behind it (issues such as race were kept in the background as much as possible) and with the quickening pace of technological advance seeming to promise a new age of prosperity. This world was about to be shattered. Within a half-dozen years, America would become involved in a Great War in Europe, black migration to northern cities (to fill the jobs made available by wartime conditions) would transform the dialogue on race, a revolution in Russia would alter American attitudes toward socialist ideas, and even the literary world of Howells would be trying to digest new and very different kinds of writing by authors such as Ezra Pound, T. S. Eliot, and Gertrude Stein. The faith in progress that had animated the nineteenth century would be deeply undermined and, for many people, irrevocably lost because of the horrors of the First World War. But before the moment passed, American progressivism would have a last turn at center stage.

The protagonist of the year's electoral drama was Theodore Roosevelt. Roosevelt had picked Taft to succeed him and had pledged back in 1904 that his time as President would end for good with the completion of his term in office in March 1909. But a long vacation spent killing big game in Africa and elsewhere had not drained politics from his blood, and his dissatisfaction with Taft's performance as President drew him back to electoral pursuits.

As President, Taft had achieved a number of progressive goals, adding public land to the national parks and forests (more than Roosevelt had) and continuing to press for closer supervision and regulation of the great trusts. Yet his temperament was essentially conservative and he could never match his predecessor's popularity, either with the common man or with the progressive wing of the Republican Party. It was easy for Taft to draw closer to the party's conservatives, and by the time he had been President for a year, he had clearly aligned himself with them.

Since the national thirst for reform and innovation was unslaked, this was a poor place for Taft to be, and there was general expectation that there would be a challenge to the incumbent President from within his own party. Throughout 1911, Republican progressives were talking about, and even getting behind, the candidacy of Senator Robert La Follette of Wisconsin. As governor of that state from 1901 to 1906, La Follette had developed the "Wisconsin idea," that of a close link between government and the universities, in which the expertise of academic specialists (in fields like agriculture, economics, and education) was brought into the daily practice of government. The perceived successes of the Wisconsin idea had helped make La Follette a national figure (and later established a model for Franklin Roosevelt's New Deal "Brains Trust" of academic advisers), but in 1911 it was clear that Republicans in other states were not as ready as those in Wisconsin to embrace La Follette's innovations, and Taft's renomination seemed secure.

Theodore Roosevelt, however, was not out of the running. His desire to challenge Taft was increased by Taft's decision, in 1911, to attack the United States Steel trust, an offensive that singled out a deal with J. P. Morgan that Roosevelt had personally approved. (This deal had been part of Roosevelt's arrangement with Morgan to help end the financial panic of 1907.) Ambition and hurt pride helped drive Roosevelt back into electoral life, and in the last week of February 1912, he told the world, "My hat is in the ring."

One consequence of the preceding twenty years of political reform was the growth of primary elections around the country, and Roosevelt used the primaries to challenge Taft's control of

> "Sometimes I think I might as well give up as far as being a candidate is concerned. There are so many people in the country who don't like me. Without knowing much about me, they don't like me."
>
> WILLIAM HOWARD TAFT, 1912

1912

PRESIDENTIAL CANDIDATE (STATE) VICE-PRESIDENTIAL CANDIDATE (STATE)	PARTY	ELECTORAL VOTES	APPROX. % OF POPULAR VOTE
Woodrow Wilson (N.J.) Thomas R. Marshall (Ind.)	Democratic	435	42% *
Theodore Roosevelt (N.Y.) Hiram Johnson (Calif.)	Progressive	88	27%
William Howard Taft (Ohio) James S. Sherman (N.Y.)	Republican	8	23%

Again among the minor-party candidates was Eugene V. Debs (Socialist), who increased his share of the popular vote to approximately 6 percent.

*Because of the Republican-Progressive split, Wilson won with fewer popular votes than Bryan received in any of his three defeats (1896, 1900, 1908).

ABOVE: *Cartoon from the Denver* Post.
LIBRARY OF CONGRESS.

RIGHT: *"When an Irresistible Force Meets an Immovable Object," by Joseph Keppler, Jr., who continued his famous father's work at* Puck *until 1914.*
LIBRARY OF CONGRESS.

OPPOSITE: *When Roosevelt announced in February 1912, "My hat is in the ring," he transferred a term from his beloved sport of boxing to the political arena, where it has remained ever since.*
DAVID J. AND JANICE L. FRENT
POLITICAL AMERICANA COLLECTION.

the Republican Party. This was the first presidential campaign in which primary elections played a significant role as the ex-President trounced the incumbent around the country, winning contests in California, Pennsylvania, New Jersey, Maryland, and Illinois and besting Taft by two to one in Taft's home state of Ohio. In primary voting, Roosevelt won 278 delegates to 48 for Taft (La Follette won 36).

The Republican organization nevertheless remained in the hands of the party's conservatives, and they demonstrated this at the convention in Chicago that June. Taft already had strong support from Republican organizations in the South and the backing of many state party leaders. The credentials of more than 250 of the 1,078 delegates were challenged, but the Taft forces were in control, and the convention awarded 235 of the disputed seats to Taft. Roosevelt branded this "naked robbery" and took the unusual step of going to Chicago himself to lead the fight. But the Republicans, led by the conservatives, nominated Taft for President and James Sherman for Vice President.

A prudent party man would have folded his hand and backed the nominee, consoling himself with the knowledge that Taft would serve only one more term and that four years hence the nomination might be his. Prudence was never Roosevelt's forte, though, and, announcing his intention to break with the party, he called for a meeting of progressives in Chicago in August to put forward a presidential candidate.

The division in the Republican ranks that broke wide open at the convention had long been apparent, and this meant that Democrats saw an opportunity to return to the White House for the first time since Cleveland's second term. William Jennings Bryan, painful as it must have been for him, realized that he could not be the party's nominee for a fourth time. Champ Clark, the Missouri Democrat who had been chosen Speaker of the House after the Democrats had won control of the House in the 1910 elections, sought the nomination. He had the support of the publisher William Randolph Hearst and widespread backing from Bryanites. Another leader in the House, Oscar Underwood of Alabama, also sought the nomination, as did the conservative Democratic governor of Ohio, Judson Harmon.

A fourth contender was New Jersey's Woodrow Wilson. Born in Virginia and educated at Princeton and then at the University of Virginia Law School, Wilson had had a brief and unsuccessful career as a lawyer in Georgia before attending graduate school at Johns Hopkins. His thesis, published under the title *Congressional Government,* was a brilliant analysis of the way American government works; it quickly became influential and, with his other writings, would have made his reputation even if he had not gone on to other accomplishments. In 1902, he was named president of Princeton University, where he reformed the curriculum and turned the university into a major innovator in higher education. But his attempts to change the undergraduate eating clubs were foiled, and in that fight and others he lost at Princeton, Wilson demonstrated what his biographer Arthur S. Link described as an "unfailing habit of converting differences over issues into bitter personal quarrels." This habit would have significant consequences for the course of the century.

In 1910, Wilson was advanced as a candidate for governor of New Jersey by his friend George Harvey of Harper Brothers publishers—later to be the sponsor of the dinner for Howells—and won the nomination and the election easily. In the frothy political spirit of the time, Wilson was a comparative conservative, and his candidacy was seen by Harvey and others as a way of preventing the state from falling into the hands of reformers. After his victory, however, Wilson, although still conservative in many ways, showed himself unwilling to subordinate himself to the state Democratic machine, and he soon won a reputation as a liberal. By the spring of 1911, his allies, Harvey among them, were plotting a campaign for the White House.

As the Democratic convention opened in Baltimore in late June, Champ Clark led Wilson by nearly 200 delegates. For the first nine ballots the vote totals remained fairly constant, but on the tenth ballot Tammany Hall switched the New York delegation from Harmon to Clark, thus giving Clark a majority of the delegates. Tammany (and almost everyone else) expected this to end the contest. It had become customary to close ranks behind a candidate once he had obtained a majority vote, even though the Democratic rules demanded a two-thirds majority. Wilson, mindful of this custom, instructed his manager to release his delegates. But before the manager could act, it became clear that Tammany's move was not triggering a mass movement of votes to Clark, and the delegates were never released.

The Progressive Party convention, Chicago, August 6, 1912.

Four ballots later, Bryan announced that he was switching his support from Clark to Wilson; still, neither candidate could win two thirds of the delegates. Wilson's men courted powerful state party leaders in Illinois and Indiana, and when, finally, on the forty-sixth ballot, Oscar Underwood went over to Wilson, the scholar-politician was nominated.

The Democrats left Baltimore exhausted but confident. Their confidence increased when Roosevelt's followers met in Chicago in August. Most of the Republican leaders who had supported T.R. in the race against Taft had stayed with the party after the convention (the major exception being Hiram Johnson, the governor of California). Roosevelt arrived for the Progressive Party gathering feeling, he told reporters, like a "bull moose," and when he was duly chosen as the Progressive candidate for President and Hiram Johnson was picked to run with him, their ticket was called the Bull Moose Party.

If the Democrats had nominated a pallid conservative like 1904's Alton Parker, the Bull Moosers might have had a good chance, given Roosevelt's personal popularity and the widespread appetite for continuing political and economic reform. But Wilson had established himself as a reformer, too, and he proved to be an effective and eloquent campaigner. He was no match for Bryan as an orator, and he failed to generate the sort of audience enthusiasm Roosevelt could call forth, but he did speak engagingly and managed to convey his intelligence without seeming to condescend. And his speeches read well in the newspapers. Taft was scarcely a presence in the campaign at all, humbly accepting the nomination and then disappearing. Roosevelt's defeat would be enough to satisfy him; he had no expectation of victory. "I think I might as well give up as far as being a candidate is concerned," he said as early as July. "There are so many people in the country who don't like me."

The power of Wilson's and Roosevelt's personalities sometimes obscures the fact that they were conducting an important debate on the future of the American economy and, therefore, on the proper shape of American society. In opposition to Roosevelt's statist New Nationalism, Wilson offered a New Freedom. Whereas Roosevelt accepted that big business was here to stay, Wilson (much influenced by the legal theorist Louis D. Brandeis) wanted to rein in bigness and felt that unfettered competition, not government regulation, was the right prescription. Even Taft's platform contained progressive elements (a ban on child labor, for

Theodore Roosevelt, the "Bull Moose" candidate, campaigning in 1912.
LIBRARY OF CONGRESS.

example). And the fourth candidate in the race was the Socialist Eugene V. Debs. It was the most left-leaning presidential contest in American history.

The final month of the race brought additional drama. In Milwaukee on October 14, Roosevelt was shot by a lunatic. T.R.'s eyeglass case slowed the bullet, and it is typical of the man that, bleeding copiously, he insisted on delivering his speech before seeking medical attention. The other candidates suspended campaigning

Woodrow Wilson on the campaign trail in 1912.
LIBRARY OF CONGRESS.

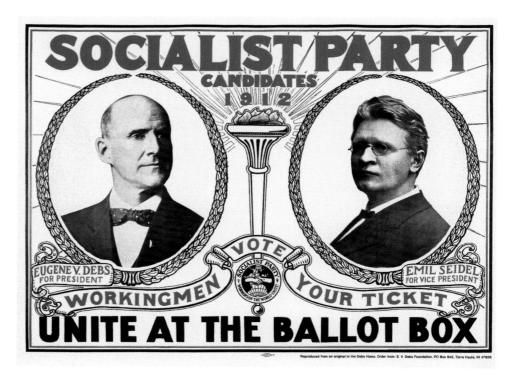

"Whether I win or lose is not the important thing. But I am in this fight to perform a great public duty—the duty of keeping Theodore Roosevelt out of the White House."

WILLIAM HOWARD TAFT, 1912

while the ex-President recovered. Then, shortly before election day, James Sherman, Taft's running mate, died, and the Republicans replaced him on the ticket with Nicholas Murray Butler, the president of Columbia University.

By October, Wilson's victory seemed inevitable, and the Electoral College results were clear-cut. He took 435 electoral votes, while Roosevelt won 88 and Taft just 8. In the popular vote, Wilson won 6.3 million votes to Roosevelt's 4.1 million, Taft's 3.5 million, and an impressive 900,000 for Debs. For the first time since the birth of the Republican Party in the 1850s, a third-party candidate had outpolled a major-party nominee. Some Progressives had hopes that their party would win next time. But the circumstances of American politics, like the genteel world of William Dean Howells's seventy-fifth-birthday party, were about to change dramatically.

"He Kept Us Out of War"

WILSON v. HUGHES, 1916

During the 1912 election there had been much discussion concerning the differences between Roosevelt's New Nationalism and Wilson's New Freedom. Taft's backers had made a case for a more conservative approach to the nation's problems, and Debs had analyzed America's challenges from a socialist perspective. But in all those discussions of 1912 little attention had been paid to the world beyond America's borders. With victory in the Spanish-American War the United States had acquired a colonial empire from Spain, and some Americans took pride in the fact that their nation now cast a global shadow, but few (even in government) gave much thought to the consequences of this new identity or the possible entanglements that might follow.

The advance of science and the rise of the expert as an adjunct to government seemed to promise a more rational age, one in which international disputes could be resolved through arbitration rather than war. Roosevelt had made a reputation as a peacemaker, brokering the end of the Russo-Japanese War (and winning the Nobel Peace Prize in the process). Although the American experience in the Philippines had been bloodier than anticipated when thousands of Filipinos joined Aguinaldo's revolt against the substitution of American colonial rule for the Spanish variety, to many in Washington that merely proved that the Filipinos were not yet ready for self-government. It seemed evident that the great powers of Europe were by now above resolving their disputes through war. Nevertheless, in the summer of 1914 Balkan conflicts led to the outbreak of what came to be called the Great War, and soon Americans were reading of bloody battles and then trench warfare on several European fronts.

For Woodrow Wilson, the turn to international concerns was unexpected, and he was ill prepared for such a challenge. An expert in the internal workings of American government, he had shown little interest in or familiarity with foreign affairs and had given little thought to the appointment of American ambassadors, using the posts in the traditional way as rewards for loyal service to the party. (His choice for ambassador to Germany was, according to Wilson himself, an "ass" and an "idiot.") He had picked William Jennings Bryan as secretary of state in order to placate the Great Commoner and his followers, but Bryan's approach to diplomacy was even more moralistic and naive than Wilson's, and, in any case, Wilson conducted his own foreign policy, scarcely consulting either Bryan or the more experienced diplomats at the State Department.

In domestic affairs, Wilson had been fairly successful, passing major legislation in his first two years in office. The Federal Reserve Act at last provided a national banking system, and the Clayton Anti-Trust Act and the establishment of the Federal Trade Commission increased federal supervision of the economy. Two constitutional amendments ratified in 1913 went far toward altering American politics: the Sixteenth Amendment allowed the federal government to collect an income tax (set at 1 percent of incomes over $4,000 a year and a further 1 percent for incomes over $20,000, progressing to a maximum of 6 percent); the Seventeenth Amendment made the election of U.S. senators the prerogative of each state's voters rather than of its state legislature, a move that helped end the Senate's archconservatism. Wilson also lowered the tariff. But in the spring of 1914, the economy stumbled, and when war broke out in Europe it weakened again. The midterm elections that fall greatly reduced the Democratic majority in the House, and the Senate Republicans, mindful of the fact that Wilson had won only 42 percent of the popular vote in 1912, felt that if the party's rift between progressives and the Old Guard could be mended, their nominee could win easily in 1916.

Wilson, too, could count. He knew that the only states where he had won more votes than the combined totals of William Howard Taft and Theodore Roosevelt were the eleven states of the old Confederacy. Unless he could broaden his own and his party's national appeal, the Democrats would once again be marginalized as a sectional party, able to gain power in the White House only under exceptional circumstances. As 1916 got under way, he prepared to change things for himself and the party by attracting progressives to the Democratic banner.

In January he named Louis D. Brandeis to a vacancy on the Supreme Court, an act that was immediately seen as significant, both because of Brandeis's reputation as one of the leading legal thinkers of the progressive movement and because he would be the first Jew to sit on the high court. To attract midwestern farmers, Wilson supported the enactment of

1916

PRESIDENTIAL CANDIDATE (STATE) VICE-PRESIDENTIAL CANDIDATE (STATE)	PARTY	ELECTORAL VOTES	APPROX. % OF POPULAR VOTE
Woodrow Wilson (N.J.) Thomas R. Marshall (Ind.)	Democratic	277	49%
Charles Evans Hughes (N.Y.) Charles W. Fairbanks (Ind.)	Republican	254	46%

Among the minor-party candidates were Allen L. Benson (Socialist) and James F. Hanly (Prohibition).

the Federal Farm Loan Act. In July, he made his move to the left plain to all. He threw the weight of his office and his reputation behind bills to limit child labor and to provide workmen's compensation for federal employees injured on the job. In August, when negotiations between railroad owners and workers threatened to result in a national strike, Wilson jawboned both sides to try to win a compromise. And when the workers agreed to their part of the proposal but the owners did not, Wilson told the latter in a White House meeting, "I pray God to forgive you, I never can," and walked out of the meeting. He then backed the Adamson Act, which established an eight-hour day for railroad workers.

Wilson campaign trucks were a novelty on the streets of New York City.
COPYRIGHT © BETTMANN/CORBIS.

Of course, the ultimate success of Wilson's efforts would depend on the identity of the Republican nominee. Had Theodore Roosevelt once again emerged as the GOP standard-bearer, Wilson would have faced real trouble winning over Republican progressives, but by the summer of 1916 Roosevelt was on the sidelines and the Republican nominee was Charles Evans Hughes, the former New York governor and Supreme Court justice, whom Roosevelt called a "bearded iceberg." Hughes had won praise as a reforming governor of New York, and his service on the Supreme Court from 1910 until 1916 had conveniently kept him away from the party schisms that had disqualified other possible contenders. He had won nomination easily at the Republican convention in Chicago in June, and when Roosevelt announced that he would not run as the candidate of the Bull Moose (Progressive) Party and suggested the archconservative Henry Cabot Lodge in his place, the Progressive Party imploded and Hughes had the happy opportunity to face Wilson in a two-man race.

Unfortunately, Hughes needed more help than that. For one thing, he had problems defining his campaign themes. He had to satisfy his party's conservatives and attack Wilson's increasingly prolabor, pro-big-government policies, but he also had to try to appeal to the progressives. Similarly, his position on the Great War was vexed by a need to appeal to both those who wanted nothing to do with it (again, this included a number of progressives) and those who, like Teddy Roosevelt, at-

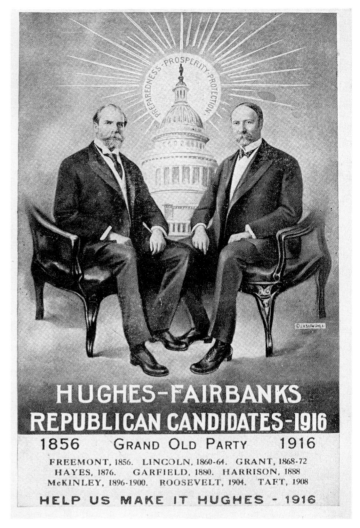

ABOVE LEFT: *The presidential election of 1916 was the last in which women were excluded from voting.*
DAVID J. AND JANICE L. FRENT POLITICAL AMERICANA COLLECTION.

ABOVE RIGHT: DAVID J. AND JANICE L. FRENT POLITICAL AMERICANA COLLECTION.

tacked Wilson for being weak in his response to German submarine attacks in the Atlantic.

The stealth attacks of submarines did not fit into the existing rules of naval warfare. In May 1915, America had become vividly aware of this new aspect of warfare with the sinking of the *Lusitania*, a British liner that was torpedoed off the Irish coast near the end of a journey from New York to Liverpool. More than a thousand people died, including 128 Americans. For a time it seemed that the sinking of the *Lusitania* would bring the United States into the war. Wilson responded to the crisis with a series of strong diplomatic notes to Germany—so strong, in fact, that Bryan resigned as secretary of state in protest. Germany felt justified because the ship had been carrying artillery shells and other war supplies, but, wishing to keep America out of the war, it moderated its submarine tactics. The issue erupted again in March 1916, when the *Sussex,* a ferry crossing the English Channel, was sunk by a German

U-boat. Although many in the German military were arguing for unrestricted submarine warfare, even if it brought the United States into the war, Kaiser Wilhelm was not yet ready to run that risk, and in May Germany agreed to search merchant vessels before sinking them. The German concession was well timed, since American feelings toward Britain were turning less friendly in the wake of the Irish rebellion that had commenced in late April. And the British, growing more confident of victory as they plotted their great July 1 offensive at the Somme, spurned American efforts to broker a negotiated settlement of the war.

If one moment crystallized America's yearning for peace, it may have come at the Democratic convention during the keynote speech of former governor Martin H. Glynn of New York. In his speech Glynn reviewed a series of past situations in which America might have been drawn into war but had resisted. As he neared the conclusion of each anecdote, the delegates began to ask, "What did we do? What did we do?" And Glynn responded, with growing emphasis, "We didn't go to war." "He kept us out of war" became one of the key points in Wilson's campaign. And in 1916 it was true.

At the same time, Wilson managed to avoid being stamped as biased. When the Irish-American leader of a German-financed organization accused him of pro-British policies, he wrote back, "I would feel deeply mortified to have you or anybody like you vote for me. Since you have access to many disloyal Americans and I

Wilson receiving official notification of his renomination, at his summer home in Long Branch, New Jersey, on September 2, 1916.
LIBRARY OF CONGRESS.

Because Hughes was ahead in early returns from eastern states, some papers rushed into print on Wednesday, the morning after Election Day, with headlines announcing a Republican victory. Not until the California vote count was completed late on Thursday was Wilson finally declared the true victor.

have not, I will ask you to convey this message to them." This reply worked beautifully to exonerate Wilson of the charge in the public mind and also to turn the attack back on Hughes, who had the open support of many German-American and Irish-American groups. (Indeed, support from these traditionally Democratic immigrant groups was part of the electoral formula the Republicans thought would bring victory in 1916.) But Hughes's attempts to satisfy these supporters while keeping on good terms with Roosevelt's more bellicose followers left him prone to embarrassing contradictions. In addition, his campaign was poorly run and at times vexed by intraparty feuds. Hughes neglected, for example, to seek out California's governor, Hiram Johnson, when both men were in the same Long Beach hotel; this "forgotten handshake" was seen as an insult by California progressives and may have cost Hughes the state. Wilson understood that his best campaign gambit was to deal effectively with the challenges he faced as President, and he did little to confront Hughes. "I am inclined," Wilson said, "to follow the course suggested by a friend of mine who says that he has always followed the rule never to murder a man who is committing suicide, and clearly this misdirected gentleman is committing suicide slowly but surely."

Hughes was able to raise more money than Wilson—the business community was upset by the Adamson Act and other intrusions of government into the workplace—but Hughes was unable to offer a coherent and attractive message. Wilson presented a progressive program linked to avoidance of war, and that was enough to take him back to the White House.

Nevertheless, the election was very close, and it was not until two days after the balloting that Wilson's victory was clear. Wilson conceded the Northeast but managed to build the electoral link between the South and the Midwest that had so often eluded Bryan. California helped secure the victory, with Wilson winning 277 electoral votes to Hughes's 254. On election night, Wilson (and much of the eastern press) was sure that Hughes had won, and the President had planned to appoint Hughes secretary of state and then resign, along with his Vice President, in order to put Hughes into office sooner and spare the nation a lame-duck period at a time of world crisis. But Wilson was left with the responsibilities of office, and the events of the next four years would prove crucial to the course of the rest of the century.

Normalcy

HARDING v. COX, 1920

During his first term, Woodrow Wilson had kept America out of war in Europe, but before his second term was a month old he called on Congress to declare war on the Central Powers, and America entered the bloody conflict. America emerged from the First World War a very different nation than it had been in 1916. Progress had been shown to have horrible new guises, a place on the world stage had proved to carry a high price, and the internal politics of the nation was now judged according to a new and more fearful set of standards.

The submarine had revealed how a technological marvel could lead to brutal slaughter and moral chaos; the machine gun, poison gas, the tank, and the airplane armed with bombs all demonstrated that the sort of ingenuity that people admired in Henry Ford and Thomas Edison could also come up with inventions that took life with new and terrible efficiency. In diplomacy, Wilsonian idealism had encountered tough European realpolitik abroad and Republican isolationism and opportunism at home. And the Russian Revolution and the establishment of a Communist Soviet Union had altered the environment in which workers' grievances and aspirations could be discussed. In the 1920 presidential race, the veteran Socialist candidate Eugene V. Debs was able once again to represent his party; this time, however, he had to campaign from a cell in a federal penitentiary in Atlanta, having been found guilty of sedition for speaking out against the war.

The war brought about major changes, some abrupt, others long brewing, such as the passage of the Eighteenth and Nineteenth Amendments (prohibition of alcoholic beverages and votes for women) in 1919 and 1920. Woman suffrage had been on the reform agenda since the Seneca Falls conference of 1848, but only now did women finally get the vote nationwide. The outcome was helped by the fact that during the war women had for the first time taken "men's jobs" in factories and elsewhere to make up for the drain of male workers to the armed forces.

Women were not alone in spotting new opportunities during wartime. African Americans in the South found that they could go north and find good jobs in the factories of Ohio and Illinois, and that they would be treated better there than in

Window decal.

DAVID J. AND JANICE L. FRENT
POLITICAL AMERICANA COLLECTION.

their home states of the old Confederacy. Although they were still confronted with prejudice and the Wilson administration did little to advance their interests, black Americans followed opportunity north in growing numbers; indeed, no change of the war years, not even woman suffrage, had a more profound effect on American politics and society over the balance of the century.

White men found new opportunities, too. During the war, farm boys torn from the soil of Nebraska or Alabama had seen the cities of the East Coast and even the marvels of France. The opportunities of the modern urban world beckoned to those whose families had struggled for generations to make ends meet. People from very different backgrounds had mingled on troopships and in trenches, and a new sort of national identity took embryonic form, which would soon be given more definite shape as movies and radio conquered the nation in the 1920s, establishing a truly national mass culture for the first time.

Assimilating all these changes was a daunting task, and when the war ended, reaction set in. It took ugly forms. In Washington, Attorney General A. Mitchell Palmer launched a series of raids against suspected subversives. Palmer's concern, particularly about the Communist menace, had crystallized on June 2, 1919, when ten bombs exploded in eight eastern cities within an hour of one another. The fact that one of these bombs had been placed at Palmer's house may have helped focus his ire. He had help in carrying out the raids from the zealous new head of the "Red squad" in the Bureau of Intelligence, J. Edgar Hoover.

1920

PRESIDENTIAL CANDIDATE (STATE) VICE-PRESIDENTIAL CANDIDATE (STATE)	PARTY	ELECTORAL VOTES	APPROX. % OF POPULAR VOTE
Warren G. Harding (Ohio) Calvin Coolidge (Mass.)	Republican	404	61%
James M. Cox (Ohio) Franklin D. Roosevelt (N.Y.)	Democratic	127	35%

Among the minor-party candidates was once again Eugene V. Debs (Socialist), who won approximately 3 percent of the popular vote.

On January 2, 1920, some six thousand aliens were arrested on suspicion of conspiring against the government of the United States. Although many were arrested without valid warrants and most were ultimately released, Palmer's raids helped established a climate of fear.

The northward migration of blacks set off violence as well. A bloody riot in East St. Louis, Illinois, in July 1917 left about fifty persons dead, most of them black. And through the spring and summer and into the fall of 1919, riots hit twenty-five towns and cities, including Chicago, when unrest claimed nearly forty lives. The death toll for the six months of rioting was more than 120. A postwar slump in the economy heightened tensions that summer. With orders for war supplies canceled and servicemen returning home, employment opportunities fell just as the number of civilian workers abruptly rose. Often, women and blacks were laid off so that jobs could be given to the returning veterans—the assumption, generally unspoken, being that providing decent jobs for blacks and women had to be understood as a temporary measure and that when things got back to normal they would return to their designated lower rungs on life's ladder.

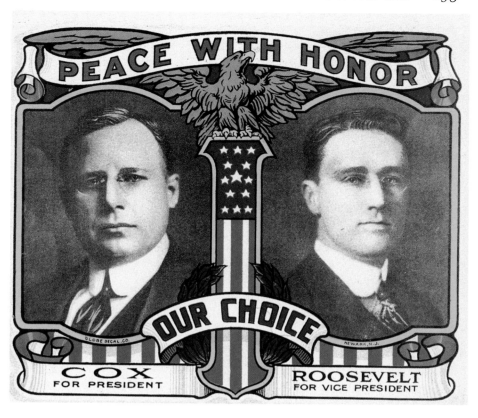

Window decal.

DAVID J. AND JANICE L. FRENT
POLITICAL AMERICANA COLLECTION.

Getting back to normal was the key idea of the immediate postwar era, and the person who managed to embody this ethos perfectly, and even to coin a new term for it ("normalcy"), was Senator Warren G. Harding of Ohio. Harding advanced to the Republican presidential nomination and then to the White House principally because of three factors: he looked the part; he was from the vote-rich swing state of Ohio, which Wilson had carried in his two presidential campaigns; and although unimpressive in office he had managed to offend almost nobody within his party. When Harding told America that he would enable the nation to return to "normalcy," people knew immediately what he was promising and believed he was the man to deliver it.

Harding's nomination at the Chicago convention had come about after a deadlock between two better-financed candidates, General Leonard Wood (a friend of Teddy Roosevelt who had the backing of the soap magnate William Cooper Procter) and Governor Frank O. Lowden of Illinois (who had married into the Pullman family, heirs to the sleeping-car fortune). The Republican barons of the Senate, who were running the convention, met in the famous "smoke-filled room" in the Black-

Eugene Debs being officially notified of his nomination, outside the federal penitentiary in Georgia where he was serving a sentence for having criticized the government's wartime antisedition policies.

DEBS COLLECTION,

INDIANA STATE UNIVERSITY.

hawk Hotel in Chicago and picked Harding. So naked was this exercise of power that when it came time to choose Harding's running mate, the convention delegates bridled. They rejected the bosses' choice of Senator Irvine L. Lenroot of Wisconsin and nominated Governor Calvin Coolidge of Massachusetts, who had won national notice for his stern handling of a police strike in Boston the year before.

If Harding was the epitome of "normalcy," Wilson was all that the nation wanted to step back from. He had enlarged the federal government beyond what anyone could have imagined, had led the nation into war in Europe, and had gone to France in person to dominate the peace conference at Versailles. Wilson's idealism, his high moral tone, and his implacable sense of his own rightness on all issues had offended first the statesmen with whom he dealt in Europe and then the senators whom he had tried to bully into accepting the peace accords as written. The story of the treaty and the ratification debate is a long and convoluted one, but a key element was Wilson's intransigence. Aware of the importance of public opinion in the debate and, as always, supremely confident of his ability to persuade, Wilson embarked on a grueling tour of the United States, seeking support for the Versailles Treaty. In Pueblo, Colorado, on September 25, 1919, he collapsed, and soon afterward he suffered a stroke. Still he harbored the idea of running for a third term, and his unwillingness to make his plans clear greatly complicated the race for the Democratic nomination in 1920.

William G. McAdoo, the former secretary of the Treasury, who was also Wilson's son-in-law, was seen as the early favorite but could not run openly as long as Wilson refused to remove himself definitively from consideration. A. Mitchell Palmer felt that his crusading anticommunism should make him a public favorite, but the response to his campaign from primary voters as well as party leaders was tepid. A third candidate was James M. Cox, the governor of Ohio (the Democrats, like the GOP, saw Ohio as crucial to victory). Cox was from outside Washington and was therefore less closely associated with the perceived failings of the Wilson administration than Palmer or McAdoo. Like Harding, his greatest gift was for not offending others, and when the Democratic convention seemed deadlocked it was to Cox that the meeting finally turned, on the forty-fourth ballot. For Vice President the convention chose the assistant secretary of the navy, a young New York politician named Franklin Delano Roosevelt. He had a reputation as a mild reformer, he was from a crucial state, and he had a famous name. Few suspected that he would later prove to be a President of uncommon distinction.

The campaign of Harding and Coolidge against Cox and Roosevelt was modern in several ways. The practice of propaganda had matured during the war years as various interest groups had tried to influence American policy. Once the United States entered the war, the government had used posters, newsreels, and other methods to rally support for the war effort. Later the pioneering public relations man Edward Bernays had been hired to help prepare the nation for the return of the troops from France. For the 1920 race, the head of the Republican National Committee, Will Hays, had a 496-page *Republican Campaign Text-Book* prepared to guide party activists in helping the ticket win. He also organized a grassroots fund-

A delegation of African–American leaders with Harding on the front steps of his house in Marion, Ohio. Until the presidency of Franklin D. Roosevelt, most African Americans—both in the North and in the South—remained loyal to Lincoln's Republican Party.

In 1920, race became a prominent issue only when, one week before Election Day, hundreds of thousands of copies of an "Open Letter to the Men and Women of America" were given to the postal service for mailing to voters. The letter included a genealogical table tracing Harding's ancestry back to a "West Indian Negro of French stock" who had lived in Ohio early in the nineteenth century. The letter, signed by W. E. Chancellor, an economics professor at Wooster College in Ohio, concluded that Harding did not qualify as white.

When President Wilson was told about the letter and about the Democrats' eagerness to play it up, he responded that he would never give his consent to such a scheme. "We cannot go into a man's genealogy," he stated. "We must base our campaigns on principles, not on backstairs gossip. That is not only right, but good politics." Wilson ordered the postal service not to deliver any copies of the Open Letter.

Harding's wife and Republican leaders advised the candidate not to dignify the Open Letter with a public rebuttal. Nevertheless, the party supplied the press with an "official" genealogy and averred that the Hardings were "a blue–eyed stock from New England and Pennsylvania, the finest pioneer blood, Anglo-Saxon, German, Scotch-Irish, and Dutch."

Despite all efforts to suppress the Open Letter, rumors about its charges spread, though they seem to have given rise to more curiosity and amusement than outrage. When a reporter for the Cincinnati Inquirer asked Harding bluntly whether he had any "Negro blood," the candidate cavalierly replied, "How do I know? One of my ancestors may have jumped the fence."

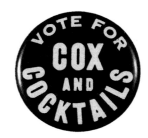

To many voters one of the most appealing planks in Cox's platform was his promise to repeal the Prohibition Amendment, which was ratified in January 1919 and went into effect in January 1920. Buttons with pictures of both Cox and Roosevelt are the rarest of all campaign buttons.

DAVID J. AND JANICE L. FRENT

POLITICAL AMERICANA COLLECTION.

raising campaign that did little to raise funds but did help deflect charges that the Republicans were using their larger war chest to buy the election.

Campaign finance was one of Cox's chief issues. He accused the Republicans of having shaken down their rich backers for first $15 million, then $30 million. Harding responded by calling the accusations "ridiculous," and there were enough problems for the Democrats in this realm (coerced donations from holders of federal appointments, money from liquor interests eager to undercut or overturn Prohibition) that the issue failed to catch fire. In the end, the Republicans spent about three times as much as their opponents.

Little of the Republican budget was spent on travel for Harding. Apart from a few carefully managed events around the country, Harding emulated McKinley and conducted his race from the front porch of his home in Marion, Ohio. Harding was a former newspaperman (as was Cox) and knew how to put reporters at ease. Jovial and courteous, he knew how to make interesting copy without committing actual news.

Cox, too, was comfortable around reporters, but Franklin Roosevelt was less adept, and from time to time he allowed his ego to overcome his judgment. He bragged about having written the Haitian Constitution ("I think it is a pretty good constitution," he said complacently) and then retreated when Harding attacked this example of American abuse of power. Cox might have done better had he distanced himself from Wilson and his policies, but the Democrats had chosen to make the election a referendum on the Versailles Treaty and the League of Nations, as Wilson wanted it to be. The problem was that this was not the issue to win on. Although the Republicans were split on it, Harding was able to say little enough on the subject to keep most of the party faithful on his side, and the nation, sick of the war and its aftermath, fearful of further change in a more dangerous world, and eager to enjoy the new consumer goods pouring forth from American industry, retreated into the comfortable arms of Harding and the Republicans.

The victory Harding won on November 2 (his fifty-fifth birthday) was stupendous. He and Coolidge won 16 million votes, while Cox and FDR got just 9 million. The House and Senate went Republican by large majorities, and even New York City abandoned the Democrats. A new America had emerged out of the war, but now the nation wanted to retreat to the comfortable world of prewar life. Harding held out the promise of a future in tune with the past, and in 1920 that seemed sufficient.

CHAPTER 33

Democrats Hot, Coolidge Cool

COOLIDGE, DAVIS, LA FOLLETTE, 1924

The dominant image of the 1920s has long been of an extravagant American bacchanal ending in well-deserved retribution in the form of the Great Depression. And with this perception comes a view of the politics of the era as having been foolishly, even crassly indifferent to the perils of the time. When it came to the election of 1924, voters appeared more interested in six-day bicycle races, flagpole sitters, and dance marathons than in the varying merits of the contenders for the White House.

To be fair to the voters, it was no wonder they wanted to enjoy themselves after the previous few decades of intense political and social strife—from the populist protest in 1892 and the depression that had begun the following year, through the Spanish-American War and the birth of a new imperial United States, to the assassination of McKinley, the strenuous presidency of Teddy Roosevelt, and on into Wilsonian moral suasion and the First World War. For those whose attention wandered, there was always the chance to hear William Jennings Bryan speak (and usually a chance that he was running for President). The return of peace meant rising prosperity and with it the spread of airplanes and automobiles, movies and radio, and a certain jubilee spirit was inevitable.

In politics, there was a retreat from the stern moral attitudes of Wilson and Bryan, and America's imperial ambitions were curbed somewhat by the isolationist spirit that had killed any hope of America's participating in the League of Nations. Linked to isolationism was a growing unwillingness to share American prosperity with those from overseas. Asian immigration had been tightly limited since the passage of the Chinese Exclusion Act in 1882, and in 1924 a new law reduced all immigration to a trickle. The law was designed to exclude those more recent immigrants—Russian Jews and Italian Catholics in particular—who were thought to be ill suited to partake of the blessings of American society. For some Americans, even strict immigration restrictions were insufficient, and the early 1920s saw a revived Ku Klux Klan reach its greatest popularity and influence ever.

The Klan used the new marketing techniques of the business world to build its membership. Klan officers called Kleagles were offered four dollars out of the ten-dollar enrollment fee required of each new member. With such sales incentives, the Klan grew exponentially, reaching a high in the mid-1920s of perhaps 4 million members. (This was the same decade in which an advertising man, Bruce Barton, wrote a life of Jesus Christ that portrayed the Messiah as the best businessman the world had ever known: "He picked up twelve men from the bottom ranks of business and forged them into an organization that conquered the world.") The Klan sponsored referendums and legislation to ban parochial schools (the courts threw these out) and managed to elect members to high office or enroll incumbent officeholders. This modern incarnation of the Klan differed from the Reconstruction-era model in that its target was as much Jews and Catholics as blacks. It was strongest in states such as Indiana, Ohio, and Illinois and weakest in the Northeast. In 1924, the Klan would play a significant role in Democratic Party politics.

The Democrats knew that they faced a difficult task in 1924. The Harding administration had taken office with great confidence, buoyed by a smashing electoral mandate to return the country to the safe harbor of Republican rule. But a recession in the early 1920s had led to major Democratic gains in the midterm elections; in addition, some in Harding's circle had been discovered to be taking advantage of high office to line their pockets, and the result was a series of scandals. Assorted members of Harding's entourage known as the Ohio Gang were driven from office or sent to jail by the revelations of corruption, and things might have gone badly for the Republicans had not Harding himself died suddenly of heart failure in San Francisco on August 2, 1923. His successor, Calvin Coolidge, had a reputation for honesty and a sour mien that seemed inconsistent with personal avarice. Untainted by the crimes of Harding's men, Coolidge had a clear path to the Republican nomination and the White House. His personal secretary, with the Marxian (Groucho) name of C. Bascom Slemp, secured enough support to nominate Coolidge on the first ballot with 1,065 votes, followed distantly by Wisconsin's old progressive voice, Robert La Follette, with 34 delegates, and California's Hiram Johnson with 10. Johnson concluded, "Money is king of politics again, as it probably has not been in our generation, and of course, it looks askance at

1924

PRESIDENTIAL CANDIDATE (STATE) VICE-PRESIDENTIAL CANDIDATE (STATE)	PARTY	ELECTORAL VOTES	APPROX. % OF POPULAR VOTE
Calvin Coolidge (Mass.) Charles G. Dawes (Ill.)	Republican	382	54%
John W. Davis (W.Va.) Charles W. Bryan (Nebr.)	Democratic	136	29%
Robert M. LaFollette (Wis.) Burton K. Wheeler (Mont.)	Progressive	13	17%

me." The convention, held in Cleveland the second week in June, turned to Charles G. Dawes of Illinois to run with Coolidge.

In contrast to the ordered progress of the Republicans, the Democrats quarreled their way through the primaries and met in New York in a convention that would become a benchmark of political futility. Convening at Madison Square Garden on June 24, the weary delegates did not finish their business until July 9, taking a record 103 ballots to choose a presidential nominee. And it was their bad luck that these inept proceedings were brought vividly before the public by means of a new consumer delight, radio.

One of the principal contenders for the nomination was William McAdoo, the former Treasury secretary who had married the boss's (Wilson's) daughter and had wanted the nomination in 1920. Although he was not a noted bigot, McAdoo drew support from a number of voting blocs that were sympathetic to, if not actually in league with, the Klan. This issue might have remained dormant if his principal opponent had not been Alfred E. Smith, the governor of New York and a Roman Catholic. The Happy Warrior (as Franklin D. Roosevelt dubbed him) had served with distinction as governor, marrying political instincts honed on New York City's

A cardboard placard to remind voters of the worst scandal of Harding's administration.

DAVID J. AND JANICE L. FRENT
POLITICAL AMERICANA COLLECTION.

"How Happy I Could Be With Either . . ." Senator Robert M. La Follette of Wisconsin, the Progressive Party's candidate, encouraged both major parties to woo him by adding progressive planks to their platforms. Cartoon by C. K. Berryman.

SWANN COLLECTION OF
CARICATURE AND CARTOON,
LIBRARY OF CONGRESS.

The Candidates and the Klan

A vote for Coolidge is a vote for the Klan.

A vote for Davis is a vote for the Klan.

A vote for La Follette is a vote **against** the Klan, **against** invisible government, **against** mob rule;

And FOR **Law and Order, Representative government** and **Democracy.**

DAVID J. AND JANICE L. FRENT
POLITICAL AMERICANA COLLECTION.

streets with a reforming zeal that dated back to his role in investigating the tragic Triangle Shirtwaist Factory fire of 1911, in which 146 workers, nearly all women, had died as the result of the owners' disregard for safety regulations.

Because the Klan was at the height of its influence, because the Democratic Party's electoral base was composed largely of white southerners, because there was a Catholic in the race, and because many in the party were reluctant to denounce the Klan, the struggle for the nomination was bitter. The fact that the convention was held in Al Smith's hometown, which the Klan called Jew York, simply raised tempers higher. McAdoo came to the convention with a lead in delegates, although his chances had been undercut earlier in the year, when it emerged that he had professional ties to one of the leading figures in the Harding-era scandals, an oil magnate named Edward Doheny. In spite of the urgings of many party leaders to withdraw, McAdoo stayed in. Smith's candidacy, which started mainly as a way to raise his profile for future elections, began to take on the feeling of a moral crusade when the Klan made his Catholicism a central issue.

The first week of the convention was taken up by the creation of a platform and the struggle over whether to denounce the Klan explicitly. The meeting resolved not to mention the Klan by name, some delegates swayed, perhaps, by William Jennings Bryan's view that such a mention would only increase the Klan's power, while others (including many McAdoo delegates) were opposed to censuring the Klan because they supported (or even belonged to) the group. The same split, largely between the Democratic Party's traditional southern and rural base and its rising strength in the industrial cities, marked the ensuing attempt to agree on a nominee.

The strategies of the individual candidates played a role, too. Smith's managers, recognizing that McAdoo would have a large lead in the early balloting, directed some Smith supporters to vote for McAdoo, so that their votes could later be switched to Smith, creating the impression that momentum was with the New Yorker. But McAdoo managed to stay in the lead ballot after ballot. The Democrats held fast to their rule that required a two-thirds majority of the delegates for nomination, and in 1924 that meant 729 votes. The closest McAdoo came was 528 delegates, on the seventieth ballot. Repeated attempts were made to cut some sort of deal to end the embarrassing agony at Madison Square Garden, but each side felt it had too much to lose. This was a battle between the past and the future of the Democratic Party, between its rural Jeffersonian roots and its urban, multiethnic future. Neither side was ready to concede. Finally, after the ninety-ninth ballot, with Smith's total drawing even with McAdoo's, both men agreed to stand aside. Then the convention turned to another kind of Democrat, John W. Davis, a Wall Street lawyer (he had represented J. P. Morgan's bank) who was a throwback to the sort of conservative exemplified by Grover Cleveland. The party balanced the ticket by choosing a fairly radical running mate, Nebraska's Charles W. Bryan, brother of the Great Commoner.

The remnants of the Bull Moose Party, along with labor groups and socialists, met in Cleveland in July to put Robert La Follette, the Wisconsin senator, forward for President. "Fighting Bob" had opposed America's entry into the war and then voted against membership in the League of Nations; he advocated public ownership of railroads and called for curbs on the power of the Supreme Court by allowing Congress to reverse a court decision by repassing any law that the Court had overturned, and by limiting justices to a maximum term of ten years. La Follette was joined on the ticket by Senator Burton Wheeler, a Montana Democrat who had been a leading investigator of the Harding scandals. "When the Democratic Party

When Coolidge ventured out on the campaign trail, his discomfort in the role was painfully evident. Here he was being made a chief of the Sioux tribe.
LIBRARY OF CONGRESS.

"Coolidge's Whirlwind Campaign."
Coolidge was the last major-party candi-
date to do very little stumping. Cartoon by
Rollin Kirby, who was awarded a Pulitzer
Prize for his graphic commentary on the
1924 campaign.
LIBRARY OF CONGRESS.

goes to Wall Street for a candidate," Wheeler explained, "I must re-
fuse to go with it."

The Progressive ticket had many disadvantages. La Follette was
aged and unable to campaign much (he died the following year).
Opposition to the war was unpopular with many voters. There
were difficulties getting the candidates onto the ballot in some
states. And the campaign had little money. Meanwhile, the Republicans had raised more than $4 million, and as the economy im-
proved during the summer and fall they were increasingly sure of
victory. Coolidge was able to use his reputation for being close-
mouthed to avoid taking stands on issues he wanted to avoid, and
he tried to instruct his running mate in that art. Advising Dawes
early in August on how to draft his acceptance speech, Coolidge
wrote, "If you keep as much as you can to an expression of general
principles, rather than attempting to go into particular details of
legislation, you will save yourself from a great deal of annoying criticism." He added a campaign tip: "P.S. Whenever you go anywhere,
take Mrs. Dawes along."

Since La Follette was nominally a Republican senator, it was
logical that the GOP had the most to fear from his candidacy. But
the Republicans did a brilliant job of portraying him as danger-
ously radical and used his Supreme Court proposals as a way to entice conservative
Democrats into the Republican camp and thus prevent the election from going to
the House of Representatives, where in return for supporting one of the two major-
party candidates La Follette might cut a deal to win his reforms. Alternatively, Republicans warned that a coalition of Democrats and Republican Progressives in the
House might choose Charles W. Bryan for Vice President, and, if the House failed
to agree on a President, Bryan might become the nation's chief executive by de-
fault.

In the event, the nation voted to "Keep Cool with Coolidge," as the party's slo-
ganeers had asked. The incumbent President won 54 percent of the popular vote
and 382 electoral votes to 136 for Davis (whose only success was in the South) and
13 for La Follette (who carried only his home state of Wisconsin). La Follette, however, won 17 percent of the popular vote, a tribute to his own reputation and a sign
that a significant portion of the electorate was dissatisfied with the party status quo.
When the bacchanal finally ended, these voters would at last find a home in
Franklin Roosevelt's New Deal. But first the man Roosevelt called the Happy Warrior would have his chance at the presidency.

CHAPTER

34

The Engineer and the Pol

HOOVER v. SMITH, 1928

So thoroughly was Herbert Hoover's reputation destroyed by the Crash of 1929 and the ensuing Great Depression that it is hard for modern readers to recapture the sense of Hoover as one of the world's great men—a sense that was widespread at the end of the First World War and into the 1920s. John Maynard Keynes judged that Hoover was the only person to come out of the Versailles Treaty process with an enhanced reputation, and praised his air of "reality, knowledge, magnanimity, and disinterestedness." Hoover's accomplishments as a mining engineer, his work to bring relief to war-torn Europe, and then his performance as secretary of commerce under Harding and Coolidge had made him at once a leading humanitarian and the virtual embodiment of the corporate prosperity of the Roaring Twenties.

As a businessman and later as commerce secretary, Hoover focused on bringing greater reason and order to economic processes while retaining private control and avoiding government interference at all costs. He cherished individual initiative (his book *American Individualism* was published in 1922). He worked to build American exports by encouraging the formation of trade associations in the United States to pool information and coordinate strategies for penetrating foreign markets.

In a decade of increasingly conservative Republicanism, when the Progressive Era seemed far away, Hoover was in many ways a vestige of progressivism, sharing the faith in experts and the sense of public duty that characterized that movement but lacking the progressives' faith in government as the ideal agent of change in American society. Hoover's strength lay in the middle of the political spectrum, and he was not a favorite of many of the other Republican powers, either in the Senate or in the state party organizations. These men (notwithstanding woman suffrage, they were all still men) would have much preferred to see Calvin Coolidge seek reelection. But on August 2, 1927, Coolidge, on vacation in South Dakota, handed out to reporters slips of paper on which was written, "I do not choose to run for President in nineteen twenty-eight." Hoover moved quickly into the gap, and his reputation was such that the nomination soon seemed inevitably his.

There was something inevitable about the Democratic choice as well. Alfred E. Smith had come close to winning the nomination in 1924, and the party was determined to avoid the sort of agonized choice that had kept that year's convention in session for weeks and had made the Democrats seem like amateurs hopelessly unequal to the task of defeating the Republicans. It was victory the Democrats wanted. They knew that they could not win without carrying New York's 45 electoral votes, and they could not hope to carry New York if they again denied the nomination to Smith, the state's governor.

Smith had been elected governor four times, and his reforms of state government had made New York a model. He was among the first American politicians to appoint women to significant government posts. He reformed treatment of the mentally ill, increased the state's commitment to protecting the welfare of children, and created a state park system. Other politicians had, of course, envisioned the sort of changes Smith was making, but Smith had a unique ability to work effectively with both principled reformers and powerful party bosses. This gift was certainly in part a legacy of his upbringing on Manhattan's Lower East Side. Smith had had to leave school when he was thirteen to help support his family, and he regretted that his only degree was "FFM," for Fulton Fish Market, where he had worked for four years in his late teens. He had also worked as a newsboy and as a laborer, and when he was twenty-one he had gotten his first job in politics, serving jury notices. Smith's facility with people smoothed his rise in the Democratic organization, and once elected to the state assembly he worked long hours struggling to master the intricacies of the legislative process. Smith's hard work and intelligence paid off, winning the respect of such unlikely admirers as Charles Evans Hughes and William Allen White, the Kansas editor, who said that nobody had "a clearer, stronger, more accurately working brain" than Al Smith.

Smith's rise from urban poverty to national prominence endowed him with as strong a faith in the American way as anyone in the nation. This faith proved to be a terrible disadvantage, because it left Smith ill prepared to discern the hate behind the anti-Catholic spew that was to stain the 1928 presidential campaign. Smith could see that there were some legitimate concerns that arose out of the Vatican's temporal powers, and he addressed those issues thoughtfully and

1928

PRESIDENTIAL CANDIDATE (STATE) VICE-PRESIDENTIAL CANDIDATE (STATE)	PARTY	ELECTORAL VOTES	APPROX. % OF POPULAR VOTE
Herbert C. Hoover (Calif.) Charles Curtis (Kans.)	Republican	444	58%
Alfred E. Smith (N.Y.) Joseph T. Robinson (Ark.)	Democratic	87	41%

Among the minor-party candidates were Norman Thomas (Socialist) and William Z. Foster (Worker's, or Communist).

honestly. But the idea that his critics might be motivated not by reasonable fears but by blind prejudice or might merely be in search of political advantage was apparently beyond the reach of his acute but generous intellect.

The notes of prejudice were being sounded around the nation not just by Klansmen but by religious leaders and respected journalists. William Allen White's admiration for Smith's brain, for example, was undercut by his fears about Smith's religion. And White's fears were both deep and influential. "The whole Puritan civilization which has built a sturdy, orderly nation is threatened by Smith," wrote White, who had previously run for governor of Kansas on an anti-Klan platform. White saw Smith as the public face of the "saloon, prostitution, and gambling."

The public face of Herbert Hoover was vastly different. His was, in fact, the first face broadcast on television, in a demonstration of the new invention in 1927. As commerce secretary, Hoover was an innovator in the use of modern communications technologies and methods. His press secretary, George Akerson, brought in advertising experts such as Bruce Barton to offer advice on how to promote Hoover's message; print, radio, and film were all marshaled, first for the cabinet member, then for the candidate.

These tools were used to project an appearance of Hoover's invincibility and authority, so as to intimidate Republican rivals and the Democratic nominee alike. When the Republican convention opened in Kansas City in June, Hoover was far in the lead and won nomination on the first ballot. Because he was not very popular in farm states (his job as commerce secretary had focused on industry, and he was, in addition, an internationalist) the GOP selected Senator Charles Curtis of Kansas as his running mate. (Hoover had been born in Iowa, and this was the first time both nominees of a major party came from west of the Mississippi.)

Smith's march to the nomination was also untroubled. In 1928 the Democrats met in Houston, so Smith's victory owed nothing to the crowds that had cheered him so enthusiastically at Madison Square Garden four years earlier. To assuage the fears of Democrats who favored Prohibition (as Smith did not), the convention selected a "dry," Senator Joseph T. Robinson of Arkansas, for Vice President. The Democrats felt that their only chance to win was with Smith, and they also recognized that they had to present themselves as responsible stewards of the nation's economic health. Fearing any proposal that might seem antibusiness, the Democrats wrote a platform that echoed Republican positions on the economy. "If a man could tell the difference between the two parties," Will Rogers quipped, "he could make a sucker out of Solomon."

There were two areas where the differences between the parties, and the candidates, were wide: Prohibition and Smith's Roman Catholicism. Many men were trying to make suckers of Solomon there. William Allen White's worries about Smith's threat to "Puritan civilization" were mild compared with those of others. Part of the problem, of course, was New York City, Smith's hometown. For many Americans, then as now, New York seemed alien, threatening, hostile. *The Denver Post* said that the city was "a cesspool into which immigrant trash has been dumped for so long

Window sticker.

that it can scarcely be considered American any more." Some of Smith's advisers urged him to work on toning down his New York accent, but Smith refused.

The issue of Prohibition was one that Smith could have dodged by merely pledging to uphold the law, but he was opposed to it, and he made his position clear even when it meant going against the plank in his party's platform that accused the Republicans of having "flagrantly disregarded" their obligation to enforce Prohibition and pledged that the Democrats would make an "honest effort" in that regard. But Smith wanted to return control over alcoholic beverages to the states, and in his speech accepting the nomination he said so. (He made this speech on August 22, for it was still the custom for nominees to accept the nomination formally weeks or even months after the conventions had made their choices, a last vestige of the tradition of the reluctant candidate.)

The larger issue, though, was Catholicism. This, of course, had been crucial to denying Smith the nomination in 1924. Now the Republicans were aided by all manner of voices that considered Smith's candidacy a threat. The Klan's popularity in the middle of the decade had been one indication of the virulence of anti-Catholic and other nativist sentiments, but there were others. Alabama had created a commission to inspect convents and determine whether Protestant girls were being held prisoner in them; a Florida governor warned that the pope was planning to invade the state and move the Vatican there. Nor were these sentiments confined to the South: a New York City minister said that Smith represented "the worst forces of Hell," and one in Oklahoma told his congregation that if they voted for Smith they would "all be damned." Others said Smith was the darling of "the northern Negroes, who lust for social equality" and of Jews, who supposedly felt that "this is the time for God's chosen people to chastise America."

Such attacks drew Smith into lengthy explanations of his views on the divide between church and state, and a campaign biography published in 1927, *Up from the City Streets*, insisted, "No responsible person can be found in the whole state of New York who can charge that the Governor has favored Catholics" (although some Catholics complained that Smith's desire to avoid seeming to favor his coreligionists had deprived worthy Catholics of government jobs). Yet Smith showed less acuity than he might have in choosing John Jacob Raskob, a Catholic, to head the Democratic National Committee. However foolish the accusations and however reasoned Smith's responses, prejudice against Catholics was widespread and deeply felt, and this prejudice seriously hurt the Democratic ticket.

Hoover, for his part, was content to campaign as little as possible, letting the booming economy and Smith's detractors do his work. He did almost nothing to criticize even the most outlandish attacks on Smith. Hoover's principal campaign speech was his acceptance of the nomination, which was broadcast nationally on the radio. This in itself was a testimony to the Republican-led prosperity—purchasing power had risen by roughly 10 percent in just five years, and one in three American homes now contained a radio. Hoover's bland delivery was not very effective, but his message was the foundation of the coming Republican victory. He recalled

the difficult adjustment from a war economy to a peacetime one and then praised the successes of his Republican predecessors. The national debt had been reduced, as had taxes, and in a progressive manner (that is, taxes on those making less than $10,000 had been lowered more than those on wealthier Americans). He apologized to those—farmers, coal miners—who were not sharing in the general prosperity and promised to do better.

Hoover's message seemed true to most voters, and Smith never managed to move the campaign off the subjects of Prohibition and Catholicism and into areas where he might do well. Hoover's victory in November was one of the easiest and

VOTE FOR HERBERT HOOVER and CHARLES CURTIS for the Prosperity of your Country and the Happiness and your home....

most complete in modern times. He won 58 percent of the popular vote and took forty of the forty-eight states, racking up 444 electoral votes to Smith's 87. Five states of the old Confederacy deserted the Democrats for Hoover. There were some promising signs for the Democrats. The urban party that Smith represented was beginning to show itself—the Democrats carried Massachusetts for the first time since the Civil War and established themselves as the majority party in the cities. But there was little consolation in this at the time. What could the Democrats do when the Republicans had presided over such unprecedented prosperity? Hoover's acceptance speech had come close to making a bold promise—that poverty might soon be abolished: "We in America today are nearer to the final triumph over poverty than ever before in the history of any land," he said. "The poorhouse is vanishing from among us. We have not yet reached the goal but given a chance to go forward with the policies of the last eight years, and we shall soon with the help of God be in sight of the day when poverty will be banished from this nation."

It was the tragedy of Hoover's life, and a turning point for the nation, when this bright promise was rendered a bitter mockery by the Crash and the dreadful depression that followed.

A New Deal for the American People

ROOSEVELT v. HOOVER, 1932

In July 1932, an insurgent army camped on the outskirts of Washington. The Bonus Army of veterans of the First World War (along with, in many cases, their wives and children) had come to the capital to ask that Congress disburse the bonuses it had voted for their military service immediately, rather than waiting until the planned payment date of 1945.

The need that drove these veterans to march on Washington grew out of the Great Depression, which by then had paralyzed the economy. America's steel plants, the vast industrial complexes that were the symbol of the industrial age, were functioning at only 12 percent of capacity. As much as a quarter of the nation's workforce was unemployed, and more than a million men were traveling the country by freight train and thumb looking for work. The veterans hoped that their thousand-dollar bonuses would give them a grubstake, a way of getting back on their feet and starting to support themselves and their families again. When the Bonus Army arrived in Washington in June, its status and its respectful demeanor won it a good deal of admiration. The superintendent of police for the District of Columbia helped the veterans maintain their camp and even used his own money to buy them food. But by the end of July, Hoover's secretary of war, Patrick Hurley, had decided that the Bonus Marchers were a sinister presence. After a police attempt to move them out resulted in gunshots (fired by panicky police, not by marchers), Hoover sent in the army. The forces, under the command of General Douglas MacArthur, included a column of infantry carrying tear gas, gas masks, and rifles with fixed bayonets, four cavalry troops, and six tanks. One infant died in the gas attack, which also set the encampment on fire, and a seven-year-old boy was bayoneted in the leg when he returned to his tent to retrieve a pet rabbit. Although the administration later claimed that it was the veterans who bore all responsibility for the violence and the burning of the camp, photos and newsreels showed that the army had attacked aggressively.

The inept—indeed, brutal—handling of the incident, as well as the poverty that had driven the marchers to travel to Washington, illustrates how far Hoover had fallen from the pinnacle of his easy victory in 1928. He had raised hopes that poverty might soon disappear from America, and now he was presiding over the greatest economic disaster in American history and was unable to demonstrate the slightest concern for the needy. The man who had been hailed as a great humanitarian when he provided relief to war-torn Belgium fifteen years before was now giving his name to every manifestation of poverty. The homeless lived in shacks known as Hoovervilles, turned-out pants pockets (denoting poverty) were called "Hoover flags," and the jackrabbits that hoboes trapped for food were known as "Hoover hogs."

Of course, a major cataclysm such as the Great Depression was hardly the fault of one man, and to hold Hoover responsible for the collapse of the American economy would be absurd. But he and the Republicans had taken credit for the prosperity that in 1928 had seemed permanent, so it was natural that some of the blame should attach to them. Indeed, some of that blame was deserved. While the economy was thriving and the stock market exploding upward in the late twenties, few, including Hoover, had worried that production was expanding faster than the ability of the nation's workers to buy what they produced. As new inventions such as radio and the automobile transformed American life, fortunes were made, and investors were confident that a new economic world had been born. In 1928, for example, the price of a share of stock in the Radio Corporation of America (RCA) went from $85 to $420, and in the twenty months before September 1929, the market overall had nearly doubled. Then, on October 24, the stock market started to fall, and only a late-day buying spree organized by the firm of J. P. Morgan stemmed the slide. On October 29, Black Tuesday, the market crashed, and as the autumn progressed it failed to recover.

Although Hoover insisted that the basic business of the nation was "on a sound and prosperous basis," by 1930 the Depression was under way in earnest. Hoover's faith in voluntary economic cooperation and his belief in individual initiative predisposed him against any bold government moves. Businessmen should put their heads together to work things out, not be ordered around by government, he thought, and individuals should never be given direct relief, like Britain's "dole," because it would sap them of self-reliance. Hoover urged businessmen to help their workers through what he expected would be only a brief downturn and pleaded with them not to cut wages or make layoffs. For

1932

PRESIDENTIAL CANDIDATE (STATE) VICE-PRESIDENTIAL CANDIDATE (STATE)	PARTY	ELECTORAL VOTES	APPROX. % OF POPULAR VOTE
Franklin D. Roosevelt (N.Y.) John Nance Garner (Tex.)	Democratic	472	57%
Herbert C. Hoover (Calif.) Charles Curtis (Kans.)	Republican	59	40%

Again among the minor-party candidates were Norman Thomas (Socialist) and William Z. Foster (Worker's, or Communist), joined by James M. Cox, of the Jobless Party.

a time employers listened, but by 1931 layoffs and wage cuts were under way across the country. Hoover's aides, eager to please their boss, relayed every positive report they could find, and the President, increasingly isolated, believed what he was told.

The midterm election of 1930 had seen the Democrats gain control of the House and come close in the Senate, and as the 1932 election approached Democratic leaders were confident that the right nominee would easily prevail. The key was to avoid factional splits and cultural divides (particularly between the party's urban ethnic base in the North and its traditional stronghold in the South). And it turned out that the Democrat with the best chance of doing this was again a governor from New York: Franklin D. Roosevelt.

Reared in comfort on his family's Hudson Valley estate and educated at Groton and Harvard, Franklin Roosevelt decided early to follow the path of his distant cousin Theodore Roosevelt: a seat in the state legislature, service in the Navy Department, New York's governorship, and then the White House. His early national prominence as the vice presidential running mate of James M. Cox in 1920 had built upon his already famous name. Yet any hint of triumphal progress and easily earned honors that might have attended such a smooth upward ascent was eradicated when in the summer of 1921 he was stricken with polio. He nearly died, and although he lost the use of his legs as a result of his illness he worked hard to restore his health. In 1924 and again in 1928, it was he who placed Al Smith's name before the Democratic convention; it was at Smith's urging that he ran for governor (successfully) in 1928, and in 1930 he was re-elected. By 1932, however, Smith had grown apart from his former protégé—in part, perhaps, because it is hard to be satisfied with the work of one's successor in a job, in part because FDR had not treated all of Smith's old pals with the respect Smith felt they deserved. In any case, Smith entered the 1932 race, and in the Massachusetts primary he bested Roosevelt by a three-to-one margin. Other Democrats, too, had their hopes. John Nance Garner of Texas, the House Speaker, was strong in his home state and in California, where Smith's old rival William McAdoo and the newspaper tycoon William Randolph Hearst were backing him. There, too, Roosevelt was defeated in the primary. But in much of the rest of the country he fared well, in spite of the efforts of Smith's man John Jacob Raskob, who was still head of the Democratic National Committee, to foil Roosevelt's plans. Roosevelt's support-

DAVID J. AND JANICE L. FRENT
POLITICAL AMERICANA COLLECTION.

Within weeks of Roosevelt's inauguration, the Democrat–dominated Congress began the process of repealing Prohibition.
DAVID J. AND JANICE L. FRENT
POLITICAL AMERICANA COLLECTION.

ers arrived at the convention in Chicago that July with a majority of delegates but lacked the two-thirds majority called for in the party rules. He moved ahead very slightly on the second and third ballots, helped by a mighty rhetorical effort from Louisiana's Huey Long, who kept the Mississippi delegation from deserting Roosevelt's camp. On the fourth ballot, California switched to Roosevelt, and the nomination was his. John Nance Garner, who had decided to do what he could for party unity and victory, accepted the nomination for Vice President (an office he famously dismissed as not worth a "bucket of warm spit").

Then Roosevelt demonstrated the genius for the bold symbolic gesture that would make him such an effective President. Knowing that his illness was a matter of concern to voters and politicians and aware, too, that Hoover's inertness in office riled many voters, FDR decided to fly to Chicago to accept the nomination in person. Roosevelt's appearance served as proof of his determination to have the Democratic Party "break foolish tradition" in politics. Speaking to the convention, he made his pact with the electorate: "I pledge you, I pledge myself, to a new deal for the American people."

Roosevelt's ability to deliver on such a promise could then only be guessed at. His record as governor had been reformist but hardly radical, and his election statements blended traditional praise of frugal government ("I regard reduction in federal spending as one of the most important issues of this campaign") with more moving recognitions of the plight of the destitute, such as a preconvention address on the "Forgotten Man" that Al Smith called "demagogical." By this time, Roosevelt was receiving regular briefings from his Brains Trust, a set of advisers headed by three Columbia University professors: Raymond Moley, Rexford G. Tugwell, and Adolf A. Berle, Jr. Historians analyzing Roosevelt's campaign speeches have found almost every position in the New Deal prefigured, as well as many statements one would more likely expect to hear from Hoover's mouth. Roosevelt, with a large lead, could afford to be vague, just as Hoover had been four years earlier.

Radio played an even bigger role in 1932 than it had in 1928,

Early in 1932 Roosevelt was only one of more than a dozen contenders for the Democratic nomination. Cartoon by Clifford Berryman, published in the Washington Star, *March 9, 1932.*
LIBRARY OF CONGRESS.

Franklin Delano Roosevelt, on the arm of his son Elliott, arriving at the Democratic convention in Chicago, as the band struck up "Happy Days Are Here Again."
LIBRARY OF CONGRESS.

and here Roosevelt had a great advantage. The warm glow of his elegant baritone voice and the naturalness of his delivery were in marked contrast to Hoover's nasal timbre and stilted phrasing. Trailing badly, Hoover tried more active campaigning but encountered little enthusiasm and even some outright hostility. Toward the end of his term, he finally tried some innovative approaches to the problems of the Depression, but his philosophical prejudices kept him from going very far, and his tone deafness to human want convinced voters that he did not care about the homeless and starving people visible in nearly every city.

Never in the history of presidential elections has there been such a reversal of fortune as Hoover suffered between his first campaign and his second. He had won a great victory in 1928, carrying forty of the forty-eight states, but in 1932 he suffered an even greater defeat, with only six states supporting him. He got 59 electoral votes to Roosevelt's 472. Perhaps the two most surprising facts of the campaign are that, in spite of the economic crisis, minor parties did not attract many voters, and the overall level of voter participation was exactly what it had been in the fat times four years before: 56.9 percent.

REPEAL UNEMPLOYMENT!

FOR PRESIDENT
NORMAN
THOMAS

FOR VICE-PRESIDENT
JAMES H.
MAURER

VOTE SOCIALIST

NATIONAL MUSEUM OF AMERICAN HISTORY, SMITHSONIAN INSTITUTION.

Between the election and the inauguration, the country plunged into the worst period of the Depression, with a harsh winter compounding the economic ills. In February, just a couple of weeks before the inauguration, a radical bricklayer named Joseph Zangara fired five shots at FDR, missing him but killing Anton Cermak, the mayor of Chicago. On March 4, 1933, Hoover turned his burden over to Roosevelt, and on the cover of that week's *New Yorker* the artist Peter Arno drew the two men riding in the open limousine to the inauguration, Roosevelt flashing his megawatt grin, Hoover looking seasick. A New Deal—and a new era in American politics and government—had begun.

"That Man" Wins Big

ROOSEVELT v. LANDON, 1936

As Roosevelt took the oath of office on March 4, 1933, states across the nation were declaring bank holidays to prevent a complete collapse of the banking system. In spite of Hoover's recurring optimism, the road from 1929 to 1933 had seemed all downhill, and people's faith in government's power to change things was dwindling. Guests arriving at Washington hotels for the inauguration were told that, owing to the banking crisis, checks drawn on out-of-town banks could not be accepted. Franklin Delano Roosevelt struggled to the podium in his steel leg braces, stood before the crowd, and said to America, "Let me assert my firm belief that the only thing we have to fear is fear itself." He then set forth on a program of legislation, known as the Hundred Days, that initiated a transformation of the role of government in American life.

First came the Emergency Banking Act, which stemmed the banking panic and eased the sense of total crisis. The Agricultural Adjustment Act established ways of limiting production of certain commodities so as to stabilize prices. The National Industrial Recovery Act tried to promote cooperation within industries and between management and labor, and its famous Section 7(a) unequivocally established the right of workers to join unions and to bargain collectively. One of the first acts signed by FDR allowed the production of 3.2 percent beer, and the repeal of Prohibition was accomplished later that year. Not all of the Hundred Days policies were well thought out; some contained huge contradictions, and key parts of the legislation were later overturned by the Supreme Court. Taken together, though, the Hundred Days gave Americans a sense that their government could do, and was doing, something about the Depression and that perhaps fear—"nameless, unreasoning, unjustified terror"—was the country's biggest problem.

It is hard to say what limits upon his actions Roosevelt faced at this time, so great was the nation's concern and so profound its need to be led. Senator Bronson Cutting of New Mexico later wrote that Roosevelt, had he wanted to, could have nationalized the country's banking system that March and regretted that FDR had chosen not to do so: "It was President Roosevelt's great mistake."

Many wealthy Americans regretted the path Roosevelt was taking, worried that the New Deal was going to destroy American industry, give too much power to labor unions, tax inheritance, and otherwise ruin their lives. Some despised him so thoroughly that they referred to him simply as "that man." On the left, too, Communists and socialists were unhappy, complaining that Roosevelt was using his power to save capitalism rather than to replace it. They drew inspiration from the Russian Revolution and the increasing confidence of the Soviet Union. In the early days of the New Deal, Joseph Stalin had not yet put his tactics of show trial, gulag, and summary execution into wide effect, and many Americans (and others around the world) were charmed by the utopian hopes of this new order of society. The economic crisis in Europe had brought another radical leader to power, Adolf Hitler, the chancellor of Germany. Like Benito Mussolini in Italy, Hitler embraced fascism. He began a program of rearmament that he hoped would build Germany's military power while helping to provide the sort of government stimulus of the economy that the New Deal was seeking to achieve through public works projects such as dams and highways.

In the United States, indigenous demagogues and would-be saviors of the nation put forth various prescriptions for healing the country's ills. One of the most influential was Dr. Francis Townsend, whose simple plan was to have the government pay each person over the age of sixty $200 a month, with the conditions that the person quit his job immediately and that he spend the full $200 each month. Thus, Townsend argued, unemployment would be reduced and money would be pumped into the economy to finance the purchase of consumer goods. By 1935, there were three thousand Townsend Clubs, with half a million members and a newspaper, the *Townsend National Weekly,* and Townsend's proposal was seriously being considered by mainstream politicians. The fact that economically the plan was completely impractical did not do much to dampen enthusiasm, and although it was never enacted, it did promote support for the creation of the Social Security system, a major New Deal program passed in 1935.

Townsend himself was a modest, grandfatherly figure whose very demeanor made his scheme seem sound and sensible. Other critics of FDR's policies were more strident and threatening. The liberal nature of

1936

PRESIDENTIAL CANDIDATE (STATE) VICE-PRESIDENTIAL CANDIDATE (STATE)	PARTY	ELECTORAL VOTES	APPROX. % OF POPULAR VOTE
Franklin D. Roosevelt (N.Y.) John Nance Garner (Tex.)	Democratic	523	61%
Alfred M. Landon (Kans.) Frank Knox (Ill.)	Republican	8	37%

Among the minor-party candidates were Norman Thomas (Socialist) and Earl R. Browder (Communist).

many of those policies and the growing threat of fascism in Europe and Japan made the left cautious in its criticisms, although many Communists and socialists had quarrels with Roosevelt's moderation. But on the right figures such as Father Charles E. Coughlin and Louisiana's Huey P. Long were vituperative in their attacks. Coughlin, a Catholic priest, reached a large national audience in weekly radio broadcasts. Radio ministries had already become common by the 1930s (Billy Sunday and Aimee Semple McPherson were among the pioneers), but Coughlin, like Roosevelt, had a particular gift for radio. "Radio broadcasting, I have found, must not be high hat," he said. "It must be human, intensely human. It must be simple." By 1936, Coughlin's message had degenerated into simple name-calling ("Franklin Double-Crossing Roosevelt"), and he was aping the mass-rally techniques of the Nazi Party.

The greatest potential challenge to Roosevelt was posed by Long, who as governor had managed to achieve nearly total control of Louisiana and was elected to the U.S. Senate in 1930. In 1934, Long, who was also a master of the radio appeal, started promoting his Share-Our-Wealth Plan, which involved levying very high taxes on the rich; this, Long said, would allow for an average wage of $2,500 a year for all American workers. He built his Share-Our-Wealth organization into a powerful political apparatus, and it was estimated in one poll in 1935 that he might take 10 percent of the vote in a presidential race, possibly throwing the election to the Republicans. Long's career ended in that September, however, when he was assassinated by a doctor who feared that he might become a dictator.

As the 1936 election approached, Long was dead, Townsend's support was ebbing (owing in part to the passage of the Social Security Act), Coughlin's increasingly rabid performances had drawn a rebuke from the Vatican, and the GOP was hardly feeling strong. In the midterm elections of 1934, the already tiny Republican presence in Congress had been further reduced—from 117 to 103 in the House, from 36 to 25 in the Senate. Republican governors, too, were becoming scarce, so that merely finding a candidate with national standing was difficult. Senators Charles L. McNary of Oregon and Arthur H. Vandenberg of Michigan had some support but were little known outside their home states and the capital. Alfred M. Landon, the Kansas governor, had managed to win his gubernatorial race in 1932 in spite of the Roosevelt landslide, and he soon received significant backing

"Come along. We're going to the Trans-Lux to hiss Roosevelt."

Automobile bumper attachment. Landon used the sunflower, the state flower of his native Kansas, as his campaign emblem.
DAVID J. AND JANICE L. FRENT
POLITICAL AMERICANA COLLECTION.

Celluloid button.
DAVID J. AND JANICE L. FRENT
POLITICAL AMERICANA COLLECTION.

from party leaders and influential journalists, including Emporia's William Allen White and the Hearst newspapers. At the convention in Cleveland, Landon won nomination on the first ballot. His running mate was Colonel Frank Knox, a Chicago newspaper publisher and, like Landon, an old Bull Moose backer of Teddy Roosevelt. (Knox had served under Teddy in the Rough Riders.) The greatest display of emotion at the convention was in response to a fiery speech from Herbert Hoover in which he urged the party to conduct a "holy crusade for liberty."

At the Democratic convention, held in Philadelphia, the only real excitement was over the abolition of the century-old two-thirds rule; now a candidate could win nomination with only a simple majority. The renomination of Roosevelt and John Nance Garner took place without opposition, but only after a national radio audience listened to a seemingly endless parade of speakers singing the praises of the New Deal and its leaders.

The futility of the Landon campaign was apparent from the start. Now that Long was dead, no third-party protest appeared to have a chance of siphoning votes away from FDR, so the Republicans would have to win on their own. The Democrats wisely chose to run against not Landon but Hoover, and the Republicans never found a way out of the trap. Even in Landon's home state of Kansas, New Deal sympathizers infiltrated Republican lines. At a Landon fund-raising dinner near Wichita that fall, a young pianist hired for the event played various medleys and the Landon campaign theme, "Oh, Susanna," but she also slipped in the Roosevelt anthem, "Happy Days Are Here Again," played in waltz time so as to slightly disguise the familiar tune. A few in the audience turned and glared at the pianist, but most seemed not to notice.

As the election neared, James A. Farley, the organizing genius of FDR's campaign, predicted that the President would carry every state except Maine and Vermont. And so it proved. (A *Literary Digest* poll forecast a Landon win; the poll takers failed to see that a telephone poll would be skewed to the more prosperous, and therefore more Republican, segment of the nation.) Even Pennsylvania, which had not gone Democratic since it had voted for its native son James Buchanan in 1856, went for Roosevelt. FDR had a popular-vote margin of more than 11 million votes, and the count in the Electoral College was 523 for FDR to 8 for Landon. Even more important was the shift that had taken place in voting patterns and in the political affiliations of certain groups. Labor unions, which in the past had been wary of partisan politics, lined up for Roosevelt, and the unions in the Congress of Industrial Organizations gave $770,000 to the President's campaign. Many black voters, who had been aligned with the Republicans as the party of Lincoln, transferred their allegiance to the Democrats. And the Democratic grip on the northern cities tightened. Of the 106 cities with a population over 100,000, Landon carried only 2.

The New Deal had transformed the relationship between the people of the United States and their government and had given the government vast new areas of responsibility. In 1936, the people embraced that change, and the balance of power between the parties was altered for a generation to come.

CHAPTER 37

A Third Term in Dark Times

ROOSEVELT v. WILLKIE, 1940

The enormous victory that Franklin D. Roosevelt won in the 1936 election seemed for a time to signal the demise of the Republicans, who were left with eighty-nine seats in the House and a mere seventeen senators (out of ninety-six). But such imbalances have a tendency to be righted, and FDR himself helped the process along with a move that seemed to belie his reputation as a political magician: in 1937, he proposed to add one new justice to the Supreme Court for each sitting justice who had passed his seventieth birthday.

The motivation for this plan was obvious: the Court had overturned many of the President's favorite New Deal programs, and there was little doubt that politics had come into the justices' calculations. Six of the nine justices were over seventy, making it the oldest Court in the nation's history, and Roosevelt felt that this gave him a justification for adding new justices (whom, obviously, he would select on the basis of their readiness to uphold the constitutionality of his programs). The proposal was quickly attacked as a plan to pack the Court with Roosevelt toadies, and conservative Democrats joined with the remaining Republicans to kill the plan. Worse than the defeat itself was the perception that FDR was beginning to think he was above the law. This, in turn, colored the reaction to his decision, in the summer of 1940, to run for a third term as President, thereby breaking the best-known unwritten rule in American politics.

Many other things changed between FDR's watershed victory of 1936 and the election of 1940. In Europe, Adolf Hitler had pushed for advantage and found the other European powers easy to bluff. In March 1936, he had sent German troops to reoccupy the Rhineland, and in March 1938 he had sent troops into Austria to effect what he termed an *Anschluss* (union) between Austria and Germany. In September, Britain and France signed the Munich Agreement, capitulating to Hitler's claims to the Sudetenland in Czechoslovakia in exchange for his promise that this was his "last territorial claim" in Europe. Late in August 1939, Germany and the Soviet Union signed a nonaggression pact; at the beginning of September, German forces invaded Poland and the Second World War began. In the Pacific, Japan was

Window sticker.

DAVID J. AND JANICE L. FRENT
POLITICAL AMERICANA COLLECTION.

at war with China and the Japanese military was making plans to confront America for supremacy in the Pacific.

The effects of these developments on American politics were complex and varied. One strain of progressive thought in the United States had concluded that American involvement in the previous world war had been brought on by Anglophilic eastern aristocrats and by munitions makers and other war profiteers. Some Americans of German, Italian, or Japanese descent took pride in the growing prominence of their nations on the world stage before war broke out and even welcomed their successes after the war began. Some Irish Americans were happy to see any development that was detrimental to the hated English. The diplomatic machinations of the period were particularly difficult for American Communists, who were expected to follow Moscow's lead and thus hold back criticism of the fascists after the nonaggression pact was signed. (This was particularly difficult for Americans who had joined the fight against Francisco Franco's fascist forces in the Spanish Civil War.) Earl Browder, the Communist Party presidential candidate in 1940, denounced any participation by the United States in the "imperialist war."

Once Germany had conquered Poland, the conflict in Europe had settled into a period of relative inaction nicknamed the "Phony War." Then, in the spring of 1940, Hitler unleashed his armored panzer divisions and other forces in an all-out attack on France and the Low Countries. By the third week in June, France had fallen, and Winston Churchill warned that the "Battle of Britain" would soon begin.

In America, as the election year moved ahead, there was confusion in both parties be-

1940

PRESIDENTIAL CANDIDATE (STATE) VICE-PRESIDENTIAL CANDIDATE (STATE)	PARTY	ELECTORAL VOTES	APPROX. % OF POPULAR VOTE
Franklin D. Roosevelt (N.Y.) Henry A. Wallace (Iowa)	Democratic	449	55%
Wendell L. Willkie (Ind.) Charles McNary (Oreg.)	Republican	82	45%

Again among the minor-party candidates were Norman Thomas (Socialist) and Earl Browder (Communist).

cause Roosevelt had not signaled what he intended to do. Early in 1940, he had said to his Treasury secretary, Henry Morgenthau, that he did not intend to run again unless "things get very, very much worse in Europe." But after France fell and the effectiveness of the German military tactics was apparent, Roosevelt still refused to declare himself a candidate. Some, including James Farley, John Nance Garner, and Cordell Hull, took his silence as encouragement to run, and even when the Democratic convention began in Chicago on July 15, the President had not yet announced his intentions. The nomination was clearly Roosevelt's for the asking, but Roosevelt did not want to ask. He wanted to *be* asked, to be drafted by his party in a

Poster by James Montgomery Flagg, playing on his famous 1917 recruiting poster for the U.S. Army.
NATIONAL PORTRAIT GALLERY, SMITHSONIAN INSTITUTION.

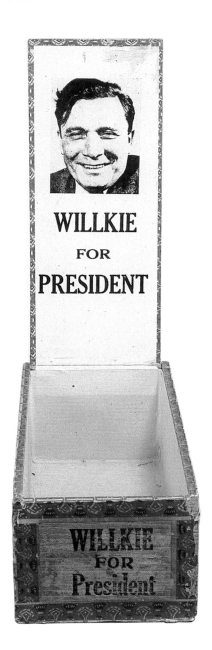

Cigar box.

show of enthusiasm that would permit him to run for a third term without seeming bloated with ambition or infected with the virus of dictatorship.

On the second night of the convention, Senator Alben Barkley of Kansas delivered a message to the convention from Roosevelt: "The President has never had, and has not today, any desire or purpose to continue in the office of President, to be a candidate for that office, or to be nominated by the Convention for that office. He wishes in all earnestness and sincerity to make it clear that all the delegates to this Convention are free to vote for any candidate. That is the message I bear to you from the President of the United States." The delegates sat in silence for a moment, and then a voice came booming over the public address system in the hall: "We want Roosevelt!" the voice said. Then "Everybody wants Roosevelt!" and "The world wants Roosevelt!" The voice belonged to a superintendent of sewers in the Chicago Democratic machine, and the demonstration that followed lasted an hour. Roosevelt was nominated on the first ballot, taking 946 votes; the second-place candidate, Farley, won only 72.

The matter was still not settled because Roosevelt, having been "drafted" by the convention, insisted on having Henry Wallace, his very liberal secretary of agriculture, as his running mate. Many in the party were reluctant to go along with this and favored the nomination of the more conservative William Bankhead of Alabama, the Speaker of the House. Roosevelt threatened to withdraw from the race unless Wallace was nominated, and the convention bowed to his wishes. Many Democrats left with a sense of having been manipulated.

In contrast, the Republican convention saw one of the few spontaneous acts of political choice ever seen at a party convention (or at least one of the few not motivated by deadlock). That year, the Republicans were looking at new faces, in part because so many of the old faces had been driven from office in the previous Roosevelt victories. Robert A. Taft of Ohio had been elected to the Senate only two years earlier, but his sharp intelligence and his famous name (his father was President William Howard Taft) marked him as a party leader. Another Republican new to the national stage was Thomas E. Dewey, who at the age of thirty-eight had been elected only to county office—he was district attorney of New York County, that is, Manhattan—but had made a reputation as a brilliant prosecutor and had nearly won election as New York's governor in 1938. His youth prompted Roosevelt's aide Harold Ickes to quip that Dewey had thrown his "diaper" into the ring, but Dewey nevertheless polled the largest number of votes on the first ballot at the Republican convention, which was held in Philadelphia in June. Taft was second, and third was a man who had never before run for political office, a businessman named Wendell Willkie. Born and educated in Indiana, he had begun his career as a lawyer in his father's firm and had risen to become president of Commonwealth and Southern, a utility company that had fought the New Deal's huge Tennessee Valley Authority. By 1939, Willkie had admitted defeat and sold the company's assets to the government. A harsh critic of what he saw as excessive government interference in private business, Willkie presented himself as the chief business victim of the New Deal.

His rise to political prominence was unconventional. He made a fine impression as a contestant on a radio quiz show called *Information Please,* and his energetic speaking style and easy, informal manner won public support and attracted hordes of campaign volunteers, an unusual phenomenon in an age when the bulk of political campaign work was still undertaken by party organizations. Willkie volunteers worked the convention hard and with imagination: delegates who sent suits to be cleaned found their pockets full of Willkie propaganda when they came back. The enthusiasm the Willkie people generated helped him gather steam, and on the sixth ballot he was nominated. Willkie's candidacy was also helped by the facts that he was an internationalist while Taft was a prominent isolationist and that neither Taft nor Dewey seemed to have the experience the country would want in a wartime leader. (To be prudent, the Republicans balanced the ticket with Senator Charles McNary of Oregon, an isolationist.)

Willkie faced a huge task in confronting Roosevelt, whom he modestly referred to as "the Champ." The task was made harder by the fact that he had supported many New Deal programs and was basically in agreement with FDR's foreign policy. So he had to make a big issue of the third-term precedent and hope that after eight years voters were weary of alphabet agencies and liberal ideas. The energetic Willkie traveled the nation giving speeches. (In fact, he made so many speeches and delivered them so robustly that eventually he had to travel with a doctor to help keep him from losing his voice.)

Roosevelt was planning to take advantage of his incumbency and run for office by simply being presidential, but by October the campaign had become closer than expected, and for the last two weeks both candidates fought hard. Willkie's chances were boosted in late October, when he was endorsed by John L. Lewis, the head of the CIO, who asked union members to join him in supporting the Republican nominee and promised to resign his post if Roosevelt won. Wild accusations were made by partisans on both sides. Democrats tried to link Willkie to Hitler and Mussolini, and Republicans called Roosevelt a warmonger.

It was, perhaps, the war that did more than anything to give the election to Roosevelt. Churchill's Battle of Britain got under way in August, with the Luftwaffe attempting to destroy Britain's fighter forces in preparation for an invasion of Britain. On September 3, Roosevelt announced a deal to trade American destroyers to Britain for long-term leases on British bases in the Western Hemisphere. That same day, Germany issued secret orders containing the planned schedule for the invasion. The Battle of Britain did not work out as Hitler had hoped, and the British navy retained control of the English Channel (aided in some small degree by the destroyers that Roosevelt had made available). Americans were awakening to the seriousness of the German threat, and the success of modern mechanized war suddenly made the Atlantic seem a less dependable defense against German ambition. In a time of such challenges, Americans felt more comfortable trusting their future to the man who had led them out of the darkness of the Great Depression, rather than a lawyer who had done well on a quiz show. Roosevelt won by 5 million votes,

Matchbook.

NATIONAL MUSEUM OF
AMERICAN HISTORY,
SMITHSONIAN INSTITUTION.

and in the Electoral College the margin was 449 for FDR to 82 for Willkie. Again, the cities were crucial for FDR, who carried every one with a population over 400,000 except Cincinnati.

Facing the challenge of preparing the nation for war, Roosevelt brought Republicans into prominent positions in his administration, naming Frank Knox (Landon's running mate in 1936) to head the Navy Department and Henry Stimson secretary of war. As Roosevelt himself later put it, "Dr. New Deal" was being replaced by "Dr. Win the War."

A Stubborn Old Man

ROOSEVELT v. DEWEY, 1944

Three consecutive defeats by huge margins at the hands of Franklin Roosevelt had only increased the Republicans' partisan ardor and their loathing for "that man" and his supporters. As the 1944 election approached, they had new reason to hope. Roosevelt was visibly worn from twelve years in office, and his radio appearances had become lackluster. Republican newspapers (and most newspapers *were* Republican) delighted in printing photos in which the President looked haggard. The requirements of the wartime economy had necessitated various unpopular measures, such as a withholding tax on wages (which went into effect in 1943). The sheer size of the war effort meant that there were countless opportunities for mismanagement or corruption in war-related industries, and when such practices were exposed it was often damaging for the administration. The social changes of the war era—black migration north, women in the workplace—together with the ideological effects of America's alliance with Stalin's Soviet Union had resulted in a set of conditions and new attitudes profoundly disturbing to conservative Americans. Many of those conservatives were in the President's own party, and as the Republicans looked toward 1944 they hoped that with a strong candidate they could unite voters in both parties who were weary of the New Deal and elect a Republican to the White House.

Roosevelt, however, was not exactly without assets as the race approached. His greatest strength was the war effort itself. The vast expenditures required had ballooned the federal budget (it had gone from $9 billion in 1939 to $100 billion in 1945), but the expenditure had revived the economy and brought prosperity not only to those who had been well off in the past but also to groups that had scarcely tasted economic success before (such as African Americans, who had found good jobs in northern defense plants). Labor unions were stronger than ever under Roosevelt and were willing to repay their debt by helping with the campaign. And beyond the economic effects, the prosecution of the war was going well in 1944, highlighted by the D-Day invasion of Normandy in June. Meanwhile, Roosevelt was meeting with his counterparts in Britain and the USSR, Winston Churchill and

Joseph Stalin, to coordinate the war effort. To win the election, the Republicans would have to put forward a candidate whom Americans could picture sitting at a conference table and defending American interests effectively.

This was a serious problem. Many of the Republican leaders had been associated with the now unfashionable dogma of isolationism, and many others had been defeated in previous elections. The leading contenders in 1944 were three newly elected Republican governors and one egomaniacal war hero.

The hero, Douglas MacArthur, had developed a real gift for public relations. Driven from the Philippines by the Japanese early in 1942, he had pledged, "I shall return," and was going to make certain that he did so. MacArthur dressed the part of war hero (his ex-wife regaled friends with accounts of him practicing heroic poses at home in front of a mirror). Arthur Vandenberg, a senator from Michigan, tried to start a "draft MacArthur" movement early in 1944, but this was derailed when an overenthusiastic backer of the general, Congressman Albert L. Miller of Nebraska, published an exchange of letters with him. Miller had written about the danger to the nation "if this system of left-wingers and New Dealers" lasted much longer, and MacArthur replied that this was a "sobering" thought. He went on, "We must not inadvertently slip into the same condition internally as the one which we fight externally." MacArthur had not intended his views to be made public, and when a furor greeted the release of the letters MacArthur withdrew his name from consideration.

In the view of many conservatives in both parties, the administration's liberal bias—its most vulnerable point—was personified by Vice President Henry Wallace, whom Roosevelt had forced upon the Democratic convention four years earlier. Wallace was a credulous man and not always the most sensible. During the 1940 campaign, Roosevelt's men had been worried that some letters Wallace had written to a former guru named Nicholas Roerich might be used against the nominee, but Willkie had blocked this tactic, in part because the Democrats had information on a mistress Willkie had in New York. (MacArthur's reluctance to run in the end may have been due in part to information the columnist Drew Pearson had on a mistress MacArthur had in Washington, a former chorus girl from Singapore.) Wallace was Roosevelt's link to the most liberal wing of his party, and many thought he was too far left. After a trip Wallace made to Latin America in 1943, the FBI's J. Edgar Hoover

1944

PRESIDENTIAL CANDIDATE (STATE) VICE-PRESIDENTIAL CANDIDATE (STATE)	PARTY	ELECTORAL VOTES	APPROX. % OF POPULAR VOTE
Franklin D. Roosevelt (N.Y.) Harry S. Truman (Mo.)	Democratic	432	53%
Thomas E. Dewey (N.Y.) John W. Bricker (Ohio)	Republican	99	46%

Again among the minor-party candidates was Norman Thomas (Socialist).

warned the President that Wallace had fallen under the influence of "Bolivian Communists" and had received "improper information concerning working conditions in the Bolivian mines."

Wallace's politics and his personality were a problem for Roosevelt, and the President moved with his usual canniness to solve it a couple of weeks before the convention. Meeting with some of his closest political advisers, Roosevelt reviewed his possible running mates. Wallace had little support (apart from Eleanor Roosevelt, who wanted him kept on the ticket). Various other candidates were considered and eliminated, and the choice finally came down to Harry S. Truman, a Missouri senator who had led a major Senate investigation into war industry mismanagement and corruption. Truman was a regular Democrat with close ties to the Kansas City machine run by Tom Pendergast. A couple of Roosevelt aides were assigned to break the news to Wallace, who refused to believe them, and when Wallace went to the President, FDR warmly (but falsely) told him that he hoped it would be "the same old team" in the election. At the convention in Chicago in July, Truman was chosen.

With MacArthur out of the race, the Republicans turned to three new governors: New York's Thomas Dewey, Minnesota's Harold Stassen (who had left the job to enlist in the navy and was stationed in the Pacific), and Ohio's John W. Bricker. The same midterm elections that had brought these three to prominence had nearly won the House for the Republicans (the margin there was 222 Democrats to 209 Republicans, with four representatives of other parties). Wendell Willkie tried to put himself forward again but was thrashed in the Wisconsin primary by Dewey, who was not a declared candidate but was allowing allies to suggest that he was available for a draft. His reputation as a racket-busting prosecutor (he had won convictions against the gangsters Legs Diamond and Lucky Luciano) combined with his post as New York's governor made him a popular choice. Stassen, too, was being considered for a draft, but with less success. And Bricker, jokingly described as "an honest Harding," looked presidential but lacked credentials. At the Republican convention in June, Dewey won almost unanimously on the first ballot and then chose Bricker as his running mate. Accepting the nomination, he denounced the Roosevelt administration as a group of "stubborn men grown old and tired in office."

The Republicans had, of course, noticed the growing dominance of the Democrats in the big northern cities and the movement of black voters from the party of Lincoln to the party of Roosevelt. Partly in reaction to that and partly owing to nobler motives, the Republican platform contained strong planks calling for stiffer action against employment discrimination, an antilynching bill, and a constitutional amendment to end poll taxes (which were used to discourage black voters in the South). Roosevelt's achievements as President had not included a single piece of

Cartoon by Rube Goldberg.
LIBRARY OF CONGRESS.

civil rights legislation, and the Republicans hoped to draw black voters back into the GOP.

But the main thrusts of the Republican campaign pointed in two directions, one against the long rule of Roosevelt, the other against supposed Communist influence in the administration. Toward the end of the campaign, Dewey played this theme up, charging at one stop that fall that "the Communists are seizing control of the New Deal, through which they aim to control the Government of the United States." Roosevelt struck back by pointing out that that same day Dewey had asked the voters to end "one-man government." "Now, really, which is it?" Roosevelt demanded, "communism or monarchy?" He went on to say that he wanted neither.

Perhaps the most remarkable thing about the election was that it was held at all. To many British observers, for a nation in the midst of a global war to subject the

The floor of the Republican Party convention, Chicago, June 1944.
LIBRARY OF CONGRESS.

leader of that war to an election campaign seemed bizarre. (Britain itself postponed its scheduled general elections.) In spite of the pressure of the election, Roosevelt managed to keep running both the war effort and the process of preparing for peace, and his biographer James MacGregor Burns judges that "winning a presidential campaign even while the foundations of a controversial postwar organization were being hammered out" was "the climactic political feat of his career."

To silence accusations that his health was too poor for another term, Roosevelt traveled to defense plants, and late in the race he endured long campaign swings in an open car through the streets of New York and Philadelphia, smiling broadly and waving to throngs who braved the foul weather to see him. But his most adroit political move may have come in a speech that September, in which he ridiculed Republican charges that he had sent a destroyer to pick up his dog, Fala. "These

Republican leaders have not been content with attacks—on me, on my wife, or on my sons. No, not content with that, they now include my little dog, Fala. Well, of course, I don't resent attacks, and my family doesn't resent attacks, but [pause] Fala does resent them." Roosevelt's timing and delivery were perfect, and the pompous Dewey (called "the Boy Orator of the Platitude" in mock reference to William Jennings Bryan) was no match for FDR.

The election was the closest of Roosevelt's four victories, and he was aided tremendously by a get-out-the-vote drive led by the labor boss Sidney Hillman, which set as its goal "every worker a voter." Most of the country's newspapers endorsed Dewey, and many potential voters in the armed forces were kept from voting by Republican legislatures concerned that (as Robert Taft was supposed to have said) the fighting men were too far from home to vote intelligently (that is, they were likely to vote for the commander in chief). The final margin of electoral votes was 432 for Roosevelt and 99 for Dewey, and the margin in popular votes was 3.6 million.

Then, on April 12, 1945, less than three months after his fourth inauguration, Roosevelt died. Those entering the armed forces in the spring of 1945 could scarcely remember any other President, and older Americans wondered what would happen now that the man who had led the nation out of the Depression and to victory in war had passed from the scene. They would have to adjust to a new and very different leader, Harry S. Truman.

Giving Hell to the Man on the Wedding Cake

TRUMAN, DEWEY, THURMOND, WALLACE, 1948

Called urgently to the White House on the evening of April 12, 1945, Harry S. Truman was greeted by Eleanor Roosevelt, who told him that the President was dead. He asked if there was anything he could do for her. "Is there anything we can do for *you*?" she replied. "For *you* are the one in trouble now."

Later in the evening, after Truman met with members of what was now *his* cabinet, Secretary of War Henry Stimson told him obliquely about the development of a tremendously powerful new explosive but did not give any details. It was not until April 25 that Truman learned of the Manhattan Project and of the potential for a new bomb of unprecedented power. Nor was this the only vital subject of which Truman had been kept in ignorance. He had not been given a thorough briefing on Roosevelt's talks with Stalin and Churchill at the Yalta Conference. In fact, Roosevelt had conducted much of the nation's foreign policy without involving, or even informing, the Vice President. Given Roosevelt's improvisational style of policy making and his fondness for pitting his aides against one another as part of the decision-making process, it was difficult for the new President to unearth the intentions of his predecessor, although that did not keep him from being accused of betraying FDR's legacy whenever he made a decision someone did not like.

Truman was still relatively unknown nationally, yet he had to deal with huge problems: the winning of the war, the decision about whether to use the atomic bomb against Japan, the problems of demobilization and conversion to a peacetime economy, and the construction of a stable postwar world order. Many Americans, Truman among them, wondered if the new President was up to the task.

The end of the war thrust the world into a new series of confrontations in Europe and Asia, this time against a former ally, the Soviet Union. Stalin was pushing for a large Soviet sphere of influence in eastern Europe, and, with the Red Army in place and Americans clamoring for U.S. troops to come home, there was little Truman could do to prevent Soviet expansion without threatening to use nuclear force. Around the world, as colonies were eager to shake off European (or American) rule, Britain and France were reluctant to lose their empires, yet unable to prevent their slow drift (or fast march) toward independence. In much of Asia, resistance to Japanese invaders had been led by Communists, and in Korea, China, Vietnam, and other countries those resistance leaders were preparing to take power.

At home, the end of wartime restrictions allowed businesses to satisfy long-unfulfilled consumer demands, and Americans delved into their savings accounts to buy what they had been deprived of during the war. The return of troops and the start of the baby boom made for a great housing shortage, and, with demand outstripping supply in many markets, prices rose dramatically. One result of the rising prices was that the increasingly militant labor unions demanded a commensurate rise in wages. Truman had attempted to deal with the domestic issues of the postwar era by offering his "Fair Deal" program, which proposed expanding New Deal initiatives and adding new social programs, including national health insurance. But conservatives of both parties blocked most of his proposals, and in 1946 the Republicans swept to power in the House and Senate behind the simple slogan "Had Enough?"

The Republican-dominated Eightieth Congress passed some parts of Truman's international program—most notably the Marshall Plan for the reconstruction of Europe—but also attempted to roll back the liberal reforms of the previous dozen years. The Taft-Hartley Act, for example, significantly undercut the power of labor unions by banning closed shops and allowing states to enact so-called right-to-work laws that permitted workers not to join a union once they were in a union shop.

The Republicans were not his only problem. African Americans' migration to the North and their demands for civil rights, together with greater sympathy for minorities in general, arising partly in reaction to Hitler's racist ideology, had put the issue of black rights onto the national agenda for the first time since the end of Reconstruction. Black votes in the northern cities had helped build Democratic power, but the Democrats were still the party of the segregationist South as well, and in 1948 this conflict was coming to a head. On the left, former Vice President Henry Wallace had broken with the President on foreign policy, which Wallace saw as

1948

PRESIDENTIAL CANDIDATE (STATE) VICE-PRESIDENTIAL CANDIDATE (STATE)	PARTY	ELECTORAL VOTES	APPROX. % OF POPULAR VOTE
Harry S. Truman (Mo.) Alben W. Barkley (Ky.)	Democratic	303	49%
Thomas E. Dewey (N.Y.) John W. Bricker (Ohio)	Republican	189	45%
Strom Thurmond (S.C.) Fielding L. Wright (Mich.)	States' Rights (Dixiecrat)	39	2%
Henry A. Wallace (Iowa) Glenn H. Taylor (Idaho)	Progressive	0	2%

Among the other minor-party candidates was Norman Thomas (Socialist), running for his sixth and last time.

much too anti-Soviet, and in December 1947 Wallace announced his intention to run for President in 1948.

As the election year began, nearly everyone had given Truman up for dead politically. He was urged by friends not to run, to spare himself the humiliation. Major Democratic leaders were publicly calling for the party to draft Dwight D. Eisenhower as its candidate in 1948, although Ike had not made his party preference known and soon issued a statement declining to be a candidate. (Ironically, three years earlier, Truman himself had offered to support Eisenhower for President in 1948.)

All this, of course, made the Republicans very happy. One poll in March showed at least four Republicans who would beat Truman easily, and by the time the Republican convention met in Philadelphia late in June the standard-bearer from 1944, New York's Governor Thomas E. Dewey, was the favorite. Clare Boothe Luce, the wife of Henry Luce, the publisher of *Time* magazine, entertained the delegates with an address in which she referred to Truman as a "gone goose." When the Republicans nominated a ticket featuring two popular and moderate big-state governors—Dewey's running mate was California's Earl Warren—it truly seemed that the Democratic goose was cooked.

Dewey spoke clearly, and his speeches were carefully constructed. But there was little in either the speeches or the man that communicated warmth or even basic human feelings. Alice Roosevelt Longworth, Teddy Roosevelt's daughter, famously likened the dapper Dewey, with his pencil mustache, to "the man on the wedding cake." Once a photographer taking a shot of him asked Dewey to smile, and the candidate replied, "I thought I was."

Matters got worse for the Democrats at their convention, when liber-

In this cartoon by Walt Kelly, Henry Wallace is carrying boomerangs and Truman is blindfolded, while efficient administrator Dewey seems on track to victory.

LIBRARY OF CONGRESS.

Truman at a whistle stop.

als refused to accept a watered-down civil rights plank in the platform. They won the ensuing struggle, but some southern delegates walked out. A few days later, a white supremacist faction of the party lined up behind South Carolina Democratic governor Strom Thurmond as the candidate of the States' Rights, or "Dixiecrat," Party. Those remaining at the convention nominated Truman for President, but with little enthusiasm, and chose Kentucky senator Alben Barkley, who had opened the meeting with a stirring keynote address, as his running mate.

But Truman was not willing to accept that the path before him was impossible, despite a party that was broken into three pieces and polls that showed him far behind. He wisely chose to run not against his opponent but against the congressional Republicans, who had refused to pass his proposals for dealing with farm problems, the housing shortage, and other national issues. As Truman accepted his party's nomination, he announced that he was calling Congress back into session to pass the legislation he wanted, and as the session opened he issued two executive orders, one to end discrimination in the armed forces, the other designed to ensure fair employment practices in the government. Congress met but refused to pass Truman's programs, and when the session ended a reporter asked if the President would say it was a "do-nothing session." Truman replied, "That's a good name for the Eightieth Congress," and much of his campaign was spent denouncing the "do-nothing Congress" that had prevented him from carrying on Franklin Roosevelt's tradition.

Dewey, meanwhile, had such a commanding lead that he was careful to do nothing that might jeopardize it. He felt he could afford to avoid pandering to the baser instincts of his party. When Congressman Richard M. Nixon of California urged the campaign to capitalize on recent revelations about Communist infiltration of the government, Dewey declined, and he also refused to make the politically easy gesture of calling for the Communist Party to be outlawed in the United States. More fundamental to the election result, Dewey and the Republicans were unable to see that they were losing support among farmers. Harold Stassen, the Republican governor of Minnesota, had accused the Democrats of not doing enough to fight inflation and said that Truman was trying to keep farm prices high. That, of course, was what farmers wanted, and Truman replied that the Republicans "are obviously ready to let the bottom drop out of farm prices." Nor could Dewey have been helped by the attitudes of some of the more conservative members of his party, such as Robert A. Taft, who had advised that the way to deal with inflation was to "eat less."

Wallace claimed that he, not Truman, represented the true spirit of the New Deal. DAVID J. AND JANICE L. FRENT POLITICAL AMERICANA COLLECTION.

This Marie Antoinette attitude was not really representative of the views held by Dewey or Earl Warren, but Truman did a superb job of associating the ticket with the reactionary elements of the party. (A Democratic memorandum written shortly before the convention had recommended keeping "a steady glare on the Neanderthal men of the Republican party.") At the same time, the fissures in the Democratic Party actually helped deflect some of the attacks the Republicans might have launched against Truman. The issue of Communist infiltration, for example, was not as harmful to Truman as it would have been had Wallace not undertaken an independent campaign. Most of the real leftists in the Democratic Party were with Wallace, so Truman was not implicated. And Soviet moves during the year (the Berlin blockade, taking over Czechoslovakia) undercut Wallace's sunny portrayal of the USSR. At the same time, the Dixiecrat campaign made it easier for Truman to move toward a more liberal position on civil rights and thus keep black voters in the Democratic coalition Roosevelt had built.

Truman kept his campaign promise of advancing the cause of civil rights. DAVID J. AND JANICE L. FRENT POLITICAL AMERICANA COLLECTION.

Truman campaigned with tremendous energy, covering more than 31,000 miles by train—aboard the Presidential Special—and speaking to perhaps 6 million people. By September, pollsters were practically ignoring the campaign, and though reporters puzzled over the large turnout Truman was getting at campaign events, they concluded that people were coming to witness the spectacle of a man who kept on fighting because he did not know he was licked. Setting off on one of his whistle-stop tours in September, he promised to "give 'em hell," and the phrase, a little risqué for the time, became part of his public persona.

Dewey, who was unwilling to trade barbs with Truman—and in any case was constantly being told that he was going to win—remained so aloof that he scarcely seemed to be running. Get-out-the-vote drives helped keep Democrats' participation high, while many Republicans (Dewey later estimated between 2 and 3 million) stayed home, thinking that the GOP ticket would win easily. The polls were predicting that Dewey would have a margin of between 5 and 15 percent, and on election night Republicans, waiting patiently for victory, wondered why Truman was still ahead in the popular vote.

Photograph by W. Eugene Smith.
COPYRIGHT © LIFE PICTURE SERVICE.

The most famous example of Republican overconfidence was the *Chicago Tribune* headline DEWEY DEFEATS TRUMAN, but it wasn't just the *Trib*'s headline writers who were surprised. The only person who seemed to take victory in stride was Truman. Across the nation, the Democratic campaign was so effective that not only did Truman win but the Democrats regained control of the House and Senate. The voters, after just two years of the Republican Eightieth Congress, had once again "had enough."

The Dawn of the Television Age

EISENHOWER v. STEVENSON, 1952

A week after the Japanese attack on Pearl Harbor in 1941, Dwight D. Eisenhower, who had just been promoted to the rank of brigadier general in the U.S. Army, was called into the office of George C. Marshall, the chief of staff. Marshall gave Eisenhower a quick summary of the situation in the Pacific and asked him what "general line of action" he thought the United States should follow. After a couple of hours Eisenhower came back with his recommendations. Marshall looked them over, said he agreed with them, and put Ike in charge of the Philippines and Far Eastern Sections of the War Plans Division. From then until the end of the war, Marshall was Eisenhower's mentor and patron. Recognizing Eisenhower's gifts as a leader, he promoted his protégé and helped prepare him for the ever-more-difficult tasks he faced. Eisenhower's performance justified Marshall's confidence, and by war's end he was the country's greatest military hero, the man who had masterminded the Normandy invasion and defeated the Nazis.

The postwar period did nothing to diminish Eisenhower's reputation. In 1948, he became the president of Columbia University, and in 1951 he left Columbia to rejoin the army as supreme Allied commander in Europe, in charge of the multinational forces of the recently established North Atlantic Treaty Organization, or NATO. So popular was the general that he could have had either party's nomination for President in 1952; in fact, Truman had offered him the 1948 Democratic nomination. But Eisenhower's views on domestic policy were too conservative for him to feel comfortable with the Democrats, and his orientation had always been Republican; thus, if he were to run, it would be as the GOP candidate.

The problem was that the Republicans remained divided between internationalists (who were centered in the party's more liberal eastern wing) and isolationists (who were more conservative and tended to be from the Midwest). The leader of the isolationists was Robert Taft, the Ohio senator who was so steeped in his party's orthodoxies that he was called "Mr. Republican." Taft had announced in September 1951 that he was a candidate, and as the election year began he was using his control of the party organization to build a large lead in delegates. The isolationists

Senator Taft looking as though he had just realized that his bid for nomination had laid an egg. One wonders whether "Mr. Republican" knew that a rooster had been the old symbol of the Democratic Party. Photograph by Alfred Eisenstaedt.
COPYRIGHT © LIFE PICTURE SERVICE.

were filled with wrath at the perceived crimes of the Roosevelt and Truman administrations, and one of the leading scapegoats for their wrath, trailing not far behind Truman himself, was George C. Marshall.

All this put Eisenhower in an awkward position. To win the nomination he would have to campaign, because otherwise Taft would have a majority of the delegates tied up long before the convention. And if he were to become the nominee, he would have to accommodate the reactionaries in the Republican Party, such as Senator Joseph McCarthy of Wisconsin, who had in essence accused Marshall of being a traitor to his country, having walked "side by side" with Stalin, and having been complicit in the "sellout" of China to the Communists. Dwight D. Eisenhower would have much preferred to be chosen by the Republicans without having to seek the nomination and to have distanced himself from the likes of McCarthy. But he wanted to be President—and was, indeed, told that he had an obligation to run—so he accepted the conditions and failed to defend Marshall, who, more than anyone else, had made his presidential hopes possible.

The stakes were high for the Republicans, because Truman's spectacular upset win in 1948 had been nearly the last good news of his presidency. Worries about Communist infiltration increased following the detonation of an atomic bomb by the Soviet Union in 1949, and charges that Communists had served in Democratic administrations appeared to be confirmed by the 1950 perjury conviction of Alger Hiss (who had served under both FDR and Truman). In June 1950, the nation was stunned by the outbreak of war in Korea and by the early success of the Communist North Koreans in pushing South Korean and American forces to a tiny defensive perimeter in the southeastern corner of the peninsula. Then, in September, Douglas MacArthur directed a brilliant landing at Inchon, a port city near Seoul, and by late November he had driven the North Koreans back almost to the Chinese border. The Chinese, joining the North Koreans, then drove MacArthur south of Seoul, and a bloody

1952

PRESIDENTIAL CANDIDATE (STATE) VICE-PRESIDENTIAL CANDIDATE (STATE)	PARTY	ELECTORAL VOTES	APPROX. % OF POPULAR VOTE
Dwight D. Eisenhower (Kans.) Richard M. Nixon (Calif.)	Republican	442	55%
Adlai E. Stevenson (Ill.) John J. Sparkman (Ala.)	Democratic	89	44%

war raged around the center of the peninsula, near the old border between North and South, along the thirty-eighth parallel. The following March, MacArthur attacked Truman's conduct of the war, and in April Truman, with Marshall's support, removed MacArthur from command. Also that March, Julius and Ethel Rosenberg were convicted of passing atomic bomb secrets to the Russians. For many Americans, it seemed that the nation was adrift—unable to win a small war in Asia, riddled with spies, and lacking courage and vision. Truman's approval ratings in the polls hovered around 30 percent, and the Democrats despaired.

Eisenhower's supporters finally brought him into the race by flying to his French headquarters a film of a draft-Eisenhower rally held at Madison Square Garden. Seeing the enthusiasm of the crowd, Ike agreed to seek the nomination actively. Other candidates who were challenging Taft, such as governors Earl Warren of California and Harold Stassen of Minnesota, essentially became stalking horses for Eisenhower. Perceiving the threat, Taft's backers started spreading stories that they thought would hurt Eisenhower—that his wife, Mamie, had a drink-

"The idea that you can merchandise candidates for high office like breakfast cereal is the ultimate indignity to the democratic process."

ADLAI STEVENSON, 1952

A new use for World War II army–surplus barrage balloons.
NATIONAL MUSEUM OF
AMERICAN HISTORY,
SMITHSONIAN INSTITUTION.

ing problem, for example, or that Ike himself was Jewish—but this did not slow the Eisenhower bandwagon. The Republican convention, held in July in Chicago, was the first to be broadcast on television. Eisenhower's personal popularity made him unstoppable, and he was nominated on the first ballot, although angry Taft backers refused to take the traditional step of making the nomination unanimous. Eisenhower selected as his running mate Senator Richard M. Nixon of California, who brought to the ticket youth (he was only thirty-nine) and a reputation as a dogged anti-Communist (he had led the attack on Alger Hiss).

Democrats were relieved when Truman announced in April that he would not run again, and the party turned to consider other candidates. Senator Estes Kefauver of Tennessee had received a great deal of attention for his investigation of organized crime, and he had the largest number of committed delegates as the

Adlai Stevenson campaign parade on Forty-second Street, New York City. Photograph by Cornell Capa.

Democratic convention (also in Chicago) approached. Other possibilities included Vice President Alben Barkley and Senator Richard Russell of Georgia. Many Democrats were hoping that the governor of Illinois, Adlai Stevenson, would run. Stevenson had made a good impression as governor and had shown a real ability for working with a Republican-dominated legislature. At first he declined to make himself a candidate, but a movement to draft him as the party's choice took off, and on the first ballot he was second only to Kefauver. As other candidates dropped out, Stevenson's support grew, and he won nomination on the third ballot. To try to appeal to the South and to avoid a repetition of the Dixiecrat revolt of 1948, Stevenson chose Senator John Sparkman of Alabama to be the vice presidential nominee.

The Democrats emerged from their convention more unified than they had been four years earlier, although the question of civil rights was eroding the party's connection to the South. The Republicans, however, were deeply split. Eisenhower, upon winning the nomination, had gone to see Taft and expressed the hope that they could work together, but Taft was distant, and it was not until September that Taft, after getting Eisenhower to endorse a document outlining what he thought were the correct stands on a number of issues, agreed to back his party's choice. Democrats blasted Ike's "surrender" to Taft, but the party was made whole. The following month,

Adlai Stevenson campaigning in Flint, Michigan, on Labor Day, 1952. Photograph by William M. Gallagher for the Flint Journal. *This picture—in which the hole in the sole of Stevenson's shoe so eloquently symbolizes the grueling and exhausting work of campaigning— became the best-known image of Stevenson and won the Pulitzer Prize for news photography. In 1956 an Eisenhower campaign button reproduced this picture with the legend "Don't let this happen to YOU! VOTE for IKE!"*

COPYRIGHT © WILLIAM M. GALLAGHER.
COURTESY OF THE FLINT JOURNAL.

1952: THE "CHECKERS SPEECH"

THE CHECKERS SPEECH is important for two reasons. First, it saved the budding career of Richard Nixon, who was the most influential American political figure of the second half of the twentieth century. And second, it was perhaps the first nationally significant political event to be televised—or, rather, the first time a politician used television in a sophisticated way. Although Nixon lacked the ease before the camera of John Kennedy, Ronald Reagan, or Bill Clinton, he showed an early and acute understanding of the rules of the TV game. An estimated 58 million Americans witnessed his effort—the largest audience in television history until 1960, when it was eclipsed by the audience for the first Nixon-Kennedy debate.

The speech was a crucial test for Nixon, his chosen means of responding to charges about a secret campaign war chest of about $18,000 that had been discovered by the press, and his genius was to understand that it was people's hearts, not their minds, that he needed to reach. Eisenhower had refused to come to his aid, and the Republican vice presidential nominee had to stand or fall on his own. Although he did deal with the substance of the charges (he said that the fund was legal, that all the money had been used for campaign purposes, and that no contributor had received special favors in return for a gift), what was memorable was his sentimental, Uriah Heep—ish portrait of his family as paragons of middle-class respectability, not wealthy big shots. He set forth his family finances in excruciating detail ("I inherited $1,500 from my grandfather") and then moved on to discuss the Nixon lifestyle.

He said that he was proud of the fact that "every dime we've got is honestly ours" and pointed out that his wife, Pat, "doesn't have a mink coat." He went on, "But she does have a respectable Republican cloth coat. And I always tell her that she'd look good in anything." And then, in a climax long to be remembered, he told of a dog his daughters had received from a man in Texas: "And our little girl—Tricia, the six-year-old—named it Checkers. And you know, the kids love the dog, and I just want to say this right now, that regardless of what they say about it, we're going to keep it."

Nixon had managed to transform an investigation into a questionable campaign fund into an attempt to tear a cocker spaniel from the arms of his six-year-old daughter. His success would have many consequences.

Eisenhower also "surrendered" to McCarthy. Preparing for a campaign swing through Wisconsin early in October, he decided to defend Marshall there, in Joe McCarthy's state, and to emphasize his continued respect for Marshall. His draft remarks on the subject said that Marshall had demonstrated the "profoundest patriotism," but he never read that part of his speech, and the press, which was aware of the planned statement, attacked him for backing down. Still, the party remained united.

The greatest challenge to the GOP ticket came in September, when the *New York Post* revealed that various wealthy Californians had given money to a secret campaign fund for Nixon. The fund was legal, and Nixon's first response was to call the report a smear devised by Communists to discredit him. Eventually, he was forced to make a national television broadcast defending his actions—the "Checkers speech." Eisenhower refused to help him, making it clear that Nixon was on his own. The public reaction to the speech was positive, and Nixon stayed on the ticket.

Nixon's speech represented a new use of television, and in general the Republicans were much quicker to grasp the importance of the new medium than the Democrats were. Since the previous election, the number of TV sets in the United States had risen from 172,000 to 15.3 million, and one in three American homes now had one. In New York, Eisenhower made a series of short TV spots in which he read prepared answers to questions on various issues; then the questions, asked by ordinary folks, were intercut. Twenty-eight of these fairly primitive ads were shown, and although they were bland and superficial they managed to project Eisenhower's charm and broad smile into American living rooms.

By contrast, Stevenson bought longer chunks of TV time and used it mainly to deliver speeches. He was an able speaker, with a quick wit and an impressive vocabulary—too impressive for many, for whom the Illinois governor came across as an

"I LIKE IKE" became perhaps the best-known slogan in the entire history of American presidential campaigns. Clever but obscure was the Republican campaign formula K_1C_2, meaning that the key issues were the Korean War, Communist influence within the federal government, and corruption among Truman administration officials. Because many Americans attributed the recent economic boom to military expenditures for the Korean War, in which so many thousands of U.S. soldiers had died, they felt guilty about the "blood money" in their pockets. Consequently, they were offended by the Democratic campaign slogan, "You Never Had It So Good."

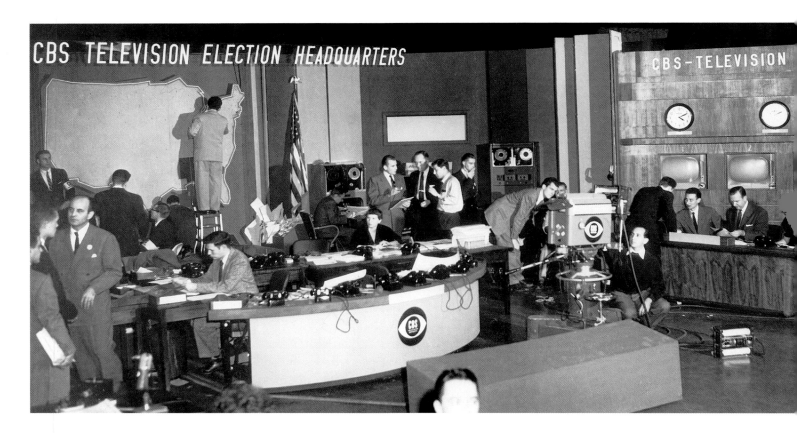

CBS election headquarters.

"egghead." He was also somewhat long-winded, with the result that he would talk longer than the time he had paid for and be cut off before reaching his conclusion.

Eisenhower was a dull speaker and given to malapropisms, but he was a hero and he conveyed a welcome solidity. When, shortly before the election, he promised that he would "go to Korea" to seek an end to the war, America was persuaded. Eisenhower won 55 percent of the vote, and his margin in the Electoral College was 442 to 89. The Republicans now controlled both houses of Congress. The nature of the problems that the President would contend with was brought into focus on November 1, 1952, when the United States detonated its first hydrogen bomb, at Eniwetok atoll in the Pacific. For a majority of Americans, Ike was the man to be trusted with such awesome power.

CHAPTER 41

Gathering Votes like Box Tops

EISENHOWER v. STEVENSON, 1956

The Republican ticket of 1956, President Eisenhower and Vice President Nixon, ran for re-election claiming to have brought the nation "peace, prosperity, and progress." And with the end of the Korean War in July 1953, a booming economy, and rapid technological advances, the Republicans' complacency was easy to understand. It was shared by many Americans, and in November Eisenhower would win a resounding victory. But there were signs that change was coming and that the verities of the 1950s would not remain unchallenged.

If commercial television was the home mostly of white middle-class families and quiz shows, other parts of the culture were showing signs of breaking loose. Some of these signs appeared only on the fringes of society. Nineteen fifty-six was the year Allen Ginsberg published the poem "Howl," in which he wrote that the best minds of his generation had been "destroyed by madness." Other signs, however, showed up in the mass culture. The sensational fiction best-seller of 1956 was Grace Metalious's *Peyton Place,* which portrayed Americans as more passionate and sexually active than they liked to admit. It was another conveyor of sexual messages who got the most publicity of the year: Elvis Presley, whose "Heartbreak Hotel" and other songs were redefining popular music and whose sexually suggestive performing style ("Elvis the Pelvis") scandalized guardians of public probity.

Part of the significance of Presley's music (and indeed of his performing style) was that it brought African-American culture into the mainstream. A white man singing black music was not a total revolution, but Americans were also listening to black men (and women) singing black music, whether in the unthreatening cadences of Nat "King" Cole or in the more edgy performances of Little Richard and Chuck Berry.

Black America was entering white consciousness in other, more political ways as well. In 1954, the legal basis of Jim Crow segregation had been struck down in the epochal Supreme Court decision in the case of *Brown v. Board of Education of Topeka,* which found segregated schools to be "inherently unequal." The following year the

Court set forth guidelines for implementing the decision "with all deliberate speed." Schools were not the only battleground. On December 1, 1955, in Montgomery, Alabama, a black woman named Rosa Parks was arrested for refusing to give her seat to a white passenger. A black boycott of the bus system followed, led by a young minister named Martin Luther King, Jr. Against tremendous pressures, the boycott continued through 1956, when a court decision overturned segregation on public transportation.

Internationally, too, there were signs of change and of future American involvements. In 1953, the Central Intelligence Agency helped overthrow a nationalist prime minister in Iran and replace him with Mohammed Reza Pahlavi, the shah of Iran. In 1954, after France was defeated at Dien Bien Phu by Vietnamese forces loyal to Ho Chi Minh, the United States stepped in as the principal support for the pro-Western government in South Vietnam under Ngo Dinh Diem. At the time, these decisions received little attention from the American press and even less from the public, and their full consequences would remain hidden for years.

With the nation at peace and prosperous, the Democratic Party needed to identify issues that would give it a chance to defeat Ike. Civil rights was one possibility—the Eisenhower administration was slow to implement the *Brown* decision, and southern resistance to desegregation was delaying matters further. But this issue would have split the party, which was an increasingly uncomfortable coalition of northern liberals and avowedly segregationist southern conservatives. The possible candidates had different positions on civil rights. Estes Kefauver, the Tennessee senator who had made his reputation investigating organized crime, was, for a southerner, fairly moderate but was certainly no champion of the movement. Averell Harriman, who had been elected governor of New York two years earlier, was a strong civil rights advocate, but as the convention drew near he dropped out of the running in spite of having received the endorsement of Harry Truman. In fact, Adlai Stevenson, the party's choice four years earlier, had matters well in hand a month before the convention opened in Chicago in August, and he won nomination on the first ballot. Eager to keep the party united and knowing that he had no chance of defeating Eisenhower without carrying the traditionally Democratic states of the South, Stevenson avoided civil rights talk when he could. Since the Republicans did not wish

1956

PRESIDENTIAL CANDIDATE (STATE) VICE-PRESIDENTIAL CANDIDATE (STATE)	PARTY	ELECTORAL VOTES	APPROX. % OF POPULAR VOTE
Dwight D. Eisenhower (Kans.) Richard M. Nixon (Calif.)	Republican	457	57%
Adlai E. Stevenson (Ill.) Estes Kefauver (Tenn.)	Democratic	73	42%

to debate civil rights, either, the most important issue in American domestic politics was essentially ignored.

The only drama of the Democratic convention came when Stevenson threw the choice of the vice presidential nominee to the convention. In doing so, Stevenson stressed the "solemn obligation" the voters had to consider "who will be their President if the elected President is prevented by a higher will from serving his full term." And he reminded his audience that "seven out of thirty-four Presidents have served as the result of an indirect selection." The convention had a number of men to consider, some new to the national scene: Senators Estes Kefauver and Albert Gore of Tennessee, Hubert Humphrey of Minnesota, and John F. Kennedy of Massachusetts, and Mayor Robert F. Wagner, Jr., of New York City. The contest came down to Kefauver and Kennedy, with Kefauver winning (narrowly) when Humphrey and Gore threw their support to him. But Kennedy had impressed the convention; given that he was a Catholic, politicos were particularly surprised at his success in winning the support of southern delegates.

He stopped the war in Korea

He proved he could keep the peace

Under his administration we have...

PEACE...not war

Not a single American boy fighting anywhere in the world. A firm foundation for *lasting* peace. American defenses at their highest peace-time level. An "atoms for peace" program.

HONESTY...not corruption

Dignity and integrity in Washington. No Communist influence in high places. No mink coats, deep freezers, five percenters. Today — a President respected and honored all over the world.

JOBS...with PEACE

The harmony that is essential to progress. Goodwill between labor and management. Strike losses down 53% over 1952. Highest employment — best wages in history.

LET'S KEEP IT THAT WAY...

An Eisenhower pamphlet.
NATIONAL MUSEUM OF
AMERICAN HISTORY,
SMITHSONIAN INSTITUTION.

Noble as Stevenson's rhetoric was on the subject of the "solemn obligation" the delegates faced in choosing a vice presidential nominee, the real motive was political. Because it was here, in the question of the health of the President and the qualifications of his potential successor, that the Democrats had their most useful campaign theme. In September 1955, Eisenhower had suffered a serious heart attack, so serious that for a time it was assumed he would not consider running for a second term. But he recovered, and on February 29, 1956, he said that he would seek a second term. His health again became an issue in June, when he suffered a severe case of ileitis and had to undergo a major operation. Although he came back strong and made a visit to Panama to show that he was up to the duties of office, his age (he turned sixty-six that year) caused people in both parties to worry that he would not live to complete a second term.

This was a potential campaign issue for the Democrats because many people, both politicians and voters, felt an unease with and distaste for Vice President Richard Nixon. Nixon's youth and his standing as an anti-Communist had been seen as assets for a balanced ticket in 1952, but with McCarthy discredited and Red hunting out of fashion, Nixon's past activities no longer seemed an ornament, and

In 1956, television advertising was already taking up a significant portion of campaign budgets.

he was hampered by his reputation as a dirty campaigner. The Republicans were concerned that Nixon might hurt the ticket, and this concern extended all the way up to the President.

Eisenhower, in fact, would have preferred to run with his aide Robert Anderson, but Anderson was a Democrat. At one point Ike counseled Nixon to take a cabinet post in order to gain administrative experience, but Nixon declined. On being asked by a reporter in March what his plans for Nixon were, Ike answered that Nixon would have to "chart out his own course." All the President had to do was say that he wanted Nixon on the ticket again, but he refused to do so. This naturally made Nixon furious. Harold Stassen, the former Minnesota governor, who was now working on arms control issues for Eisenhower, came to the President with private polling information showing that Nixon might cost the ticket many votes—not enough to defeat Ike but enough to give the Democrats control of Congress. Eisenhower did not stop Stassen from pursuing this dump-Nixon quest, and Stassen subsequently called a press conference to share his poll results and to urge Republicans to nominate Governor Christian Herter of Massachusetts for Vice President. But Nixon had not been idle; he had built ties to local party leaders across the country and in Congress, and that was sufficient to ensure his renomination when the Republicans met in San Francisco near the end of August.

Eisenhower's age and ill health and the unease about Nixon were issues that had to be exploited very carefully if the Democrats were to avoid a backlash. After all, Ike was the nation's father figure, and it hardly seemed nice to tell the family it was time to think about what would happen when Dad died. The Democrats eventually decided to attack Ike as a "part-time President." Stevenson, speaking in Los Angeles late in October, laid out a long list of examples of Ike's being on a golfing or hunting vacation when a world crisis had occurred. Stevenson's wording was careful but pointed: he began the speech with a remark about an "administration without heart, and without heart in its work," which may have reminded listeners of the President's heart attack. But he was careful to say that this catalog of truancies "left out every case where the President's absence from Washington or his ignorance of crucial facts could be traced to his illnesses." The Democratic nominee spoke with apparent concern about the President's "need to conserve his energies" but worried that a less energetic President would mean less control over Republicans in Congress and that "into this vacuum would come Richard Nixon—beloved by the most reactionary wing of Old Guard Republicanism." At the end of the speech, while not directly addressing the possibility of the President's death, Stevenson called up the sobering image of "Richard Nixon's hand on the trigger of the H-bomb."

Unfortunately for Stevenson, this was not enough. The Republicans were outspending the Democrats by a factor of two to one, and in television ads, which were coming into their own, the Republicans' advantage at the end of the race was huge;

they had $5 million to spend compared with $100,000 for the Democrats. The Stevenson campaign's final group of ads was never broadcast because there was no money to buy the airtime. Stevenson was not fond of this new form of campaigning—he denounced the use of "slick slogans and advertising arts" in choosing a President. "The idea that you can merchandise candidates for high office like breakfast cereal—that you can gather votes like box tops—is, I think, the ultimate indignity to the democratic process," he said. Yet he himself became part of the problem, appearing in ads that featured the "Man from Libertyville" (an Illinois town where he had once lived) doing such things as shopping with a daughter-in-law and discussing the high cost of living.

As the election neared, world events conspired against Stevenson. An uprising in Hungary was met with an invasion of Russian troops the weekend before the vote, and on the eve of election day British and French troops parachuted into Port Said and elsewhere along the Suez Canal. Americans decided they were more comfortable keeping Dwight Eisenhower in office than they would be with Adlai Stevenson. The election was a landslide for Ike, who

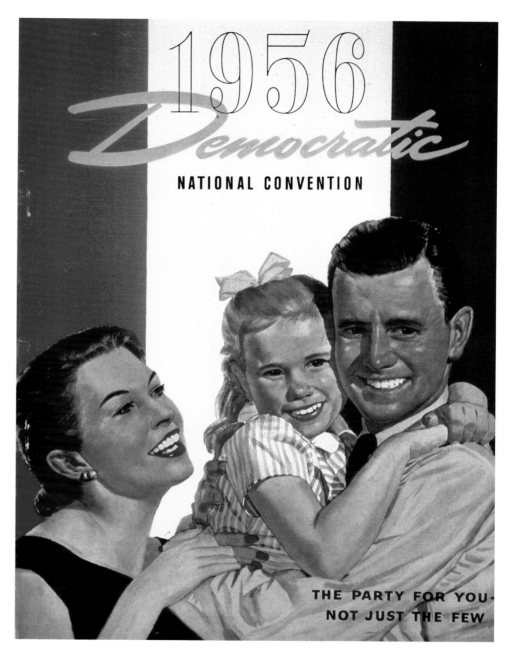

won by nearly 10 million votes. His margin in the Electoral College was 457 to 73. But the Senate and House, as Stassen had warned, went to the Democrats.

Late on election night Stevenson still had not conceded, and Eisenhower, gleeful and perhaps a bit resentful of some of Stevenson's rhetorical thrusts at him, asked, "What in the name of God is the monkey waiting for? Polishing his prose?"

CHAPTER

42

Achilles' Knee?

KENNEDY v. NIXON, 1960

The Kennedy-Nixon contest of 1960 has become so freighted with symbols, so laden with signs of the tumultuous decade that followed, and so emblematic of the emergence of the televised presidential campaign that we must remind ourselves that it was also one of the closest elections in American history. Nixon's biographer Stephen Ambrose has observed that with a few breaks in his direction we would be congratulating him on "staying away from the religious issue" (of Kennedy's Roman Catholicism), "admiring his good political sense in saving Ike until the last minute," and generally dismissing incidents, such as Kennedy's superior performance in the first of their four televised debates, that now seem central. While the keepers of the Kennedy flame have at times portrayed the election in almost Manichean terms, Camelot versus Golgotha in prime time, the closeness of the contest has caused some historians to focus on the small events that might have tipped the victory the other way. Historians and political scientists fond of statistical analyses have shown that being Catholic cost Kennedy votes—and that his religion helped him win. More than anything, this race was a confrontation between two supremely ambitious, ruthless men who fought tenaciously, and on the whole fairly, for the right to succeed Dwight D. Eisenhower as President.

Ike's shadow loomed over the contest at the time and still affects the way it is viewed. Because Eisenhower had won two presidential races by large margins and because Nixon was in second place on the ticket in those two wins, Kennedy's triumph in 1960 is often seen as a difficult feat, if not a stunning upset. But as Kennedy's aide Theodore Sorensen noted in a memo in August 1960, the Democrats were the majority party in the country, and given a good campaign Kennedy should win. (The wild card for Sorensen was religion, and he felt that Kennedy would have to respond effectively to this to ensure his victory.) Eisenhower's lack of enthusiasm for his Vice President was fairly obvious, as had been shown in 1952, when he had refused to help Nixon extract himself from his "secret fund" scandal, and in 1956, when he had allowed Harold Stassen to foment a dump-Nixon movement. In August 1960, with Nixon the nominee of his party, Ike was asked in a press conference what policy ideas Nixon had contributed to the administration. "If you give me a week, I might think of one," the President said. "I don't remember."

In 1956, Eisenhower had been able to run on a platform of peace and prosperity, but his second term had been rough. The fall of 1957 had seen two major crises. The first had concerned school desegregation in Little Rock, Arkansas, where an unwilling Ike had had to call in army troops and nationalize the Arkansas National Guard to protect black students. Orval Faubus, the governor of the state, was attempting to build his popularity by blocking school integration and brazenly appealing to racist sentiment. Although Eisenhower had no wish to hasten desegregation, Faubus's challenge to his authority was overt, and he felt he had to act.

The second crisis had come in early October, when the Soviet Union had launched the first man-made satellite to orbit the Earth, *Sputnik*. This triumph of Russian rocket engineers punctured America's assumption of scientific superiority and led to worries, exploited by Kennedy in the 1960 campaign, that there was a "missile gap" that the United States desperately needed to close if it was to remain secure. Also, by the end of 1957 and on into 1958, the economy was in recession, and this helped the Democrats make substantial gains in the midterm congressional elections, increasing their majorities in both the House and the Senate. The only bright spots for the Republicans came with the election of a new governor of New York, Nelson Rockefeller, and a strong re-election effort by Arizona senator Barry Goldwater.

Both parties were turning to a new generation of leaders, men (only men were considered presidential timber) who had fought in the Second World War but had not been, like Ike, in positions of great responsibility. The leading Democratic hopefuls all came from the Senate. The majority leader, Lyndon Johnson of Texas, was respected and feared by his colleagues and had done a capable job of managing legislation, helping achieve the compromise that had led to the passage of the Civil Rights Act of 1957, the first such piece of legislation since Reconstruction. But Johnson was from the South, and this

"MIRROR, MIRROR, ON THE WALL, WHO'S THE FAIREST ONE OF ALL?"

Cartoon by Herblock (Herbert Block), published in The Washington Post *on January 2, 1960.*

COPYRIGHT © BY HERBERT BLOCK.

1960

PRESIDENTIAL CANDIDATE (STATE) VICE-PRESIDENTIAL CANDIDATE (STATE)	PARTY	ELECTORAL VOTES	APPROX. % OF POPULAR VOTE
John F. Kennedy (Mass.) Lyndon B. Johnson (Tex.)	Democratic	303	49.7%
Richard M. Nixon (Calif.) Henry Cabot Lodge (Mass.)	Republican	219	49.5%
Harry F. Byrd (Va.)	Independent	15	

Among the minor-party candidates was Orval Faubus (States' Rights).

A supporter of Lyndon B. Johnson at the Democratic convention. Photograph by Cornell Capa.

COPYRIGHT © BY CORNELL CAPA.

was still considered a drawback to winning. Hubert Humphrey of Minnesota was the most liberal candidate in the race but was perennially short of funds. John F. Kennedy, who had been given a huge victory by Massachusetts voters when he ran for re-election in 1958, had shown heroism as a PT boat captain in the Pacific war and in 1957 had won a Pulitzer Prize for his set of essays on American history, *Profiles in Courage.* Missouri's Stuart Symington was an expert in defense matters and had the support of Harry Truman. Also available, but not actively running, was Adlai Stevenson, twice the loser to Eisenhower but still with a large following.

Although primary elections were becoming more important, many delegates were still chosen by party insiders rather than voters, and both Johnson and Symington were resting their chances on their connections within the party. Kennedy and Humphrey had no hope except by contesting primaries, and it was the matchups between the two in Wisconsin and West Virginia that decided the nomination. Wisconsin was adjacent to Humphrey's home state of Minnesota and also had a large Catholic population, and Kennedy knew that a victory there would help establish him as a candidate who could appeal across the nation. He spent much of the month of March in Wisconsin, shaking hands, meeting voters, honing his campaign form. All this paid off, and his winning in Wisconsin brought attention to his campaign. The next major battleground was West Virginia, where the salience of Kennedy's Catholicism as a campaign issue would be tested. Humphrey made it clear that he would not use the issue against Kennedy; in fact, he said he would not want anyone to vote for him because of concern over Kennedy's religion. But Humphrey's campaign was poor, and Kennedy had a rich father to bankroll his effort; easily outspending Humphrey, Kennedy also beat him easily, and Humphrey withdrew from the race.

Still, Kennedy arrived at the Democratic convention in Los Angeles uncertain if he had enough votes to win, and there was the chance that if he didn't win on the first ballot, delegates would bolt to another candidate, such as Stevenson or Johnson. On the eve of the convention, Johnson's campaign leaked the news that Kennedy had Addison's disease, an adrenal condition, and was receiving daily cortisone treatments. Kennedy's aides denied the story (they lied), and the issue was

The floor of the 1960 Democratic Convention, Los Angeles. Photograph by Cornell Capa.

passed over, in part because Kennedy looked so healthy and his publicists stressed his outdoor lifestyle. When the balloting took place, the outcome was not certain until the final state in the roll call, Wyoming, put Kennedy over the top, with 806 votes; Johnson was second, with 409. Then Kennedy asked the Texan to accept the second spot on the ticket, and Johnson, to general amazement, did.

Two weeks later, the Republicans met in Chicago to nominate Richard Nixon. Any other possibility had long been foreclosed, and the meeting was a carefully scripted celebration of Eisenhower and Nixon. For his running mate, Nixon chose Henry Cabot Lodge, the former Massachusetts senator (he had been defeated by Kennedy in 1952), who had been appointed by Eisenhower to represent America at the United Nations. Although a respected man, Lodge could hardly have been expected to bring much to the ticket, since Kennedy's strength in New England was unassailable. And Lodge proved to be a reluctant campaigner, unlike Johnson, who carried the Democratic message throughout the South.

However different from each other Kennedy and Nixon look to us today, at the time many saw tremendous similarities: both were young men (JFK was forty-three, Nixon forty-seven) practiced in the arts of politics and unhindered by discernible principles. If Eisenhower had trouble recalling Nixon's contributions in the White House, so Kennedy's colleagues on Capitol Hill had trouble recalling what he had done there. "The Processed Politician has finally arrived," the veteran newsman Eric Sevareid commented.

For the Processed Politician the testing ground would be television, in a series of four debates beginning in late September. But before Richard Nixon got to the debates, he had some bad luck. He banged his knee on a car door in August and finally, after ignoring the pain for some time, consulted a doctor. He was told that he would have to spend two weeks in the hospital to fight a serious infection. So at the beginning of September, as the race was beginning, Nixon had to lie on his back and watch Kennedy get a head start. Nixon lost ten pounds and, stubbornly refusing to deviate from a pledge to make campaign appearances in all fifty states, he pushed himself even harder than usual when he was well enough to resume campaigning, in mid-September.

The first debate took place in Chicago on September 26. Nixon was tired and underweight, and he banged his ailing knee again getting out of the car at the studio. Kennedy, who had been campaigning in California, spent the afternoon tanning himself and came to the studio looking fit and rested. Nixon refused to have any but the most rudimentary makeup, and the heat of the lights, combined with his poor condition and the pain in his knee, turned him into a sweaty, hollow-eyed, pasty, and nervous adversary for the calm, handsome Kennedy. Ike had told Nixon that he should not debate Kennedy: Nixon was better known and would inevitably lose ground simply by appearing on equal terms with his opponent. Nixon, however, felt that

Kennedy and Nixon during their first television debate.
LIBRARY OF CONGRESS.

he had to meet the challenge and was confident that his command of facts would be crucial. But images, not facts, were what mattered. Those listening on the radio thought Nixon won the first contest, but television viewers—around 70 million of them, attracted by this new phenomenon of American politics—gave the advantage to Kennedy. Henry Cabot Lodge's reaction was to the point: "That son-of-a-bitch just lost us the election."

That explanation, however appealing, is not sufficient. Nixon, after all, was a canny politician with many resources to draw on, and a misstep in late September was hardly conclusive, particularly since his entire strategy rested upon a crescendo of appearances and announcements in the last few weeks of the campaign. That was when he intended to use Eisenhower, who was not enthusiastic but was willing to do what he could (given his poor health) for the GOP. And that was when, Nixon hoped, some dramatic event in foreign affairs might swing voters his way. The year before, Cuba had come under the control of Fidel Castro, who had drawn close to the Soviet Union and was nationalizing American holdings in Cuba. Nixon advocated a military strike against Castro's regime, but Eisenhower decided that the time was not right. Then, after Kennedy proposed the sort of military adventure that Nixon was hoping for, Nixon was put in the unpleasant position of having to defend the administration's inaction.

Surprisingly, given Nixon's reputation as a dirty campaigner, he avoided using Kennedy's Catholicism as an issue. Others tried to use it for him, and Kennedy decided to face the issue head-on by addressing a group of Protestant divines in Houston on September 12. He was eloquent, telling his listeners, "If this election is decided on the basis that 40,000,000 Americans lost their chance of being President on the day they were baptized, then it is the whole nation that will be the loser in the eyes of Catholics and non-Catholics around the world, in the eyes of history, and in the eyes of our own people." From a tape of the performance, Kennedy's aides made various short spots and a long version and broadcast them in selected markets around the nation. They also made use of clips from the first debate, so that their candidate's best moments and Nixon's worst ones were kept in the public eye. The Democratic campaign had to go into debt to make the ads and broadcast them, but it was willing to take the risk (as were its suppliers, at least one of whom was never paid).

The three other debates were more even, but fewer people watched. Kennedy had already gained a decisive advantage in the first contest, for now that he had won a face-to-face contest, his less impressive credentials no longer seemed as important. Nixon's people learned their lesson from the first encounter, and at the second debate Nixon submitted to a full regime of makeup. (His aides lowered the thermostat in the building where the debate was being held; Kennedy's aides then sneaked out and raised it.)

Nixon had more bad luck. On October 25, just as he was launching his final offensive, Dr. Martin Luther King, Jr., was sentenced to four months in jail as a consequence of a minor traffic infraction. John Kennedy called King's wife, Coretta, to offer his support, while Robert Kennedy, without consulting his brother, called the judge in the case and persuaded him to free King on bail. Nineteen sixty was a year

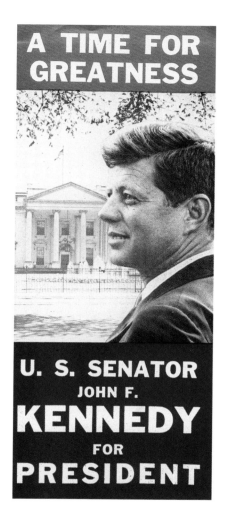

DAVID J. AND JANICE L. FRENT
POLITICAL AMERICANA COLLECTION.

The shadow of John F. Kennedy. Photograph by Cornell Capa.
COPYRIGHT © BY
CORNELL CAPA.

of increasing activism among southern blacks, with lunch counter sit-ins by college students drawing international attention. Both parties had similar civil rights approaches: they endorsed the principles of equal rights and opportunity and avoided any more concrete commitment as much as possible. In this atmosphere, Kennedy's phone call, small gesture though it was, attracted a lot of attention in black America. Reverend King's father said he had "a suitcase of votes" and that he would take them to JFK and "dump them in his lap," and the Sunday before the election Democratic workers distributed pro-Kennedy literature in black churches across the nation. African-American voters supported Kennedy in much greater numbers than they had Stevenson four years earlier.

If one looks at the campaign as a whole, the safest conclusion to be drawn is that issues mattered little. Kennedy and Nixon both ran as Cold Warriors, the only question being which candidate was truer to the cause. Kennedy's call to Coretta King was about the only thing he did to signal his support for civil rights, and Lyndon Johnson, campaigning for the ticket in the South, routinely mentioned his family's Confederate roots to appeal to white voters there.

On the final weekend, it was clear that the election would be very close. Nixon, however, had still not set foot in his fiftieth state, Alaska, and he spent valuable time fulfilling his pledge rather than visiting states such as Illinois, where the race was close and many more electoral votes were at stake.

Kennedy's popular-vote margin was thin—119,450 votes out of more than 68.8 million cast. His electoral-vote margin was 303 to 219, with 15 electors casting votes

Photograph by Cornell Capa.
COPYRIGHT © BY CORNELL CAPA.

Kennedy on his campaign train.
Photograph by Cornell Capa.
COPYRIGHT © BY CORNELL CAPA.

for the Dixiecrat Harry F. Byrd of Virginia, whose noncampaign had attracted about half a million segregationist voters. The question of what had made the difference—Nixon's performance at the first debate, Kennedy's call to King, or the Democratic majority nationwide, which reflected the continuing strength of Roosevelt's New Deal coalition—is impossible to answer, just as it is impossible to be certain whether Kennedy's Roman Catholicism helped bring Catholic voters to the polls for the Democrats or energized anti-Catholic Protestants to vote for Nixon.

But the campaign did change the face of American politics and made it clear that the place to be was not on a whistle-stop tour or in a union hall but on TV. As the political process evolved over the next few decades, the place of television grew in importance. Politics was emerging from smoke-filled rooms, conventions were changing from places where choices were made to places where choices were ratified, and substance was losing ground to image. Above all, candidates now needed to find huge amounts of money to buy television time in order to present their painstakingly selected and tested messages to the American public.

"In Your Guts You Know He's Nuts"

JOHNSON v. GOLDWATER, 1964

The possibility of nuclear war between the United States and the Soviet Union was a constant worry during the Cold War, and discussion of the issue could be found everywhere, from the most serious journals to the most sensational science fiction films. Into this nervous atmosphere in 1964 strode the new darling of Republican conservatives: Senator Barry Goldwater of Arizona. The Republicans had been conducting internecine struggles over foreign policy since the war, with the isolationist, midwestern Taft wing wishing to disengage as much as possible from the rest of the world and the internationalist eastern Republicans embracing a more active policy of containment, as put forth by the Truman administration. Eisenhower had on occasion embraced the aggressive rhetoric of seeking to "roll back" the advance of communism, but his actions were cautious. In Goldwater the party found a candidate who advocated "total victory" over communism and seemed willing, even eager, to use nuclear weapons to achieve that goal.

In May 1963, as American involvement in the Vietnam War was just beginning to grow, Goldwater suggested a way of dealing with supplies going to Viet Cong forces in the South: "I'd drop a low-yield atomic bomb on the Chinese supply lines in North Vietnam or maybe shell 'em with the Seventh Fleet." Then, in November, he suggested that America could reduce the number of troops stationed in Europe "if we gave the NATO command the right to use nuclear weapons—tactical weapons—when they were attacked." Not long afterward he tried to clarify the statement, indicating that he meant to limit this discretion to the top commander of NATO, but he went on to say, "Under the present system, red tape makes our nuclear deterrent almost unusable." The paranoid visions of Stanley Kubrick's movie *Dr. Strangelove* seemed to have come to life in Goldwater's battle-ready rhetoric.

It became increasingly clear that Goldwater, however extreme some of his ideas might seem, was emerging as a front-runner for the GOP nomination. His main opponent was Governor Nelson Rockefeller of New York, a liberal, internationalist Republican. Rockefeller had been an early favorite, but he was divorced, and when, in May 1963, he married a much younger woman (who was also divorced), his lead

Johnson buttons.

DAVID J. AND JANICE L. FRENT
POLITICAL AMERICANA COLLECTION.

evaporated. (The Gallup Poll showed him ahead 43 to 26 percent before his marriage and trailing 35 to 30 percent after it.) Still, the biggest threat to Rockefeller's chances was not his marital status but the dedicated band of very conservative Republicans who were working to take control of the party and move it to the right, and who saw Goldwater as the man to help them do this.

The crucial insight the group brought to Republican politics was that Democratic actions to enforce and expand civil rights laws were creating a "white backlash" in the South as well as in northern cities and suburbs. In April 1963, these conservatives, with the Texas Republican chairman Peter O'Donnell as their spokesman, announced a National Draft Goldwater Committee. This committee argued that the Republicans had a chance to break the old Democratic dominance in the South and endorsed a "southern strategy" for the 1964 election.

The Democrats had not taken up the cause of civil rights quickly or eagerly. John F. Kennedy had done little early in his administration to advance African Americans' rights; he was by temperament and training more interested in foreign policy, and he was also aware that the issue threatened to destroy the Democratic hegemony in the South. But, as had happened to Eisenhower in school integration in Little Rock in 1957, whites' defiance of federal court rulings and outrage in the North over violence against civil rights workers prodded the administration to act. Moreover, black activists made sure the Democrats knew that black people were impatient for change. In August 1963, King spoke to a crowd of perhaps a quarter of a million people in Washington, telling them and the world, "I have a dream." In June of that year, President Kennedy had proposed a civil rights bill, but it had stalled in the Senate. How things might have played out under Kennedy's leadership is impossible to know, for on November 22 he was assassinated in Dallas, and Lyndon Johnson succeeded him as President.

This posed problems for Goldwater's "southern strategy," since Johnson himself was a southerner. Johnson made the promotion of Kennedy's civil rights legislation a high priority, and, using his mastery of the congressional process and the emotional surge of support that followed Kennedy's assassination, he managed to win the votes needed to end a southern filibuster and pass the bill. His moves caused dissension within his own party, and Alabama governor George Wallace announced that he would run in some presidential primaries. Liberal Democrats reeled when he won significant followings: 30 percent in Indiana, 34 percent in

1964

PRESIDENTIAL CANDIDATE (STATE) VICE-PRESIDENTIAL CANDIDATE (STATE)	PARTY	ELECTORAL VOTES	APPROX. % OF POPULAR VOTE
Lyndon B. Johnson (Tex.) Hubert H. Humphrey (Minn.)	Democratic	486	61%
Barry M. Goldwater (Ariz.) William E. Miller (N.Y.)	Republican	52	39%

Wisconsin, 43 percent in Maryland. The showing in normally liberal Wisconsin was a sobering indicator of how widespread and deep the "white backlash" was.

As the conventions approached, the polarization of the electorate continued. In June, three civil rights workers involved in the Freedom Summer voter registration drive in Mississippi disappeared (their bodies were not found until August). On July 18, a riot erupted in Harlem, and the next day the Republican convention opened at the Cow Palace in San Francisco. Goldwater's supporters not only nominated their candidates—Representative William E. Miller of New York was chosen for Vice President—but also showed a raucous intolerance of figures such as Nelson Rockefeller, whose speech to the convention was jeered. Goldwater, accepting the nomination, made it clear that he was not interested in compromise: "Extremism in the defense of liberty is no vice!" he proclaimed, and "Moderation in the pursuit of justice is no virtue!" The battle lines were drawn, more starkly than in almost any other election.

Between the Republicans' convention in July and the Democrats' in Atlantic City late in August, more riots broke out in northern cities, and a naval incident in the Gulf of Tonkin provided justification for a wider American involvement in

Goldwater campaigning in his home city of Phoenix, Arizona.
Photograph by Cornell Capa.

The quotation on this button, from Goldwater's nomination acceptance speech, polarized the Republicans into conservative and liberal camps. Another popular Goldwater button bore the slogan "In your heart you know he's right," which the Democrats countered with buttons stating "In your guts you know he's nuts."

DAVID J. AND JANICE L. FRENT
POLITICAL AMERICANA COLLECTION.

Vietnam. Johnson's desire to have the convention function as a coronation was undercut chiefly by the efforts of Mississippi blacks to gain the voice there that they had been denied at home through voting restrictions and intimidation. But Johnson was eager not to jeopardize his hopes in the South any more than he already had. (Signing the Civil Rights Act earlier in the year, he had said to his aide Joseph Califano, "I think we delivered the South to the Republican party for your lifetime and mine.") He offered a compromise that would give the black delegates—who called themselves the Mississippi Freedom Democratic Party—two at-large seats at the convention, but they rejected the offer. Johnson told the convention that he would like Senator Hubert H. Humphrey of Minnesota to have the second spot on the ticket; he had earlier ruled out members of his cabinet in order to block any move to give the slot to Attorney General Robert Kennedy, with whom he was at odds.

In contrast to Goldwater's divisive and ideological speech, Johnson extolled the opportunities before America: "This nation, this generation, in this hour has man's first chance to build a great society, a place where the meaning of man's life matches the marvels of man's labor." Sincerely eager to build a better nation, Johnson pictured a society where "every man can seek knowledge and touch beauty and rejoice in the closeness of family and community." Johnson's dreams were large, and some certainly lay outside the compass of what any government could achieve, but they were inspiring.

The campaign settled into a routine in which Johnson stayed in the White House and acted presidential while Goldwater campaigned vigorously around the country. Goldwater sought to play on the white backlash without resorting to racist language (he himself was tolerant, but he nevertheless had to appeal to the segregationist vote if his southern strategy was to succeed), and he found in the phrases "law and order" and "violence in the streets" useful code words that could appeal to whites without branding him a racist.

The Democrats, for their part, stressed Goldwater's irresponsibility and used nuclear terror as the ultimate danger arising from Goldwater's extremism. In a famous ad, broadcast just once, on September 7, but replayed frequently on news programs, a young girl is plucking petals from a daisy and counting "One, two, three, four, five, seven, six, six, eight, nine." Then a man's voice recites a rocket countdown: "Ten, nine, eight, seven, six, five, four, three, two, one, zero." The frame dissolves from a close-up of the girl's face to a shot of a nuclear explosion, and against the mushroom cloud Lyndon Johnson is heard saying, "These are the stakes: to make a world in which all of God's children can live or to go into the dark. We must either love each other, or we must die." Although the ad did not mention Goldwater at all, the effect was devastating. The Democrats pulled the ad after one showing, figuring the expected news coverage would be more effective than further showings would be and allowing them to avoid a long-running controversy over airing it. An estimated 40 million people saw the spot at some point during the campaign.

Goldwater's best hope—and it was a slim one—came when a White House aide was arrested for homosexual relations in a Washington YMCA. For the moralistic Goldwater campaign, the scandal, with its aura of degeneracy (at the time, homosexuality was still widely seen as a perversion or, at best, an affliction), seemed perfect, and there was the further possibility that government secrets might have been compromised, since a homosexual could so easily be blackmailed. This was an old idea that had been given currency in the 1950s by Joseph McCarthy, of whom Goldwater had been a staunch defender.

The matter might have proved important, but it disappeared when three huge international stories broke in the forty-eight hours following the aide's arrest: Nikita Khrushchev, the Soviet leader, was deposed; the People's Republic of China detonated its first atom bomb; and the Tory government in Britain fell. In addition to pushing the scandal off the front pages, these events reminded voters of the fragile international situation and probably made them even less willing to entrust the country's nuclear arsenal to Goldwater's possibly overeager hand. On being asked by a reporter in 1963 how he felt about the possibility of becoming President, he had said, "Frankly, it scares the hell out of me." In 1964, most Americans agreed. Johnson's margin of victory was 16 million votes, and he won more than 61 percent of the popular vote. In the Electoral College he won by 486 to 52. Johnson's coattails helped other Democrats; the new Senate was Democratic by a 68–32 margin and the House by 295 to 140. There was one sobering note for the Democrats: although Goldwater had won in only six states, five of them were in the South (the other was his home state, Arizona). For the Republicans, the southern strategy was beginning to show real promise.

The Goldwater campaign produced many novelty items with the candidate's name expressed as a chemical formula, using the scientific abbreviations for gold (Au) and water (H_2O).

NATIONAL MUSEUM OF AMERICAN HISTORY, SMITHSONIAN INSTITUTION.

Helter Skelter

NIXON, HUMPHREY, WALLACE, 1968

Many Americans felt that in the middle 1960s the country they thought they knew was disappearing. The Vietnam War, still a minor consideration for most people when Lyndon Johnson was elected, had become a major conflict involving half a million American troops, and by the fall of 1967 scenes of warfare had become routine on the nightly news. Black protest moved from the towns of the South to the cities of the North. In August 1965, a riot in the Watts section of Los Angeles (touched off when police stopped a black motorist) lasted five days and was suppressed only when some 14,000 National Guard troops were brought in; thirty-four people died. In 1966, there were 38 riots, and in 1967 there were 164, 8 of them serious enough for National Guard troops to be summoned. Large riots in Newark, New Jersey, and Detroit in July threw both cities into a prolonged decline. An emerging youth culture had quickly evolved from the cuddly pop images of the Beatles to an angrier, louder, and more drug-laden counterculture. Birth control pills and changing attitudes spawned a "sexual revolution," and the idea that the nation was suffering from moral blight grew stronger among conservatives.

Yet the period also saw lasting reforms of American law and the initiation of social programs that have become as central to American society as the New Deal measures establishing Social Security and protecting the rights of organized labor. Following the Civil Rights Act of 1964, the Great Society programs passed between 1965 and 1967 included the Voting Rights Act, Medicare, Medicaid, important environmental legislation, aid to education (such as federally financed college loans), and food stamps. For a significant number of Americans, the world that disappeared in those years was the world of no health coverage, too little food, and no right to vote.

Yet for all the upheaval that occurred between 1964 and 1967, the events of 1968 made for an election year of unparalleled drama and tragedy. The first shock came from Vietnam. As 1967 ended, American commanders and administration spokesmen were saying that they could finally see "the light at the end of the tunnel." This was easy for many Americans to believe—after all, the nation that had defeated Germany and Japan was surely equal to the task of subduing a small Asian country. But at a little before three in the morning Saigon time on January 30, at the start of the traditional Vietnamese New Year, called Tet, a detachment of soldiers from the National Liberation Front, or Viet Cong, broke into the American embassy compound and tried to break into the embassy building. Although the attack was driven back, other attacks were simultaneously taking place across Vietnam. Weeks of fighting followed, with losses—huge for the Viet Cong and their North Vietnamese allies—on both sides. The effect on American public opinion was significant: both citizens and reporters grew more skeptical of the official line on the war.

The Tet offensive was a problem for Lyndon Johnson in two ways: he had to figure out how to respond to it militarily, and he had to manage the political damage at home. Opponents of the war had been protesting America's involvement for some time, and at the end of November 1967, Eugene McCarthy, a senator from Minnesota, announced that he would run against President Johnson and his Vietnam policies in some of the Democratic primaries. Tet sent many voters to McCarthy's side, and in the New Hampshire primary, on March 12, he received 42 percent of the vote. Johnson (as a write-in candidate) received 49 percent. Owing to the nature of the delegate selection process there, McCarthy secured most of the state's votes for the Democratic convention. Four days later, Robert Kennedy, now a senator from New York, entered the race, finally confronting his brother's successor in a struggle for the White House.

The confrontation would not last long. While the political landscape was being altered by McCarthy's strong showing in New Hampshire, Johnson was weighing a request from his military advisers to increase the number of American troops in Vietnam by more than 200,000. Others told him that he could not afford to pay

Lyndon Johnson announcing that he would not run for reelection, March 31, 1968. LIBRARY OF CONGRESS.

1968

PRESIDENTIAL CANDIDATE (STATE) VICE-PRESIDENTIAL CANDIDATE (STATE)	PARTY	ELECTORAL VOTES	APPROX. % OF POPULAR VOTE
Richard M. Nixon (Calif.) Spiro T. Agnew (Md.)	Republican	301	43.4%
Hubert H. Humphrey (Minn.) Edmund Muskie (Maine)	Democratic	191	42.7%
George C. Wallace (Ala.) Curtis LeMay (Calif.)	American Independent	46	13.5%

Among the minor-party candidates were Eugene McCarthy (New Party), Eldridge Cleaver (Peace and Freedom), and Dick Gregory (various parties).

Poster by Ben Shahn.

for so many troops and that in any case it seemed unlikely that escalation would lead to a defeat of the Viet Cong and the North Vietnamese. On March 31, Johnson addressed the nation on TV, announcing that he was cutting back the bombing missions against North Vietnam (he did not mention that at the same time strikes against enemy targets in the South would be stepped up) and making overtures for peace talks with the North Vietnamese. Then he surprised his audience by announcing, "I shall not seek, and I will not accept, the nomination of my party for President."

The nation was still processing this news when another, even greater shock came. Four days after Johnson's speech, Martin Luther King, Jr., was assassinated in Memphis. The civil rights movement was not as unified in 1968 as it had been five years earlier, when King had delivered his "I have a dream" speech, but King was still its most prominent leader, and he had remained committed to nonviolence even as younger and more militant leaders advocated more confrontational approaches to the problems of racism and inequality in America. The murder of this apostle of nonviolence provoked riots in more than 130 cities across America; more than forty people died, and around twenty thousand were arrested.

As the riots burned out, Democratic Party leaders were assessing the effect of Johnson's withdrawal on the coming election. Robert Kennedy's forces tried to persuade Johnson's allies to support his candidacy, but his rivalry with the President and his liberal positions made that unappealing, and many of them turned to the Vice President, Hubert Humphrey, and encouraged him to run. One of the great ironies of the 1968 race is that Humphrey, who was both by temperament and by record the most liberal of the Democratic contenders, became the choice of the party's conservatives because he supported Johnson's Vietnam policy. As Vice President, he could hardly lead the opposition.

Or perhaps it should be said that he was the choice of the Democratic conservatives who remained with the party, because the conservatives would actually have two champions in November, one a longtime Democrat, George Wallace. Wallace's strong showing in the 1964 primaries had persuaded him to mount a full-scale race in 1968 as the candidate of the American Independent Party. Although he knew he could not win, he hoped to do well enough to deny either major-party candidate a majority in the Electoral College and then use his votes as leverage to win policy commitments and other favors. He managed to get onto the ballot in all fifty states, and polls showed him to have significant support—as high as 20 percent at times.

The Republican candidate for conservatives to turn to was Richard Nixon. After his 1960 defeat, he had returned to California. In 1962, he had run for governor but had lost by a large margin to Edmund G. "Pat" Brown. Telling reporters after his defeat that they wouldn't have "Nixon to kick around anymore," the maudlin loser moved to New York to practice law (which he found colossally boring). He devoted much of his time to cultivating Republican leaders across the nation, making countless appearances to support candidates in local races, speaking at fund-raising dinners, and generally doing the party's work. He had not run away from the Goldwater campaign in 1964—in fact, he had helped it—and this had won him the gratitude of many GOP conservatives. Governor George Romney of Michigan was planning to oppose Nixon in the primaries, but polls showed him doing so poorly as the New Hampshire vote neared that he withdrew. Two other governors were considering a run for the nomination. On March 21, Nelson Rockefeller announced that he would not run and then, a month later—following Johnson's withdrawal, King's death, and the riots—announced that he would run after all. Ronald Reagan, who had been elected governor of California in 1966, entered the race after the primaries were over, hoping to win at the convention.

On the Democratic side a strange contest was developing. Humphrey had announced too late to get on the ballot for any primaries, but he hoped that delegates selected by or loyal to state party leaders would give him the votes he needed. In the primaries, Eugene McCarthy and Robert Kennedy were fighting bitterly. Kennedy was greeted enthusiastically on his campaign stops, and he did well in early contests. McCarthy won a major victory in Oregon, and then, in the vital California primary, Kennedy won narrowly. But as he left a Los Angeles hotel ballroom after his victory speech he was shot by an Arab nationalist named Sirhan Sirhan. Twenty-five hours later, he was dead.

The Tet offensive, the assassinations, and urban riots were just part of the atmosphere of turmoil that year. In Paris in May, a student-led insurrection nearly shut down the city and led to the fall of the government of President Charles de Gaulle, while in America campus protests intensified. Students at Columbia University seized offices to protest various university policies; Co-

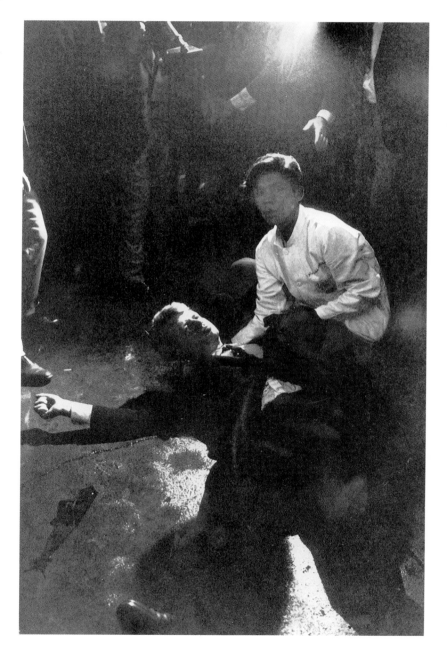

Robert F. Kennedy, moments after he was fatally shot, in a kitchen hallway of the Ambassador Hotel, Los Angeles, June 6, 1968. Photograph by Bill Eppridge/Life Magazine.

George Wallace, the American Independent Party's candidate.
LIBRARY OF CONGRESS.

lumbia called in the police to remove the protesters, and they did so with such gratuitous violence that many on the campus who had been indifferent or opposed to the original protest were radicalized.

By the time the Republican convention convened in Miami early in August, the sensation of life spinning out of control was palpable across the nation. As the delegates gathered, Rockefeller's campaign tried to persuade them that, according to the polls, only he could defeat the Democrats in the fall. Nixon's losses in 1960 and 1962 had branded him as a loser, and the lack of primary opponents after Romney's early withdrawal had deprived him of the chance to post the sort of victories that could eradicate that reputation. Reagan hoped that the convention would turn to him as a more electable candidate, one whose indisputable conservatism would attract potential Wallace voters. But Nixon's long years of political networking paid off, and he won the nomination—narrowly—on the first ballot. For Vice President he chose Spiro T. Agnew, the governor of Maryland. One columnist mocked Agnew's obscurity, suggesting that Nixon had used a Ouija board to find him. Indeed, Agnew proved detrimental to the ticket, owing chiefly to his verbal blunders, such as "You've seen one slum, you've seen them all."

The Democratic convention, in Chicago, was the last major act in the country's nervous breakdown that spring and summer. As a badly divided party debated what its platform should say about the Vietnam War and as feuds erupted between backers of McCarthy and Humphrey and those still loyal to Bobby Kennedy, protesters of various persuasions attempted to demonstrate in downtown Chicago. The police department, under Mayor Richard J. Daley, grew increasingly violent in its reaction to the protests. On the third night, police attacked demonstrators in front of the Hilton Hotel, beating them with nightsticks while protesters chanted, "The whole world is watching." Inside the convention hall, Senator Abraham Ribicoff of Connecticut nominated Senator George McGovern of South Dakota for President, saying that if McGovern were in the White House you would not have "Gestapo tactics on the streets of Chicago." TV viewers could see Mayor Daley in the audience, his face contorted with rage, shouting at Ribicoff, "Fuck you, you Jew son of a bitch, you lousy motherfucker, go home!" By the time Humphrey accepted his party's nomination (with Maine's Edmund Muskie, a respected senator, as his running mate), it hardly seemed worth having. McCarthy refused to endorse the nominee, and the Republicans were awash in campaign contributions while the Democrats were lagging badly. In early September polls showed Humphrey trailing Nixon by about ten percentage points, with Wallace another ten points back, in third place.

The truly remarkable thing about the last two months of the campaign was that Humphrey, with all his disadvantages—a divided party, meager campaign funds, the challenge from Wallace, the need to distance himself from Johnson's policies without going so far as to enrage the vindictive President, and a well-financed opponent with a carefully plotted campaign strategy—came very close to victory, losing to Nixon by only half a million votes out of more than 73 million cast.

Humphrey's revival had several causes. One was the comparative merits of the two major-party vice presidential nominees. Muskie appeared dignified and intelligent and proved a capable defuser of the hecklers who were a constant presence on the campaign trail. Agnew, in contrast, called Humphrey "squishy soft on communism" (and later professed to be unaware of the McCarthyite—Joe McCarthy, not Gene—associations of the charge) and was a purveyor of ethnic insults, speaking of "Polacks" and calling a Nisei reporter a "fat Jap." Democratic ads contrasted the

Protesters and police outside the Democratic Party convention, Chicago.
AP/WIDE WORLD PHOTOS.

vice presidential candidates, asking whom the voters would prefer to have "a heart-beat away from the presidency."

Even more important was a major effort made by organized labor to win union voters back to the Democrats. Labor attacked Wallace as the governor of a "right-to-work" state and stressed the long service the Democrats in general and Humphrey in particular had provided to labor. By mid-October, Humphrey was cutting into Wallace's support, while Nixon remained steady in the polls. As the Democratic contender began to show promise, money started flowing to the party, although the amounts were in no way comparable to what was going to the Republicans.

Nixon, for his part, had learned the lessons of his exhausting 1960 campaign. He kept to a moderate pace, and his campaign stops were planned for maximum television exposure and press coverage. He studiously avoided specific proposals, sticking to bland statements of principle and offering to speak for the "forgotten Americans"—those whose views were being ignored by news media that focused only on the protesters.

Humphrey's late surge fell short, and Nixon won with 301 electoral votes to 191 for Humphrey and 46 for Wallace. Nixon entered the White House the following January having been elected by only 43 percent of the voters. He faced Democratic majorities in both houses of Congress and a nation severely split over Vietnam and civil rights. A student of history, however, he proceeded to use the time-honored tactic of dividing and conquering to consolidate his power. Along the way, he would invent some new techniques for practicing this old art.

Shadow Play

NIXON v. McGOVERN, 1972

On the surface, the story of the 1972 election is quickly told. The Democrats nominated a representative of the party's left wing, Senator George McGovern of South Dakota, who selected Senator Thomas Eagleton of Missouri as his running mate, then ditched him when he turned out to have received electroshock treatment for depression. McGovern never recovered from this blunder and spent the rest of the race on the defensive as his fringe positions were skillfully exploited by President Nixon and Vice President Spiro Agnew, who racked up one of the great electoral victories in American history: Nixon and Agnew carried forty-nine of the fifty states, with McGovern able to win only Massachusetts and the District of Columbia.

If a security guard in Washington's Watergate complex named Frank Wills had not noticed that a door had been taped open, that might have remained the story of the 1972 campaign. But Wills's discovery led to a string of discoveries that exposed the secret history of the Nixon administration and its 1972 campaign activities and ended with Nixon's resignation in disgrace in 1974. But in 1972, the American electorate was truly like Plato's prisoners, seeing the shadows on the wall of the cave but unable to perceive the substance that cast the shadows.

Richard Nixon was acutely aware that his victory in 1968 had been narrow and that he had become President with only 43 percent of the popular vote. As he looked ahead to 1972, he sought a new, more secure strategy for winning. One of the principal strategists of the Nixon re-election effort was Patrick Buchanan, a speechwriter and later an aspirant for the presidency. Buchanan recognized that the Republicans remained a minority party (the Democrats controlled both houses of Congress throughout the Nixon years) and believed that Nixon's chances depended on dividing the Democrats. The White House, preparing for 1972, assumed that George Wallace would make another run for the presidency and that this would help Nixon. At the same time, the Republicans were eager to avoid having the Democrats nominate a strong centrist candidate, and the man they feared most was the Democrats' vice presidential nominee from 1968, Edmund Muskie. Muskie had performed impressively as Hubert Humphrey's running mate and, in the view of many Democratic Party leaders, had the best chance of pulling together the now-drifting elements of the New Deal coalition.

But Democratic Party leaders had far less power in selecting the presidential nominee in 1972 than they had had four years earlier. The black civil rights movement, the women's liberation movement, and the efforts of other minorities—Hispanic Americans, Native Americans, Asian Americans—to win a greater voice in the nation's political life all exerted pressure on the party to open its procedures for choosing delegates and to make those delegates more representative of the voters they were supposed to speak for. After the disastrous Chicago convention of 1968, the party appointed a committee, headed by George McGovern, to ensure "adequate representation" of women and minorities. Although the committee declared itself opposed to quotas, there was nonetheless tremendous pressure for previously underrepresented groups to be chosen in force for 1972. At the same time, the selection of delegates at state party conventions was losing favor, and more states were making primary elections the center of the process. More than half the delegates at the convention in 1972 had been chosen in primaries.

In theory, primaries are a more open and objective method of selecting delegates; in fact, the Nixon White House was conducting a covert campaign that aimed to ensure that the Democrats chose the candidate Nixon had the best chance of beating. In October 1971, Pat Buchanan wrote a memo outlining ways of keeping the Democratic Party divided, proposing that the White House seek ways of making sure that George Wallace entered the Democratic primaries and noting that a fourth-party candidate, particularly a black one, would do more than anything else to "advance the President's chances of re-election." The White House and the President's electoral organization, the Committee to Re-Elect the President (CREEP), were resourceful, if unethical, in their methods.

Nixon's helpers drafted letters to reporters and columnists planting derogatory information about Democratic contenders and produced reams of letters to the editor endorsing Nixon's positions on the issues. Policy questions were assessed on the grounds of their ability to divide the Democrats; for example, Nixon spoke in favor of aid to parochial education, an issue that was ex-

1972

PRESIDENTIAL CANDIDATE (STATE) VICE-PRESIDENTIAL CANDIDATE (STATE)	PARTY	ELECTORAL VOTES	APPROX. % OF POPULAR VOTE
Richard M. Nixon (Calif.) Spiro T. Agnew (Md.)	Republican	520	61%
George S. McGovern (S.Dak.) Sargent Shriver (Md.)	Democratic	17	8%
Joseph Hospers (Calif.) Tonie Nathan (Oreg.)	Libertarian	1	

John Mitchell, Nixon's campaign manager, pulls back the curtain to reveal his candidate. The Republicans meticulously choreographed their 1972 convention to make a show of unanimous political moderation with all the key events timed for television prime time. The Democratic convention, in Miami Beach, was in striking contrast, as McGovern began his nomination acceptance speech at nearly three o'clock in the morning. The Great G.O.P. Middle of the Road Show, *painting by Richard Hess, 1972.*

pected to separate the Catholic segment of the Democratic coalition from those who took stronger positions on the separation of church and state. G. Gordon Liddy, the chief legal counsel to CREEP as the year began, proposed a set of adventurous activities that included hiring muggers to attack any demonstrators outside the Republican convention and kidnappers to spirit away leaders of the demonstrations. Prostitutes, he suggested, could be hired to compromise delegates to the Democratic gathering. The plan was rejected—not, as one might hope and expect, because it was illegal but because it was too expensive.

More economical misdeeds were actually carried out by a campaign operative named Donald Segretti. At a rally for George Wallace at the time of the Florida Democratic primary, cards were handed out comparing Wallace to Hitler and urging a vote for Muskie. Also in Florida, an ad, supposedly for Muskie, was placed on a Spanish-language radio station by Nixon's people, saying, in Spanish, that Muskie "was born in Maine and is a good American"—a sure way of offending members of the Cuban immigrant community. Perhaps the most influential White House trick was a letter to the hyperconservative *Manchester Union Leader,* which charged that Muskie had acquiesced when an associate had referred to Canadians using the derogatory term "Canucks." Muskie's emotional denial of the charge caused members of the press to raise the question of whether he could "take the heat" and endure the pressures of high office. Muskie's victory in the New Hampshire primary, with 46 percent of the vote to McGovern's 37 percent, was portrayed as a loss for him, since he was from a neighboring state and had been expected to do better.

Segretti and other Nixon aides were tireless in their disruption of the Democrats' activities and in sowing mistrust among the contenders. Calls were placed to the press announcing events that had never been scheduled and canceling those that had. A fake letter printed on "Muskie for President" stationery accused Hubert Humphrey of sexual misconduct. A Nixon agent found a job as a driver for Muskie's campaign and had campaign documents copied for the White House before delivering them.

But the Nixon campaign's activities involved far more than espionage and dirty tricks. In 1972, there was, in the words of Jonathan Schell, whose book *The Time of Illusion* remains the most thoughtful analysis of the subject, "not only a rigged campaign but a rigged America and a rigged world for the campaign to take place in." The Vietnam War was the center around which the rigged world revolved, and Nixon's conduct of the war and the peace negotiations was duplicitous on many levels. A secret air war against Cambodia was part of his strategy, as were secret peace negotiations that shadowed the public peace talks taking place in Paris. Although the Vietnam War was undertaken as part of the long-standing American policy goal of containing the spread of communism, in 1971 and 1972 Nixon was drawing closer to China and the Soviet Union, the two great Communist powers. In the spring of 1972, a North Vietnamese offensive began to crack the allied defenses in South Vietnam, and Nixon announced that the United States would mine North Vietnamese harbors to keep war matériel from arriving. At the same time, he was signing a deal to sell vast amounts of American wheat to the Soviet Union at bargain prices. When *The New York Times* found fault with Nixon's Vietnam policies, a Nixon aide arranged for an ad headed "The People vs. *The New York Times*" to run in the paper. (The ad did not, as was required by law, show that it was paid for by the President's campaign, and in 1973 CREEP was fined for that.)

Two days before the fake ad ran, George Wallace, campaigning in Maryland, was shot by a would-be assassin and left paralyzed below the waist. Wallace's withdrawal from the race meant that Nixon would not face a general election in which a right-wing candidate would siphon off some of his conservative support. Add to this the Republicans' traditional advantage in fund-raising and the opportunities that incumbency offers a President, and Nixon was well situated to meet any opponent. When the Democrats nominated George McGovern, the candidate the White House wanted and had worked to get, Nixon's operatives prepared for an easy race.

The magnitude of McGovern's defeat in November obscures his gifts as a politician. In a heavily Republican state, South Dakota, McGovern had managed to win election to the U.S. Senate two times and had built a solid party organization. An able speaker, he was the only Democrat to emerge from the 1968 convention in Chicago with his reputation enhanced. His role in reforming the party's rules for delegate selection meant that he had the best understanding of the new order, and he had the service of an inventive campaign manager, Gary Hart, who would himself go on to be a senator and presidential hopeful. McGovern's early and strong antiwar position had alienated him from Lyndon Johnson, Hubert Humphrey, and most of the party's other leaders. With the new rules for delegates and the greater

The Nixon campaign's Committee to Re-Elect the President had the unfortunate acronym CREEP.

importance of primaries, this was not as great a liability as it would have been in the past, but there was still the question of how to raise money. With traditional party sources closed to him and business hostile, McGovern pioneered a new sort of campaign finance, appealing directly to voters through the techniques of direct-mail marketing. This innovation would later be copied, with even greater success, by conservative candidates.

Just before McGovern's last big primary victory, in New York, the Watergate break-in took place. (The Watergate "burglars" were actually replacing a defective listening device that had earlier been planted in the offices of the Democratic National Committee.) *The New York Times* ran the story on page 30, and most reporters seemed to be in agreement with Nixon's spokesman Ron Ziegler, who characterized the episode as a "third-rate burglary." When *The Washington Post* ran a story about Segretti's dirty tricks, Ron Ziegler called it "hearsay" and "innuendo." When McGovern suggested that there might be more to these events than Nixon admitted, he was charged with having paranoid delusions.

The White House succeeded in keeping the Watergate issue out of the campaign. There were some embarrassments (as when the script for the Republican convention fell into the hands of reporters, who gleefully related how "spontaneous demonstrations" of enthusiasm for the President had been assigned exact durations, so that all the important convention speeches would happen in prime television hours). The nation's newspapers were overwhelmingly for Nixon, his campaign was better run and better financed, and McGovern's positions, both on the war and on domestic issues, were to the left of the majority of American voters'.

National security adviser Henry Kissinger's announcement in late October that peace was "at hand" in Vietnam (it was not) gave the President a last-minute boost. On election day, he won nearly 61 percent of the popular vote, and in the Electoral College his margin was 520 to 17. Richard Nixon had, by hook and by crook, won one of the great victories in the history of American presidential campaigns. But he would not be able to savor his success for long.

The Praline President

CARTER v. FORD, 1976

In the drama Richard Nixon made of his own life, he often cast the press as his nemesis; in 1962, when he was defeated in the California gubernatorial race and his political career had apparently ended, he petulantly cried that reporters would no longer be able to kick him around. At first glance, Watergate seems like the perfect climax of the play, with the press finally bagging Nixon for good. That is the view of many in the press, then and now. But during the 1972 campaign the press was certainly more lapdog than watchdog, and the ultimate exposure of the Watergate crimes was the result not of relentless reporting (although there was much of that) but of the unfolding of the legal process. It was the threat of harsh prison sentences, the danger of perjury indictments, and the subpoena power, not the power of the press, that caused the disintegration of the White House machinery and laid bare an administration without moral standards, devoted only to its own perpetuation. Nixon's true nemesis was not *The Washington Post* but Federal District Court Judge John J. Sirica, in whose courtroom the Watergate "burglars" were tried and, in January 1973, convicted.

Judge Sirica's threat to hand out stiff prison terms started the process by which the full dimensions of the secret and illegal activities carried out by the Nixon White House were revealed. In the summer of 1973, the nation followed the hearings of a Senate committee chaired by Sam Ervin of North Carolina. A crucial moment came when a former White House aide named Alexander Butterfield told of the existence of a taping system in the Oval Office, and the pursuit of those tapes by Ervin's committee and the Watergate special prosecutor, Archibald Cox, became a key element of the political drama. In October, Nixon directed his attorney general, Elliot Richardson, to fire Cox; Richardson refused and resigned, as did his deputy, William Ruckelshaus, and it was finally the solicitor general, Robert Bork, who fired Cox.

Beyond Watergate, Nixon and the Republicans had other problems. Vice President Spiro Agnew had to resign after a no-contest plea to charges of tax evasion, and Nixon nominated Representative Gerald Ford of Michigan to succeed Agnew.

The Watergate investigations continued under a new special prosecutor, and on March 1, 1974, seven top Nixon aides, including former attorney general John Mitchell, were indicted, with Nixon himself named as an "unindicted co-conspirator." On April 30, Nixon released cleaned-up transcripts of the White House tapes. These had many "expletives deleted," but they also omitted key segments that (it ultimately proved) made clear the President's complicity in the cover-up. The prosecutor and others sued for release of the full tapes, and late in July the Supreme Court ruled in their favor. By the end of the month the House Judiciary Committee had voted to impeach Nixon, with a significant number of Republicans supporting the move. The release of the tapes on August 5—they revealed that, among other things, the President had tried to get the CIA to intervene and block the FBI investigation of the break-in—sealed Nixon's fate. He announced his resignation on August 8, 1974, and the next morning Gerald Ford was sworn in as President.

The personification of orthodox midwestern Republicanism, Ford, with his open demeanor and palpable lack of Nixonian deviousness, initially won a great deal of support from a nation that wanted to accept his assurance that the "national nightmare" was over. But a month after taking office, Ford appeared on television on a Sunday morning to announce that he was granting Nixon a presidential pardon for any crimes he might have committed while in office. Ford's popularity plummeted, and that November the Democrats gained five seats in the Senate and nearly fifty in the House, electing a number of young liberals called the "Watergate babies."

In the mid-1970s, America was a nation considerably less confident than it had been two decades earlier. Urban riots and rising crime had contributed to a white exodus to suburbia that was underwritten by federal housing and tax policies, leaving the nation's cities maimed and seemingly doomed to become holding pens for the nation's nonwhite poor. Lyndon Johnson's attempt to have both "guns and butter"— an expensive war in Vietnam and expensive social programs at home—had weakened the American economy. In 1973, inflation was propelled upward by sharply rising oil prices and an embargo declared by OPEC, the Organization of Petroleum Exporting Coun-

1976

PRESIDENTIAL CANDIDATE (STATE) VICE-PRESIDENTIAL CANDIDATE (STATE)	PARTY	ELECTORAL VOTES	APPROX. % OF POPULAR VOTE
Jimmy Carter (Ga.) Walter Mondale (Minn.)	Democratic	297	50%
Gerald Ford (Mich.) Robert Dole (Kans.)	Republican	240	48%

Ronald Reagan, who was not a candidate, received 1 electoral vote, from the state of Washington.

Among the minor-party candidates were Eugene McCarthy (Independent), Roger L. MacBride (Libertarian), Lester G. Maddox (American Independent), Gus Hall (Communist), and Lyndon H. LaRouche (U.S. Labor).

tries, in reaction to the 1973 war between Israel and its Arab neighbors. And finally, in the spring of 1975, America's long involvement in Vietnam ended with the triumph of the Communist forces.

The candidates for President would have to contend both with these problems and with a profound distrust of government that had resulted from the Watergate revelations. One outcome of the previous decade's political experiences was a new set of campaign rules, including a greater reliance on primary elections. Between 1968 and 1976, the number of delegates chosen in primaries rose from 30 percent to 70 percent of the convention total. And 1976 saw the first federally financed election under the provisions of the Federal Election Campaign Act. To win in 1976, a candidate would have to understand the new rules and would also have to project an image that somehow promised relief from the Washington scandals and a reinvigoration of the nation's confidence.

With the Republican Party wounded by Watergate, many Democrats were eager to run, and most political professionals assumed that the Democratic nominee would win easily, as long as there were no major mistakes along the way. Liberals in the race included Senators Birch Bayh of Indiana, Fred Harris of Oklahoma, and Frank Church of Idaho; Representative Morris Udall of Arizona; and California governor Jerry Brown. At the more conservative end of the scale were Senator Lloyd Bentsen of Texas, Senator Henry M. "Scoop" Jackson of Washington, and Jimmy Carter, the former governor of Georgia. The most conservative contestant was George Wallace, who, although confined to a wheelchair, was sufficiently recovered from the assassination attempt on him four years earlier to run. Not a declared candidate but available to his party if wanted was former Vice President Hubert Humphrey.

Jimmy Carter's success in winning the nomination that summer had many sources. He was, as he stressed in his campaign, a Washington outsider. Being from the South, he held out the promise of a return of Democratic victories there. He was a centrist, but he managed to clothe his more conservative stands in ways that avoided offending the liberal elements in the party. Furthermore, he and his advisers showed a strong grasp of the new primary system and knew how to use the press.

The key elements of Carter's plan were to start early and to try for better-than-expected showings in the first tests: the Iowa caucuses and the New Hampshire primary. Expectations, in fact, turned out to be crucial. Carter and his advisers proved adept at seeming indifferent to losses in major primaries as they pointed out the supposedly greater significance of their carefully plotted wins. It hardly took genius to figure out the strategy—after all, McCarthy in 1968 and McGovern in 1972 had chalked up major "wins" in New Hampshire in spite of coming in second. But Carter's plan was to take this a step further and put a lot of work into the previously insignificant Iowa caucuses. Since Carter was out of office, he could devote himself full-time to the race, and he crisscrossed Iowa during 1975; his efforts were rewarded with a first-place showing there on January 19, 1976. This allowed him to emerge from the crowd of Democratic contenders and thus brought him greater

The best of all the Jimmy Carter caricatures—in the form of a coin bank. NATIONAL MUSEUM OF AMERICAN HISTORY, SMITHSONIAN INSTITUTION.

Betty Ford was more widely popular than was her husband.

DAVID J. AND JANICE L. FRENT
POLITICAL AMERICANA COLLECTION.

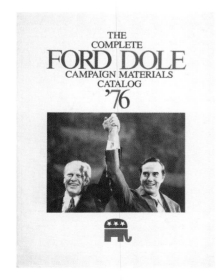

DAVID J. AND JANICE L. FRENT
POLITICAL AMERICANA COLLECTION.

press attention in the days before the New Hampshire vote. Winning in New Hampshire made Carter the candidate with momentum, and by manipulating expectations Carter was able to stay in front. A fourth-place showing in Massachusetts (a much more populous state than New Hampshire) was downplayed because Carter had not made the state a priority. Similarly, in April, Carter was badly beaten by Jackson and Udall in New York, but his backers could point to a win the same day in Wisconsin to deflect attention from that loss. Carter's campaign had put him on the ballot in every primary, so by directing its resources carefully it could, on any given Tuesday, usually produce a win in one state to balance a loss in some other state or states.

Toward the end of the primary season, Carter's major opposition came from Udall and from two late starters, Church and Brown. But they were no more successful in derailing him than his earlier opponents had been, and the one-term former governor of Georgia won nomination on the first ballot at the convention in New York that July. For Vice President he turned to Minnesota's Senator Walter Mondale, a Humphrey protégé who had strong ties to the party's traditional leadership and to the labor unions, which had long provided funds and workers to the Democratic cause.

Gerald Ford faced a tough challenge for the Republican nomination and nearly became the first incumbent President since Chester A. Arthur to fail to win his party's nomination. His opponent was Ronald Reagan, the former governor of California and the favorite of the party's right wing. Gerald Ford was no liberal, but to the true believers of the Republican right Ford's choice of Nelson Rockefeller as Vice President and his continuation of the Nixon-Kissinger policy of détente with the Soviet Union signaled a dangerous streak. Besides, Reagan turned sixty-five in 1976, and there was a feeling that he should run before he became too old to campaign. Ford had the advantage of incumbency, but in Republican primaries it is the conservatives who are most faithful about getting to the polls, and Reagan's gift for delivering speeches powerfully provided great material for his TV ads.

All the candidates were featuring themselves in their ads. The voters, disgusted by Nixon's now painfully obvious lack of character, wanted to elect a President who was decent, moral, and not distorted by ambition. Jimmy Carter capitalized on this mood when he promised not to lie to the American people. Others tried to make the same point indirectly, and Reagan's sincere on-screen demeanor was a crucial part of his appeal. Ford, on the other hand, was a mediocre speaker, and at one point his campaign tried ads that showed ordinary people (played by actors) discussing his achievements. But the evident phoniness of the ads undercut the message that Ford was sincere, and later ads tried to use him in ways that stressed his presidential status without letting him talk too much.

Throughout the primary season, Ford and Reagan remained closely matched. As the Republicans gathered in Kansas City in mid-August, fewer than 40 votes out of more than 2,000 delegates separated the two men. Late in July, Reagan had tried to swing doubtful delegates to his side by endorsing Senator Richard Schweiker of

Pennsylvania, a fairly liberal Republican, as his choice for Vice President. This merely made Reagan appear unprincipled, alienating his conservative base without bringing him support from moderates. At the convention Ford managed to win the nomination on the first ballot, and, after checking with Reagan, he selected Senator Bob Dole of Kansas as his running mate.

Carter started the fall race with a rally in Warm Springs, Georgia, invoking the memory of Franklin D. Roosevelt while emphasizing his distance from recent events in Washington. Polls showed that he had a comfortable lead, which evaporated in the two months of the fall campaign, so that on election day the race was too close to call. This decline owed almost nothing to Ford's campaign, which remained lackluster. Nor, unlike in previous elections, could the Republicans' strength be attributed to outspending the Democrats, since each candidate received the same amount of federal money—$21.8 million. Carter made one big error: he gave an interview to *Playboy* magazine. In the interview, he admitted to feeling "lust in his heart" for women other than his wife, and he also used terms such as "screw" and "shack up," which seemed at odds with his much-publicized born-again-Christian faith.

It was, perhaps, the dissonance between the sort of person Carter claimed to be—religious, moral, a man who would "never lie," and a polymath (peanut farmer, nuclear physicist, author, and so forth)—and the sort of person one has to be to get elected that began to erode his support. As Carter's portrait of himself became less plausible (thanks in part to *Playboy*), other doubts about his presidential qualifications began to weigh on the minds of undecided voters. But Ford, making blunders of his own, was unable to take advantage of them. His most notable misstep was his statement, in the second televised debate, that there was "no Soviet domination of Eastern Europe" and his tortured attempts to explain away the gaffe. Ford was tormented by his image as a stumblebum, and a series of pratfalls made him a running gag in skits by Chevy Chase on television's *Saturday Night Live*. A politician can be shifty and still be elected, as Richard Nixon had shown, but becoming a laughingstock is another matter.

Television, of course, was the main battleground, both in the debates between the candidates (which included, for the first time, a debate between the vice presi-

It's here! The Jimmy Carter PLAYBOY interview!

Read it for yourself in November PLAYBOY. On sale now.

282 THE PRALINE PRESIDENT

Ford and Carter during their television debate on September 29, 1976.
LIBRARY OF CONGRESS.

dential candidates) and in the candidates' ads. Ford's campaign wisely saved money for an ad blitz at the end of the race, and that no doubt helped his final surge to parity with Carter in the polls. Because the candidates had less money to spend than in earlier campaigns (Nixon had spent $60 million four years earlier, McGovern half that much) and TV would consume most of what they had, such standbys as bumper stickers and buttons were largely ignored. Carter's people made clever use of radio ads on black radio stations to get his message to blacks, particularly in the South, in a medium that received little attention from white voters or reporters. As it turned out, blacks' votes proved crucial to his victory in the South and therefore in the nation.

The race was very close, with fewer than 2 million votes separating Carter and Ford out of more than 80 million cast. A third-party candidacy by Eugene McCarthy might have tilted the race to Ford if McCarthy had not been kept off the ballot in New York, which went for Carter by a small margin. The final Electoral College tally was 297 to 240, with one Ford elector voting for Reagan. Despite the narrowness of Carter's victory, the Democrats remained strong in Congress, keeping control of the House by a better than two-to-one margin and of the Senate by 62 to 38. With Nixon off-stage for good and the Vietnam War over, it seemed that the new President would have an opportunity to advance the nation in new directions.

"Ronald Reagan? The Actor?"

REAGAN, CARTER, ANDERSON, 1980

The era of Lyndon Johnson and Richard Nixon had raised fears of what Arthur Schlesinger, Jr., has called the Imperial Presidency, in which a White House, unchecked by Congress and independent even of the executive departments, made and carried out policy based on the judgments and whims of a small inner circle. Johnson's expansive interpretation of the Tonkin Gulf Resolution had sanctioned a deeper involvement in Vietnam, and Richard Nixon's secret bombing campaign against Cambodia had been an extension of that logic. Foreign policy had become too important to leave to the diplomats (to paraphrase Talleyrand), so in the Nixon White House it had been Henry Kissinger, the national security adviser, who had made policy while the secretary of state, William Rogers, tried to discover what that policy was. Nixon even commissioned a sort of Ruritanian uniform for the White House guard to wear at formal events.

Against this background, Jimmy Carter's inauguration in January 1977 set a refreshing new tone. Not only were the ceremonies more folksy than those of the recent past but the inaugural parade took a decidedly untraditional turn when the President and his wife, Rosalynn, chose to walk the parade route rather than riding in a limousine. The symbolism was easily understood, and editorials praised Carter for his informal approach and his disdain for the trappings of office. After a dozen years of war, assassinations, riots, and scandals, America wanted a quieter time and a more trustworthy President, and Carter initially seemed to promise both.

Carter's promises, however, proved to be one of the biggest problems of his presidency. He had said that he would not lie to the American people, but governing seems to require telling at least white lies, and one lesson of American politics is that too much truth telling can hurt a candidate as badly as a pack of lies. When people close to Carter (such as his budget director, Bert Lance) were found to have behaved unethically, the President, in his defense of them, often seemed to skirt the truth, if not actually to lie. Having professed a higher standard than his predecessors', Carter, to his disadvantage, was held to it.

He had also promised to provide "a government as good and honest and truthful and fair and competent and idealistic and compassionate and as filled with love as are the American people." A pessimist might argue that that was what the nation had had in Richard Nixon, but Carter was assuming that the national character was unblemished and that all corruption of the national spirit was contained within the Washington Beltway and could be excised. Arriving in the capital as a self-proclaimed outsider, Carter tried to shape the government to his will. But there were too many power sources in Washington that he could neither understand nor control. In particular, the economic problems of high inflation and stagnant growth that Carter inherited from Gerald Ford proved to be more than he could handle. In the summer of 1979, as OPEC raised oil prices and the inflation rate went up with them, the administration began asking prominent Americans for help in understanding what was wrong in the country. Meetings were held at the White House and at Camp David, and eventually Carter emerged from these meetings to deliver an address to the nation. (It was called the "malaise" speech, although the President did not use the word himself.) The gist of the speech, as later summarized by the Harvard sociologist Daniel Bell (whose views Carter had sought in the weeks before the speech) was "not that the President was doing anything wrong, but that the people were wrong." The problem, in Carter's view, was that the people needed to be "as good and honest and truthful and fair and competent and idealistic and compassionate and as filled with love" as he was. It was a remarkable—and disastrous—performance.

Carter did score some triumphs in his years in office, in particular with his strenuous and successful efforts to bring about a peace agreement between Egypt and Israel, but economic problems and the inability of his administration to solve them left the President's approval ratings in the cellar and attracted a large band of Republicans eager to run against a damaged President. Among them were Bob Dole, the Kansas senator who had been Gerald Ford's running mate in 1976; two Illinois congressmen, the conservative Philip Crane and the maverick John Anderson; John Connally, a former governor of Texas and former Democrat; Senator Howard Baker, a consummate Washington insider from Tennessee; and George Bush, whose résumé of appointive offices included being chairman of the Republican National Committee, the United States' diplomatic

1980

PRESIDENTIAL CANDIDATE (STATE) VICE-PRESIDENTIAL CANDIDATE (STATE)	PARTY	ELECTORAL VOTES	APPROX. % OF POPULAR VOTE
Ronald Reagan (Calif.) George Bush (Tex.)	Republican	489	51%
Jimmy Carter (Ga.) Walter Mondale (Minn.)	Democratic	49	41%
John B. Anderson (Ill.) Patrick J. Lucey (Wis.; Democrat)	Independent	0	7%

representative in China, and director of the Central Intelligence Agency ("George Bush: A President we won't have to train" was one of his slogans). Former President Ford was also considered a possibility. But the clear front-runner was former California governor Ronald Reagan.

After narrowly losing the nomination to Ford in 1976, Reagan had given a unity speech at the end of the convention, bracing Gerald Ford and the Republicans with the admonition "There is no substitute for victory." This had been General Douglas MacArthur's rallying cry in his battles with the Truman administration during the Korean War, and its invocation was appropriate, for Ronald Reagan wished to return American government and society to an earlier, simpler time.

The speech demonstrated the fundamental difference between Reagan and his predecessor as the leader of the Republican Party's right wing, Barry Goldwater. Goldwater would rather be right than President, while Reagan was willing to make the sort of compromises required by practical politics in order to win. He was willing to place party loyalty over his own feelings and to work with Republicans with whom he disagreed in order to have the best chance of defeating the Democrats.

On the Democratic side, the presumption that a sitting President eligible for re-election should be renominated by his party was challenged by Senator Edward M. Kennedy of Massachusetts. As the surviving brother of John and Robert Kennedy, Ted Kennedy had long been considered a presidential contender but had long refused to campaign. But Carter's more conservative policies and his political vulnerability persuaded Kennedy to run.

On November 4, 1979, the hopes of both Kennedy and Carter were deeply undercut by two different events. For the President, it was the seizure of the American embassy in Teheran by Islamic militants protesting the admission of the former shah of Iran into the United States for medical treatment. The militants took members of the embassy staff hostage, and the drama of this crisis would provide a crucial context for the election. For Kennedy, the wound was self-inflicted. In an interview with Roger Mudd, of CBS News, he was unable to answer the most obvious sort of soft question: "Why do you want to be President?" Kennedy ended a dis-

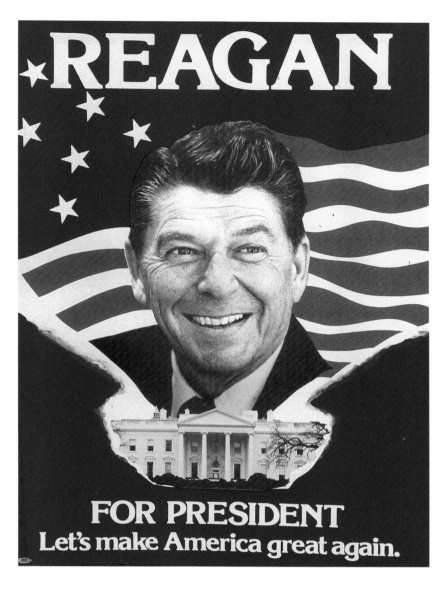

Poster featuring Reagan's effective campaign slogan.
DAVID J. AND JANICE L. FRENT
POLITICAL AMERICANA COLLECTION.

Re-Elect
Carter-
Mondale

A Tested and
Trustworthy Team.

Uninspired publicity like this poster made
Carter and Mondale seem hopelessly boring.
DAVID J. AND JANICE L. FRENT
POLITICAL AMERICANA COLLECTION.

jointed answer by saying, "And I would basically feel that—that it's imperative for this country to either move forward, that it can't stand still, or otherwise it moves back." Mudd also took his viewers to Chappaquiddick to retrace the route Kennedy had taken on the night in 1969 when he drove off a bridge and a young woman in his car died. Kennedy's explanations of his actions had generally been held to be unsatisfactory, and the tour with Mudd made his story seem even more unlikely. (Mudd showed, for example, that Kennedy had made a sharp turn off a paved highway onto a rough road, making his claim to have found himself on the wrong road by mistake seem dubious.)

Although few wanted to emulate Jimmy Carter's performance as President, most of the Republican hopefuls sought to match his early victory in the Iowa caucuses. George Bush's campaign, in particular, devoted a great deal of attention to that state. The Reagan campaign, directed by John Sears, was trying to keep its candidate above the fray and, having failed to perceive that Carter's success in 1976 had changed the rules of the game, was surprised when a much larger turnout at caucus meetings helped give the victory there to Bush.

In New Hampshire, Reagan recovered, largely through his own skill in handling a public confrontation with Bush. A New Hampshire paper, the Nashua *Telegraph,* had offered to sponsor a debate between the two men who now appeared to be the leading contenders. When this was ruled out, owing to objections from the Federal Election Commission, Reagan's people suggested to Bush's team that they split the cost of the debate. The offer was rejected, and Reagan's advisers decided to pay the entire cost, at the last minute inviting other candidates as well and thus denying Bush the prominence he would have in a one-on-one debate. With Reagan and Bush seated at their microphones, Reagan began to make the case for including the others. The moderator, Jon Breen, the editor of the Nashua *Telegraph*, told the sound engineer to turn off Reagan's mike. "I'm paying for this microphone, Mr. Green [*sic*]," Reagan responded as Bush sat there looking petulant. Bush eventually got his way, with a two-man debate, but the damage had been done by Reagan's deft performance and Bush's sullen passivity. Reagan overwhelmed Bush and the other candidates in New Hampshire; his misstep in Iowa was one of the last the campaign would make (Sears, who was blamed for Iowa, was fired the day of the New Hampshire primary), and he won nomination easily. Bush's chief contribution to the year was to describe Reagan's plan for the economy as "voodoo economics," a term later cited gleefully by the Democrats after Reagan chose Bush to be his running mate.

In seeking the Democratic nomination, Kennedy was handicapped by Carter's attempt to use the Iran hostage crisis and the 1979 Soviet invasion of Afghanistan as reasons to avoid campaigning and to remove those and other foreign policy matters from the debate in order to protect American diplomacy. Most of Kennedy's efforts to challenge Carter backfired, and in the end the campaign centered on the conflict between Kennedy as the guardian of the party's liberal tradition and the more conservative Carter. In April, the President's campaign was hurt by a botched military effort to rescue the hostages in which eight servicemen died.

DAVID J. AND JANICE L. FRENT
POLITICAL AMERICANA COLLECTION.

Kennedy did well in the later primaries, winning large states such as New York, Pennsylvania, California, and New Jersey. But Carter was better organized and had the advantage of incumbency. When the Democrats convened in New York in August, Kennedy's supporters made a last effort to throw the convention to the senator by asking that the rules be changed to permit delegates to vote as they pleased on the first ballot, rather than being bound by primary or caucus results. With polls showing Carter trailing Reagan by a big margin, this might have worked, but Carter had enough strength to win the rules fight and thus secure the nomination.

In the general election, the basic challenge for Carter was to persuade voters that, however unhappy they might be with things as they were, Reagan was too radical, too dangerous, and too likely to involve the United States in a war to be trusted with the office of President. Another Carter strategy had to be employed more subtly: the suggestion that Reagan was mentally vague and—although it could not be said outright—perhaps too old for the office. (He would turn seventy within a month of the inauguration.) Reagan himself fueled such thoughts with his frequent misstatements of fact, the consequences of a mind unfriendly to detail and a tendency to conflate reliable and unreliable sources. (Eventually, two aides, Stuart Spencer and Michael Deaver, were assigned to travel with him to try to prevent or minimize his verbal blunders.)

Carter, with his keen mind and his close, even excessive, attention to detail (he went so far as to personally supervise the schedule of the White House tennis courts), resented the fact that Reagan's blunders eventually became a nonstory. As the fall campaign progressed, his attacks on his rival grew harsher, charging that in

Reagan did the best acting job of his life playing the role of an avuncular president.
NATIONAL MUSEUM OF
AMERICAN HISTORY,
SMITHSONIAN INSTITUTION.

President Reagan's nation "Americans might be separated black from white, Jew from Christian, North from South," and so on. This squandered one of Carter's few assets—that most people, even those who considered him a poor President, thought he was a decent man. The attacks on Reagan made him seem nasty and did more harm to him than to his opponent.

Reagan's television ads accentuated the candidate's polished TV presence and showed him speaking to the camera sincerely and cogently. Although the two candidates were restricted to the same amount of funds, the independent ad campaigns financed by political action committees, or PACs, spent about $12 million to support Reagan, while pro-Carter PACs managed a mere $50,000. And Carter spent money on ads at the start of the race, hoping to discredit Reagan early. At the end of October, Reagan had far more money left for a final push.

The only debate between the two candidates occurred late in the race, on October 28, and was won by Reagan on two points. (Although Republican dirty tricks again played a role—Reagan's team had obtained copies of Carter's briefing books for the debate—this was not revealed until after the election.) First, as Carter was pointing out that Reagan's political career had been launched in part with attacks on Medicare, Reagan said, "There you go again," suggesting that Carter was unfairly distorting his record (in fact, Carter was correct). Reagan won the second, more substantial point in his summation, when he asked Americans to consider whether they were better off in 1980 than they had been four years earlier and to vote on that basis. With inflation up and interest rates nearing 20 percent, the hostages still being held in Iran, and the American industrial establishment apparently headed toward rusty obsolescence, voters decided that the risk of a President Reagan was less worrisome than the continuation of President Carter.

The chief worry of the Reagan people toward the end of the campaign was that Carter would engineer an "October surprise," securing the release of the hostages and causing voters to surge toward the President. To guard against this, the Republican campaign constantly warned that such a plot might be in the works and even had ads made, ready to run in case the surprise happened. But a diplomatic offer from Iran on the final weekend of the race was rejected by Carter, and election day—the first anniversary of the seizure of the embassy—came without a resolution of the crisis.

That final weekend saw a significant improvement in Reagan's numbers, and in the end his margin was 51 to 41 percent, with the Republican congressman John Anderson, running as an independent, collecting 7 percent. Reagan's Electoral College tally was 489 votes to 49 for Carter. Unexpectedly, the Republicans also gained control of the Senate.

Reagan was inaugurated with more pomp and with fancier parties than Carter had been, and no casual walk along the parade route was attempted. Minutes after he took the oath of office, the hostages were released, and the Reagan Revolution got under way on an auspicious note.

Electing a Bar of Soap

REAGAN v. MONDALE, 1984

The Republican campaign of 1984 may have been the most effective—and the most cynical—in American history. President Ronald Reagan was packaged for public consumption like a soft drink or a detergent, and any attempt to take the product off the shelf and test it—say, by making the President answer questions from the press—was assiduously avoided. The President's painstakingly choreographed appearances and his campaign ads were designed to work together to convey the impression of a confident leader in charge of a reviving nation. Reagan's handlers worked hard to avoid any brush with the unrehearsed, and the only real threat to his re-election came when the campaign had to "let Reagan be Reagan" (as his more zealous conservative backers kept urging) during the two presidential debates.

Ronald Reagan was a willing participant in his own packaging. Early in the planning for the advertising campaign, he dropped into a White House meeting on the subject and said to the ad executives there, "Since you're the ones who are selling the soap, I thought you'd like to see the bar." He was equally docile in his campaign appearances, hitting his mark and saying his lines like the old trouper he was. Throughout, the campaign kept striking a few harmonious notes: the nation was at peace, the inflation rate was down, the economy was moving forward. It was "morning again in America," as one of the Reagan ads stated, and that was that.

Advertising campaigns that are completely divorced from reality won't work, as anyone in the ad business will tell you. An ad campaign for Tiffany's that stressed the store's "low, low prices" would not make it very far. Reagan's ad campaign would not have worked for Jimmy Carter four years earlier, because in 1980 most people had been worried that it was twilight in America. Reagan's ads succeeded because they were based on a general perception that the country was indeed "better off" than it had been four years earlier.

Reagan's first term had seen dramatic ups and downs. The most dramatic, of course, was the assassination attempt on the new President on March 30, 1981. The bullet came within an inch of Reagan's heart, and his surprising good humor in the face of the attack, combined with his rapid recovery, set an optimistic tone that took off from the nation's mood upswing that had begun on Inauguration Day with the release of the hostages in Iran. Reagan's legislative successes in his first year—cutting taxes, paring the budget—and his forceful handling of a strike by air traffic controllers established him as a President who could both take definite stands and move legislation through Congress. Even those who disagreed with his positions (such as union members angered over his firing of the striking controllers) admired his decisiveness. Compared with his predecessor, Reagan appeared to provide a model of executive determination.

Carter's attempt to blame a national malaise for the country's problems and his misfortunes in Iran had made him an easy act to follow. In addition, his own shortcomings provided a heaven-sent antidote to Reagan's. For example, Reagan had at best a hazy grasp of the specifics of his job. His wildly inaccurate statements on the campaign trail in 1980 had required major efforts at damage control by his staff, and stories from the Reagan White House told of a leader who seemed disengaged from the issues at hand, lost when forced to depart from his script, and unable to remember the names of those around him, including members of his own cabinet. This was a President who liked to nap. However, since the micromanaging Carter had, by general agreement, been a flop, perhaps Reagan's disconnected style had some merit.

For the Democrats, the challenge was to make the most of Reagan's weaknesses and to put their candidate forward as the best hope for America's future. Many Democrats were eager to challenge Reagan, and since the decision to run has to come early if a candidate is to have time to raise funds and assemble a staff, a number of these potential nominees were making their plans as early as 1982, when the nation was mired in a serious recession and Reagan looked vulnerable. Unemployment was around 10 percent, the President's approval rating was in the low forties, and in the midterm election that year the Democrats won back most of the House seats they had lost in the Reagan victory of 1980. The early favorites among the Democrats were former Vice President Walter Mondale and John Glenn, the Ohio senator and former (and future) astronaut. Other senators in the race were Colorado's Gary Hart, California's Alan Cranston, South Carolina's Fritz Hollings, and former senator (and former party nominee) George McGovern of South Dakota. The

1984

PRESIDENTIAL CANDIDATE (STATE) VICE-PRESIDENTIAL CANDIDATE (STATE)	PARTY	ELECTORAL VOTES	APPROX. % OF POPULAR VOTE
Ronald Reagan (Calif.) George Bush (Tex.)	Republican	525	59%
Walter F. Mondale (Minn.) Geraldine Ferraro (N.Y.)	Democratic	13	41%

BRINGING AMERICA BACK

PROUDER ★ STRONGER ★ BETTER

REAGAN-BUSH'84

DAVID J. AND JANICE L. FRENT
POLITICAL AMERICANA COLLECTION.

Reverend Jesse Jackson, the civil rights leader, also announced his candidacy, as did former governor Reubin Askew of Florida.

Mondale's advantages included name recognition and long associations with key figures in the Democratic Party's leadership, as well as close ties to organized labor. But he had to contend with the usual press expectations of a front-runner and had to try to manage those expectations so as to guard against the sort of problems Muskie had faced in 1972, when narrow primary wins had been seen as losses. Learning from Carter's 1976 campaign, Mondale concentrated on the Iowa caucuses and won. But in New Hampshire he was defeated by Gary Hart, who urged the party to reinvent itself in line with the emerging postindustrial economy rather than cling to the loyalties and assumptions of the New Deal era, with its attachment to smokestack industries and big labor. By early March, the race was between Mondale and Hart, with the other candidates having either withdrawn or become marginalized, except for Jesse Jackson, whose solid base in the black community allowed him to remain in the race, drawing attention to the views of his supporters. Hart might have blocked Mondale's march to the nomination had he not made several blunders, such as his explanation of why he had changed his last name from Hartpence to Hart. Well before the convention, Mondale was assured of nomination.

Although Mondale was an able and even appealing candidate in some ways, from Reagan's viewpoint he was an ideal opponent. For one thing, his service as Carter's Vice President allowed the Republicans to associate him with the discredited Carter. And as an old-fashioned New Deal Democrat, Mondale represented exactly the sort of big-government policies Reagan opposed. Even better for Reagan's purposes, these were the points that Gary Hart had attacked in the primaries and on which Mondale had already been shown to be vulnerable.

In an effort to overcome Reagan's large lead in the polls, Mondale decided to try to capture the nation's imagination with his choice of a running mate. After interviewing a number of candidates, including members of various minority groups, Mondale named Representative Geraldine Ferraro of New York as his choice a week before the convention was to open. Then, with remarkable ineptitude, he tried to install Carter's former budget director Bert Lance as head of the Democratic National Committee. Lance had been forced to leave the job after a scandal involving his financial dealings in Georgia, but he had avoided conviction in the subsequent trial. By bringing him forward, Mondale tied himself even more closely to the Carter administration and to one of its least popular figures. The convention, held in San Francisco, featured an address by Governor Mario Cuomo of New York that ignited the crowd and also marked Cuomo as a possible future presidential aspirant. Surprisingly, the Mondale forces were for the most part successful in keeping the usually bickering Democrats in harmony.

With an admirable faith in the fiscal sophistication of the American voter, Mondale decided to make the growing budget deficit a key target of his campaign. It seemed a promising issue. Republicans, including Reagan, had criticized the deficit in the past yet now were allowing it to increase significantly. By painting the deficit as a sort of economic quick fix, a Ponzi scheme that would lead to trouble in the future, the Democrats could attempt to undercut Reagan's most powerful advantage, the renewed health of the economy. The obvious way of lowering the deficit was by raising taxes, although that was a risky course in an election year. Flying in the face of political wisdom, Mondale told the Demo-

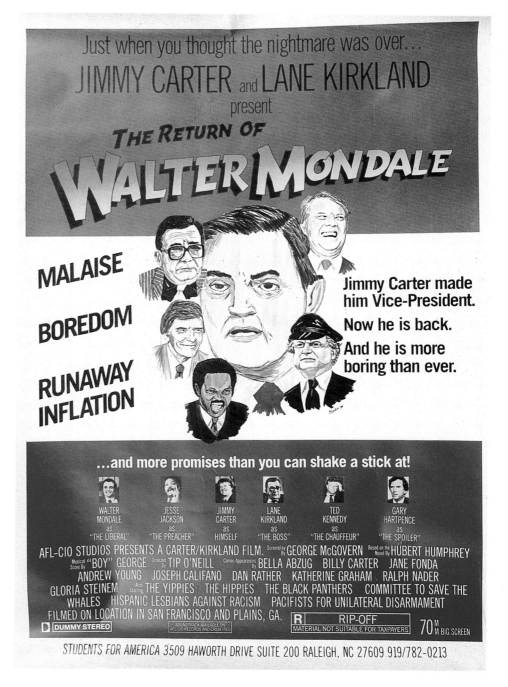

An anti–Mondale poster produced by a conservative Republican student organization. Almost anyone other than a right-winger could find at least a few things in the small print at which to take personal offense.
DAVID J. AND JANICE L. FRENT
POLITICAL AMERICANA COLLECTION.

cratic convention, "Mr. Reagan will raise taxes, and so will I. He won't tell you. I just did."

President Reagan was not telling Americans much about his plans for taxes or anything else. His last press conference before the election came in late July, and his aides continued to work hard (sometimes with the help of the Secret Service) to keep the press at a distance. The logic and customs—and finances—of the news business demand that reporters cover a candidate and that their bosses use their reports. Reagan's people understood this, and they made sure that the only news reporters would have to file at the end of the day was the set of images and themes the campaign wanted to get across. Even if there was no "news" in a Reagan appearance, it could seem unfair for the media to cover a newsworthy Mondale event and then not show Reagan's activities for the day. The White House used the powers of incumbency deftly, announcing, for example, the allocation of funds to clean up a toxic waste site in Missouri the very day Mondale planned to go there and attack Republican environmental policies.

Alongside the Reagan team's careful planning, the Democratic effort seemed amateurish. Even though Mondale had been the front-runner through the spring and had the nomination in hand by June, on Labor Day he still did not have an ad team in place. His press operation was naively open to reporters, constantly making the candidate and his top aides available. Minor misstatements or internal squabbles were therefore easier to find, and reporters could file their own stories, not just those choreographed by the campaign.

Of course, reporters did write about the Reagan campaign's manipulation of the press, but by 1984 this was an old story, and even when the subject made it into the news, the public's interest was small. The press also had to be careful that criticism of the President did not seem lacking in patriotic spirit, for Reagan was doing his best to wrap himself in the American flag.

Mondale's big chance came in Louisville, Kentucky, on October 7, in the first of two scheduled presidential debates. Mondale had received extensive advice on debate strategy from Patrick Caddell, one of Carter's top media advisers, and had taken much of it to heart, finding an effective balance between respectfulness and aggressive attacks. Reagan, out of practice for such a confrontation after nearly four years in the White House and always more comfortable with a script, did poorly. In one exchange, on Medicare, Reagan finally had to lower his eyes; the veteran Reagan watcher Lou Cannon of *The Washington Post* later wrote that it was something he "had never seen Reagan do in any other public encounter." Reagan appeared tentative, rambling, sometimes even incoherent, and old.

Age was a delicate matter for the Democrats to bring up, but after the debate the issue was raised, most forcefully by *The Wall Street Journal*, which questioned the President's fitness for a second term. Although Mondale was still trailing badly, Reagan's performance injected hope into the campaign, and the following day Mondale crowed, "We have a brand-new race." Unfortunately for Mondale, the

PRO LIFE
PRO FAMILY
PRO REAGAN

The Roe v. Wade *Supreme Court decision of 1973, legalizing abortion, gave rise to a powerful new political force in America, the right-to-life movement.*

DAVID J. AND JANICE L. FRENT
POLITICAL AMERICANA COLLECTION.

press was more interested in handicapping the new horse race than it was in exploring the more substantial issue of the incumbent President's health, both physical and mental.

The second debate, in Kansas City on October 21, was seen as the final test, the basic standard being whether Reagan could survive the evening without making a terrible blunder. It was not a very high standard, and by managing to look more relaxed and avoid serious embarrassment, Reagan ensured his re-election. During the last weeks of the campaign, with the Democrats low on funds, inspiring Reagan ads dominated television. Patriotic music played as happy families bought new cars, got married, and celebrated their lives. Attacks on the Democrats were often indirect, as in the brilliant "bear ad." A bear approaches a man holding a rifle. The voice-over says, "There is a bear in the woods. . . . Some people say the bear is tame. Others say it's vicious and dangerous. Since we can never really be sure who's right, isn't it smart to be as strong as the bear—if there is a bear?" The tag read, "President Reagan: Prepared for Peace." It was a clever way of defusing the common concern that Reagan was more likely to start a war with the USSR, which, only a year earlier, Reagan had called an "evil empire." Now his ad campaign conceded the point—"if there is a bear"—but defended an expensive military buildup that was helping to inflate the budget deficit. The ad even managed to carry a subliminal anti-gun-control message for those who wished to find it.

In the end, most Americans decided that there was a bear and that Reagan was doing a pretty good job of handling it, as well as of keeping the wolf from the door. Mondale (to continue the animal theme) was forced to play Chicken Little, pointing to the budget deficit and saying that if the sky was not falling now, it soon would be. Ultimately, Reagan played the hog, garnering 525 electoral votes and taking forty-nine states (Mondale just managed to win his home state of Minnesota and the District of Columbia). Soap had triumphed over soapbox, and the presidential product was returned to the White House.

DAVID J. AND JANICE L. FRENT
POLITICAL AMERICANA COLLECTION.

CHAPTER

49

Meet Willie Horton

BUSH v. DUKAKIS, 1988

Few aspects of American political history are as consistent, and as consistently troubling, as the role of racial, ethnic, and religious prejudice in national campaigns. Much of the time, the prejudice is hidden, as in the period between the end of Reconstruction and the 1960s, when the problems of black America were almost completely excluded from the national political debate. Similarly, rules against Asian immigration, which started in the late nineteenth century, were accepted by the leaders of both major parties and were not addressed in presidential campaigns.

At other times, appeals to prejudice have been overt, as in the accusations that Thomas Jefferson had an affair with Sally Hemings, a slave, or the attacks on Richard M. Johnson, Van Buren's running mate, who had lived with a mulatto. Anti-Catholicism gave rise to major political movements, such as the nativist Know-Nothing Party of the 1850s, and found vent against the candidacies of the Democrats Alfred E. Smith in 1928 and John F. Kennedy in 1960.

De jure segregation and legal restrictions on black voting continued into the mid-1960s, and social limits and prejudice, of course, continue to this day. But with the civil rights movement and the integration of major American institutions (including television), the sort of blatant racism that was once commonplace became unacceptable. By 1968, both Richard Nixon and George Wallace were using "crime in the streets" and "law and order" as code phrases meaning "Blacks, particularly in the cities, need to be kept under control." Politicians had to be careful not to become too overt in their use of such code words, and those who needed black votes had to take particular care.

One student of presidents and race, the historian Kenneth O'Reilly, described George Bush's campaign against former governor Michael Dukakis of Massachusetts in 1988 as "so implicitly racist that it appeared suited to a prior century." The Bush campaign in the general election was essentially a creature of its television ads, which reinforced and repeated messages that the candidate was delivering in his stump appearances. These were supplemented by ads sponsored by ostensibly independent political action committees. The PAC ads—which the Bush people were always able to say were not under their control—amplified the campaign's themes and presented the racial message in stark clarity. In this way, the dominant figure of the fall campaign was neither Bush nor Dukakis but a convicted murderer and rapist named William J. Horton, Jr.

Horton was convicted of first-degree murder in 1974 in the death of a seventeen-year-old boy during a robbery. Under a prison furlough system in Massachusetts, Dukakis's state, Horton was given a pass to leave prison for a short time. He failed to return and was arrested in Maryland for the kidnapping and rape of a woman and the kidnapping and assault of her fiancé.

In view of the potency of Horton as a campaign symbol, it is ironic that Horton's record was first used against Dukakis in the Democratic primaries. The man who raised the issue was Albert Gore, Jr., then a senator from Tennessee. But the ultimate source of the story was a small Massachusetts newspaper, the Lawrence *Eagle-Tribune*, which published a series of articles about crimes committed by furloughed inmates. Horton's was far from the worst story—in fact, the paper led its coverage with an account of how a (white) former policeman on furlough had murdered a friend—but Horton became the symbol of (black) crime in America and of supposed Democratic tolerance of criminals.

The Horton story did not play a significant part in the Democratic primaries (if it had, Dukakis might have failed to become the nominee); victory simply went to the candidate who managed *not* to do major damage to his cause. Gary Hart, the Colorado senator who had performed impressively in the 1984 primary race, was forced to withdraw in the spring of 1987 when he was found to have been extra-maritally involved with a model named Donna Rice. Another hopeful senator, Joseph Biden of Delaware, had to quit after it became known that he had plagiarized a speech by a British politician for his own campaign. In addition to Al Gore, candidates for the Democratic nomination included Richard Gephardt, a representative from Missouri; Paul Simon, a senator from Illinois; and the Reverend Jesse Jackson. Dukakis had a superior campaign organization and greater success in fund-raising, and he won the nomination with relative ease.

The Republican contest was between Vice President George Bush and Senator Bob Dole of Kansas. Dole did well in the Iowa caucuses, but

1988

PRESIDENTIAL CANDIDATE (STATE) VICE-PRESIDENTIAL CANDIDATE (STATE)	PARTY	ELECTORAL VOTES	APPROX. % OF POPULAR VOTE
George Bush (Tex.) Dan Quayle (Ind.)	Republican	426	54%
Michael S. Dukakis (Mass.) Lloyd Bentsen (Tex.)	Democratic	111	46%

One electoral vote from West Virginia went to Bentsen for President and Dukakis for Vice-president.

Bush won the New Hampshire primary and then swept the Super Tuesday primaries in March, and by the end of that month he had the nomination in hand. The central figure in the Bush campaign was a young political operative named Lee Atwater, a blues-guitar-playing conservative who saw race as an issue the Republicans could use to attract working-class whites, who would normally vote Democratic. By playing on fear and resentment of blacks, Atwater figured, the Republicans could appeal to such white voters by making them more resentful of black Americans than they were of wealthy Americans.

Sizing up the threat from Dukakis, Atwater said, "We're going to have to use research to win this campaign." His staff came up with the pollution of Boston Harbor, Dukakis's veto of a bill that would have required all Massachusetts students to recite the Pledge of Allegiance each day, and (thanks to Al Gore) the furlough program and Willie Horton, all of which became issues in the fall race.

George Bush began mentioning the Horton case in his campaign speeches in late spring, but it was in television ads during the fall that Atwater's message was put forth most clearly. The campaign was handled so deftly that Bush never had to defend himself against charges of race-baiting. As Atwater later said, and truthfully, "Our campaign made no TV commercials about Willie Horton." The Republicans did, however, run many times an ad portraying "revolving-door justice" under Dukakis and the Democrats: a line of prisoners files into prison through the right side of a revolving door, while an equally dense and fast-moving line of criminals emerges toward the viewer from the left side of the door. Since campaign speeches and news coverage had planted the Willie Horton story, the message was clear. At the same time, the National Security Political Action Committee produced an advertisement that included a mug shot of Horton and attacked Dukakis's use of the furlough program. Another PAC ran print and TV ads in which Horton's victims spoke out against the Democratic nominee. It hardly mattered to anyone that such furlough programs were common in the United States, that the one in Massachusetts had been established by a Republican predecessor of Dukakis, or that under the Constitution the primary responsibility for law enforcement lies with the states and not with the federal government. Lee Atwater had succeeded in making Willie Horton into Michael Dukakis's running mate.

His actual running mate, Senator Lloyd Bentsen of Texas, was chosen at the Democratic National Convention in July. That convention was a notable success, in spite of a seemingly endless speech nominating Dukakis by the governor of Arkansas, Bill Clinton. (The biggest applause line in Clinton's speech, which lasted for more than an hour, came at the words "In closing . . .") Revelations of malfeasance in the Iran-*contra* affair were hurting the Republicans and Bush, and the Democrats emerged from their convention with a seventeen-point lead in the polls. Bush did not help himself by choosing Indiana senator Dan Quayle as his running mate. Quayle was widely seen as a Senate lightweight and verbal blunderer. Bush himself was prone to malapropisms, as when, speaking of his partnership with Quayle, he said, "We have had triumphs, we have made mistakes, we have had

sex . . ." The word he was reaching for was "setbacks," and he soon corrected himself, to the relief of a gasping Republican crowd.

The two principal struggles of the race took place on television: the debates and the war of TV ads. There were two presidential debates and one between the vice presidential candidates. The crucial moment in the presidential debates came in the second debate, when CNN's Bernard Shaw asked, "Governor, if Kitty Dukakis [the candidate's wife] were raped and murdered, would you favor an irrevocable death penalty for the killer?" The question represented the sort of idiotic personalization of a complex set of issues that characterized the Atwater strategy and was consistent with the press's adoption of the Republican frame of reference on the issue. Rather than denouncing the offensive question, Dukakis launched into a boilerplate statement of why he opposed the death penalty, sounding like the robotic policy geek his opponents said he was. On the other hand, Bentsen's confrontation with Quayle was a devastating blow for the Republican. Quayle's youthful appearance added to the challenge he faced in appearing to be a credible person to sit "a heartbeat away from the presidency." He tried to defuse this by saying, "I have

A photo op that gravely injured what little was left of Dukakis's chance of winning. One Republican strategist observed that the fact that Dukakis was wearing a tie was what made the picture so laughable.
AP/WIDE WORLD PHOTOS.

Willie Horton.

as much experience in the Congress as Jack Kennedy did when he sought the presidency." Bentsen responded, "I served with Jack Kennedy. I knew Jack Kennedy. Jack Kennedy was a friend of mine. Senator, you are no Jack Kennedy."

The Bush campaign did a superb job of integrating the messages of the campaign trail and the messages of its ads. Positive spots showed Bush as a sort of father of the country, the proper heir of Ronald Reagan. Negative spots concentrated on the issue of crime and did a good job of linking it to military preparedness, the logic being that a person who could not figure out how to protect American citizens from common criminals would be no match for larger-scale threats posed by hostile nations. The Republicans were aided in this effort by Dukakis himself, who took part in a "photo opportunity" that featured him riding in an M1 tank at a defense plant in Michigan. The picture of Dukakis perched in the top entry hatch of a tank and wearing a helmet made him look fatally ridiculous. Roger Ailes, the leading strategist of the Bush TV ads, caught the absurdity when he spoke of Dukakis riding in a tank "with a silly hat and tie on." It was the tie that made the image painfully incongruous, and Ailes was smart enough to use footage from this event to trumpet Dukakis's supposed opposition to major new weapons. (Although the specifics of the ad were inaccurate, it ran often.)

Dukakis was unwilling to use similar tactics, feeling that such a cynical and inaccurate ad campaign would ultimately backfire. He eventually approved an ad attacking Bush for a crime committed by a prisoner in a furlough program the Republican nominee was associated with and an ad protesting the tank ad, but throughout the campaign he remained on the defensive. Issues such as health care, housing and homelessness, Iran-*contra,* and foreign policy in the post–Cold War world received little attention. Instead, voters and the news media focused on Willie Horton and other peripheral matters. Dukakis briefly ran a series of ads purporting to show Bush's political handlers developing their cynical ad strategy, but the message was too subtle and continued the Dukakis campaign's defensive posture. On election eve, he was still trying to dig himself out from the barrage of negative ads and charges. Bush promised a continuation of Reagan's budget policies: "Read my lips—no new taxes."

On election day, November 8, Bush was victorious, taking nearly 54 percent of the vote and winning 426 electoral votes. Toward the end of the campaign, Bush, tired of all the negative ads, had urged that the candidates get back to the real issues. Roger Ailes replied, "We plan to do that November ninth."

"The Economy, Stupid"

CLINTON, BUSH, PEROT, 1992

George Herbert Walker Bush took a New England heritage and education with him to Texas, where he built a career in business and Republican politics. The son of a Republican U.S. senator from Connecticut, Bush was a patrician who affected some of the habits of the good ol' boy, but in spite of his years in Texas he never really looked at home in cowboy boots and hat. His political career had been built largely on appointive offices, and his greatest patron had been Richard Nixon. Like Nixon, Bush as President was far more interested in foreign policy than he was in the details of domestic matters, far happier meeting with other world leaders than trying to wrangle with Democrats in Congress to pass domestic legislation. Fortunate in his timing, Bush presided over the final disintegration of the Soviet Union and its satellites in the Warsaw Pact, the "evil empire" that Ronald Reagan had decried. The Cold War that had defined the world since the late 1940s was over.

This ought to have been a triumphant moment for an old Cold Warrior like Bush, and in foreign policy he did win general approval from Americans. His invasion of Panama in 1989 to overthrow General Manuel Noriega, who was accused of complicity in narcotics trafficking, was relatively popular, despite, as some critics pointed out, long-standing support of Noriega by Republican administrations eager to find allies against leftist elements in Central America. The same sort of awkward history emerged in Bush's major foreign policy involvement, the 1991 Persian Gulf War, which followed Iraq's invasion of Kuwait in August 1990 and was dominated by American airpower. Bush had successfully lobbied for UN sanctions against Iraq and for a concerted military effort, even though, as in Panama, American geopolitics had historically supported Iraq.

In both Central America and the Middle East, a major component of the decision to support dictators such as Noriega and Hussein had been an assessment of how useful they were as counterweights to Soviet ambitions. But as the former Soviet satellites moved away from the influence of Moscow and then the Soviet Union itself dissolved, the old threats no longer seemed to matter. The sort of accusation that the Republicans had made against Michael Dukakis in 1988—that he was soft on crime and, both directly and by inference, soft on defense—no longer had much force. Republicans had been Red-baiting Democratic candidates since at least 1944, when Thomas Dewey had charged that Franklin Roosevelt's New Deal was being run by Communists. Richard Nixon's career had been founded on attacking Democrats as being "soft on communism." Now there were hardly any Reds left to bait, and the Communist Menace was becoming out of date, the political equivalent of a leisure suit.

Another difficulty was the rightward drift of the Democratic Party. Nearly a generation of defeats in presidential elections had persuaded many in the party that government programs to help the poor were both unpopular politically and ineffective practically and that most voters viewed championing the rights of the accused as encouraging criminals. A group of Democratic moderates formed the Democratic Leadership Council to try to pull the party toward the political center. Among the leaders of that effort were Bill Clinton, the governor of Arkansas, and Albert Gore, Jr., a Tennessee senator. These Democrats saw an opportunity to take back issues that the Republicans had held for a generation. For example, a Democrat who favored the death penalty, like Clinton, could exploit the Republicans' opposition to gun control more effectively than a more traditional liberal could. Three decades of rising crime rates, culminating in the crack cocaine epidemic of the early 1990s, had greatly weakened support for liberal views on criminal justice, and the successful use against Dukakis of Willie Horton's crimes in 1988 had driven the point home to even the dullest Democrat.

The Willie Horton issue had helped Bush win the presidency in 1988. And the end of the Cold War constituted the greatest diplomatic victory of the late twentieth century. But just as that victory undercut the traditional Republican campaign strategy, so did the success of Willie Horton. As the press reviewed its own performance in 1988, it came to feel that it had been deftly manipulated by the Republican strategists Lee Atwater and Roger Ailes, and as the 1992 campaign approached reporters wrote of an increasing hunger, in the public and in the press, for a campaign based on the real issues facing the country, not on the images that tested best for negative ads. Bush had needed negative ads to overcome Dukakis's lead following the Democratic convention, in part because he himself had a

1992

PRESIDENTIAL CANDIDATE (STATE) VICE-PRESIDENTIAL CANDIDATE (STATE)	PARTY	ELECTORAL VOTES	APPROX. % OF POPULAR VOTE
Bill Clinton (Ark.) Al Gore (Tenn.)	Democrat	370	43%
George Bush (Tex.) Dan Quayle (Ind.)	Republican	168	37%
Ross Perot (Tex.) James Stockdale (Ill.)	Independent	0	19%

lackluster image (he was constantly battling the so-called wimp factor), in part because of the difficulty of succeeding the Great Communicator, Ronald Reagan. In spite of the diplomatic and military successes of his administration, voters continued to feel unenthusiastic about George Bush as the 1992 campaign got under way.

The principal cause of this unpopularity was a serious economic recession—a recession that Bush barely seemed to be aware of. As the unemployment rate grew and the number of personal bankruptcies climbed, the President remained insulated inside the Secret Service cordon that he had inhabited for a dozen years. In February, when he went through a checkout line in a store that used a scanner to read the price of each item, he marveled at the new technology—new, of course, only to a person who had not shopped for himself in a decade. It was a vivid illustration of his distance from the American people.

It was exactly on this point that Bush would be attacked, first by an opponent within his party and then by others. Bill Clinton's skill in persuading voters that "I feel your pain" helped him win the election, and Ross Perot's skill in seeming to explain the causes of that pain allowed him to mount a successful third-party candidacy. The slogan of the successful Clinton campaign was three words written on a whiteboard in the campaign's "war room" in Little Rock, Arkansas: "THE ECONOMY, STUPID." Anyone who hoped to defeat the incumbent President would have to make the state of the economy the centerpiece of the campaign.

The attack on Bush from within the Republican Party came from Patrick Buchanan, the former Nixon speechwriter who had served President Reagan as well and was a popular television commentator. Although Bush had moved far to the right in the years since he had attacked Reagan's plans for the federal budget as "voodoo economics," he was still too far to the center for the Republican right, and Buchanan tried to tap that support as a means of raising his own profile as a candidate, perhaps with 1996 in view. He did not concentrate on the economy; instead, he devoted himself to promoting the agenda of the more conservative social policies: making abortion illegal, opposing affirmative action, championing school prayer. His immoderate remarks—calling AIDS a divine punishment of homosexuals, making statements that were widely seen as anti-Semitic—made him a certain loser in any general election but appealed to right-wing elements of the Republican coalition. In the New Hampshire primary, Buchanan's underfinanced campaign won 37 percent of the vote as Republicans frustrated with the President cast protest votes. It was an embarrassment for the incumbent, but his renomination was never in doubt, and he easily secured a first-ballot victory at the Republican convention.

The contest among the Democrats was wide open, and for them, too, New Hampshire was a vital test. Their early field included a traditional Democratic liberal, Senator Tom Harkin of Iowa; a war hero, Nebraska's Senator Bob Kerrey; a neoliberal of Greek descent from Massachusetts (this time named Paul Tsongas); a New Age visionary, former California governor Jerry Brown; the African-American governor of Virginia, Douglas Wilder; and the governor of Arkansas, Bill Clinton. For Clinton, the challenge of New Hampshire was dealing with rumors that he had

Gennifer Flowers at her press conference at New York's Waldorf–Astoria, January 1992.
AP/WIDE WORLD PHOTOS.

been unfaithful to his wife. In Arkansas, a woman named Gennifer Flowers had denied rumors that she had slept with him, but shortly before the New Hampshire vote she confessed publicly that her earlier statement had been a lie. A headline in the tabloid weekly *The Star* advertised Flowers's account of "MY 12-YEAR AFFAIR WITH BILL CLINTON."

In response, the Clinton campaign agreed to an interview with both Clinton and his wife, Hillary, on the popular CBS television newsmagazine *60 Minutes*. On the show, Clinton said that he had caused "pain" in his marriage, but he refused to be maneuvered into actually admitting adultery. Then Flowers held a press conference and played tapes of intimate conversations between her and Clinton. Her story would have been even more damaging had it not been revealed that she had been paid by the tabloid and that she had been encouraged to speak by Republican operatives. Voters in New Hampshire were notably less concerned with the story of the alleged affair than were the reporters or the Clinton campaign team, and Clinton finished a strong second in the primary, behind New England's favorite son, Paul Tsongas. Clinton declared that he was the "comeback kid" and moved into the next round of primaries in a strong position.

Tsongas was Clinton's most effective primary opponent, but Clinton proved to be a master campaigner, and by the time of his victory in the California primary, at the beginning of June, he seemed headed for a first-ballot victory at the convention. Polls tracking the likely outcome in November, however, showed him trailing Bush badly—in fact, he was running third, behind the President and a third-party challenger, the Texas businessman Ross Perot.

Perot had one crucial qualification for the office of President—a vast personal fortune that he could devote to his election, regardless of federal campaign finance laws. He also had a cause, reduction of the federal deficit, which allowed him to attack both the past fiscal profligacy of the Democrats and the more recent deficit-bloating effects of Ronald Reagan's "voodoo economics." Perot's campaign was a weird amalgam of a modern television candidacy and nineteenth-century political notions. He revived the dormant tradition of the reluctant candidate, asking his supporters to "draft" him by getting his name on the ballot in all fifty states. He professed hesitancy about running while building a campaign organization and making all the moves associated with candidacy. He possessed a relaxed, aw-shucks style of speaking that permitted him to appear the simple country billionaire. Combined with the voters' widespread dissatisfaction with the political process, Perot's money and manner promised to present a serious challenge to the two-party status quo.

But between Clinton's California win early in June and the Democratic convention in New York in July, his campaign managed to knit the victory-hungry Democrats together, and the convention was a highly successful presentation of the new, more moderate Democratic Party. Clinton was nominated by Mario Cuomo, the New York governor and a favorite Democratic convention orator. The nomination of Al Gore as the number two on the ticket placed a second moderate southerner there and was well received by party professionals and by some in the Washington press corps who knew and were impressed by Gore. The Democrats managed to demonstrate compassion (for those suffering from AIDS, for example) without appearing determined to tax the country to death to fund that compassion.

In Texas, Ross Perot had followed the Democratic convention with interest. He had not enjoyed the increased press scrutiny he had drawn as his presidential aspirations jelled, and Clinton's resurgence seemed to dim his chances of victory. In July, Perot announced that he was not running (he had never actually announced that he was) and pointed to the "revitalization of the Democratic Party" as the cause.

Perot's departure was a boon for Clinton. The convention had proved successful for the Democrats in large part because it had been taken as an opportunity to project a new image of the nominee. Polls had revealed that people thought the Clintons were childless and that Clinton had had it easy in life. So the script for the convention brought the Clintons' daughter, Chelsea, forward, and a biographical film about Clinton broadcast to the convention dwelled on his humble roots and the deprivations of his childhood. This emphasis on lesser-known aspects of the candidate's life helped mitigate the negative "Slick Willie" image he had for some voters. With the nation in recession and Bush apparently unconcerned about the plight of the average citizen, those who wanted to vote *against* Bush now had only one reasonable alternative.

Voters were given more reasons to vote against Bush and the Republicans at the party's convention in Houston in August. The party, stuck with the relatively moderate Bush as the nominee, allowed its more extreme elements to have their say at the convention as the price of party unity: Give me airtime, Patrick Buchanan promised, and I will endorse you. But the endorsement was hardly noticed amid the fulminations against those Buchanan saw as the nation's enemies. His opening-night speech was a declaration of war against liberals, working women, prochoice voters, and gays, among many others. The Republicans thus presented a public face of intolerance, a sharp contrast to the careful messages sent out of the Democratic convention the month before. Hillary Clinton was a particular target of the Republicans, and postconvention polls showed an upward jump in public esteem for her.

The "culture wars" aspect of the campaign had been there since the start, and talk shows, both on television and on radio, were particularly prominent battlegrounds. Ross Perot made Larry King's CNN program his own special slot, while Clinton attracted attention and criticism for appearing on MTV and, in particular, on Arsenio Hall's show, where, in dark glasses, he played saxophone with the house band. Even President Bush succumbed to the lure of broadcast chat.

The natural tendency of the Bush campaign to go negative was undercut by several factors. One, already mentioned, was the press's retrospective denunciation of the 1988 campaign and its Willie Horton manipulations. Then the bloody riots that broke out in 1992 in south central Los Angeles after the acquittal of officers accused in the videotaped beating of Rodney King, a black motorist, made it clear yet again that the divisions in America needed to be reduced, not expanded. The Republicans tried their best to make an issue of Clinton's draft status and his not always frank accounts, past and present, of his efforts to avoid service in Vietnam. But public interest in events of more than twenty years earlier was not great, and the

Ross Perot infomercial, October 1992.
AP/WIDE WORLD PHOTOS.

White House had to respond to revelations about campaign aides searching State Department files for information about a trip Clinton had made to Moscow as a student in 1969.

The brightest moment for the Republicans came early in October, when Ross Perot announced that he would, after all, be a candidate. With thirty-three days left until the election, he began spending huge amounts of money to broadcast television messages. Ignoring the advice of experts, Perot favored half-hour lectures—infomercials—using charts and graphs to present his arguments about the need to control the federal deficit. In spite of the amateurish quality of the programs, voters were interested in hearing the nation's problems discussed, and Perot drew respectable audiences. His money helped make him a credible candidate, and that credibility bought him a place at the presidential debates.

The debates had been a subject of long negotiations, with the Bush camp repeatedly avoiding any commitment. Democrats began appearing at Bush events in chicken costumes, challenging "Chicken George" to debate. (Chicken George was a character in Alex Haley's book *Roots*.) Much of the discussion had been about format, with the Bush team favoring a panel of reporters (who were deemed likely to press Clinton on his marital and draft histories), while the Clinton camp wanted the questions to come from audience members (who would be more likely to ask about issues). There were three debates in October. In the second, the questions came from the audience, and Clinton was able to connect with the questioners and show that he could understand the concerns of average Americans. Bush, glancing at his watch as if he had better things to do, fared poorly, while Perot did reasonably well. (Perot's chances were diminished by the performance of his running mate, James Bond Stockdale, in the one vice presidential debate. "Who am I?" and "Why am I here?" Stockdale asked rhetorically; unfortunately, he seemed not to have the answer to either question.)

By now presidential debates were part of the furniture of the fall campaign, and the crucial thing was not to stumble, as, for example, Gerald Ford had done in 1976 by stating that there was no Soviet domination of Poland or Nixon had done by just being himself in his first debate with Kennedy in 1960. In the campaign's last weeks, the Bush ads did become increasingly negative, pointing out some of the shortcomings of the state of Arkansas and attributing them to Clinton's performance there as governor. The race tightened slightly, but the voters were even more aware of Bush's performance as President, and the continuing sense of economic hardship was hurting him. Then, in the closing days, the special prosecutor in the Iran-*contra* scandal indicted former Reagan defense secretary Caspar Weinberger, and the indictment contained evidence that then–Vice President Bush had known of the arms-for-hostages deal in spite of his public contention that he had been "out of the loop." Republicans denounced the timing of the disclosure, the Friday before the election, but the story dominated the news in the final weekend of the race.

Bill Clinton won a decisive Electoral College victory, receiving 370 electoral votes to Bush's 168, with Ross Perot getting none. Yet Perot won 19 percent of the popular vote, the best showing by a third-party candidate since Teddy Roosevelt in 1912. Clinton had 43 percent of the vote and Bush 38 percent. The voters had rejected Bush decisively, but the results, in spite of the Electoral College tally, demonstrated serious reservations about Clinton.

George Bush checks his watch during a debate in Richmond, Virginia.
AP/WIDE WORLD PHOTOS.

Dullness Visible

CLINTON, DOLE, PEROT, 1996

Over the course of more than two hundred years, presidential elections have varied in interest and importance, and perhaps the most charitable thing to say about the 1996 campaign is that such a dull contest could have occurred only in a time of relative peace and prosperity. Decisive elections, such as Lincoln's triumph in 1860 and Franklin Roosevelt's defeat of Herbert Hoover in 1932, have usually taken place in times of national crisis. On a slightly lesser scale, the conservative victories of William McKinley over William Jennings Bryan in 1896 and of Ronald Reagan over Jimmy Carter in 1980 occurred when times were hard and the divisions in American society quite clearly drawn. So perhaps the dullness of 1996 should be seen as a powerful testimony to the general health of American society at the end of the twentieth century.

Many would reject this Panglossian assessment, arguing that the campaign was an indication of the failure of American politics and a triumph of hypocrisy and poll worship in our electoral life. The principal challenger, Senator Bob Dole of Kansas, was a witty Washington insider who for some reason was persuaded that he had to repudiate both his experience and his sense of humor to campaign successfully. The incumbent President, Bill Clinton, did his best to drain the Democratic Party of any last reservoirs of liberal standards, working hard to drag it to the dead center of American politics in spite of any beliefs, liberal or conservative, that he himself might hold. The political professionals who handled both campaigns had studied the past well, and the lessons they learned and passed on to their clients were that avoiding a gaffe is more important than having an idea and that the actual dynamics of a campaign have virtually nothing to do with the issues and real choices facing the government and everything to do with images and symbols.

In fact, Clinton and Dole had significant policy differences—on gays in the military, on government's proper role in the economy, on judicial appointments, on foreign affairs—but each took care to disguise any idea that varied from the statistically determined midpoint of public opinion. Clinton wished to help the poor but not at the expense of the middle class; Dole wanted to lower taxes but still provide a safety net for the poor. Both men had a real command of the intricacies of government policy, but neither wished to flaunt that expertise before the voters.

As an incumbent President with unsurpassed political gifts and with the economy strong, Clinton faced no serious opposition for the Democratic nomination and was favored to win re-election. Bob Dole, as a war hero and longtime leader of his party, was the early favorite to win the Republican nomination. Dole had been a prominent figure in the party for more than a quarter of a century and had been the GOP vice presidential nominee in 1976, when Gerald Ford lost to Jimmy Carter. But he was old for a candidate—at seventy-three he was four years older than Ronald Reagan had been in 1980—and many Republicans hoped that this and Dole's tendency to lash out at critics might allow someone else to win the nomination. Among Dole's challengers were his Senate colleagues Phil Gramm of Texas and Richard Lugar of Indiana; the former Nixon aide Pat Buchanan; Lamar Alexander, a former Tennessee governor and cabinet member; and Steve Forbes, the millionaire business-magazine publisher.

Dole's presumed front-runner status was self-fulfilling, bringing him the endorsements and the campaign contributions that allowed him to run television ads and put a smooth political operation into place. Buchanan's message of hard-core conservatism, with an emphasis on isolationist foreign policy and protectionist economic policy, hit some of the notes that Republicans of previous generations, such as Robert Taft, had played to the Republican faithful. Buchanan, with little chance of winning the nomination, had no need to cater to the center of the electorate, and his straightforward rhetoric, although offensive to many, was terribly appealing to Republican conservatives uncomfortable with Dole's more moderate views. Buchanan managed to beat Dole in the New Hampshire primary, but Dole's greater resources soon quelled the challenge, and he won the nomination easily. He selected Jack Kemp, the former football star and congressman, who was a champion of supply-side economics, as his running mate, in spite of the fact that Kemp had endorsed a fellow supply-sider, Steve Forbes, in the primaries.

Clinton, facing no primary challenge, was able to use some of the federal funding for his race in late spring and early summer to broadcast ads that portrayed Dole and the Republicans as a threat to Social Security, Medicare, and other

1996

PRESIDENTIAL CANDIDATE (STATE) VICE-PRESIDENTIAL CANDIDATE (STATE)	PARTY	ELECTORAL VOTES	APPROX. % OF POPULAR VOTE
Bill Clinton (Ark.) Al Gore (Tenn.)	Democrat	379	49%
Robert Dole (Kans.) Jack Kemp (Calif.)	Republican	159	41%
Ross Perot (Tex.) Pat Choate (Tex.)	Independent	0	8%

popular social programs. Dole had had to spend money to hold off the challenges from Buchanan and Forbes, who devoted nearly $40 million, most of it his own money, to his quest for the nomination. Clinton's ads were able to put the Dole campaign on the defensive, and there Dole stayed for most of the race.

In spite of the strength of the economy and the near absence of foreign threats, Bill Clinton was far from invulnerable. Serious issues had been raised about his character and judgment, and investigations of his involvement in a land deal in Arkansas ("Whitewater") and a sexual harassment suit brought by a former Arkansas state employee named Paula Corbin Jones held possibilities of derailing his re-election. But neither issue seemed to rate very high on the list of voters' concerns, and although polls showed that most Americans had a higher estimate of Bob Dole's character, the same polls showed a continuing tilt toward Bill Clinton in any vote. Revulsion against negative campaigning was strong enough to make it hard for Dole to capitalize on the character issue in his TV ads. (Similarly, Clinton's campaign did not dare to make any explicit reference to Dole's age, although it did characterize his *ideas* as old.)

Yet it was age—or rather, an event that could be interpreted as being about Dole's age—that was the defining moment of this lackluster race. In Chico, California, on September 18, Dole was leaning over a railing to shake hands when the railing gave way and he fell to the ground. A Reuters photographer took pictures of the nonplussed candidate, and the image conveyed to the nation a message about Dole's age that no Clinton ad could dare to suggest.

Similarly, the Dole campaign had to rely on others to make an issue of Clinton's character, and between congressional and legal investigations and the publications of the conservative press, plenty of material was aired about Clinton's finances and sex life. But voters remained unconvinced of the salience of these issues, and Clinton moved imperturbably along, running a cautious campaign and relying on his political gifts to control the situation. With Al Gore again the vice presidential candidate, Clinton and the Democrats did a successful job of claiming the political center. No longer the champions of Keynesian economics or social experimentation, the Democrats had mastered the art of assimilating Republican themes and making them their own. In the middle of the summer, Clinton faced a crucial legislative test—whether or not to sign a welfare reform bill that the Republicans had passed. Although many of his advisers urged a veto, Dick Morris, a political operative whose previous clients had been Republicans, warned that a veto would lose Clinton the election. Clinton decided not to veto the bill, so welfare reform, too, became part of the Democratic agenda. (Soon afterward, Morris resigned when it was revealed that he had patronized a prostitute and had even let her listen in on his conversations with the President.)

Perhaps the Dole campaign's greatest weakness was the candidate's inability to enunciate a reason for voters to elect him. George Bush had faced the same problem in 1988, and then a barrage of negative ads had obscured it. But in 1996, Dole avoided harshly negative ads, and the reason to vote for him seemed to boil down to his being a nice fellow who had been in Washington a long time and had earned his chance. It was not enough.

On election day Clinton won 49 percent of the votes to Dole's 41 percent. Ross Perot was again on the ballot but received only 8 percent. The campaign for President in 1996 was tedious, with each side straining not to give offense to anyone. While few would lament the absence of the sort of personal attacks that had marred the 1988 race (or, for that matter, the 1828 race), the lack of serious debate on the issues, the fear of leading opinion rather than following it, and the general disengagement of the electorate (only about half the eligible voters bothered to cast ballots in 1996) pointed to serious problems in American politics.

Yet the history of presidential elections has demonstrated a powerful dynamism over time as the excesses and shortcomings of one election or era have been gradually corrected—even though such corrections have invariably led to new difficulties. At the close of the twentieth century, new attention was being paid to the way campaign finance practices were distorting politics; the Reform Party, founded by Ross Perot, was proving more lasting than political professionals had expected; and new ways of reaching voters on the Internet were reshaping American politics and government. If the past is any guide, future elections will reveal new ways of carrying out—and thwarting—the will of the majority.

Bob Dole after falling from the stage at a campaign rally in Chico, California, on September 18, 1996.

COPYRIGHT © REUTERS.

Edward Sorel's cover for the election issue of The New Yorker.

Index

About the Authors

EVAN CORNOG is the author of *The Birth of Empire: DeWitt Clinton and the American Experience, 1769–1828,* and is currently an associate dean at Columbia University's Graduate School of Journalism. He lives in New York City.

RICHARD WHELAN, an independent cultural historian, is the author of numerous books, including acclaimed biographies of Robert Capa and Alfred Stieglitz. He lives in Brooklyn.

About the Type

This book was set in Baskerville, a typeface which was designed by John Baskerville, an amateur printer and typefounder, and cut for him by John Handy in 1750. The type became popular again when The Lanston Monotype Corporation of London revived the classic roman face in 1923. The Mergenthaler Linotype Company in England and the United States cut a version of Baskerville in 1931, making it one of the most widely used typefaces today.